Measured Words

Measured Words

The development of objective language testing

Bernard Spolsky

Oxford University Press 1995

Oxford University Press
Walton Street, Oxford OX2 6DP

Oxford New York Toronto Madrid
Delhi Bombay Calcutta Madras Karachi
Kuala Lumpur Singapore Hong Kong Tokyo
Nairobi Dar es Salaam Cape Town
Melbourne Auckland

and associated companies in
Berlin Ibadan

Oxford and *Oxford English* are trade marks of
Oxford University Press

ISBN 0 19 437201 4

© Bernard Spolsky 1995

Set by Wyvern Typesetting
Printed in Hong Kong

Dedication

This will be in agreement with what Rabbi Hanina said: I have learned much from my teachers, and more from my colleagues than from my teachers, and from my students, more than from them all.

Babylonian Talmud, *Ta'anith*, 7A

Contents

Acknowledgements

The opportunity to work on this book came with a sabbatical leave from Bar-Ilan University. Once again, I am deeply grateful to the institution for its wise and generous sabbatical policy, and to my departmental colleagues and students who graciously and efficiently dealt with my absence from teaching. In particular, I acknowledge the extra burden placed on doctoral students who accepted electronic rather than personal guidance.

Atmosphere and facilities to work were provided by a Mellon Fellowship at the Institute of Advanced Studies of the National Foreign Language Center at the Johns Hopkins University, Washington DC, just a block from the building where TOEFL started out. I want to express my deepest thanks to the director of the Center, Professor Richard Lambert, and his colleagues for their hospitality and intellectual stimulation, and to the staff members of the Center for their constant and willing help and support.

The three libraries where I did the bulk of the research were the Library of Congress, Georgetown University Library, and the George Washington University Library. For access to Georgetown University Library, with its vital collection transferred from the Center for Applied Linguistics, I am grateful to Dean James Alatis, with whom I am also happy to acknowledge more than twenty years of friendship. I especially thank him for handing over to me, from his personal papers, a number of key documents from the early years of TOEFL which he rescued.

During the course of this study, I have been permitted to read and copy archival material at the Educational Testing Service, the Ford Foundation, the University of Cambridge Local Examinations Syndicate, and the College Board. Without these institutions' willingness to open up these records, much of this book would have remained speculation. While I may have bared some of the skeletons in their cupboards, I hope my admiration for their devotion and service to the field of language testing continues to shine through.

A number of other scholars have also searched their own archives or memories. I thank in particular: John B. Carroll, Leslie Palmer, David Harris, Sydney Sako, Robert Lado, and John Roach, all of whom deservedly have starring roles in parts of the story that follows. I am grateful to William G. Shephard for valuable leads to written and unwritten archives at the University of Cambridge Local Examinations Syndicate.

In my struggles to fit all the fascinating or important data I found into a book, I was especially grateful to Henry Widdowson and a number of anonymous readers who challenged or encouraged me to overcome my reluctance to sculpt and pare a large amount of data into a readable form and manageable size. I also acknowledge, with deep gratitude, John Carroll's reading of an early draft and his effort to help me correct some of the errors and biases in it, and Alastair Pollitt's perceptive commentary on a near-final draft that has enabled me to grasp more clearly what I am trying to say.

While I may have for a little been tempted to look elsewhere, I appreciate the continued association with Oxford University Press and the encouragement, co-operation, and efficiency it has guaranteed from Cristina Whitecross and her colleagues. I wish in particular to thank Antoinette Meehan for painstaking editing of a complicated manuscript.

I have been particularly fortunate that my work on this book has been paralleled by my wife's own studies of the relevance of scepticism to understanding the literature and painting of the Renaissance, and our conversations and shared readings have played a major role in my own clarification of the issues I have been working on. Although we have not yet sat down to the joint authorship that more than thirty years of sharing family and careers might have been expected to induce, in writing this book, in particular, I have sensed the intellectual overlap that matches other common values and pursuits.

The author and publisher are grateful to the College Board, the Educational Testing Service, and the Ford Foundation for permission to reproduce material held in their archives.

Preface

When, somewhat early in my career in language testing, I was first honoured with an invitation to be a plenary speaker at an International Congress of Applied Linguistics, the dignity of the event so affected me that I allowed myself to make *ex cathedra* pronouncements on the history of the field. Although my speculations then seem to have been quite well received and are widely cited without complaint, I have from time to time returned with some anxiety to the paper that I presented in Stuttgart and wondered if the notions in it would stand up to more careful scrutiny, or if the data would demolish the theory. Thus, this book is both an exploration and an expiation.

It is also a small contribution to the professionalization of a field in which it has been a pleasure to work. Without knowing our past, we have all enjoyed regular discoveries of round objects or other similar novelties. I hope I will not be felt to be spoiling the fun of colleagues who have provided such a sympathetic fellowship. I acknowledge a debt, as any historian of language testing must, to my predecessors in the field and to the countless people who suffered or gloried in the tests that they gave or inspired. This book is dedicated to the students who, over my years of teaching, have provided me with opportunities to try out my burgeoning ideas, and justified the paid employment that has allowed me to continue my research.

Bernard Spolsky
Jerusalem 1994

Acronymns

ASTP	Army Specialized Training Program
CEEB	College Entrance Examination Board
CITO	(Centraal) Instituut voor Toestonwikkelling (National Institute for Educational Measurement)
CPE	Certificate of Proficiency in English
ETS	Educational Testing Service
EUROCERT	English Proficiency Certification Program
FCE	First Certificate in English
FSI	Foreign Service Institute
(I)ELTS	(International) English Language Testing Service
IIE	Institute of International Education
MLA	Modern Language Association of America
TOEFL	Test of English as a Foreign Language
TSE	Test of Spoken English
TWE	Test of Written English
UCLES	University of Cambridge Local Examinations Syndicate

1   Prolegomena

Read this carefully before starting the test

'There is no blessing to be found', the Babylonian Talmud remarks (in Treatise *Ta'anit*, 8B), 'in something that has been weighed, or in something that has been measured, or in something that has been counted'. None the less, the last century has seen a determined effort to weigh, gauge, and count not just obvious and visible physical objects but also unseen forces and conjectured abstract concepts. The flowering of modern scientific language testing has been one facet of the attempt to measure an aspect of human ability, and a further application of the rationalistic Cartesian search for certainty to an area perhaps better left for a healthy humanistic scepticism.

Since the days of World War I, psychometric principles and practices have come to dominate the testing of foreign language proficiency, and a movement that initially blossomed in the United States has spread throughout the world. As long as testing was confined to helping students learn or to determining the qualifications of individuals seeking employment, there was a strong ethical case to be made for it, as the ends justified the means. But, from its beginnings, testing has been exploited also as a method of control and power—as a way to select, to motivate, to punish. The so-called objective test, by virtue of its claim of scientific backing for its impartiality, and especially when it operates under academic aegis and with the efficiency of big business, is even more brutally effective in exercising this authority. Clothed in the respectability of psychometric objectivity, and with powerful institutional support, the Test of English as a Foreign Language (TOEFL) was able to capture the market and become industrialized. It is only by taking full account of the institutional or political context that one can appreciate how the psychometric controversies have distracted attention from more serious social (or anti-social) motivations and impact.

This point can be illustrated by any of a number of modern language testing programmes. One might choose the pioneering work of Henmon and his associates in the late 1920s, the development of the Foreign Service Institute Oral Interview in the 1950s, the Modern Language Association Cooperative and Proficiency tests created in the 1960s, the British work resulting in the International English Language Testing Service test battery in the last few years. Interesting as all these are, I found that it is the early history of TOEFL that best demonstrates the tendency for economic and commercial and political ends to play such crucial roles that the assertion of authority and power becomes ultimately more important than issues of testing theory or technology.

My main intention in this study, then, has been to widen the current perspective by looking at one aspect of the field of language testing in its historical, sociological, and political context. Most recent books on language testing have been written ahistorically, to put it politely, as if the field rose Venus-like out of the waves of applied linguistics sometime after 1960.[1] While this book was in manuscript form, I gave a copy to a colleague who was just preparing to teach a course he had labelled 'A history of language testing'. His first surprised comment was that he had planned to start with 1961, a year I reach half-way through this book. Clearly, one writer's history is another's pre-history.

Not only are our horizons restricted, but there has been another limitation in our understanding. Most historical references read as though advances in methodology and theory had been the driving force behind the development of language teaching and language testing. We regularly talk and write (I know because I have done it) in terms of progress and periods. We see the Audio-Lingual Method as the result of the application of structural linguistics and Skinnerian learning theory. We interpret the cognitive approaches as products of the theoretical revolutions of transformational-generative grammar. We regard the notional-functional syllabus as related to theories of pragmatics and communicative competence. We lament the failure of British applied linguists to agree a model in place of Munby. We propose three periods of language testing, one traditional, a second modern or psychometric-structuralist, a third as post-modern or psycholinguistic-sociolinguistic (Spolsky 1977, 1981a).

With such a restricted outlook, almost new historical in its egocentricity, we have difficulty in recognizing why a theoretical breakthrough (especially if it is one that we have just proposed) does not immediately win absolute acceptance and total implementation. Only recently has a handful of scholars—Richards (1984), Pennycook (1989, 1990), and Phillipson (1992)—forcibly diverted attention to some of the external, non-theoretical, institutional, social forces that, on deeper analysis, often turn out to be much more powerful explanations of actual language teaching practice.

Without this reminder, we too easily forget, for instance, the enormous power of institutional inertia; it is much easier to think up reasons against a change than to provide arguments in its support. There are, of course, important and valuable reasons why institutions resist change. They are explainable as much through their history as through the logic of their present operation. They function because of their constancy, their imperviousness to other than minor changes. It is much easier to come up with a new theory than to find a way of fitting its implementation into an existing establishment. The decisions more often represent political compromise than theoretical principle. In debate, statements of principle serve as rhetorical devices or rallying cries rather than as the basis for empirical proof or logical argument.

A clearer account of a field depends on willingness to look carefully not just at the history of the ideas that underlie it, but also at the institutional, social, and economic situation in which they were and are actualized. In the field of language pedagogy, for instance, the development of language laboratories was a commercial offshoot of innovative technology rather than an answer to theoretical needs. The enormous growth of the demand for English language teaching throughout the world is explained, at least in part, by the hugely profitable language teaching industry and related publishing (and testing) businesses, where new theories hold interest as sales pitches. The move towards a European economic community clarified, as no theoretical approach would have done, the requirement to define language teaching goals as precisely as did the notional-functional syllabus.

In the study of fields like language testing and teaching, scholars need to be ready to draw not just on the obvious theoretical disciplines that underpin applied linguistics, such as the various language sciences and education, but also on fields like economics, political science, and sociology that furnish methods of investigating the context in which language and education exist.

I should stress that this book is not a general or complete history of language testing theory and practice but a history of some highly institutionalized and industrialized tests and test batteries. Because it focuses on the *objective* language test in some institutional-industrial contexts, it is essentially a history of the attempts to develop tests that place their highest value on technical reliability, efficiency, and commercial viability. It thus does not attempt to chart the evolution of the kind of post-modern testing that many testers (among whom I number myself) have come to favour as an alternative to the model described here. It is because TOEFL marks the acme of this development in language testing, as well as revealing the forces that led to it, that the second part of the book is so narrowly focused. Because of this focus, events since the institutionalization and industrialization of TOEFL are only sketched. The main emphasis is on testing in America, where industrialization and objectivity have been most developed, but parallel British progress is also described.

Language testing is of particular interest because of the various competing factions that contribute to it. One of the reasons for my continuing fascination has been the way that it constantly forces practical and theoretical issues into fruitful tension. The needs of the tester regularly challenge the theorist, just as the findings of the theorist repeatedly tempt the tester. While it is fairly easy to come up with new assessment procedures, it remains difficult to explain exactly what is being measured,[2] a situation that guarantees a continuing productive stress. As if this first cause of strain were not enough, there is a second one provided by the fact that at least two disciplines have proprietary claims on the theory behind language testing: both language learning theorists and measurement experts have their own independent (and perhaps unresolvable) notions of what is involved. It is a field whose lush complexity promises stimulating exploration.

Answer in 500 words: What is a test?

My goal in this book is to chart some aspects of the genesis of some public, institutional testing, and of one test in particular. This is not intended to be a history of disembodied language testing theory. I start with the assumption that a public language test needs to satisfy several different sets of criteria, representing the interests of divergent and often competing groups. The language tester is expected to be responsible for and responsive to theories derived from two unrelated and fundamentally inharmonious fields, linguistics (which wants to describe language knowledge) and psychometrics (which hopes to measure it and other human attributes), and at the same time is directed and constrained by rival practical institutional, economic, social, and even political demands. Any large-scale test or examination battery is the result of hard-fought compromises between these many theoretical and practical demands. By understanding how this has happened in the past, language testers and test consumers should be in a sounder position to face present and future tasks.

The techniques for testing ability to understand written and spoken texts that the TOEFL programme applied finally[3] had been known and were described a decade earlier by Thibault (1953) and Carroll (1954), but the development of satisfactory testing of spoken and written expressive ability continued to reveal the underlying paradox that is at the heart of this book. As Carl Brigham, one of the founders of the objective testing movement, expressed it in 1934, what can be measured reliably is not necessarily the same as the ability one is interested in (College Entrance Examination Board 1934a). Peter Skehan in a talk at the 1992 Language Testing Research Colloquium made this point even more dramatically by telling about the person who preferred to search for a missing object in the living room where there was a light rather than in the dark kitchen where it had been lost. Our failure to develop the perfect language proficiency test, I now believe, is because of the nature of the task we are unwisely accepting.

My earliest essay in dealing with the history of language testing was a plenary lecture I gave at an Applied Linguistics Congress (Spolsky 1977). In that talk, I proposed an analysis of language testing history as moving through three periods or approaches. I have tinkered with the idea, from time to time, but only in the last few years have I started to look at the evidence that will support or reject it. The reading I have done in the pro-

cess of writing this book has, inevitably, influenced my thinking. My analysis has changed by becoming more complex because the various
approaches I tried to arrange in order of time have continued to operate,
as I first sensed, throughout the period. In some respects, the analysis has
also changed by becoming more simple. If I were to try to sum up my
overall impression—and I do it at this stage in the book so that readers
can recognize in advance the prejudices that have influenced my reading
and historiography—it would go something like this.

First of all, there are two major ideologies underlying the testing and
assessment of human characteristics, which I might characterize as the
humanistic-scepticist descriptive approach on the one hand, and the ration-
alist-empiricist measurement approach on the other. The former, which
corresponds to what I first named the *pre-scientific approach* (Spolsky ibid.)
and later (Spolsky 1981) the *traditional*, on the shaky grounds that it had
at least a forty-year lead on the other, is the one that is associated with
examinations of the British university style. It is the direct ideological heir
of the pluralistic and sceptical humanism of the Renaissance described in
Toulmin (1990). Characterized in the 1920s as old-type questions, it used
open-ended interviews or, more typically, essays, marked intuitively by
selected judges, and it produced results, the probable error of which has
been studied and publicized clearly and repetitively (though often with minimal effect) ever since Edgeworth (1888).

The latter approach is that typified by the true-false or multiple-choice
test, with large numbers of items whose statistical qualities produce acceptable standard deviations (the more recent term for the older *probable error*)
and whose internal consistency and other technical kinds of reliability can
be demonstrated. It represents what Toulmin would consider the counter-
renaissance, a rejection of scepticism and a claim for the power of rationalism and empiricism to permit absolute certainty, that has been associated
since Descartes with the natural sciences and has proven to be enormously
powerful in its grip on the social sciences where psychometrics is placed.
Outside of the United States (and even in Britain where in 1888 Edgeworth
was its spiritual founder and in 1921 Burt was one of its most eloquent
proponents) it is popularly known as the American test, and not altogether
incorrectly associated with such other modern technological innovations as
television, computers, and mass-market hamburgers.

In the course of my studies, I have come to believe that there is some
value in each of these ideologies, and many problems with both of them.
To oversimplify, with the traditional examination we think we know what
we are assessing, but remain happily or unhappily uncertain about the
accuracy or replicability of our assessment; with the modern examination,
we are sure enough of our measurement, but are, or should be, uncertain
as to what exactly we have measured. The confrontation, properly recognized, is potentially a fruitful and useful one, each view working to correct

the tendency of the supporters of the other to a dangerous complacency and over-certainty.

While I was writing this book, the Olympic Games took place in Barcelona, and I was struck by the thought that testing has many analogies with the two kinds of events that athletes participate in. One class of events has strictly measured results: the time of the 100 metre race, the distance the shot is put, the weight that is lifted, the number of goals scored in a hockey or football match, are all precisely measurable (for timed events, electronic accuracy has even replaced the averaging of human timekeepers). Other events, however, continue to depend on subjective scores awarded by judges: the diving, the gymnastics, the skating, the dressage.[4] In these terms, the field of language testing faces the question of whether language proficiency can be measured or judged, or perhaps only described. This book will show some of the answers that have been given to that question. It will also show, in the way TOEFL took its shape, the temporary triumph of quantified measurement.

Technology and its uses or misuses

What I have been talking about so far is the development of the *technology* of testing, to apply the term suggested by Madaus (1990). But it is a mistake, and a misleading and potentially dangerous one, to look at a technology alone, decontextualized, without considering the *use* to which it is put, and the *effect* of the use. A medicine that cures some may well kill others; a gun can be used for self-defence or for murder; a test can help some people but cause harm when its results are misapplied or its aims distorted. The sympathy that I felt for a system of examination by interviews by committees of judges has, for instance, been severely curtailed by stories told me by students who experienced such testing in the former Soviet Union. One student, a recent immigrant to Israel from Russia, recounted the traumatic experience she had suffered when, at the age of seventeen, she applied for admission to a university programme that used its oral examination to exclude Jews. The examining committee continued asking questions until they found something she did not know, and then failed her. We must be ready to look then at the uses and misuses, the intended and the unintended effects, of the never-neutral technology of tests and examinations.

In the pragmatic and political world in which assessment takes place, there has not been the luxury of the reasoned blending of theoretical approaches. Rather, economic pressures or bureaucratic needs or personal ambitions or commercial interests have often led to the imposition of inadequate and injurious systems of testing on unsuspecting subjects. For tests and examinations exist in the context of complex and dynamic societies.

They are the 'encroaching power' that can revolutionize education as Latham (1877: 2) pointed out more than a hundred years ago. They could offer a solution to the problems of governing India, as Macaulay argued (1853: 185), or the control of primary education in Britain, or of schools in Boston. Madaus (1990: 3) put this well in saying that 'tests are a social technology, and historically are mechanisms of control and power deeply embedded in education, government, and business'. The nature of our study then must be as Latham (1877: iii) expressed it, to inquire 'as to what we want to effect by Examination and how far we can succeed'.

Pedagogical testing

One employment of tests and examinations that is so intimately associated with the pedagogical process as to require no other justification is the use made by a teacher or student to check the progress of learning. The purely pedagogical test, whether given at the beginning of a learning session to see what needs to be taught and to predict areas of difficulty, or given in the course of learning to see how much progress has been made, is a natural concomitant of even the most informal methods of teaching and learning.[5] The good learner is one who constantly tests and examines his or her changing skill or knowledge; the good teacher is one who continually observes the learner to be sure that successful learning is taking place. The purely pedagogical test use, then, is any form of testing used by a teacher or learner to check on the learner's progress in order to modify the course or nature of instruction.

The force of this definition might be made clearer by considering the speech act called a question. A normal conversational question (see Searle 1969) is an attempt to obtain direct information that the speaker does not have but has a right to, from an interlocutor who may reasonably be expected to know the answer and give it. In the course of an instructional procedure, such a question might take the form 'Do you understand what I am telling you?' or even 'Do you remember what I told you last time?' As Searle pointed out, examination questions do not fit this definition, for it is normally the case that the speaker knows the answer better than anyone else: the focus is on establishing whether the interlocutor also knows it. I have characterized examination questions of this kind not as *requests for information* but as *requests to perform*. I now propose a further distinction, between questions posed by a speaker who will then modify his or her teaching strategy as a result of the answer, and any other uses of examination questions.

There are many other uses of tests. Even in the classroom, a test may be used with the alternative or additional purpose of motivating or punishing or classifying or grading a student. Fundamental to this 'enriched' (and at the same time impoverished) use of tests is an uneven power relation. In the purely pedagogical test as I have defined it, I assume learner and teacher to be in a mutual relationship where the only difference between them is that the teacher has some special knowledge or skill that the learner wishes to obtain. In many societies, the formal context for learning is unequal, it must be admitted, with the teacher required to force learning on the unwilling learner. Thus, new uses are found for tests, to motivate or discipline or otherwise control the learner. Tests are not restricted to pedagogical uses, and it is to this wider scope that I now turn.

Qualifying tests

A second class of uses of tests and examinations that I believe to be sufficiently obvious and natural to be considered 'pure' and unarguable is the appropriate inspection of an individual who is seeking recognition as being qualified for some role. A pure qualification test might be of a doctor seeking to practise medicine or a pilot wishing to fly a plane or a person offering marriage. It is in its simplest sense, the result of an agreement between two individuals, one of whom is offering the service and one of whom is considering its use, that the former will offer some evidence of being qualified. This certification may come from an individual, such as the letter of reference from a former employer or the individually transmitted authority of a rabbi or a bishop. It may alternatively be a certificate issued by a trade or guild or profession, or a designated governmental agency, or a teaching institution. A pure qualification test is any germane examination of an individual who claims qualifications to perform certain services for another individual.

Again, in actual situations there can be disagreement about what is *germane*. Should one be permitted to ask the political opinions of a person who offers to mow a lawn or repair a watch? What sorts of question is it reasonable to ask of someone wanting to be a doctor? Or a teacher? Or married? Should gender or religious persuasion or sexual preference or ethnic origin be relevant to employment? Each of these clearly goes beyond the pertinent, nor is there easy justification for the widespread tendency to use tests and examinations to restrict entrance to lucrative occupations, or exert power over certain members of the population, such as the use of French language tests as requirements for taxi licenses in Quebec in the 1970s.

Wider uses and stronger

As these last cases showed, the main extension of the purely pedagogical and qualificational use of tests is the assertion of power. An early example, already observed in the Middle Ages and of continuing importance, is the use of tests by people outside the classroom to exert power over it and over the school as a whole. One special case of this use, and a central issue in modern foreign language testing, is the use of tests and examinations to control the curriculum of a school.[6] The temptation to do this is strong, but as Gregory Anrig, President of Educational Testing Service until 1993, put it, to use tests to drive a curriculum is dangerous driving.[7] A second use is the blend of pedagogical and qualificational testing that occurs commonly when students are required to take external examinations at given career points; the design of the system has obvious social implications in determining which groups have access to the kind of education that permits economic advantage or social mobility.

The tendency to concentrate on technology, on the nature of the test, rather than on its use, has made it difficult to ask intelligent questions about the quality of tests. We spend a lot of time worrying about the technical reliability and technical excellence of our instruments, and too little worrying about their validity for the purposes for which they are intended (or about the ethical justification for those uses). In the history that follows, I will do my best to put at least as much emphasis on test use as on test form.

There is a further aspect that one dare not ignore, and this is the unintended effect of tests. Whatever the test-makers (or even the test-users) intended, the side-effects of a test (like many medicines) are sometimes even more striking than its primary use. I will look at these effects later, but simply mention a few obvious examples now. Foucault (1975, 1979), in the brilliantly stimulating few pages he devotes to examinations, shows how the very disciplines of medicine and education can be explained as results of formal medical and school examinations. Critics of examinations as early as Latham (1877) have shown how formal examination systems lead to cramming and cramming schools, and to the narrowing of educational goals. Others, like Gould (1981), have denounced the unjustified and pernicious effects of mental measurement and the reification of its results.[8] There are less striking but distressing effects of the use of modern language tests and the unquestioned belief in the unqualified fairness and meaningfulness of their results.

A short history

Essentially, the general picture that will emerge in this history is something like this. In Europe, examinations flourished first in the universities: from the seventeenth century, the disputations that had been required for degrees were first supplemented by and later replaced by written examinations as part of a Cartesian move for decontexualization and certainty. In Prussia, examinations were first used for selection of civil servants in the eighteenth century; the idea was adopted in France after the Revolution. In Britain, written examinations in emulation of the major university examinations (especially the Cambridge Tripos) were first used in the middle of the nineteenth century as a means of selecting candidates for the upper grades in the Indian Civil Service, and later adopted for admission to the Home Civil Service and other professions. In France, Napoleon introduced oral examinations at the end of secondary school. In England, similar examinations were established some fifty years later under the control of various universities. They were subsequently further democratized, and their use in elementary schools served to maintain centralized control of education By the end of the nineteenth century public examinations were firmly established in Western Europe as methods of controlling education and selecting civil servants. By the 1890s, the element of uncertainty and chance still involved in written examinations had been recognized, and minimal efforts were being made to overcome them.

The notion of testing mental ability emerged in a different context in order to solve the problem, recognized as popular education grew at the end of the century, of determining what to do with children who appeared mentally unprepared for school. Mental testing originated as a method of diagnosing retardation. Once it was found that test results could be quantified, and that the resulting numbers had somewhat less uncertainty than the scores given in traditional examinations, the way was clear for the birth of the new-type test. After mental tests had been used with some effect in World War I, their use was widely encouraged in both the United States and Britain.

The objective modern language test derived its appeal from the belief that the methods of mental testing could be satisfactorily applied to specific cognitive abilities as well as to general intelligence, and the associated belief that objective new-type tests were fairer than the older traditional examinations. The first new-type language tests appeared in the United States at the beginning of the 1920s, and received a strong stimulus from their utilization in a major US study of language teaching at the end of the decade.

During the 1930s, the growth of the psychometrics industry encouraged the use of objective testing techniques, but, reflecting current socially motivated goals for foreign language instruction, this was largely confined to the written language. By 1954, objective testing of this limited skill seemed to be triumphant on one side of the Atlantic at least. These arguments were particularly effective in setting the model for the development of TOEFL, and its later incorporation into the range of highly successful tests offered by Educational Testing Service in Princeton. They were much later in their effect on some parallel batteries offered by the University of Cambridge Local Examinations Syndicate. However, the changed goals of language teaching required the development of techniques for testing communicative control of the spoken language, a task that has challenged the effectiveness of objective testing.

In all this development, the central question in language testing theory has been a mirror of that in mental testing: are we measuring a single factor or a number of factors? Are we really measuring something (language ability or proficiency) or is the construct we are working with simply an unjustifiable reification, an artifact of the statistics we use? There have been many theoretical answers, but the practical ones have tended to follow Macaulay's recognition that the examinations used 'are not infallible tests' (1853: 185) but that they are the best way to do the job, or as Edgeworth put it, 'It is a species of sortition infinitely preferable to the ancient method of casting lots . . .' (Edgeworth 1888: 626). One of the goals of this book is to draw attention to the limitations of scientific objective testing and to the need for responsibility and care in the use of its results.

A second and related goal, most fully developed in the second part of the book, is to understand the working of political, institutional, economic, and practical factors in effecting the development of a test. Whatever the state of testing theory and technology, the shape of a major institutional test like TOEFL is strongly influenced by non-testing factors. Part II, then, will attempt to trace these pressures and the events that help explain why the test developed in the 1960s did not attempt to exploit the notions of integrative testing that were already well matured. It will, by sketching parallel developments at the University of Cambridge, show the way in which institutions may variously cope with the demands of language testing.

Notes

1 Bachman (1990), an excellent survey of current theory, has no language testing reference earlier than 1961, although his psychometric references go back twenty years earlier.
2 Or, as Douglas Stevenson put it, it is easy to invent a new kind of language test, but hard to explain what the old kinds measure.
3 See Chapter 13.
4 This analogy is even more fully developed, I have not been surprised to learn, in Pollitt (1991).
5 For fuller discussion, see Spolsky (1981b, 1992) and the book in which the second of these appeared.
6 Recent studies of what is called washback or backwash raise questions about the efficacy of this approach (Alderson and Wall 1993).
7 From remarks made at a panel on 'Uniform Standards and Tests' at the Brookings Institution, 12 May 1992.
8 Carroll (1993: 23) defends psychometrics against the charge of reification. He sees no necessity of assuming any specific neurophysiological

function underlying an ability: 'For our purposes, a cognitive ability can be viewed as an intervening variable, i.e. a calculational convenience, as it were, linking together a particular series of observations.' He does not see it necessary to assume that an ability is 'a thing or entity that somehow resides in the individual' (22).

PART ONE

The history of the objective language test

2 The encroaching power of examinations

Shibboleths and other punishments

While the first modern language test is less than a hundred years old, study of its pre-history reveals some of the major trends. The Book of Judges (12: 4–6) in the Bible records an early language test.[1] Guarding the fords on the River Jordan, Gileadite patrols asked anyone approaching to say the word *shibboleth*, by most accounts the word for a stream and pronounced *sibboleth* in the transjordanian dialect spoken by the Ephraimite enemies they had just defeated in battle. The Shibboleth test[2] was, technologically, a single-item, objective, oral, phonological test, individually administered: the 42,000 who failed it were slaughtered on the spot. There was nothing educational about the test, which served an immediate political purpose.

Social or political purposes lend tests and examinations their critical weight, as Michel Foucault indicated in a book he called *Surveiller et punir: naissance de la prison*.[3] The first section of his book deals with torture, the second with punishment, and the third with discipline, and it is here that examinations are discussed. Examinations, Foucault explained, provide 'a normalizing gaze, a surveillance that makes it possible to qualify, to classify and to punish' (Foucault 1975: 186–7).[4] He proposed an analogy to the way that doctors developed authority over hospitals. Before the seventeenth century the hospital was essentially dominated by the nursing and administrative staff, with only occasional visits by doctors. The innovation of a series of regular daily examinations by physicians gave doctors pre-eminent power over the establishment, and changed the hospital into 'a place of training and of the correlation of knowledge' (ibid.: 188).[5] In the same way, the institution of regular examinations in the eighteenth century transformed the school into 'a sort of apparatus of uninterrupted examination' (ibid.).[6] As a result of examinations, knowledge started to flow not just from teacher to pupil, but back from pupil to teacher, establishing a science of education, in much the same way that the information flowing from examined patients to their doctors had instituted a 'discipline' of medicine.

The examination, Foucault suggested, was a mechanism linking power and knowledge. It was a ritualized ceremony that required the subjects to be seen, and transformed them into objects under control. It built an archive of documentation: the mark-book of the teacher, the papers and scores of the candidates became 'a whole meticulous archive' (ibid.: 191)[7] in which the population of the school could be ordered and fixed for ever in its place, and it transformed the individual into 'a case'[8] preserved as an object. Foucault considered his book to be a first step in a study of 'the power of normalization and the formation of knowledge' as the footnote that concludes it remarks.[9] The emphasis he placed on the *norm* is critical. While examinations often deal with the non-normal (selecting the best student, determining who is retarded), they do so by assuming a norm. Much testing is 'norm-referenced', so that scores are awarded on the basis of a subject's rank in a large group rather than on the basis of any explicit criterion.

The Chinese principle

The examinations that Foucault was writing about were presumably the daily or regular examinations of the French seventeenth-century religious schools.[10] In the late medieval universities, the purely pedagogical tests and examinations that accompanied classroom teaching came to be combined with qualification tests, as public oral disputations and examinations came to be used to determine the award of degrees. In the eighteenth and early nineteenth centuries in both France and Prussia, formal examinations evolved into methods for selecting civil servants and controlling the educational process. This new emphasis, Madaus (1990) believes, matured from an idea that the Jesuits had brought back to France from China.[11]

In China during the Han dynasty (201 BCE to 8 CE), examinations on classical Confucian doctrine replaced patronage as a method of selecting civil servants. To avoid corruption, all essays were marked anonymously, and the Emperor personally supervised the final stage. With some modification, the system survived until the end of the nineteenth century. The first Western scholar to give a detailed (and admiring) account of the Chinese examinations was the late sixteenth-century Jesuit explorer and missionary, Matteo Ricci (1942). French *philosophes* such as Voltaire and Turgot quoted the example of these competitive examinations in order to attack the privilege and patronage that were the basis for political appointments in contemporary France.

The Catholic schools of eighteenth-century France conducted elaborate and orderly forms of examination. The rules for Christian schools laid down then by Jean-Baptiste de la Salle (1838, 1935)[12] transformed the classroom into a highly organized place, with precise ordering and arrangement of every word and gesture for teacher and pupil, and close factory-like control of all instruction, monitored by monthly examinations conducted by teachers and principal.

The justification for using examinations for external supervision of the classroom is clear, but the pernicious and inevitable outcome of narrowing the educational process has been repeated over and over again.[13] Once the content of an examination has been bruited abroad, it becomes a more or less precise specification of what knowledge or behaviour will be rewarded (or will avoid punishment). No reasonable teacher will do other than focus his or her pupils' efforts on the specific items that are to be tested; no bright pupil will want to spend time on anything but preparation for what is to be in the examination. The control of the instructional process, then, is transferred from those most immediately concerned (the teacher and the pupils) to the examination itself. This may be appropriate and harmless when the goal is the rote learning of a specified body of material—a sacred text, a spelling list, a catechism, a multiplication table—but it is constraining and rigid when it pertains to the less defined and more creative aspects of a curriculum. The greater the uniformity, the more the danger of crystallization and stultification.

Liberty, equality, and examinations

The system of examinations in France spread from the Catholic schools to secular institutions, and gained in significance. The *agrégation* was introduced as a competitive examination for selecting teachers in 1766; the *concours générale*, a prize competition for the Parisian *lycées*, dates from 1747 (Anderson 1975). After the French Revolution, examinations continued to grow in importance and were seen not as methods of controlling the masses but as a way of giving the educated élite access to power. In 1795, an entrance examination for teachers' colleges was established (Madaus and Kellaghan 1991). Under Napoleon, examinations became the method of controlling a centralized educational system, with the introduction in 1808 of the *baccalauréat*, used to admit students to a university-level school or faculty, to the *grandes écoles* (which by mid-century had their own competitive entrance examinations), and to government service. Modern languages made their way into the system when, in 1848, a special *agrégation* for modern languages was established. Modern languages formed part also of the scientific *baccalauréat*, an examination whose importance grew during the century as it became required for many posts (Anderson 1975: 13).

In Germany, too, examinations played a major role in the 'systematization' and centralization of education (Müller 1987). The Chinese principle was especially important in Prussia, where around 1830 examinations were developed not just to control schools, but also to select civil servants (McClelland 1980).

In England, the university examination system spread into public life in the nineteenth century, becoming 'a major tool for social policy' (Roach 1971) by its end. Displaying an ethnocentric disregard of continental developments that must be the envy of many of his compatriots, Roach (ibid.: 3) considered public examinations to be 'one of the great discoveries of nineteenth-century Englishmen'. Originally, those taking degrees (a small

proportion of students) had demonstrated their worthiness in public disputations conducted in Latin. As the Reformation destroyed the oral teaching
of Latin, the disputations lost their value, and were first supplemented, and
then replaced, by written examinations (Latham 1877). The most important of these examinations was the Cambridge Senate House Examination,
later called the tripos. The name referred to the three-legged stool on which
the senior bachelor sat for his disputation with the senior wrangler (ibid.:
129). The form of this examination changed, in the eighteenth century,
with the written examination becoming more important than the public
oral disputations. After 1747, the results were published, with the candidates (after 1752) listed in order of merit led by the senior wrangler. In
1774, the examinations were conducted by moderators, who had controlled (moderated) the original disputations; they set and marked the written examinations, conducted the *viva voce* and determined the order of
candidates (ibid.). The examination was conducted in English, and was
mainly concerned with mathematics; the classical tripos was introduced
only in 1824.

By the middle of the nineteenth century, it was widely appreciated that
those who had achieved outstanding results on the Cambridge and
Oxford[14] examinations were likely to gain high status in later life as leaders
of the professions, so that 'the public caught from the Mathematical Tripos
the idea of introducing competitive examinations' Latham (ibid.: 124). In
a speech reported in Hansard (1833) and given in the House of Commons
on 10 July 1833 on the East India Company Bill, Thomas Macaulay made
this clear in his argument for using competitive examinations to select
cadets for the Indian senior civil service. Twenty years later, Macaulay
made the same case in his speech at the second reading of the India Bill
on 24 June 1853 (Hansard 1853). He listed men of distinction who had
already made their mark by being 'first in the competition of the schools',
among them governors-general of India, lawyers, and judges. Even the
Leader of the Opposition, Lord Stanley, agreed to 'a principle unknown in
this country, but which was said to prevail in China, and therefore it might
be called the Chinese principle, namely, that of unlimited intellectual competition for admission to civil offices', although he noted that 'there would
also be a practical difficulty in submitting to a proper examination such an
enormous and unwieldy number of persons'. He had doubts about making
decisions about a man's future on the basis of 'the precocious efforts of
youth' (ibid.: 620), but because it was so much better than patronage, he
would go along with the proposal. The system should not be too rigid, for
there would be 'some risk of flooding India with over-educated mediocrity'.

Speaking in the continuing parliamentary debate a day or so later, Vis-
count Jocelyn agreed that it was necessary to rectify the evils of the existing
patronage system, but he was not in favour of selection by examination:
'It was not a man's passing an examination creditably here that should

give him a right to a place, but proofs given to his character and ability' (ibid.: 728).

In spite of these doubts, the Act passed, but it took five years before the system was in place. The first Indian Civil Service examinations were held in 1858, with sixty-seven candidates, twenty-one of whom were selected for cadetships. The examination marks totalled 6,875; 1,500 being for English language, literature, and history; 750 each for the language, literature, and history of Greece and Latin; 375 each for the language, literature, and history of France, Germany, Italy, and for each of Sanskrit and Arabic language and literature; 1,000 for mathematics; and 500 each for natural and moral sciences (Roach 1971: 196).

The fact that the largest proportion of successful candidates came from public schools and universities relieved the fears that a competitive examination might open up the Indian Service to men who were not gentlemen. In the 1865 report, the Commissioners were proud to report that of the 458 successful candidates in the first decade, 101 had been at educated at Oxford, 80 at Cambridge, 37 at the University of London, 27 at the University of Edinburgh, and 76 at Trinity College Dublin. One Brahmin of high caste 'though unacquainted, as might be expected, with the classical languages of Europe' passed well enough in Sanskrit and Arabic to succeed in the competition. The Commissioners, Roach (ibid.: 199) noted, were pleased especially with the effect that the examinations had as a stimulus to education.

The competitive examination, then, was a democratic but élitist tool, making it possible, superficially at least, to replace patronage with an objective selection procedure in which ability and not birth or connections would determine the result. It was the primary technology employed in the slow transformation from aristocracy to meritocracy, the start of the establishment of a mandarin class in Prussia and Britain and France made up of brilliant and liberally educated senior civil servants. Their very prominence and public success brought distinction to the technology of tests and examinations, and encouraged in turn their wider use and acceptance.

The triumph of the competitive examination

One realm into which the examination moved in England was pre-university education. Booth (1847), vice-principal at the Liverpool Collegiate Institution, wrote a pamphlet proposing a national examination system, with district examining boards awarding certificates without which no person should be eligible for public appointment. A decade later a group of citizens living in Exeter took the initiative which resulted in the Oxford and Cambridge local examinations for secondary school pupils, given first in 1856, by convincing both universities in 1857 to pass statutes establishing a Syndicate to examine students under the ages of 15 and 18 outside the university in 'the English language and literature, history, geography, the French, Latin and German languages, arithmetic, mathematics, natural philosophy, and such other branches of learning as the Syndics . . . may determine' (Roach 1971: 82). The examinations were prepared by a committee of dons who consulted also with schoolmasters.

As the years passed, the Local Examinations grew in status. From the beginning, the Syndics at both universities were concerned about consistency in marking. For the 1858 Oxford examination, a committee worked with the examiners to ensure 'the general consistency of the examination as a whole' and its appropriateness to the variation in candidates and their preparation.[15] In 1864, two committees were set up, one to revise the total marks in the various subjects and the other 'to devise a better method of checks to insure accuracy in the conduct of the examinations'.[16]

The Local Examinations provided a method of honouring the academic prowess of the more successful élite secondary schools. It served also to co-ordinate the curriculum of the various schools. The lack of centralization and the fact that schools could choose which Local Board should examine their pupils avoided the uniformity that reigned in France. However, with the examination sovereign, curricular control was taken out of the school.

The Home Civil Service did not follow the example of the Indian Civil Service for some years, because of the much greater impact of patronage in home positions. Only in 1870 did Gladstone's Order in Council require open competition by examination for a large number of Home Civil Service positions. In the next decade, examinations were a regular topic for public comment in Britain, as has been memorialized in a Gilbert and Sullivan opera:

Peers shall teem in Christendom,
And a Duke's exalted station
Be attainable by Com-
Petitive Examination!
W. S. Gilbert, *Iolanthe* (1882)

There was serious criticism of the dangers of competition, the confining of education, and the inappropriateness of using an honours system to measure average students. In the nineteenth century, examinations were a matter, Roach (ibid.: 285–6) argues, of politics, with the central struggle between individual and collective claims. One early critic was Henry Latham (1877), whose book was 'an enquiry as to what to effect by Examinations and how far we can succeed' (ibid.: iii). By the time it appeared, he was happy to note that many of the 'evils' that had existed in the setting and marking of the Indian Civil Service selection examination when he began to write it had been remedied. None the less, he was convinced that 'within the last thirty years, the agency of Examinations has worked a revolution in the whole province of Education' (ibid.: 1) He characterized examinations as an 'encroaching power' that was influencing education, blurring distinctions between liberal and technical education, and narrowing the range of learning through forcing students to prepare by studying with crammers and in cramming schools. Teaching in England was becoming (just as it was, he said, in France) subordinate to examinations rather than its master.

Latham recognized that 'No particular sort of Examination will produce one kind of effect or test one quality and that alone' (ibid.: 349). He had a number of more specific recommendations about how to make good examinations: he remarked that 'answers that are erroneous throw much light on the state of a student's knowledge' (ibid.: 346). He also said that examinations should be related to use: 'Examinations employed to test the value of acquirements should turn on the exercise of those acquirements as much as possible in the way in which they are employed in actual practice' (ibid.: 349). With stylistic modification, that statement would fit easily into current debates over authenticity (see Spolsky 1985; Stevenson 1985; Bachman 1990). Latham was aware, too, of some of the problems of technical reliability that were to become a central issue in the debate on objectivity. He noted the difference between examinations that were scored 'by impression' and those that were scored 'by marks' (ibid.: 472), and drew attention to the existence of different standards in marks of different examiners. Latham's complaining voice was the first in a long line of critics who were to bewail and, by their complaints, corroborate the new power of examinations in Britain at the end of the nineteenth century.

Not surprisingly, the evolution of examinations in the United States paralleled that of Europe, for their democratic basis, their claim to replace influence by merit, made them especially apt for a radical and revolutionary society. At Harvard, examinations were almost as old as the university itself, Buck (1964) noted in a history of their use. He cited a 1650 statute that required an oral examination every year. For four hours a day, twice a week, for three weeks in late spring, all but first year students were required 'to sit in the Hall to be examined by all Commers in the Latine, Greek and Hebrew tongues and in Rhetoricke, Logike and Physicke' (ibid.: 5). In 1790, detailed regulations were set for public examinations to be conducted by professors and tutors 'in the presence of a joint Committee of the Corporation and Overseers' (ibid.: 7). During the first half of the nineteenth century, the oral examinations continued. In 1857, however, noting problems of oral examining, a committee of four Overseers and four faculty members recommended replacing them by written examinations. In March of that year, the Overseers accepted the proposal to establish annual written examinations, set and marked by the instructors, but approved in advance by committees appointed by the Overseers (ibid.: 11).

In 1869, the award of a Harvard degree was made contingent on the candidate having passed examinations. In 1870, an elective system was introduced and honours were recognized (ibid.: 12). By the end of the century, the notion of examinations in courses was established, but continuing dissatisfaction led to a 1909 proposal to supplement course tests by a general examination 'designed to measure intellectual power and grasp of a subject'. Such a test was implemented gradually between 1909 and 1927 (ibid.: 19).

The interest went beyond Harvard. Beginning in 1709, the town of Boston began the practice of sending 'a certain number of Gentlemen of Liberal Education, Together with some of the Revd. Ministers of the Town' to visit the town school and examine methods and proficiency. Written examinations were introduced into the Boston public system in 1845 by Horace Mann, the Superintendent of Instruction for the Commonwealth of Massachusetts 'for bureaucratic accountability and political purposes' (Madaus and Kellaghan 1992).

The unavoidable uncertainty of the traditional examination

By the end of the nineteenth century, then, the written examination in its traditional form had become stable and entrenched in Europe and the United States. It served three main purposes. First, within an instructional context, it could provide a 'stimulant', a 'spur to better performance' (Buck 1964: 7). Second, as the 'encroaching power', to use Latham's (1877) term, it permitted any external body—a university or a governmental agency—to exert control over the internal operations of educational systems that were becoming increasingly complex. Third, as a 'species of sortition', to use Edgeworth's (1888) phrase, it was arguably preferable to lotteries or patronage in the selection of civil servants or in the certification of professional qualification.

Examinations were firmly fixed in Britain, France, Prussia, and the United States as essential instruments in the control of education and in the certification of qualification for employment and further education. Technologically, they had moved from oral to written form, with the open-ended essay and answer the customary item. There were critics of these purposes, who argued that they led to undue pressure and cramming and over-narrow education, and in both countries there was resistance to centralized examination bodies that would have set too rigid a strait-jacket on local education.

These same debates continued for the next hundred years, but a more momentous attack came not on the *purpose* but on the *technology* itself, when it was demonstrated that the marking of essays and open-ended questions could never reach complete internal consistency or inter-rater reliability. It was this lack of technical reliability that came to worry the scientists who chose to establish the discipline of measurement.

How could one avoid unfair manipulation of the system, critics asked, that would favour certain candidates over others? Fairness remained a somewhat nebulous issue until the quantification of test results permitted formal analysis and proof. Quantification invaded examinations when numerical marks were awarded rather than simply identifying the level or class of a student or his performance. The idea of awarding partial marks for different items in a test and then adding them up to provide a total is attributed by Madaus (1990) to William Farish, an innovation that meant that qualitative scoring 'yielded to the precision tool of the mark'. Quantitative scores, Madaus pointed out could 'accumulate and aggregate student marks, organize them, rank them, classify them, form categories, determine averages, fix norms, describe groups, compare results across units of aggregation, and fix individuals and groups in population distribution' (21 ms.). The analysis of numbers permitted the major assault on the technical reliability (and by implication, fairness) of what had become by the end of the nineteenth century the customary method of examining.

The first published consideration of the effect of error on examinations was a paper read by Professor F. Y. Edgeworth to the Royal Statistical Society in 1888, in which he argued that the general opinion that an examination was only a rough test of merit could be made more precise by application of a part of probability theory, the theory of errors. Physicists, he pointed out, had already demonstrated the existence of error in the measuring of time, distance, and weight. Any series of measures had been shown to deviate from the correct measure in a regular fashion, so that small deviations were more common than larger ones. The resulting observations formed what, he said, 'a lively French statistician' had presented as the *gensd'armes' hat,* an elegant image for the normal curve first postulated by Carl Friedrich Gauss. The assumption, Edgeworth said, was that the highest point showed the true measure. He went on: 'Now there is reason to believe that a similar grouping of divergent estimates prevails when we are weighing—not physical mass—but intellectual worth' (Edgeworth 1888: 601). One might expect the marks given a Latin prose by different examiners to deviate in the same way, clustering around a mid-point. In physics, it was possible to check the correct weight with an atomic balance, but in the 'intellectual ponderation' of examining, one must rely on a Standard of Taste, so that the 'mean judgement of competent critics' was the true score, and any deviations were errors.

The truth emerged from these errors: 'By the cumulation of erroneous observations, it is possible to approximate to the truth' (ibid.: 602). Variations in a typical examination resulting from the fluctuating health of the candidate or the special suitability of the questions were not his first concern; the variation that worried him resided in the examiners' readings. The first cause of error was *minimum sensibile*, the limit in the number of degrees of quality that any human being could perceive, as Galton (1883) had noted. For this he estimated 5 per cent, namely the difference of one point on a twenty-point scale. Idiosyncrasies of the examiner produced the variation of 13 per cent that he had observed between his marks and those of a colleague. Even allowing for the control provided by chief examiners, he assumed an error of 5 per cent, citing in a footnote a number of examples he had seen of much larger variation. His paper included a study of English language papers, some marked hastily and others more slowly, showing the error effect from the rate. He estimated a total 2 per cent error. When the actual error was calculated for some candidates who were marked by different examiners, the error turned out to be higher, 3.5 per cent. Further error, he said, would be attributable to the sampling effect, the assumption that the sample in the examination represented the universe of knowledge being tested. As a result, he believed, a proportion of candidates was awarded honours by chance. He had no simple solution to offer to this problem, but concluded that a public examination is 'a sort of lottery' in which 'the chances are better for the more deserving ... It is a species of sortition infinitely preferable to the ancient method of casting lots for honours and offices' (Edgeworth 1888: 626).

In a second paper, Edgeworth (1890) continued the analysis of the element of chance in competitive examinations. He collected data where two examiners both marked several pieces of work. First, he found that the differences in the averages between two sets of forty papers marked by the same examiner twice, with a 'considerable interval of time intervening' was about 2.5 per cent. He calculated the probability, in various hypothetical situations, that a candidate a certain number of points above the level at which honours were awarded, would have been below the line with a different examiner. By this calculation, he proposed setting a 'security' level. Setting the security level at four times the average discrepancy between the examiners, the chances would be 300 to 1 against a candidate being misplaced.

In another study, this time of a batch of 400 pieces of composition, Edgeworth calculated a much higher error, 6 per cent, meaning that a candidate would have to be 24 per cent above the honours line to exclude the chance that the result was accidental. In two other studies of marking of compositions, he reported error levels of 8 per cent and even 10 per cent.

In his conclusion, Edgeworth (ibid.: 660) cited approvingly the words 'Whatever it is impossible to correct is alleviated by our bearing it patiently.' Accepting that there is 'unavoidable uncertainty in examinations', one should report classes of scores (as in the Oxford system) rather than attempt to rank all candidates (as in the old Cambridge system), the goal being to tell as few lies as possible. The most important thing, he concluded, was to publicize these findings, so that the public would recognize the degree of chance involved in these examinations. It was important, he believed, to recognize not just the fact of uncertainty and error, but the various sources. His peroration called for a 'liberal curiosity' about the accuracy of their examinations among examiners.

There was no direct response to Edgeworth's challenge. In spite of this, his work had to be repeated regularly in the next hundred years, and still failed to convince many examining bodies. For those who were concerned, however, the issue of reliability raised serious doubts about the fairness of the all-powerful examination. It was this fact that prepared the way for the objective test that was to be presented as a seemingly effective and for a time triumphant solution to the challenge of 'unavoidable uncertainty' that Edgeworth had identified.

For the Numbers came

The invention of this major technological innovation was a product of related attempts to measure human cognitive ability. The growth of the mental test, as it was called, had begun at least a decade before Edgeworth's papers, but in a paradigm that he was akin to, with the work of Francis Galton, who, as Gould (1981) has remarked in his popular study of the whole movement, assumed that anything could (and probably should) be measured. A cousin of Darwin, Galton was the founder of modern statistics and the coiner of the term 'eugenics'. Galton's primary objective was a technique of measuring human attributes that would overcome the limitations on human powers of discrimination.

> We inherit our language from barbarous ancestors, and it shows traces of its origin in the imperfect ways by which grades of difference admit of being expressed ... I once took considerable pains in the attempt to draw up verbal scales of more than five orders of magnitude, using those expressions only that every cultivated person would understand in the same sense; but I did not succeed. A series that satisfied one person was not interpreted in the same sense by another.
> (Galton 1883: 33)

Once these abilities had been measured, one would have created (as Foucault 1975: 186 remarked) a science and a discipline. Individual objects, Galton (ibid.) remarked, cluster around a norm, forming a smooth curve, with more variation the further from the average. His approach not only objectivized the individual (as Foucault noticed), but objectivized and reified (in Gould's tendentious term) any measurable or observable quality. This is the basic belief on which mental and other testing is built, explaining

Galton's reputation as the founder of a new field. As Woodworth (1918: 12) acknowledged, 'Galton introduced the conception of mental tests.'

Galton's studies were non-institutional, for he was a man who as Gould (1981: 75) mentions, 'had the rare freedom to devote his considerable energy and intelligence to his favourite subject of measurement'. It was an American scholar, James Cattell, who studied in Europe and with Galton,[17] who showed how they could be transferred to the educational arena. Cattell sounded the battle cry for quantification and measurement in psychology loudly: 'Psychology cannot attain the certainty and exactness of the physical sciences, unless it rests on a foundation of experiment and measurement' (Cattell 1890: 373).[18] To build such a foundation, he offered ten tests which he himself was giving to anyone he could find at the University of Pennsylvania, the full series being taken by all students in experimental psychology. The series started with bodily measures such as dynamometer pressure and rate of movement, and moved through psychophysical (reaction-time for sound) to mental (number of letters recalled on a hearing) measurements. The battery took an hour to administer. Cattell also listed fifty other tests that he had devised.

Cattell's paper was published in *Mind*, where it was followed by some 'Remarks' by Francis Galton, in the first of which Galton questioned Cattell's enthusiasm for collecting data and proposed a more theoretical approach:

> One of the most important objects of measurement is hardly if at all alluded to here, and should be emphasized. It is to obtain a general knowledge of the capacities of a man by sinking shafts, as it were, at a few critical points. In order to ascertain the best points for this purpose, the sets of measures should be compared with an independent estimate of the man's powers. We may thus learn which of the measures are the most instructive.
> (Cattell ibid.: 378)

Even if these verbal estimates were based on only a few minutes' talk, he thought that they could be used; if based on systematic observation over months or year, 'they ought to be exact'.

Cattell (1905) made the transition from theory to practice by showing the relevance of developments in psychology to the determination of individual differences and the selection of individuals. His motivation was strongly social, and evinced recognition of the social effects of unfair or inaccurate testing. His cry is one that is still valid today:

> It is quite possible that the assigning of grades to school children and college students as a kind of reward or punishment is useless or of worth; its value could and should be determined. But when students are excluded from college because they do not secure a certain grade in a

written examination, or when candidates for positions in the government service are selected as the result of a written examination, we assume a serious responsibility. The least we can do is to make a scientific study of our methods and results.
(ibid.: 376)

He concluded with a comment that remains unfortunately widely true: 'Grades assigned to college students have some meaning, though just what this is remains to be determined' (ibid.). At the beginning of the century, there had already been study in America of school marks and grades. Wissler, and Thorndike and his students had observed high correlations between grades a student received in different fields, arguing that the grades had probably been awarded as much for 'moral traits' or 'general impression' as for subject-specific ability and performance. Cattell remarked on the differences in 'examinability' between subjects. While mathematics could be graded with 'considerable accuracy', literature and psychology were more difficult. He drew attention to the use of written examinations for college admission: 'It seems scarcely possible to determine what students are fitted for a college course by means of a written examination; and I fear that the systematization of entrance examinations under the auspices of a board will be harmful to secondary education' (ibid.: 378). Rather, he would prefer the German system of leaving the decision to the secondary schools. While he would agree that almost anything was better than appointment for party service, he believed that decisions must include information on 'past performance, character, habits, heredity and physical health'. To make appointments of professors on the basis of written examinations, he believed, 'would be nearly as absurd as to choose a wife as the result of a written examination on her duties' (ibid.).

Cattell's work in the United States added to that of others like Thorndike and Wissler was slowly introducing objective measurement into the examination business, but the major breakthrough in testing came from the work of a French doctor with a pragmatic need to deal with a real problem. 'More than anyone else', Terman (1925: 2) remarked, 'it was Binet who taught us where to search among mental functions for significant intellectual differences'.

The measurement of intelligence

Binet's work first appeared in *L'Année psychologique* in 1905. In 1904, the Ministry of Public Instruction had required an examination to determine which children were retarded and needed special education. When Binet took on the task, assisted by Théodore Simon, he found the field confused and haphazard. All existing methods of classification were subjective, and there was no agreement in applying terms like idiot, moron, and imbecile. What was lacking, they remarked, was a 'precise basis for differential diagnosis' (Binet and Simon 1916: 14). Up until then, all approaches had been descriptive. A more useful approach was suggested by the work of Dr Blin and Dr Damaye, who had composed a list of questions on twenty topics that they posed to a subject; but they too made subjective decisions after the interview, and the topics were arbitrary.

Binet's innovation was to propose 'a measuring scale of intelligence' (ibid.: 40) based on a series of tasks of different difficulty for which he had determined the age at which a 'normal' child could perform the task or answer the question. These normal scores would make it possible to determine the 'mental age' of any new subject in relation to the norming population. Binet and Simon recognized that this artifact was not a real measure, 'because intellectual qualities are not superposable and therefore cannot be measured as linear surfaces are measured, but are, on the contrary, a classification, a hierarchy among different intelligences' (ibid.), but for practical needs, they believed, it could be considered as equivalent to a measure. The main purpose of Binet's work, then, was to deal with mental retardation, of which he believed only a multiplicity of tests would give a clear picture. He introduced the notion of mental age, but it is clear that his tests were meant to be used diagnostically and to provide descriptive rather than strictly scalar results.

The new technology of testing received a major (and some would argue deceptive) boost from the invention of a new technology for statistical analysis. Going beyond correlation, the idea of hierarchical order in correlations led to the discovery of factor analysis. In 1904, Charles Spearman, professor of education at the University of London, published two papers on correlations, in the first of which (1904a), he set out to explore the basis for a developing field of 'Correlational Psychology', as he named it, showing the advantage of correlating ranks and not just raw measurements, and discussing how to reduce the effects of error. In the second (1904b), he considered the existence of correlations found between various mental tests and claimed to have discovered a general factor (General Ability or General Intelligence, named g) in a hierarchical relationship with a number of Specific Intelligences.

Even those scholars who opposed Spearman, like William Brown, considered his work 'epoch-making'. But his claim to have proved the existence of general intelligence was disputed: Brown and Thomson (1921) were among the first to argue that it was an unjustified reification to identify the first factor as intelligence. In his preface to what was the second edition of Brown's original 1914 book (the first had also opposed Spearman), Thomson argued that 'hierarchical order is the natural order among correlation coefficients, that it only expresses the well-known fact that correlation coefficients are themselves correlated, and that the degree of hierarchical order found among psychological correlation coefficients is merely that which occurs by chance'.

Thomson demonstrated that the same hierarchical order emerged when he set up a table of random variables produced by throws of the dice. He argued then for what he called a sampling theory of ability. In what was to be a lifelong dispute, he accepted the existence of *g* as a mathematical entity, but considered it dangerous to reify it (Thomson 1939); the factors that emerged in factor analysis could not be assigned to individuals (Thomson 1954). More strong attacks on Spearman were to come later, in the work of L. L. Thurstone, University of Chicago professor of psychology, who pointed out in his 1935 work, *The Vectors of the Mind*, the meaninglessness of *g*, proposing rather a technique of rotating the matrices of factor analysis to produce what he called primary mental abilities. Gould (1981) argues that factor analysis does not in fact permit one to decide how many factors there are, for it allows a number of different solutions according to the wish of the researcher. Carroll (1993), reporting on a lifetime working with factor analysis, shows a way of reconciling some of these contradictions. But the damage had been done: the notion of general intelligence, once let out of its box, came to dominate the thought of laymen and form the basis for a new industry of mental measurement.

When reports of Binet and Simon's work first reached the United States in 1906, they made little impact. However, on a visit to Europe in 1908, Henry Goddard, psychologist at the New Jersey Training School for Feeble-minded Boys and Girls, in Vineland, saw the new technology. Although he was not fully convinced of the value of the scales published in 1909, he decided to try them. He was so impressed with the results that he immediately published an outline, and was successful in 1910 in persuading the physician-dominated American Association for the Study of the Feeble-minded to adopt the Binet tests as the way to diagnose mental subnormality (Zenderland 1987: 46).

The spread of the Binet scale was furthered by the work of Terman, who, in 1910, when he received an appointment to the psychology department at Stanford University, began work to revise it. He published a tentative revision in 1912 and a finished version in 1916, which he called the Stanford-Binet scale (Terman 1916).[19] The Stanford revision, Terman explained, was intended to correct 'imperfections' in the scale, now becoming widely used, and to provide sufficiently detailed explanation for the 'rank and file' of teachers, doctors, and social workers to be able to use it. The mental tests, he believed, would save money by permitting more focused teaching for the retarded and so reduce crime and the cost of prisons. The first saving would be $40,000,000 annually. The second would be a good proportion of the $500,000,000 that he estimated vice and crime cost the United States each year. 'A little psychological research would aid the united charities of any city to direct their expenditures into more profitable channels than would otherwise be possible' (ibid.: 18). Intelligence, he agreed with Binet, was the sum total of the processes, which needed to be measured functionally and dynamically.

Leahey (1987) suggests that US psychology had an applied bent from the beginning, in the work of Cattell and Goddard. In England, the Binet-Simon scale was introduced to widespread use by Cyril Burt (1921) who, in the years immediately after World War I, was psychologist for the education department of the London County Council. But its wide public acceptance came in the United States after World War I, thanks largely to the organizing and public relations work of Robert Yerkes, who firmly established mental measurement with the American public.

The modern language test, with its goal of providing objective and reliable measurement, was to grow in an atmosphere of respect not only for the natural and unchallengeable authority of the examination, but also for the flowering of psychology and associated psychometrics with its promise of scientifically achievable objectivity and fairness. One clear sign of this growing interest was the founding in 1921 of the Psychological Corporation: two of the signatories of the charter of incorporation were Cattell and Thorndike. The incorporation agreement required that stock owners carry out active research for the Corporation, the goal of which was to make it possible for psychologists to do business with businessmen (some of the earliest studies were in marketing and advertising, but others involved testing) (Joncich 1968: 385). Cattell told the first annual meeting of the new corporation that the army tests had put psychology on the map. The powerful examination gained even greater power when it was believed to be based on the accurate measurement of knowable qualities and abilities.

Notes

1 A number of language testers have independently noted this case, and as is usually the case with biblical interpretation, each has derived a different understanding. Robert Lado cited it at the beginning of his doctoral dissertation, noting that the 'mispronunciation of the Ephraimites is well understood in modern linguistic terms' (Lado 1949: 6). He assumed that because their language lacked the sound represented by [S], they substituted the nearest sound. His thesis, he said, was based on a systematic study of similar effects of differences between a native language and one being learnt. My own explanation, it will be noted, is sociolinguistic rather than structuralist. Alan Davies (1992) also quoted the story, considering the test to be 'quite useless, too powerful' to be a good language test, missing the fact that users prefer tests to make clear binary decisions.

2 A more modern version is the little poem beginning 'Bûter, brea en griene tsiis' used by Friesians to recognize Dutch speakers.

3 I am grateful to Madaus (1990) for drawing my attention to the treatment of examinations by Foucault. But I suspect Madaus is wrong in concluding that Foucault is talking specifically of 'written examinations'. He talks of the 'age of the "examining" school' ('l'âge de l'école "examinatoire"' (Foucault 1975: 189), which he sees as marking the beginning of educational science. The important records are those kept by the teachers, so that the register of results of daily catechisms and *viva voce* class tests are the basis for the new discipline. But obviously, the technology of written examinations (and even more of the machine-read answer sheet) made possible the growth of education as a scientific field. Foucault's obvious dislike for examinations may reasonably be blamed in part on his own dramatic failures with the *agrégation*, a full account of which is given by Eribon (1991: 36–8), and his earlier similar problems with examinations.

4 'un regard normalisateur, une surveillance qui permet de qualifier, de classer et de punir'. The translations are from the English edition (1979) unless otherwise stated.

5 'lieu de formation et de collation des connaissances'.

6 'une sorte d'appareil d'examen interrompu'.

7 'une archive tenue et minutieuse'.

8 'un cas'.

9 'J'interrompis ici ce livre qui doit servir d'arrière-plan historique à diverses études sur le pouvoir de la normalisation et la formation du savoir dans la société moderne' (p. 315).

10 There is an earlier account of examinations being used to control schools from outside. Madaus and Kellaghan (1992) describe a medieval language test, a *viva voce* examination with such a purpose: under the terms of a contract between the city elders of Treviso and the schoolmaster, the latter's salary depended on the pupils' level of attainment.

11 Madaus (1990) cites Webber (1989) as tracing the source of French examinations to China through the Jesuits, who appear to have used written examinations as early as the sixteenth century.

12 The form was revised regularly for the next century and more.

13 Coffman (1993) attacks the unwillingness to learn from past experience in the current US concern for national goals and national testing.

14 Oxford established a single examination for the bachelor's degree in 1800, which was entirely oral. In the 1807 statute, examiners were authorized to give written papers too; by 1819, there were two days of written examinations followed by one of oral, while in 1842 there were five days of written examinations followed by the *viva voce* examination (Clarke 1959: 98–9).

15 Cited by Roach (1971: 148) from the 1858 minutes of the Local Examination Delegates.
16 Cited by Roach (1971: 148) from the minutes of the Syndicate.
17 Born in 1860, James Cattell studied at Johns Hopkins from 1882–3 before spending three years in Leipzig with William Wundt. Later, he spent some time with Francis Galton, then returned to the United States to take up a position at the University of Pennsylvania.
18 Reprinted in Cattell (1973).
19 The book was dedicated to the memory of Alfred Binet, who had died in 1911, and who was described in the dedication as 'patient researcher, creative thinker, unpretentious scholar; inspiring and fruitful devotee of inductive and dynamic psychology'.

3 The new-type language test: 1913–1935

Beginnings of language tests

The modern language test, like other objective tests, emerged in the context of the continuing tension between the unmistakably effective and awesome power of the examination and the manifest uncertainty of its scores. The technological innovation was accepted reluctantly at first by only a few educators, but rapidly became the dominant force in American institutional testing.

While it is probably true that the experience with mental testing in the US Army in World War I[1] was the major impetus for the success of objective testing with the American public, the story started some twenty years earlier, with the proposal by J. M. Rice, in 1894, that spelling could be measured objectively by giving students a list of words to spell, and awarding them a score based on the number of their correct answers (Ruch and Stoddard 1927). Rice also prepared tests in arithmetic and language, but did not attempt to standardize them. While his tests removed human subjective judgement from the marking process, they made no effort to consider the selection of items or the relative standing of students, nor did they attempt to establish a criterion for interpretation of the results.

The earliest attempt to create tests that were at once objective and standardized was made by Edward L. Thorndike, who after some studies of school grades (Thorndike 1903), published a textbook for the social sciences and education on measurement (Thorndike 1904), in which he dealt with the problem of what should be the units of measurement in a test. Thorndike thought that Rice had been wrong to assign a single point to each answer in his spelling tests without considering the variation in difficulty between the items. Two scores on the same test would have quite different meanings if one student had answered only easy questions and the other only hard ones. Believing that 'any mental trait in any individual is a variable quantity' (ibid.: 22) and normally distributed, Thorndike argued for the use of scales[2] as the best method of achieving standardized and more objective scores, arguing that 'Amongst school abilities, achievements in handwriting, drawing, painting, writing English, translation . . . etc., are readily measured by serial rating, and the agreement is such that great reliance can be put on the results' (ibid.: 20). The handwriting scale that he published a few years later (Thorndike 1910) has good claims to be the first standardized test. To develop it, Thorndike collected a thousand samples of writing, from the worst to the best, from pupils in grades five to eight, and had thirty judges rank them; a sample showed the levels of the scale.

This dispute between Rice, who gave a score based on the number of individual items correctly answered, and Thorndike, who sought a way of scaling integrated skills, has many echoes in the history of language testing, with its classic statement in John Carroll's paper at the 1961 conference that led to the development of the Test of English as a Foeign Language.[3] Thorndike's argument related directly to the sampling problem. If we test a subject's ability to spell all the words in the language, the claim that the subject knows a certain percentage is meaningful. But if the test contains only a selection of words, how can we justify the weight given to any one word? Are not some words harder than others? Might not one student have answered all the easy words, and another all the hard words? From his early work, Thorndike took the position that the scaled subjective grading of integrative performance was preferable to the objective counting of unweighted items.

Thorndike (1904) was well aware of the problems of reliability that resulted from the decision to assess integrative performance. Any source of constant error must be avoided if the measurement was to be pure. While 'probable error' inevitably remained, it should not give rise to too much concern:

> Much time may be wasted in refining measures in cases where no advantage accrues. And much ignorance is shown by the many students who disparage all measurements that are subject to large variable error. They either do not know or forget that the reliability of a measure is due to the number of cases as well as to their variability, and that in the more complex and subtle mental traits, it is always practical to increase the number of measurements but often impossible to make them less subject to variable errors.
> (ibid.: 158)

Thorndike thus echoed Edgeworth's (1888) recognition of the 'unavoidable uncertainty' of testing, agreeing also that such error would survive the most careful refinements. In practice, however, the pursuit of the will-o'-the-wisp of near-perfect reliability seems to have dominated the work of psychometrists who gained control of institutional testing, at the expense of paying attention to what was being measured and to the use of the measures. Rice's spelling tests produced numerical scores that seemed accurate, but the interpretation of which was an act of faith. Thorndike's less objective scales made explicit their dependence on human judgement; their very lack of perfect objectivity was a constant reminder of the need for responsibly cautious interpretation.[4]

Thorndike (1910: 41) made also the crucial but often ignored point that in the 'science of human nature' (the *discipline* of education or psychology, in Foucault's terms), the measurement of an individual is made only in order to get measures of groups. The very inaccuracy that is an essential feature of measurement means that any confidence about group decisions cannot responsibly or ethically be carried over automatically to any individual decision.

By 1912, one of Thorndike's students had developed a scale for composition, which provided samples for judgement by comparison (Thorndike 1912). The first important steps had thus been taken in proposing objective ways of measuring language abilities, in the hope of reducing or eradicating 'unavoidable uncertainty'. Ideas like these already emerged in the work of one of the first committees set up, in 1913, to study modern language testing.

The 1913 committee

The plan to add measures of spoken language abilities to the requirements for college admission was, Carroll (1954)[5] suggested, one of the earliest published calls for 'objective psychological testing'. A committee appointed in 1913 by the Association of Modern Language Teachers of the Middle States of Maryland, proposed an Aural and Oral Test in French, German, and Spanish, which it circulated to a thousand schools for comments. The majority of respondents agreed that it was the only fair way to recognize and encourage the widespread direct method teaching which emphasized speaking the language. The committee reported[6] that the influential College Entrance Examination Board (its full title) had given 'hearty approval' to their idea but 'technical difficulties in securing absolute uniformity' had prevented action (Committee on Resolutions and Investigations 1917).

Their 1914 questionnaire included three specimen tests, consisting of a ten-minute dictation, the written reproduction, in the foreign language, of a short prose passage read by the examiner, and written answers, in the foreign language, to questions read by the examiner. The committee recognized 'that no actual oral test is included in this examination' but they were confident 'that no candidate could pass it who had not received abundant oral, as well as aural training' (ibid.: 252). An earlier plan had included 'an individual test in pronunciation and speaking' but as this had not proved feasible, schools could do this as they wished.

Three points deserve comment. The first is the motivation of the test developers, which was to win back curricular control from a written examination that was working against a teaching technique that was concentrating on the spoken language. It demonstrated thus a struggle for power over the curriculum, showing an attempt to benefit from what is now called the washback (or backwash)[7] effect, or curricular emphasis, of a test.

Second, the pattern of feasibility overcoming desirability in this case was to be regularly repeated. Even though everyone agreed that it was beneficial to test the use of the spoken language, it turned out to be more practical to do this indirectly by using a pen-and-paper test. In the interests of efficiency or feasibility, then, a quite different set of skills was tested. Regularly, we will find ease triumphing over principle.

Third, as early as 1914 the committee wanted an objective test and was concerned with finding 'uniformity'. This interest in objectivity was to be strengthened greatly as a result of the activities of psychometrists in the war. It was the successful selling of the myth of the usefulness of the Army Alpha tests that established in the American public its faith not just in intelligence testing but also in the possibility of objective testing of other human abilities.

The Army Alpha tests

The Army Alpha tests were the brainchild of Robert M. Yerkes. When, before the war, he wrote an introduction to psychology, Yerkes (1911) had made no mention of measurement, or testing, or Binet. Two years later, however, he started work on something that he considered an improvement over the method of Binet, a 'point scale for measuring mental ability' (Yerkes, Bridges, and Hardwick 1915). At the same time, Otis had started working on an objectively scorable group intelligence test for elementary school children (it was published in Otis 1918). The influence of this work followed from the opportunities provided by World War I. Two days after the United States entered the war, on 6 April 1917, Yerkes rushed to organize the psychological war effort. At a somewhat fiery meeting, from which Walter Scott walked out (leaving Yerkes without substantive majority support), the Council of the American Psychological Society endorsed Yerkes's plan for 'the Psychological Testing of Recruits to eliminate the Mentally Unfit' (von Mayrhauser 1987).

Though Yerkes himself would have preferred to have all tests administered individually, the press of numbers and lack of time and resources led to the adoption of the group testing of over a million recruits, using group tests developed on the basis of the work of Charles Otis. While it is now generally agreed that the tests had little practical or military[8] worth, Yerkes and his assistant, Brigham,[9] were successful in publicizing the programme and in developing a myth of the significance of its data (Reed 1987: 84). The scoring was far from error free,[10] and different scales were used. The Army Alpha tests, though, with all their weaknesses and confusion, were the beginning of mass objective testing of mental abilities[11] and were to be sold to the general public as the solution to the unreliability of traditional examinations. For Yerkes, man was just as measurable as machine.[12]

In some quarters, there was strong criticism of the new intelligence tests, especially as their racist implications emerged. Brigham (1923) emphasized the racial implications. 'We must now frankly admit the undesirable results which would ensue from a cross between the Nordic in this country with the Alpine Slav, with the degenerated hybrid Mediterranean, or with the Negro, or from the promiscuous intermingling of all four types' (ibid.: 208). American intelligence, he concluded, would continue to decline as long as immigration was free: 'Immigration should not only be restrictive but highly selective' (ibid.: 210). The journalist Walter Lippmann was one of the most outspoken of the opponents (Block and Dworkin 1976). Lippmann noted the problem of how the norms had been set, the lack of a clear definition of what was being measured, the fact that the tests could be right for the group but wrong in individual cases, the danger of abuse in using them to label children, their claim to be measuring something that was inherited and so fixed, and the social implications of this claim. In spite of his concern about the serious potential misuses and misinterpretations, he did see their values in school situations, as a better method of grading than normal and as a good way of helping children fit into school. Terman's response (in his replies published in the *New Republic* and reprinted in Block and Dworkin 1976), disclaimed any responsibility for potential misuse, an argument that continues to be made by testers, just as it is made by gun and cigarette manufacturers.

Objective testing captures American education

If even such an eloquently outspoken critic as Walter Lippmann could see some redeeming value in the new tests, it is no wonder that the movement spread with such rapidity. By 1920, most state universities were offering courses in educational measurement, and by 1923 half the business of the Teachers College Bureau of Publications was in test and scales, with over 12,000,000 copies sold in the previous ten years (Joncich 1968: 389). Test publishing was becoming big business.

The movement gained more power when Brigham and his psychometrically inclined colleagues became involved in the growth of centralized college admission in the United States. While he was a teacher at Princeton in the 1920s, Brigham had begun to experiment with objective intelligence tests that he gave to incoming freshmen. Under his influence, Princeton began to require the test of all candidates for admission in 1925; in the same year, the College Entrance Examination Board commissioned Brigham and other university psychologists to start constructing the tests that became the Scholastic Aptitude Test (Whitla 1964: 57).

The College Board had been conceived during the last decades of the nineteenth century to remedy the lack of co-ordination or consensus among colleges in requirements or methods of selecting students for admission. Formally constituted in November 1900 by the founding group of a dozen colleges (Farrand 1926), the College Board set up nine groups, each consisting of two college professors and one secondary school teacher, to conduct its first examinations in June 1901 for 973 candidates at 67 locations in the United States and two in Europe. By 1925, 35 colleges had joined and there were twenty examining groups, 316 centres, 20,000 candidates, and 600 readers.

At first, the College Board had planned to leave the specifications and requirements for the examinations and the resulting power over the school curriculum to authorities in each field of study, such as the Modern Language Association for English and languages. However, as these bodies were more interested in scholarship than in the teaching of their subject, in 1907 the College Board appointed its own commissions of specialists in each of the fields. The first tests were traditional, but there was an early interest in objectivity. Thus, in 1920, a Commission on New Types of Examinations was set up, but by 1925, no conclusions had been reached about the effectiveness of its experiments (ibid. 1926).

The early philosophy of the College Board was expressed by Lowell, for whom examining was an art: 'The value of an art depends on the purposes for which it is used, and the intelligence and precision of its application' (Lowell 1926: 31). Examinations, he believed, should have three purposes: to measure progress, to control instruction, and to set a standard. The College Board saw control of the curriculum and of the pupils as its key mission.

In the preface to the book published to mark the twenty-fifth anniversary of the College Board (College Entrance Examination Board 1926), the secretary, Thomas Fiske, wrote that there were two important messages to be learnt from the experience of the College Board. The first was that educational problems were best solved with the co-operation of all institutions and individuals who were 'vitally concerned' in the issue, and the second, that the best measures of students' attainments and the greatest value for education would be derived from examinations conducted by a body that was outside the school and free of any local or provincial control.

Quite different arguments started to be heard when Brigham joined the College Board as assistant secretary. Carl Brigham chaired the committee on the Scholastic Aptitude Test. In a report (ibid.: 44–63), he explained the psychometric principles behind testing:

Studies carried out in the early twenties had shown the usefulness of psychological tests as predictors of college success. The validity of these predictions was shown by correlations. For many reasons, there were no chances of reaching perfect prediction; rather, any tests could be reported as achieving a certain per cent of perfect prediction or a per cent of the factors measured. In actual practice, Boards of Admission, therefore, are not confronted with the problem of perfect prediction, but with the prob-

lem of devising a method that gives the best possible predictions, or one
with as high a correlation as possible with the most reliable combinations
of academic grades obtainable.
(ibid.: 53)

Part of the problem, he admitted, resided in the tests, which did not
(and could not) measure all the relevant factors with perfect accuracy.
But this imperfection was not to be blamed only on the tests. The grades
that showed success at college were themselves far from reliable measures. Nor, without an impossible experiment of letting all applicants in,
including those normally screened out by the test, was there any way
to know the full benefit of the screening and the predictive power of
the test. The committee did stress the need for multiple measures, knowing that any single measure could be wrong. Until World War II, the
objective Scholastic Aptitude Tests were sometimes given alongside the
old essay examinations, but after that they reigned alone, although with
continuing challenges.

There was objectivization of examining in New York State, too, where
the Board of Regents had since 1878 been conducting secondary school
examinations that were based on detailed syllabuses. Starting in 1923, the
Department of Education began to experiment with *new-type* objective
examinations. In 1924, half the questions in algebra and some in social
science were new type. In 1925, under the direction of Ben D. Wood, new-
type examinations were tried in modern languages and physics, and subsequently extended to other subjects (Kandel 1936).

These attacks on traditional examinations in the United States were
bolstered by a pack of studies conducted between 1912 and 1920,
summarized by Kandel. Three studies by Starch and Elliott showed wide
variation in marks in English (Starch and Elliott 1912), mathematics
(Starch and Elliott 1913a), and history (Starch and Elliott 1913b). Finkelstein (1913) reported that different instructors gave different grades to
the same student in a year course at Cornell, and Starch (1913), reported
that teachers at Wisconsin gave different marks to a paper when they
regraded it without knowing former marks. Sandiford (1928: 303–4)
reported on major variation in the grades assigned a single paper. These
continuing attacks on the reliability of examinations, Kandel remarked,
tended to bring traditional examinations into disrepute and establish the
powerful seductiveness of the objective test.

The modern language test started to flourish in the United States during
this period of objectivization. A study of its history reveals the continuing
tension between the demands of psychometric theory and practice for
objectivity and reliability in measurement, and the fact that what is being
measured is that most flexible, multidimensional, fugitive, and complex of
human abilities, the ability to use language.

The growth of new-type testing

In the decade that followed World War I, there was a prolific outpouring of new objective tests and scales for all school subjects. One of the early writers was Daniel Starch, [13] who printed three foreign language tests, one in each of Latin, French, and German. Each test had the same form, consisting of a list of foreign words to be matched with their English translation, and a group of sentences to be translated into English, the latter labelled a reading test. Starch's tests seem to have been the first published version of an objective modern language test.

American developments had their parallel in Britain. The transition from intelligence to achievement testing, from mental testing to educational or scholastic tests, was formally proposed by Cyril Burt (1921) in a report to the London County Council. The first two sections dealt with the Binet-Simon scale. The third memorandum, headed 'Tests of Educational Attainments', argued for the need of a scheme of tests measuring school progress with the same standing as the Binet-Simon scale. Teachers' judgements were good as far as they went, but for 'quantitative exactitude' something more precise was needed. In his essay, Burt remarked on the 'eagerness, perhaps too great an eagerness' that had been evinced in America to 'supplement traditional examinations by psychological tests, and to apply the new statistical methods to the survey of educational systems' (ibid.: 257). He made a clear distinction between the 'extemporized test' of the teacher and the 'standardized test' of the psychologist; each had its appropriate role. He then went on to present and discuss a number of standardized tests of reading, arithmetic, spelling, dictation, and composition. Burt's ideas had also appeared in a book published a little earlier by Ballard (1920), who was also aware of Thorndike's composition scale, though he remarked that 'If it ever comes to England it must be put in English garb.' Burt's arguments were clearly stated, but his message was not widely accepted in Britain. It was in the United States that the movement had its greatest success.

The case for the new-type tests was put forward in the United States by a number of books. Ernest Horn[14] noted the need for more standardized tests, which had so far been very beneficial to educational practice. Ruch (1924) himself believed that while examinations in their traditional form were 'almost or quite as old as formal education', only in the last twenty-five years had important reforms been introduced in testing methods. The three kinds of examinations he recognized were the traditional essay-type, the standardized educational test or scale, and the newer objective examination, where the questions were of a true-false, multiple-choice, completion, or matching variety, and he demonstrated how effective objective tests could be developed in all school subjects.

By the mid-1920s, the objective test was firmly established in American education. In a manual for teachers summarizing the 'best rules' for

new-type examinations, Paterson (1925) was able to list some fifty-five articles and books, most written in the previous few years, that had argued
for or described new subject-matter related examinations in fields ranging
from algebra to woodworking. Ruch and Stoddard (1927) reported that
they knew of more than 500 tests and scales.

The first language tests published for sale appeared just after World War I.
Ignoring for some reason the language tests that Starch (1916) had printed
earlier, pride of place is usually given to Carl Handschin (1919), who published silent reading tests in French and Spanish, followed shortly by
Henmon (1921), who published French vocabulary and sentence translation tests.[15] In 1923, Columbia University published the Méras-Roth-Wood
French Scale.[16] Pressey and Pressey (1922) commented that the modern
language tests that had been published generally covered vocabulary, silent
reading, and sometimes grammar. These pioneering efforts at language testing were soon to be supplemented and swamped by the first major effort
by the North American foreign language teaching profession to reassess
and plan its field of activity.

The Modern Foreign Language Study and the American Council Alpha tests

Two other standardized tests were published in the next year or so, but
when planning for the Modern Foreign Language Study began in 1924,
there were few standard tests available. Testing perforce became a crucial
part of the project when the Study commenced. The tradition of committee
projects in foreign language education, foreshadowed by the 1913 committee described at the beginning of the chapter, was carried to an unappreci-
ated high mark by the pioneering efforts, from 1924 to 1927, of two committees, the Modern Foreign Language Study and the Canadian Committee
on Modern Languages. With grants from the Carnegie Corporation of New
York, these committees of scholars made a thorough and thoughtful
inquiry into the situation of modern foreign language teaching in the United
States and Canada (Coleman 1929). It is regrettable that they are remembered not for the score or so of excellent volumes that their exertions produced, but for their reluctant decision to recognize that the existing reality
of the allocation of time and resources to foreign language in schools and
colleges did not justify continuing a full coverage of skills. Seeing that most
students took one or two semesters of college foreign languages, it was
decided that it was more efficient to limit the goal of these courses to developing reading ability.

> Experimental data in the modern-language field warrant the hypothesis
> that there is a close correspondence between limited reading experience

and the poor attainment in reading by large numbers of second- and third-year students as attainment is evaluated by the American Council reading tests and by teacher opinion . . . Since reading ability is the one objective on which all agree, classroom efforts during the first two years should center primarily on developing the ability to understand the foreign language readily through the eye and through the ear. The goal must be to read the foreign language directly with a degree of understanding comparable to that possessed in reading the vernacular. In order that students may attain this goal, reading experience must be adequate and the results of all other types of class exercises must converge toward the same end.
(ibid. 1929: 170)

As a result, the members of the Committee of Modern Foreign Language Study appear in recent language testing histories as the villains who discarded the direct method rather than as the realists who saw no way to increase the amount of time students would give to language learning, and as the researchers who established the basis for empirical study of language teaching and testing.

From the beginning of its intelligently planned studies, the goal of which was to assert professional control over language teaching, the committee acknowledged the need for 'devising and standardizing objective tests for measuring achievement in the foreign languages' (Henmon 1929: v). Only with such tests could accurate statements be made about the achievement levels of teaching, and the relative value of competing types of organization or methods. A good part of the effort of the study, then, was devoted to creating both achievement and prognostic tests. Working under the direction of Professor Vincent Henmon, committees developed tests in three languages, from experimental to final form. Known as the 'American Council Alpha Tests', two test forms were later published by the World Book Company in each of French, German, and Spanish, covering vocabulary, grammar, and reading. A scale for rating compositions was also prepared.

Henmon saw the work of constructing the tests as a team effort, an approach that was to be the mark of much work in modern language testing in the United States, where committees of teachers became the commonplace vehicle for test planning and writing. His underlying philosophy was clearly stated: a study of overall achievement in modern language teaching required some reasonable hard data as its base. He believed that 'Without more objective and impersonal measures than opinion or the highly subjective, variable, and unreliable system of school marks, no fruitful or convincing analysis can be made of many important problems' (ibid.: 2).

Henmon recognized four basic criteria for a good test: validity (it should 'measure what it purports to measure'), reliability, comprehensiveness, and administrative feasibility. The order is worth noting: for the purposes of

the study, it made little sense to have measures that were not clearly interpretable. If the study was to be able to make comments on the level of
achievement in foreign language reading, it would want measures that obviously represented this. The first priority, then, was to try to measure what
the study was interested in. In practice, as will be seen, the fourth criterion,
administrative feasibility, did conflict with the first.

Henmon believed that a fairly complete profile of achievement would be
obtainable with a nine-part battery that would ideally include vocabulary,
silent reading or comprehension of sentences and of paragraphs, translation
into and from English, a written composition scale, a grammar test of 'functional' knowledge, an aural comprehension test, a pronunciation test, and
an oral composition test. Only the last two, Henmon felt, would be difficult
to prepare: 'Standardized group tests for pronunciation and oral composition which could be administered widely seem almost impossibilities' (ibid.:
3). All the others were feasible, and while some abilities might prove to be
highly correlated (a fact that was to create continual havoc in the field), it
was necessary to create a complete battery in order to check this empirically. This was to be the main thrust of the work of the testing committees.

As it worked out in practice, the Alpha testers concentrated their efforts
on the five subjects that were most readily measurable: vocabulary, grammar, silent reading, written comprehension, and aural comprehension. The
main purpose of the tests was to measure group achievement, as was fitting
for their use in a study of the contemporary state of language teaching,
but they could give evidence of individual achievement and progress. Lack
of time prevented standardization of the aural comprehension tests, including plans to put them on phonograph records for group administration and
uniformity; here, then, 'administrative feasibility' (which probably could
be translated as insufficient time and funds) became the deciding factor.

The Alpha tests were not based directly on teaching material but on
'determination by actual count of the frequency of occurrence of words,
idioms, and syntactical phenomena in the literature the students will read'
(ibid.: 8). This was one way to overcome the problem pointed out by
Thorndike (1904) in deciding what weight should be assigned to individual
test items. Following this principle, the French vocabulary test consisted of
75 words selected from a frequency list based on a count of 400,000 running words of text (textbooks and normal material) that Henmon had
made earlier; the list was being extended to a 1,200,000-word corpus by
the project. The German vocabulary test was based on a 10-million-word
corpus from 1898 (Kaeding's *Häufigkeitswörterbuch der deutschen
Sprache*); the Spanish on a 1,200,000-word count. Only the Italian was
based on words in beginning texts.

Recognition was the technique chosen to test vocabulary. The test gave
a foreign word followed by five English words, and instructed candidates
to mark the correct translation. The English words chosen were selected

from incorrect answers in earlier administration of the items as completion tests. Henmon was fully aware of the arguments for testing words in context, and the equally strong arguments for completion or recall items rather than multiple choice, but answered them readily:

> The reply is that the recognition method gives more pupil response in the same length of time, that scoring is easier and more objective, and that while the absolute scores by the completion or recall method are considerably lower, the correlation between results of this with those obtained by the recognition are almost as high as the reliabilities of either technique.
> (Henmon 1929: 10)

The issue of open-ended versus multiple-choice items remains with us to this day. Most of the grammar items in the Alpha tests were of the completion type, but alternative completion and recognition forms were developed. The issue of which to use remained unresolved in the study. Henmon's decision was a pragmatic one. Because he was designing a test for a large-scale survey, there would not be individual decisions to be made. The technique enabled him to achieve reasonable technical reliability at fairly low cost. But the limitations are obvious, and there would be no justification for using this test for other purposes.

Henmon considered the silent reading test to be important, and in spite of the difficulty, decided to concentrate on a paragraph-question technique, that is to say, questions that selected a few issues that tested understanding at the paragraph level rather than a larger number of questions relevant to the sentence and word level. The Alpha reading tests therefore consisted of seven or eight paragraphs intended to be of increasing difficulty, each followed by from four to seven questions presented in the foreign language, but to be answered in English as briefly as possible. In actual practice, 'pressure of time prevented accurate scaling of the paragraphs and a detailed analysis of each answer' (ibid.: 10), and the score given was the total number of items answered correctly in the time.

Believing that 'free composition is the best test of knowledge of a language' (ibid.: 34), a notion that he cited approvingly from E. C. Kittson (1918), Henmon and his colleagues spent a lot of time and effort in developing composition scales, which would 'reduce as far as possible the subjective element in scoring' (Henmon 1929). They considered gathering the samples to be the easier task: students were presented with 'an interesting picture' nd told to write in French 'the best composition you can about the picture' in the thirty minutes allowed. Because there was no agreement on the specific objectives of writing compositions, the committee decided to develop a 'single scale for measuring the general merit of pupils' compositions' (ibid.: 35).

A number of 'competent judges' read the first batch of compositions collected in this way and judged them on an eleven-point scale ranging from 'worthless' to 'the very highest quality'. While large numbers fell into the middle groups, three essays were selected from each of the eleven levels; to these thirty-three essays were added another nine that were either from the lowest group but artificially made worse, or from the highest group artificially improved. Henmon had some 125 experienced French teachers rank the resulting batch of forty-two sample essays from 1 (the worst) to 42 (the best) on the basis of general merit, allowing whatever weight they thought appropriate to the various factors. After analysing their results carefully, the researchers established a scale of sixteen selected compositions, that represented the collective judgement of the judges.

The Alpha tests thus combined discrete items in vocabulary and grammar and more integrative skill items in reading and especially writing. For the discrete items, internal consistency was obtained by quantitative methods; the validity and the inter-rater reliability of the integrative items depended on the technique of collectively formulating a scale of graded samples that had been pioneered by Thorndike for his handwriting test.

The main claim of the Modern Foreign Language Study was to have shown 'the fallacy of measuring achievement in terms of units, credits, or time spent in the classroom' (ibid.: 209). The tests demonstrated the existence of an 'extraordinary range' in school, class, and individual differences. As more accurate achievement tests were developed, it was hoped that their results would be used instead of the unit credit system to place students. Henmon presented strong arguments for the use of multiple-choice tests and for the use of tests where 50 per cent of the students made a score of 50 per cent correct.

Henmon (ibid.) listed the problems that were still unsolved: the comparison of various test batteries: a controlled study of the effect of oral-aural ability on the reading ability that had become the proposed goal for the first four semesters of college study; the need for additional forms of standardized tests; and the need for improving existing tests and developing tests for additional abilities. His committee recognized the limitations of the tests, which measured 'only a small number of the complex capacities involved in language learning' (ibid.: vi). In spite of this, they believed that they added up to 'a picture of modern language achievement in the United States and Canada that is mathematically correct in detail and complete in its general features' (ibid.).

Considered as a battery intended to provide an overall picture of achievement in foreign language teaching, the Alpha tests were a fine piece of work. Their failure to characterize oral ability was a disappointment, but one can imagine that such a test would simply have confirmed the committee's final judgement that this ability was not being developed in the limited amount of time allocated to foreign language study in American schools and colleges. From the point of view of the development of modern language tests, their work was a major advance: a good deal of important research and development was carried out, and a great deal of fundamental importance was learnt. The inclusion of integrative items made these tests better than many that would follow them. If anything important was missing, it was the concern for language use that was to be stressed by later testers. In their use as part of the Modern Foreign Language Study, they provided the factual basis that bolstered the committee's authority to propose a major change in curricular emphasis in American language teaching.

Other standardized tests

In the late 1920s and early 1930s, a large number of other standardized tests appeared, intended more for school level control of instruction. The Bureau of Educational Research at the University of Illinois published a revised list of tests that were on sale for use in high schools (Odell 1929), including more than a dozen foreign language batteries, and advertising their prices.[17]

One battery of great importance was that developed for the Cooperative Test Service under the direction of Ben D. Wood. Where the Alpha tests had focused on providing a method of surveying group achievement, Wood's tests were concerned with tracking individual learning, and provided ten or more comparable forms of tests in the fundamental subjects of the school curriculum in order to permit systematic evaluation of progress at semester or year intervals in junior college and senior high school (Wood 1928). In doing this, he was carrying on the kind of orderly control of student progress that had been demonstrated in the Christian schools in France mentioned in the previous chapter.

Wood had begun his experimentation with new-type tests for modern languages for the New York Board of Regents examinations in 1925, at the same time that Henmon's work for the committee was going on. His tests, written after three years of experimentation with twenty different item-types, had parallel forms in French, Spanish, and German. Each consisted of a hundred-item multiple-choice vocabulary test (the foreign words were followed by five English words), a reading comprehension test, consisting of seventy-five sentences in the foreign language 'of an obvious truth or an obvious fallacy', and a hundred-item test of grammar, idioms, spelling, word-order, capitalization, and accents. Vocabulary was controlled. The grammar items were checked on the basis of an 'extensive synthesis' of standard materials. Each test contained items to cover the full range of achievement, as determined by pre-testing. Thus, nothing was left to 'subjective opinion and to chance'; everything in the test capable of objective verification had been verified experimentally. As Carroll (1954:

2) remarked, there were detailed analyses of individual items published 'with a thoroughness and detail for which current publication costs would be nearly prohibitive'. The test was still available in 1954.[18] The extensive item analysis and the use of discrete items only in the Cooperative tests assured a higher internal consistency than the Alpha tests, but this was achieved at the cost of omitting integrative items. The tests fitted, then, the class of tests driven by the pursuit of technical reliability that produced accurate measures of items the exact relevance of which to higher level skills remained to be shown.

Except for the American Council Alpha Tests that included a scale for rating written composition, the standardized batteries available in 1930 measured only vocabulary, silent reading, and grammar. In his report at the conclusion of the Modern Foreign Language Study, Henmon (1934a and b) pointed out that much more complete batteries would need to be developed before one could obtain 'a reasonably adequate picture of an individual's achievement and progress in learning a foreign language' (Henmon 1934a: 193a). There remained a number of 'gaps in the testing program'. Some experimental aural tests existed, and steps had been taken to measure pronunciation and oral composition, but not fluency in oral composition. Some attempts had been made at developing scales for scoring translation, but nothing of significance was yet available. Work had begun on proposing methods of classroom testing.[19]

Henmon (ibid.) complained that only a few published studies showed correlations between existing tests. The new-type examinations that Wood (1928) had developed had shown in trials in New York (in city junior high schools and in the Regents Examinations) reliabilities of 0.94, compared to 0.70 for the old-type examinations. Even unstandardized new-type tests were more reliable than old-type tests.

A number of studies offer support for the claimed superior reliability of new-type tests. In one study,[20] Cheydleur (1928a) administered the American Council Alpha French Grammar Test to 13,000 high school students and 12,000 college students. The tests took less time to administer (18 minutes compared to 42 minutes for the older essay-type tests), and marking was twelve times faster.

There were other comparisons of old- and new-type tests. Tharp (1927) used both new- and old-type items, the former consisting of 40 French sentences with one word in English to be translated correctly, and the latter of 100 words of English to be translated into French, as a final examination for second- and third-semester French students. The objective test was quicker to mark, and placed 64 per cent 'correctly' compared to the old-type, that placed 53.3 per cent correctly. Tharp (1929) reported that a number of teachers were asked to grade a set of French papers in their own way and in a way he laid down. Most teachers marked all errors and based the grade on the percentage of correctness. The Alpha tests were also used as the basis for international comparisons. Ford and Hicks (1929) reported that, through testing 6,000 pupils in Britain, 4,000 in Canada, and 2,500 in the United States, they had been established norms for the American Council Alpha French tests. Students in the United States, who began language study some years later than those in Britain, and a bit later than those in Canada, did better in reading and grammar than the others; British students did slightly better in composition. In Britain, instruction began at the age of 11; in Canada at 14, and in the United States at 14, 15, or 16. There was greater uniformity of standards in Canada. In the absence of oral tests, no comparison could be made of the development of speaking ability.

Research was also carried out with the Stanford standardized Spanish tests, prepared by Aurelio Espinosa and Truman Kelley (1927), which were partly multiple-choice and partly completion tests of grammar, vocabulary, and paragraph comprehension. Fraser and Crawford (1931) gave them to fifty adults and fifty junior high students who had learnt the language for the same amount of time: in all tests (grammar, vocabulary, and comprehension, but not speaking), adults scored significantly higher. Miner (1931) gave the tests to fifty-three classes from first to fourth year high school and first and second year college and showed that one year of college was about equal to two years of high school.

Other tests in Spanish were developed in California. Broom, Contreras, and Kaulfers (1927) developed and normed a silent reading test consisting of short passages of connected discourse, with high frequency words, each passage followed by a question (in English) to be answered by one of five Spanish words. There were two forms of the test, with items ranked in difficulty on the basis of advice from teachers and checked by a group of Mexican scholars. The first form was checked with 200 high school pupils. The final form, consisting of twenty paragraphs in Spanish, each followed by a multiple-choice question in English, was administered to 4,000 high school students. Broom (1927a, 1927b) prepared a silent reading test in French, too, which consisted of paragraphs in French followed by two questions in French, with four possible answers each.

In just over ten years, modern language tests had made their mark. Working within the objective or standardized paradigm, a good number of individual scholars and of teams of teachers and testers had explored various technologies for testing second language proficiency and knowledge. The weight of practice seemed to favour the new-type objective test, with its claims for internal consistency easily attainable by increasing the number of discrete point items, but efforts were being made to test writing by using scales, and speaking[21] by using a board of examiners. Many of the issues that were to remain critical in language testing had already been broached. The most notable was the tension between authentic tests of integrative skills (with the difficulty of achieving technical reliability and the high expense involved) and the objective testing of discrete items of linguistic knowledge (with the problem of establishing validity and inter-pretability of results).

Lowering the temperature of the debate, as it were, was the intended use of the tests. Essentially (with the exception of the Modern Foreign Language Study), the tests were to be used largely for school- and teacher-based evaluation of progress. Thus, teachers seem to have had no qualms about continuing to use even incomplete batteries a quarter of century after they were prepared and long after more adequate substitutes were available. In the Modern Foreign Language Study, the tests were being used not for individual decisions but as part of a national survey of the state of language teaching, but again the task was under the control of the profession, with no suggestion of external review. In the next decade, this changed when external testing bodies such as the College Board were persuaded to use objective tests in career-influencing tests. It was in these bodies that the major debate over objectivity took place, focused more especially on the use of essay examinations in the native language than on foreign language testing.

Notes

1 Jacques Barzun (1962) traced the objective test to World War I and complained that anyone who attacked these tests (as he did) was labelled 'obscurantist' or unscientific.

2 For Thorndike's later notion of an absolute scale, see Chapter 8 below.

3 Oller (1991a and 1991b: 35) misses the point in blaming discrete point 'surface-oriented' items on the 'structural linguistics of the 1930s through the 1950s'.

4 Later (see Chapter 8), Thorndike was to express faith in the feasibility of developing absolute, zero-based, equal-unit-interval scales for abilities like language, but even these, he would recognize, had serious limitations.

5 Carroll (1992, personal communication) said he offered this manuscript to Leon Dostert, then Dean of the School of Languages and Linguistics at Georgetown University, for publication, but it was turned down. How much was missed by this decision will become even more obvious as I continue to cite it in the course of this book.

6 The committee's inquiry also provided interesting information on the teaching of modern foreign languages in those days. Of the 260 teachers who replied to the questions, 84 were men and 176 were women. Some 40 had been born in France, Germany, or Switzerland, the rest in the United States, Canada, or Britain. There were 170 with BAs, 54 with MAs, and 6 with PhDs. Of the respondents, 106 had had some time

for study abroad, 67 in Germany, 35 in France, and 4 in Spain. Altogether 177 had heard the language spoken, 127 had had opportunity in their training for practice in oral reading and pronunciation; only those who had studied abroad (or who had foreign parentage) had had opportunities to practise speaking.

7 See, for example, Alderson and Wall (1992).

8 Another programme was considered more useful. Walter Dill Scott had been appointed to chair a committee on motivation, which became the committee on classification of personnel of the War Department. In the Adjutant-General's office, it came to employ a staff of 175, classified 3.5 million men, and developed proficiency tests for 83 different jobs: Scott was awarded the Distinguished Service Medal for his work.

9 When Robert M. Yerkes, as chief of the Division of Psychology in the Office of the Surgeon General of the Army, visited Canada in 1917, he had found Carl Brigham working as a psychologist to the Military Hospitals Commission; in October 1917, Brigham was appointed to the Sanitary Corps of the United States army as a psychologist, and was later transferred to the Office of the Surgeon General to help with test revision. Brigham (1923), influenced by a book by Charles W. Gould called *America, A Family Matter*, which argued for the need of pure breeding to preserve the nation, re-analysed data that had been collected for the army and published by Yerkes (1921) and claimed to be 'the first really significant contribution to the study of race differences in mental traits'. Brigham disowned the racism before his appointment to work for the College Board.

10 See Leahey (1987) and Gould (1981).

11 Carroll (1987a: 90) points out that these tests were among the first to use the multiple-choice item.

12 Preface to Brigham (1923).

13 In 1912 and 1913 he published a number of studies showing the unreliability of normal marks; the following year, he published a set of tests for measuring 'efficiency in reading, writing, spelling and English' (the last seeming to mean grammar). Starch combined these in a larger volume published in 1916, in which he summarized work on the unreliability of marks and, although he felt that it was 'undoubtedly premature to write a book on educational measurements because most of the measurements are in the experimental stage', none the less included a number of tests which had had some initial standardization.

14 In a general preface to Ruch (1924). Giles M. Ruch was associate professor of education and psychology at the State University of Iowa.

15 Starch appears to have consulted Henmon.

16 This was tried out by Andrade (1922).

17 The modern language tests that appear on the list were: American Council on Education: Alpha, Beta, and Grammar tests for French;

Alpha test and reading scale for German; Alpha and Beta tests for Spanish; Columbia Research Bureau French, German, and Spanish tests; Contreras-Broom-Kaulfers Spanish tests; De Sauze Standardized French test; Henmon French tests; Iowa Placement Examinations, Revised, for French, Spanish, and Foreign Language (English grammar and Esperanto); Stanford Spanish tests; Twigg French Vocabulary test; and Wilkins Achievement tests in Spanish.

18 For reviews published then, see Chapter 5.

19 See, for instance, Baker (1928).

20 In other studies, Cheydleur (1928b) gave the American Council Alpha French Grammar Test to 1,366 students at the University of Wisconsin in May 1925, showing a steady increase in the median by semesters; Cheydleur (1931) administered the Columbia Research Bureau (CRB) tests in French vocabulary, comprehension, and grammar to 1,700 University of Wisconsin students in their first through seventh semesters and found that the three tests correlated about 0.80 with each other, but the whole test correlated only 0.55 with teachers' marks, meaning that 'the predictive value of teachers' marks as to the probable score of a student on the CRB test is about only 18 per cent better than chance'; Cheydleur (1932) used the American Council Alpha French Grammar Test to compare knowledge of functional grammar with knowledge of formal grammar by requiring students not just to answer the regular questions, but also to indicate the grammatical principle involved in each item.

21 Speaking tests will be discussed in Chapter 5.

4 Spreading the psychometric hegemony

Objectivity or control?

Modern objective language testing evolved at a time when the new-type tests were starting to offer a tempting solution to the statistical challenge to examinations implicit in Edgeworth's assertion of the 'unavoidable uncertainty' of measurement. The quantifiable results provided by the mechanistic scoring of short true-false or multiple-choice questions, and the opportunity that large numbers of marks afforded of replacing judgements of individual performances by statistical norms, gave every appearance of solving the problem of reliability. Whatever it was that was being measured, at least it was being measured consistently.

There remained opposition to the psychometric movement, especially from those who hoped to use tests and examinations as a means of controlling the school curriculum. Edgeworth's papers, brilliant though they were, and accepted by psychologists like Burt in Britain and Brigham in the United States, did not immediately and everywhere carry the day. In much the same way that there would be objection to a suggestion to drop diving and gymnastics and other judged events from the Olympic Games, so demands continued to be made for persisting with the use of the essay that had become the archetype of the nineteenth-century English examination.

One opponent of objective testing was Edward Jones, director of personnel research at the University of Buffalo, who regretted the headway that the innovation had been making in the United States, 'because of the ease with which wordiness has proved to count for more than real substance' (Jones 1933: 20). He believed that the difficulty of grading essays was overstated and that better examinations, with questions that do not encourage cramming, and more thoughtful marking, should solve the problem. He praised the techniques that had been adopted at Antioch College, using three independent judges.

The battle was hotly waged inside major testing institutions, where psychometrists were starting to be heard. In a democratic gesture mitigating their power, the College Entrance Examination Board had always recognized[1] the need not to 'hamper the independence and initiative of individual teachers' by allowing its examinations to become too firmly set. They also wanted to permit a candidate to show understanding and power of expression, and not just 'test his ability to reproduce in a more or less mechanical manner bits of information imparted to him by a drillmaster'. To this end, they avoided precise prescription of requirements or of the form of examination, and regularly changed the membership of examining commit-tees 'to facilitate variations in the form of its examinations and to give suitable recognition to the different shades of opinion that exist among American scholars and teachers'. In answer to criticism of the introduction without notice of comprehension questions into the 1929 Latin examina-tion, the Secretary remarked that 'an examination would be quite worthless if it were reduced to a ceremony for which candidates could be prepared by a series of rehearsals' (College Entrance Examination Board 1929: 10).

Given these quite liberal and humanistic views of the examiners, one can readily imagine the uphill battle that Carl Brigham, its new associate secret-ary, faced in trying to convince the College Board of new psychometric truths. In the 1933 report (College Entrance Examination Board 1933), he presented the objectivity versus control issue and drew the Board's atten-tion to the two 'partially incompatible' purposes of the Board, the one to control institutions and the other to measure individuals. The Board's 'definitions of requirements', which had been questioned by teachers as interfering with the schools' freedom, could be written more generally, but they would still 'collide with the nature and composition of the examina-tion papers'. Brigham reminded the Board of the unreliability of measuring devices. Testers had long been aware of this problem, and so they thought of a grade not as a fixed point but rather as 'one particular grade drawn by chance from a hat which contains all of that candidate's grades obtained from an infinite series of examinations set and read to measure exactly that same trait'. Unlike the colleges, which acted as though a reported grade were an exact and fixed number, testers saw it as surrounded by its stand-ard error, 'which would include two-thirds of the grades above and below it'. The purpose of the 'new-type' testing movement was essentially to reduce this error and so to rate an *individual* more fairly. To testers with this aim, concern for control of the curriculum would be 'heretical'.

The Board's Examiners, however, considered that 'their duty is to exer-cise a benevolent control over the curriculum'. From this point of view, questions should be included in the examination simply because schools must train students to answer them. But such questions, Brigham said, were often quite unsuitable to 'describe an *individual* with a respectable mini-mum of variation in rating'. Brigham thought the underlying concern of the objective testing movement was reasonable, but 'the crusader spirit has converted good devices for measuring into a prescription of what should be measured'. Thus, some testers had come to assume that whatever they could measure was what should be taught.

Brigham argued for a better scale, that would do away with the notion of a passing point at 60 per cent, and for the experimental use of a larger number of questions, which would make it easier to achieve reliability. Requirements should be written less restrictively, as had been done perhaps in modern languages. The Board should recognize its research function, and be prepared to assume an ever-changing form of examination. In the next few years, the Board was persuaded to accept its research function. $1,193.97 was allocated for research in 1933. Brigham's title was changed to Research Secretary and in 1936, John Stalnaker was appointed Consultant Examiner with the task of providing technical and research advice to the various Committees of Examiners. The Board was also slowly persuaded to deal with the problem of the unreliability of essays and their grades.

The College Board examination to test competence in the English language

The English Competence examination prepared by the College Entrance Examination Board in 1930, probably the earliest test intended specifically for English as a second language in the United States, provides a good view of contemporary approaches to language testing.[2] Indirectly, psychometrics had played a role in the need for the test, intended to deal with a loophole in the Immigration Act of 1924 which was intended to cut down on immigration from areas other than northern Europe. Psychometrists, among them Carl Brigham, gave evidence in Congress on the deleterious effects of permitting non-Nordic immigrants to 'contaminate the American gene pool', but Sokal (1987: 7–8) believes they had little if any real influence on the decision.

The Act permitted special visas to any foreign alien whose only purpose was to study in the United States at a school, college, or university approved by the Secretary of Labor; on receipt of a certificate of admission from such an institution, the local American Consul was empowered to issue a student visa. The loophole was quickly spotted, and the number of foreign applicants seeking admission to US institutions grew rapidly. In 1926, the Commissioner General of Immigration had written in a memorandum that:

> The experience of the bureau in the past two and one-half years is to the effect that many non-quota immigrant students gain admission to the United States totally unfit, because of insufficient knowledge of the English language . . . THEREFORE, IT IS REQUESTED THAT ALL SCHOOLS INDICATE IN THE CERTIFICATE OF ADMISSION THE EXACT KNOWLEDGE OF THE ENGLISH LANGUAGE A STUDENT MUST HAVE BEFORE HE CAN BE ACCEPTED.[3]

As a result, a number of requests were made to the College Board for a test to measure their knowledge of English (College Entrance Examination Board 1929). These were formalized when, in December 1927, the American Association of Collegiate Registrars adopted the following resolution:

Whereas, it is required that a certificate of admission be furnished to a non-quota immigrant student prior to his admission to the United States, and difficulties have arisen both in defining the exact knowledge of the English language required for admission and in determining the ability of the student in this respect . . . Be it resolved that the American Association of Collegiate Registrars request the College Entrance Examination Board to consider the addition to their service of a special examination designed to test the ability of a foreign student in such use of the English language as is required for attendance by an American collegiate institutions, and to offer this examination to prospective foreign students in connection with their regular June examination.
(ibid. 1929)

In April 1928, the College Board set up a commission[4] which reported seven months later that it would be desirable to have an examination to test the student's ability to understand written English, to read English intelligibly, to understand spoken English, and to express his thoughts intelligibly in spoken English'. The aural comprehension test should include 'simple English prose read slowly' and 'simple directions given conversationally'. The report suggested that instructors in English departments were not the best qualified to develop a test, because of their concern with correct grammar. New-type tests might be suitable. The test should include passages of varying difficulty and 'with different subject matters'; the report should break down the results by section. Such an examination was 'financially feasible' but the candidates should bear its full cost.

A second commission, appointed to plan the examination,[5] at first assumed that half the test would be oral-aural. A 1928 memorandum for the commission assumed four parts, of equal weight: reading of college material, writing of college reports, understanding lectures and class discussions, and speaking well enough to take part in class discussions. In April 1929, the committee presented a detailed outline to the College Board:

1 Four one-paragraph passages (about 150 words each); one of them narrative and simple, a second historical or topical or journalistic and more difficult, a third 'of some critical weight on a matter of specific social import' and a fourth of scientific prose. The questions should be quite straightforward, and could be answered with plus or minus (true-false) answers.
2 A longer passage (about 400 words) perhaps from Mill or Lowell, dealing with 'debatable or conditioned ideas', the questions to look for capacity to 'isolate salient ideas, and to deal critically with hypothetical and adversative statements and the like'.
3 A direct dictation, and the reproduction from memory of a dictated passage.

4 An oral test, with ten topics prepared for the examiner. The examiner was to report, using a three-point scale for each (proficient, satisfactory, or unsatisfactory), on 'fluency, responsiveness, rapidity, articulation, enunciation, command of construction, of connectives, usable vocabulary and the use of idiom'; examiners should also report if the candidate appeared 'diffident or shy'.

5 A 250–300 word composition to be written on a selected topic.

Time should be given for revision; reports should be given for each part of the examination. The commission believed that the main value of the examination would be its diagnostic accuracy. 'It is important to know the candidate's strength or weakness in knowledge of words, command of English construction, and grasp of the logic and continuity of English speech.' There was no point in giving absolute percentage grades, but rather percentile standing by country. This was believed to be especially important for students whose language differed greatly from English, like Chinese or Japanese. Formal tests of spelling or grammar would give little evidence of the ability of a foreigner to carry on American college work. The reading passages of varying difficulties might show that candidates who did not express themselves with facility might still be fitted for certain work, for instance, at the graduate level. Therefore, it was thought advisable for the examination papers to be sent directly to the colleges.

A grant of $5,000 from the Carnegie Endowment for International Peace helped to cover the costs. Preparing the first examination scheduled for April 1930 was not easy, and 'no little correspondence was necessary in order to secure the services of suitable persons in the administration and supervision of the examination' (College Entrance Examination Board 1930: 8). Finally, help was received from a number of ambassadors and consuls. Thirty candidates took the examination, which was judged to be 'very carefully prepared and especially well planned' in 1930, and the work of most of them was said to have been 'very creditable'. Seven candidates were examined in China, eight in Belgium, four in each of Poland and Italy, three in Hungary, two in Germany, and one in each of Beirut and France. Six were women. Five candidates planned to go to Columbia University, three to each of Harvard, Stanford, and Michigan.

In the second year, 1931, the fee was $10 and 139 candidates were examined in seventeen countries. The largest group (eighty-two) was in Moscow, where engineering students were required by the Soviet Government to take the examination. (College Entrance Examination Board 1931). The secretary of the American-Russian Chamber of Commerce, Spencer Williams, supervised the Moscow administration, with three assistants to help with the oral interview Williams reported that he had enjoyed the experience though it had been hard work. The candidates represented that 'new class of technicians rising up for the proletariat' and had been spending twelve hours a day for five months to learn English (Saretsky 1984: 3). The average for all candidates for the oral test was 85 per cent, for the reading 77 per cent, for the composition 56 per cent, and for the dictation 47 per cent.

In 1932, the test was offered in twenty-nine countries, but as a result of the worldwide depression, only thirty candidates offered themselves at twelve centres. At the suggestion of the 1932 examiners, a commission[6] was set up to revise the examination. It proposed the use of 'indeterminate' as well as true-false items and wanted to give broad classifications rather than scores, and to continue the stress on spoken English. A new description was approved for the 1933 examination (College Entrance Examination Board 1932). Part 1 was changed to consist of several passages with about thirty true-false and other questions testing understanding. For the second dictation, the candidate was allowed to take notes. The oral test was to be based on 'ten or fifteen minutes of discussion or conversation'. The revised examination showed the acceptance of the need for objective items, but not at the cost of more face valid assessment of what Carroll (1961) later called integrative skills.

In any event, the examination did not survive the worsening international economic crisis, as the numbers of candidates continued to fall. In 1933, seventeen candidates took the examination; in 1934, twenty (College Entrance Examination Board 1934a). The secretary of the College Board had written once again to colleges asking if the examination should be continued. In 1935, the funds were exhausted (College Entrance Examination Board 1935). In fact, the 1935 report admitted, the 1933 questions had been carefully guarded and used again in 1934 and 1935, but as they could not be used for a fourth time, the examination was 'at least temporarily' discontinued.

It was hoped that conditions would improve, but in fact they did not. In 1938, a Dr Heinrich Selver called the College Board to ask about the English examination. A school he had been associated with in Berlin offered courses in English for German Jewish doctors and lawyers seeking to emigrate. The New York State Department of Education would recognize the University of Cambridge Local Examinations Syndicate (UCLES) Certificate of Proficiency in English or the College Board's English examination. As many of the students wanted to come to the United States, the American examination seemed more appropriate. He was told that it was no longer being given. It was not until after the war that interest in the test was rekindled.

This account of the first American institutional test in English for foreign students prefigures in miniature the development of TOEFL that will take centre stage in Part II of this book. Some of the features that stand out in hindsight are the dependence on the support of foundations (provided to start up the examination but lacking at the critical point), the intelligence and wisdom of the original examination proposal, tempered by practical and institutional reality, and the slowness of users to see the value of the test. The College Board responded cautiously to the mounting pressure to include objective items in standardized examinations. This was in marked contrast to the examinations in English for foreigners conducted by the University of Cambridge; another major difference between the American and the British test is that the former was (of necessity) quite curriculum-free and seen first and foremost as a proficiency examination.

It is important to note that the purpose of this test, like the Shibboleth test cited at the beginning of Chapter 2, was in fact political and restrictive, namely, to enforce an immigration act intended to close the gates to 'undesirables'. A well-established testing agency wrote it at government request. Its ultimate ineffectiveness resulted not from any formal opposition, but from an unwillingness of government or foundations or prospective users to keep paying for it.

Essay grading

The struggle over reliability and objectivity continued to focus on the essay. In a special report on the comprehensive English examination written for the College Board, the associate secretary Carl Brigham referred negatively to the old goal of examinations 'to force a certain form of preparation in the schools' and 'to use the examinations as a device for institutional control' (College Entrance Examination Board 1934b: i). He eloquently praised the College Board examinations which had 'long relinquished this police power' and had 'sought instead to embody in the examination itself an inspiring goal for youth', providing 'greater freedom' and representing 'a new spirit'. Even though the College Board might have abdicated the control of the curriculum, Brigham noted that there still remained problems, for the examinations had now been opened up to the criticism of 'those versed in the art of "mental measurement" '. The fluctuations in levels of the English examinations had been particularly cited in earlier reports of the Secretary (College Entrance Examination Board 1926: 213).[7]

Brigham (College Entrance Examination Board 1934b) summarized earlier attempts that had been made to overcome this 'unwarranted condition' by writing 'new-type or objective' tests of items of grammar or spelling or vocabulary. However, these objective items, Brigham commented, were 'silly' and when you tested only what could be tested reliably, you did not measure 'English'. The College Board had therefore accepted the continuing need for open-ended items, and set out to increase the reliability of the grading, choosing thus Thorndike's solution over Price's.[8] Brigham gave 'a running record of the first major attack on the problem of grading the written examination', looking for sources of error in the reading of the written examination that could be eliminated by developing a new grading method.

In the first three years of the study, readers read and graded each other's scripts. In 1929, the correlation between the first reader's tentative grade and the second reader's grade was calculated; most correlations fell around 0.75, but there was a wide range. In 1930 and 1931, correlations between the tentative first grading and the final grading (changed after considering the second grading) continued to show what were considered to be unsatisfactorily low correlations, and the cost of this double grading was high ($3 a booklet). With the reduced number of candidates in 1932, it was possible to decrease the number of readers, keeping only those readers with the highest degree of agreement. The second reading was restricted to a sample only, lowering the cost of grading to $2 a booklet.

The first step in increasing reliability, then, was to limit the scoring to readers who already tended to agree. This decision was quite contrary to the position of the eminent pioneer of testing, E. L. Thorndike (Monroe 1939), who believed that not much could be done to the content of traditional examinations (examining boards were already composed of 'able and conscientious persons'), but the fairness could be improved by increasing the number of readers. In borderline cases, or where marks were published, each examination should be rated by two sets of examiners, working independently with a full range of papers. He disapproved strongly of the idea of having examiners confer:

> In general all procedures designed to cause examiners to agree more closely with one another are very dangerous. They are likely to favor a conventional orthodox system of ratings which may penalize candidates who are notably original, subtle, or eccentric. Efforts should be directed rather toward causing each examiner to use all the good judgment he has and to agree more closely with the truth.
> (ibid.: 242)

Discussions between examiners before marking, then, should be concerned not with arriving at agreement but at 'the truth'. He believed that marking part of a paper made sense in many fields, including foreign languages, but not in history or literature, where scripts should be re-examined globally. He set out five 'axioms' for traditional examinations: any rating contains some error; the more work there is to examine and the more independent examiners there are, the smaller the error; the better the examiners are, the smaller the error; 'departures from complete independence in the ratings are usually extremely pernicious'; and overall, inter-rater reliability (among independent raters) is valid, but in individual cases there are seldom enough such raters.

In contrast to Thorndike's views, the College Board testers continued to pursue reliability.[9] A second important cause of low reliability recognized in 1932 was the offering of alternative items in the essay. Analysis showed that the average grade for the different choices varied, so that the very process of selecting which question to answer introduced error; the solution was to 'drop alternative questions entirely and ask all the candidates to run the same race' (College Entrance Examination Board 1934b: 9). Two other modifications were to mark each question on an 8-point scale. Some questions had allowed 35 points, but in practice, the vast majority of grades on these questions covered a 15-point range. On a 20-point scale, no more than 10 points were used; on a 10-point scale, no more than 4 seemed useful. Furthermore, the most popular place on the scale for a grade to fall seemed to be at the three-fifths point. Because there had been errors in mechanical addition (sometimes quite high) in over 4 per cent of the scripts checked, it was decided to have clerical workers do the adding up of points. With all these correctable errors, the correlation between the items encouraged confidence in the existence of a measurable underlying factor.

In the 1933 examination, more changes were instituted. Each script was split in half, and each half was marked by two different readers so that a candidate's final grade was a composite of four opinions. Alternative questions were cancelled and all were graded on an 8-point scale, ranging from X (bad failure) through F (not ready for college English) to A+ (exceptional work throughout). Final numerical scores were assigned, by a committee, in accordance with the College Board's frequency curve. In spite of all these improvements, the inter-rater reliability was only 0.75 and the correlations at the item level between readers remained too low (from 0.46 to 0.58) for results on individual questions to be reportable (ibid.: 30). There was evidence of a halo effect in the marking of individual items together, so that a reader tended to give similar scores to a candidate; the splitting of the scripts helped overcome this (ibid: 38). There was still a great deal to be done:

> The study also shows the absolute necessity of revising the examining procedures and reading techniques in a way such that the general factor is increased at the expense of the now greater chance factor. The factors making for unreliability are now so great that the examination should be discontinued unless progress can be made in getting a single stable score which is descriptive of the candidate.
> (ibid.: 41)

The study, then, left Brigham and the College Board firmly seated on the horns of a dilemma: they believed in an underlying factor of 'English' and in its measurability, but they had to choose between unreliable methods of measuring it, and reliable methods of measuring something different.

Studies of the use of essays in examinations by the College Board continued in 1936 and 1937 (Noyes and Stalnaker 1938).[10] In an echo of the principle accepted by Macaulay (Hansard 1833), that performance in an examination is evidence of both past achievement and future promise, their aim was 'to describe the candidate's ability and knowledge in the field by a single grade or score, an index which is valuable in indicating not only the extent and nature of his past training but also the promise of the future' (1938: 5). But Noyes and Stalnaker went further than Macaulay: the English examination administered by the College Board aimed to measure in a single examination three kinds of ability: ability to read, literary knowledge and judgement, and written and oral expression (including thinking).

In this hope for a multi-purpose testing technique, they were also in opposition to Thorndike (Monroe 1939), who believed that a key quality of a good objective test was its 'purity', its ability to measure just one ability at a time.[11] Sometimes one might want an adulterated test, such as an examination in mathematics that is 'contaminated' by intelligence, but it would be preferable to have two unadulterated scores, and then to decide later how to weight them. In a test of art appreciation, one would not like to include intelligence.

But the College Board examiners persisted, and the 1937 examination was changed to meet the criticisms that had been made of the 1936 examination, such as narrowness of range of the literary questions and the problems of allowing alternative subjects for the essay. A major effort was made to obtain high reliability. All papers, with the candidates' names carefully hidden from readers, were returned to New York for marking. For greater efficiency, the ninety-eight readers were divided into four groups, each of which read a single section of the paper. The readers were housed for the time of reading in dormitories at Barnard College and Columbia University and fed there. Their reading time was limited to six hours a day. The cost of the reading came to $13,925, which included $9,239 in salaries for the readers, $1,309 for travel expenses, $2,031 for room and board, and $1,016 for clerical assistance. Thus, each book cost about $2.00 to read, a reduction of $0.41 per book from the previous year.

For grading, each group was divided into tables of six or seven readers, with a table leader in charge. Grading scales had been prepared by group and table leaders in advance, after study of answer books. Detailed instructions laid down the allocation of points and were accompanied by model answers. When the readers arrived, a day and a half was devoted to standardizing their judgements. Each section of a book was graded independently at different tables by different readers, with table leaders checking for standardization and a sample of papers given a second independent reading. A week later, all reading finished, table leaders stayed on for another day for check-reading and for another small experiment in which they gave single letter grades to a hundred or so books. Inter-rater reliabilities were calculated for 1,149 books which had two independent readings, and reached 0.84 overall (the reliability in 1936 had been 0.80) with part scores ranging in reliability from 0.54 for question 3 through 0.68 for the essay to 0.87 for the mechanics question. By contrast, the report noted that in science papers it was usually between 0.96 and 0.99, and in history 0.93.

This elaborate and expensive method of marking essay examinations had still not produced the reliability that the psychometrists sought, but the demands of the test users meant that the essay was allowed to continue. The psychometrists were to continue their assaults.

The Cambridge examinations in English for foreigners

The notion of reliability was much less influential in Britain. In spite of Cyril Burt's early support for the objective achievement test and the continuing growing acceptance of intelligence testing, traditional examining in Britain remained virtually uncontaminated by psychometric notions. This may be seen from the contemporary forms of the Cambridge tests in English for foreigners.

Testing of the English of foreigners started much earlier in Britain than in America. In fact, the University of Cambridge became involved in overseas testing within a few years of starting the Local Examinations, when, in 1862, there was an inquiry from Trinidad to Cambridge. The first papers were sent out ('in sealed parcels to the Governor through the Colonial Office') in 1863, and ten candidates were examined (Roach 1971: 146).

Cambridge continued to develop its overseas examinations, and by 1898 Cambridge had 36 colonial centres and 1,220 colonial candidates (ibid.: 145). Its formal entry into testing the English of foreigners was not until 1913, when it instituted the examination for the Certificate of Proficiency in English, [12] meant to be for 'foreign students who sought proof of their practical knowledge of the language with a view to teaching it in foreign schools' (Roach 1945: 34). Reflecting the growing interest in direct method teaching, which required of teachers 'reliable command of the language for active classroom use' rather than academic or descriptive ability, it was however, modelled on the traditional native-speaker language syllabus, with the essay as the key feature. As well as a paper on Phonetics, there was a Literature paper on a period studied in advanced classes in English secondary schools (ibid.). Another paper examined translation: the two languages regularly offered were French and German.

The examination was small to start with, and being offered only at one centre, London,[13] it 'teetered along' with about 15 candidates a year. There was probably a pause in the activities of the certificate during World War I, and its growth came after 1925, when John Roach first became involved.[14] At first, Nalder Williams[15] and Roach handled the final decisions on the award of grades for the English examination, 'a hole-in-corner affair of fifteen minutes' (Roach 1983: 5).[16] The examination remaining so small, there may well have been discussions, Roach recollected, of closing it, but instead, full responsibility was handed to Roach, who prophesied that he would spread the examination round the world in ten years. By 1939, he later triumphantly noted, it was being offered in 30 countries.

The growth and development of the examination was slow but steady. In 1926, translation papers were offered as a matter of course in Italian and Spanish as well as French and German. In 1930, a special Literature paper for foreign students was written. In 1932, the Phonetics paper was dropped, and centres other than London were added, with the result that the numbers of candidates started to rise rapidly.[17] In 1935, the examinations was offered in December as well as in July, and there were centres at Cambridge, London, Edinburgh, and Rome. In 1936, a paper in Economic and Commercial Knowledge[18] was an alternative to the English Literature paper, and three levels of pass (special mention, good, and pass), were instituted. In 1935, the Board of Education gave official recognition to the examination. Roach (1934) proposed extending the notion of a Certificate of Proficiency by reintroducing (they had been offered from 1917–22) examinations in languages other than English; he suggested such certificates in French, German, Spanish, and Italian. There was opposition from the British Association for Commercial and Industrial Education who thought that existing examinations offered by the London Chamber of Commerce and the Royal Society of Arts covered the area fully. Roach (1977) argued for national tests in foreign languages. In 1936, it was offered at Hamburg, Naples, Paris, and Rome and in the Netherlands, Sweden, and Switzerland.

The certificate received a major boost when in 1937 the University of Cambridge recognized it as 'the equivalent of the standard of English required of all students, British or foreign, before entrance to the University'. Oxford took a similar step in 1938. More and more centres were opened,[19] and translation papers offered for more and more languages.[20] A new alternative to English Literature in 1938 was a paper on English Life and Institutions. The examination was offered five times in the year.

With the growing demand for certification in English, Roach proposed the introduction of a new Lower Certificate of English. The newly established British Council, Roach (1983: 6) later recalled, opposed this development, and sent a Colonel Sullivan to see him at Cambridge; Roach was taken by Sullivan to Corpus Christi College, where Spens, 'arch bully and puller of wires', and probably a member of the British Council, attempted to browbeat him. Spens 'had the guns' in England, as he was chairman of the School Council;[21] but Roach had support, he was sure, in the Foreign Office. He decided to continue with his plans for the Lower Certificate, but introduce it only at overseas centres, which he did in 1939.

In 1943, the examination was also given at home centres for members of the Allied forces. The Lower Certificate examination in June 1939 consisted of a dictation, a two-hour English Composition and Language paper, and a two-hour Literature paper. Candidates were required to write a letter of between 80 and 100 words; there were three alternative topics, the first being 'A letter of thanks for a present you have been given on your birthday. Say what other presents you were given and what you did that day.' There were also three topics offered for the required 250–300 word composition; one involved a narrative account of teaching a younger brother or sister to ride a bicycle, a second was a detailed description of a picture hanging in a house or a school, and the third was a description of what the candidate saw while waiting at a railway station for a missed train. This was followed by a short narrative; candidates were asked to give it a title, demonstrate knowledge of the meaning of six out of twelve underlined words, write a four-sentence summary of the main points of the story, and rewrite in good English some sentences in Aboriginal pidgin in the story. The literature questions (two out of four had to be chosen) were based on the prescribed texts, which were *A Tale of Two Cities, The Oxford English Course: Reading Book Four, Gulliver in Lilliput,* and *Arms and the Man.* There was also an oral examination.

Just before the outbreak of World War II, then, the Cambridge English examinations reached a high point, with centres in twenty-four overseas countries (Germany was omitted at the last minute) and twenty regular centres in Britain. In the last months before the war, Roach made visits to Belgium, Italy,[22] France, and Switzerland to establish new centres. With the war, there was a rapid decline, as so many foreign centres became inaccessible.[23]

In the development of the Cambridge test, the issue of reliability that Edgeworth had raised in 1888 continued to be of only marginal interest, and the examinations remained untouched by psychometric notions. One can see this by comparing the 1931 College Board's examination, with its true-false questions, its concentration on language, and its lack of curricular concern, with the forms of the Cambridge papers described above, with their emphasis on curriculum, their inclusion of literature, and their absolute reliance on subjective grading. The Cambridge examiners continued until quite recently to be more concerned about what to test (i.e. about curriculum) than about how to test it.

But there were some people in Britain unhappy with this established view. Valentine and Emmett (1932) summarized several years of research into the reliability of various examinations.[24] Like Latham, they were disturbed by the 'cramping' effect of examination syllabuses, but even more important for them was Edgeworth's questioning of their reliability. The most patent causes of unreliability were luck in being asked the right questions and 'adventitious variation' in the state of the candidate at the time of the examination. Other major causes were the instability of essay marking and variability in and among examiners. Valentine and Emmett (ibid.) found very little relation between the way students were ordered on secondary school entrance exams and their School Certificate examination results five years later. They remarked on the tendency to teach those things most easily examined: thus, composition in a foreign language, though less important than reading, made for easier discrimination and was more likely to be examined. In spite of this and other studies,[25] British practice continued to resist calls to apply Edgeworth's findings.

Repatriating reliability

The erratic, persistent, and largely ineffective British concerns for fair examinations received a major boost in the 1930s as the result of an American philanthropic initiative. Established respectively in 1905 and 1911, the Carnegie Foundation for the Advancement of Teaching and the Carnegie Corporation conceived a new interest in international educational activities about 1930. As this overseas activity went beyond the scope of their charters, they established and funded the International Institute at Teachers College, Columbia, under the direction of Paul Monroe, to carry it out.

Their earliest foreign venture was the first of three International Conferences on Examinations, which was held at Eastbourne, England in 1931 (Monroe 1931), with delegates from England, France, Germany, Scotland, Switzerland, and the United States. In his opening remarks,[26] Monroe, the conference chairman, stressed the importance of examinations and the four major purposes that they served: as a means of instruction, as a form of educational administration, for the control of admission to employment and the civil service, and as a means of social control. He referred to the invention of new techniques in the United States; in fact, he said, 'it is only in my country that this question of technique has assumed paramount importance' (ibid.: 2).

Professor Edward Thorndike, who talked about the various US activities, such as the efforts of the Bureau of Test Construction of the American Council of Education to develop objective tests, also cited Edgeworth's classic study of the statistics of examinations. Sir Philip Hartog, a member of the English delegation who had had extensive experience with examinations in India, was also very conscious of the failure to learn from Edgeworth's forty-year-old papers. He sketched a possible study of examination marking of the kind his committee later carried out. He was impressed with the 'new-type' or 'objective' tests, and considered, for instance, that Ben Wood's work had 'pushed the foreign language test into higher levels than I should have thought it could reach' (ibid.: 34), but still saw a place for essay examinations.

Each national committee subsequently received a grant for a three-year research project from Carnegie, the results of which were reported to a second conference which was held in Folkestone, England, in 1935

(Monroe 1935). By then, the English committee had prepared for publication a bibliography and two other monographs on examinations in general, but their main work was a study carried out by the subcommittee under Sir Philip Hartog. In their first report, the Hartog subcommittee pointed out the high seriousness and topicality of their concern:

> No element in the structure of our national education occupies at the present moment more public attention than our system of examinations. It guards the gates that lead from elementary education to intermediate and secondary education, from secondary education to the Universities, the professions, and many business careers, from the elementary and middle stages of professional education to professional life.
> (Hartog and Rhodes 1935: 6)

A 'whole congeries of examinations' had grown up, private and public, and examinations had become 'a familiar topic in our newspapers and homes'. The subcommittee's goal had been to follow up on the variation that Edgeworth had found in the marks given by examiners by undertaking a systematic investigation of the marks given by experienced examiners to authentic examination scripts.

Both the English and a related French study found evidence of major variation. The method they generally used in their studies was to select about fifteen scripts that had received the same 'middling' mark and ask fifteen experienced examiners to read the scripts and assign a mark and a classification (fail, pass, credit). Just over a year later, the same examiners were asked to read and mark the same set of scripts again. One of the most dramatic results was in a School Certificate History examination; the marks on the first reading varied from 21 to 70, and on the second from 16 to 71; in 92 cases out of 210, the examiners gave a different fail-pass-credit decision on the second reading from the one they had individually given on the first. In a separate study, two experienced boards of examiners gave a *viva voce* examination to thirty volunteer candidates, following the procedure laid down in Civil Service regulations, and the correlation between the marks of the two boards was 0.41 (ibid.: 35). They concluded that 'the element of chance in examinations still exists to a dangerous degree in the subjects which have been investigated' (ibid.: 10).

In the face of this evidence of inconsistency and unfairness, the committee not unnaturally asked, should examinations be abolished? Not at all, they answered:

> The Committee are clearly opposed to the root and branch policy. They are of opinion that examinations as a test of efficiency are necessary. They are further of opinion that, in addition to those examinations which yield identical results when applied by different examiners (e.g. 'New Type' or 'Objective' examinations), the traditional 'essay' examination

should be preserved. But they hold it is as impracticable to recommend an *a priori* cure for the defects of the present examination system as it would be to recommend an a *priori* cure for a disease. It is only by careful and systematic experiment that methods of examination can be devised not liable to the distressing uncertainty of the present system. (ibid.: 10)

Expenditure would be needed for such research, but it would be 'justified in the public interest'. To help raise standards of examining, the first long report included a sixty-seven page article on the analysis of examination marks by Cyril Burt, professor of education at the University of London and psychologist to the London County Council, setting out in simple language the quantitative statistical methods that could be used to check the reliability of examination results.

The difficulty of convincing others of the need for reliability was recorded by Hartog at Folkestone, who noted that he had been told the night before that the Americans already knew and accepted everything he had to say and would no doubt want to sleep through his presentation. But they were not his real audience: when he had visited one English university, the president of the examining board there had told him 'We think that here we know everything that there is to know about examinations' (Monroe 1935: 5). It was this attitude he hoped to change. In subsequent discussions, the difficulty of this task became evident. Sir Percy Nunn cited the Marquess of Linlithgow: 'I detest examinations as much as anybody in this room, but I distrust profoundly the man who cannot pass them.' This was echoed by another Englishman present, Dr P.B. Ballard, an inspector with the education committee of the London County Council, who said:

We have known that they [examinations] are precarious for a long time; we have been whispering it to other people for many years; and now we are beginning to shout it, and this document [Hartog's report] conveys our shouts. Though we are convinced, and though psychologists are convinced, the general public in England are by no means convinced. (ibid.: 39–40)

In America, things were better, reported Professor I. Kandel from Teachers College, Columbia University, who pointed out the more restricted role of external examinations in the United States, and who described the development of standardized and of new-type tests there. Auguste Desclos, chairman of the French committee and director of the Collège Franco-Britannique in Paris, summarized the French committee's work, a study of the *baccalauréat*; they had found divergences in marking of scripts greater than they had thought possible. They proposed to improve things by dropping unreliable examiners. Professor Erich Hylla of the Prussian Ministry of Education recounted the German committee's study of university selection, and on selection for the secondary schools. For the latter, it was considered that including intelligence testing would have made a better selection.

A third international meeting was held in Dinard, France, in September 1938 (Monroe 1938). Meeting this time 'in the shadow of the war, in the tense fortnight preceding the days of Munich'[27] as the book reporting a further English study,[28] delayed by the war, finally recounted, the third and final Carnegie-sponsored meeting of the International Enquiry started with a brief account of the work of the project by Monroe. He found it hard to realize that their work had been going on since their first meeting in Eastbourne seven and a half years before.

Some French examining procedures were described. Talking about a system with the same objective of determining who was the very best candidate that had marked the Cambridge tripos and the Indian Civil Service examinations, Celestin Bouglé, director of the École Normale Supérieur, described the testing procedures followed at this élite institution. The central feature was the dissertation, the essay, which 'permits one to evaluate general culture and mental alertness' (ibid.: 45). Three essays written by the candidates were marked by two examiners who conferred and agreed on the final marks; in case of dispute, the director himself would adjudicate. Difficult subjects were preferred, for the examination was basically competitive. Later, Sir Phillip Hartog reported on the continuation of the English committee's study. Five books had been published and a sixth was in preparation. Other countries too reported that they had made progress.

At the eighth conference session—a Sunday evening—Professor E. L. Thorndike, near retirement as professor of education at Teachers College, gave a paper that he characterized as part elementary and part idiosyncratic. The elementary part dealt with traditional examinations, in which he gave the ideas on the increase of reliability by multiple marking already cited. More substantial improvement could only be achieved, he thought, through replacing traditional examinations with objectively scorable new-type examinations. It would be valuable to develop modern language tests which concentrated on the bits of knowledge that made up language— words, phrases, even sentences—rather than connected prose, which calls for intelligence to treat as a whole. While essay and letter writing might be closer to life than objective test items, the measure provided is not purely linguistic.

Thorndike returned to the issue of scales. Students of mental measurement agreed on the need for an equal-unit scale from an absolute zero to as high a point as was to be measured. He believed such a scale could be constructed, consisting of a 'graded series of tasks in German . . . arranged so that any person who succeeds with task n in order can be guaranteed to succeed with task n_1, n_2, n_3, etc.' (Monroe 1939: 250). While the German scale might never be perfect, it would have valuable attributes. Such an examination could be developed by testing 2,000–3,000 persons, each with from 1,000 to 5,000 items, requiring about 2,000 hours work by an expert with 6,000 hours of routine assistance. Because this would be costly, he could understand why Dr Ben Wood and others were spending their time on objective scoring rather than on the equalization of units. But even having such an examination might not lead to it being used: 'The authorities in control of examinations are in general not interested in the fundamental veracity of examination measures' (ibid.: 252) and they would be unlikely to become enthusiastic about absolute scores of language proficiency. Indeed, he wondered if even the 'expert and progressive group' to whom he was reading the paper would agree with him.

In the discussion that followed, he did find doubters. Auguste Desclos, the head of the French committee, raised basic questions about the notion of 'absolute knowledge' of a language. What would it be? How would it work in pronunciation, with the different standards? Even the BBC could not agree between London and Oxford Standard English! He found it difficult to imagine absolute measurement of language knowledge, or of other imponderable values. Thorndike agreed that at the higher levels of language, measurement would not be possible. Only at the levels of ability with which schools were concerned could it be done. At higher levels, how could one scale the thousands of terms used in English as names of animals? With pronunciation, by making recordings and comparing them with standards, one could achieve uniformity on the lower levels, as when nobody could tell whether it was 'English or Chinook', but at higher levels, there would have to be separate scales for Eastern Seaboard English or General American English or Oxford English, all of which were sociologically defensible.

Carl Spearman, by now emeritus professor of psychology at University College, London, accepted Thorndike's distinction between intelligence and verbal ability, but wondered how to measure them separately, given the difficulty of getting agreement on definitions. Thorndike agreed that he should have said 'as pure as possible'. G. H. Thomson, professor of education at the University of Edinburgh, was also concerned about this notion of purity. Even if you could distinguish the g factor from the V (or Verbal) factor, and develop a German test that did not require g to answer it, surely intelligence would have helped the candidate learn German before the test, and so be present as a factor? In answer to this and further prodding by Spearman, Thorndike was forced to concede that he could only eliminate part of intelligence. Sir Philip Hartog found Thorndike's theory 'excellent', but regretted only that he could not understand it without examples. Thorndike said that if his courage were good, he would make a scale when he retired in 1940.[29] When it was suggested that the absolute zero level in a foreign language would vary in such matters as preparedness and previous experience, Thorndike replied that he did not think that his scale needed to include aptitude or intelligence.

He was asked about how the scale would handle the differences between a child who had learnt some German in a country where it was spoken and one who had learnt German in school. Thorndike was fairly sure it would work with reading ability; he imagined that it would be possible to reach a balance, as had been done with the old Binet examination, where the scale was not absolute. No mental scale was absolute in this, but statistically it was possible to treat it as absolute.[30]

In the final exchange of a session that was prolonged beyond the normal hour, Desclos asked if the scale would include more than vocabulary. Thorndike assured him it would include 'the relations, the syntax, word order, and all that sort of thing'. Knowledge of French, he conceded, was not something like space, of which you simply had more or less, but it was near enough for the purpose of building a scale. The scale would be formed of levels of difficulty, but not every level would be identical.

The ninth session was opened with a telegram bringing the news that Dr Hu Shih of the National University of Peking, who was to speak, could not come because he had just been appointed Ambassador to Washington. Professor Monroe expressed regret that they would thus not hear an expert discussion of the original Chinese examination session. The conference closed quietly, depressed not just by realizing how difficult it was to persuade their public to accept the dangers of the examination systems that had come to control much of European education, but also by the even greater threat to European civilization in the face of rising Nazi power. As Auguste Desclos put it, they had 'awakened, at least, the interest of the public and of the authorities' and 'put up landmarks, useful guiding stones for those who will carry on the work'. Over the years of the conferences and their committees' work, a great deal of research was carried on that showed once again the unreliability of the traditional examination, but it would be rash to assume that this work had any quick or lasting influence on the established European testing institutions.

In England, the Hartog committee's assaults on institutional examinations did not go unanswered. One of the early defences of traditional examinations was written by John O. Roach, criticizing the unnaturalness of the way that the experiments were conducted. Roach (1936) accepted the general criticism voiced by others that their work had failed to reproduce the system it was purporting to study: the examiners in it were given too few papers, no chance to agree on a marking scheme, and were presented with papers that had received the same scores but were told to separate them into pass, fail, and credit. The results then were as one might predict: 'Apparently, that if a team of examiners do not agree beforehand on what is required, and if there is no adequate control over them as a team, they will show alarming divergences' (ibid.: 114). But, he pointed out, examining boards had a number of ways to deal with these problems: marking schemes were discussed, sample papers were exchanged, there were meetings, and constant supervision from the chief examiner. The whole process of moderation, then, was intended to overcome this danger.

Even with these safeguards, Roach recognized that there could be difficulties in guaranteeing standards: two different chief examiners might have different notions of the standard, and a chief examiner's standards are subjective. He admitted that borderline decisions might not have the reliability of such consistent tests as those for normal eyesight, or qualification for a first-class shot in the army, or well-designed intelligence tests. To overcome uncertainties produced by borderline scores in single subjects for the school certificate, then, he presented the system adopted by UCLES, of basing order of merit not on aggregate or on individual examinations, but on a system of scaling that equalized the weight of the various subjects. But imperfections could remain: 'The Syndicate therefore endeavour to counteract any imperfections in the system by giving the fullest consideration to each individual' (ibid.: 117). If a candidate's score on one paper was out of line with his or her overall results, the 'offending' paper was sent back to the chief examiner to be re-marked.

Joseph Brereton, Roach's fellow assistant secretary at UCLES, carried this further in a book precisely labelled *The Case for Examinations* (1944). Brereton argued for the stimulating effects of examinations on learning. An Allied soldier in Britain could go only so far in his learning of English without formal academic study, and a public examination like the Certificate of Proficiency in English might well provide the incentive to such study. Examinations must offer some kind of reward (like a certificate), be given at convenient times, be fair (as can be guaranteed by the training of oral examiners with gramophone recordings of typical examiners)[31], and of an appropriate standard (hard enough to extend but not so hard as to discourage).

Brereton presented the converse of the argument that Brigham had made to the American College Entrance Examination Board a decade earlier. The examination, he claimed, was in fact 'the lynch-pin' of the instructional system. Objective testing had led to useful statistical understanding, but reliable measurement divorces the test from the preparation. While this was understandable in intelligence testing, it was not true of examinations, and accounted for the negative attitude of the Hartog inquiry. He argued then for clear and precise spelling out of the syllabus to be examined, pointing out that teachers favour such certainty; if it is not made explicit, it will be deduced from past examinations. At the same time, he did not wish a syllabus to become too rigid, but to be open to continual revision in discussions between examiners and teachers. It was also a mistake to assume the possibility of an absolute standard: examination standards can only be relative. His fundamental criticism of the measurement approach can be seen, then, in its attempt to decontextualize testing. For Brereton and UCLES, the examination gained its meaning in the context of the curriculum. He was equally convinced that examinations involved competition, placing the candidate in the context of his fellows.

In the United States and in Europe then, the decade from 1930 to 1940 saw a continued debate over the possibility of using new-type tests in place of the older, subjectively scored essays. In modern language testing, the discussion raged and the quandary remained unresolved. In Europe in particular, examining boards were reluctant to give up control over the curriculum, and assumed that bright students would continue to emerge from the system. In the United States, with its stronger concern for individual rights of fairness, the psychometric hegemony was more firmly in place, and the deification of reliability was proceeding rapidly, among language testers as well as others.

Notes

1 See the Secretary's report for 1929, for instance, (College Entrance Examination Board 1929: 6).
2 After preparing an account of this test on the basis of published material, I was pleased to come across a short history of the test by the former archivist of the Educational Testing Service, Gary D. Saretsky (1984).
3 Excerpt included in the file of English Examination for Foreign Students, Educational Testing Service Archives.
4 The commission was chaired by Professor Adam Leroy Jones (director of admissions at Columbia University), and consisted of Dr Claude Fuess (English instructor at the Phillips Academy), J. Wilson Hobbs (English junior master at the Boston Public Latin School), Ralph Minor (university examiner with the University of California), Dr Kenneth Murdock (assistant professor of English at Harvard University), David Robertson (assistant director of the American Council of Education), Ira Smith (registrar of the University of Michigan), and Edwin Stevens (registrar of the University of Washington).
5 The membership of the second commission differed from the first in that Hobbs, Minor, Smith, and Stevens were replaced by Professor Jack Crawford (Yale University), Professor Sophie Hart (Wellesley College), Professor Ada Snell (Mount Holyoke College), and Professor Harrison Steeves (Columbia University), making it thus an essentially academic committee.
6 It consisted of Professors Jones, Hansford, Snell, and Steeves, joined by the associate secretary of the Board, Professor Carl Brigham of Princeton University.

7 The earliest formal study of the problem was probably Hopkins (1921), who had shown that there was a strong effect of readers and years on examination scores.

8 See Chapter 3.

9 From the account of the Test of Written English in Chapter 13, it will be seen that this remains Educational Testing Service policy.

10 Edward Noyes was at the time associate professor of English and chairman of the Board of Admissions at Yale University; he was, in addition, chief reader in English for the College Board. He later became vice-president of the Board. John Stalnaker was a psychologist at Princeton University and consultant examiner for the College Board.

11 In a later lecture on mental abilities, Thorndike (1941) made clear his rejection of general ability, and his acceptance of the notion of many mental abilities.

12 A survey of the history of the examinations is given in a supplement to Roach (1945: 34–7).

13 Roach (1983: 4) surmised that it must have been a breakaway by Exeter University College from the London examination; both examinations, he recalled, were based on a course for foreigners, and both were 'heavily academic', including the paper on Phonetics set by Professor Daniel Jones.

14 In 1925, John Roach was appointed additional assistant secretary to UCLES, just before he took his second tripos and qualified for a degree in French and German. Roach, after studying classics at school, had served as a professional soldier in the Indian Army from 1917 until 1922, with wartime service in the Middle East.

15 A classicist, he was secretary of UCLES.

16 In fact, Williams had charge of examining in English; Roach's area was 'modern languages, geography and oddments' and as he later remarked, 'it was not then realized that English was, for foreign candidates, a "modern" language'.

17 Candidates for the Cambridge Certificate of Proficiency in English (Roach 1945: 34):

1931	1932	1933	1934	1935	1936	1937	1938	1939
15	33	66	140	202	278	412	675	752

18 This syllabus was to be written in consultation with the Head of the Day Department at the City of London College (Roach 1934).

19 In 1937, centres listed included Dublin, Paris, Berlin, Marburg, Hamburg, Florence, Rome, Naples, Milan, Hilversum, Lausanne, Basle, Malmö, Helsinki, Budapest, Belgrade, Zagreb, Ljubljana, Sarajevo, Vienna, Gdynia, Warsaw, Bucharest, Athens, Smyrna, Rabat, Beirut, Baghdad, Jerusalem, Shanghai, Oslo, Stockholm, Amiens, Bordeaux, and Dakar.

20 By 1938, translation papers were regularly set in Arabic, Chinese, Dutch, French, German, Greek, Hebrew, Italian, Serbo-Croat, Spanish, and Swedish, and other languages were available on request.

21 When Roach came in, Spens was just signing the famous Spens report, *Secondary Education with Special Reference to Grammar Schools and Technical High Schools*, which was to form the basis for the major reconstruction of the British state school system in the Education Act of 1944.

22 The close connection between English teaching and testing and the Foreign Office may be illustrated by a side-note on that trip by Roach (1989):

> Perhaps the most remarkable thing I wrote was a report that I wrote in French (it had been requested by the French Intelligence in Paris) on Mussolini's Italy. I wrote it in one evening at the end of a ten-day tour of Italy on the Syndicate's business at Christmas 1939, Italy still being semi-neutral. Professor Deseignet of Reading said, 'The style is extremely good. It should be published at once.' Certainly not! Had I published, every Intelligence Service, including our own, would have said, 'He talks.' All that I gathered in Italian (and in German from Polish refugees in my hotel) I transmuted that evening in French. It caused a stir in the French Intelligence, our Embassy in Paris, the Foreign Office. That was enough.'
> (The original report is in the library of Magdalene College, Cambridge.)

23 While inaccessible, the examinations appear to have been continued underground in enemy-occupied territory. Roach (1983) listed several such cases: Sister Pauline who kept them going in Italy and sent in the scripts after the war for validation and the award of certificates, Mrs Stansfield Popovic of Belgrade who took the examinations into Civilian Internment Camp and forwarded the scripts through the Red Cross, and a nun in Brussels who continued the examinations in her convent 'under the noses' of an occupying German unit.

24 Valentine was professor of education at the University of Birmingham, and was for twelve years a member of the Joint Northern Matriculation Board. This book was an account of:

> ... an enquiry, extending over several years, into the reliability of examinations so far as this can be tested by the performance in subsequent years of those examined ... this is no tirade against examinations in general. They seem to the writer an inevitable part of our educational system at some stages and for some purposes. What is urgent is that they should not dominate, and that we should know where their strength and weaknesses lie.
> (Valentine and Emmett 1932: 9)

25 In a study of the marking of weekly compositions in French written by first-year honours students, Benn (1936) concluded that composition seemed to be too complex a notion to be measured.

26 The first session was chaired by Paul Monroe, director of the International Institute, and Sir Philip Saddler, at the time Master of University College, Oxford.

27 After the conference, Thorndike was advised not to return to Paris, as war was expected momentarily (Joncich 1968: 583).

28 This second English study, which was finished by the third conference in 1938 but published later (Hartog *et al.* 1941) was also intended to be constructive rather than critical. It recommended that 'essays' should be replaced by 'compositions on subjects of which they may be reasonably expected to have a fund of ideas and a sufficient knowledge which they could express for a given audience and with a given point of view (ibid.: 142).

29 I have found no evidence that he did this.

30 Similarly, Henning (1992) distinguishes between psychometric and psychological unidimensionality.

31 The references are clearly to the work of John Roach. See Chapter 6.

5 New technologies and consumer protection

Testing of aural comprehension

With the inexorable spread of the psychometric hegemony, testing the ability to speak a modern language set a daunting challenge. The 1913 committee's proposal for language tests[1] had incorporated tests of speaking, but they themselves failed to produce anything that could be widely used. The Modern Foreign Language Study, fifteen years later, was also frustrated in its goal of finding a reliable way of testing for the control of the spoken language that was a central feature of the direct method. But efforts were made to test listening comprehension, including the New York Regents' examinations in 1925 (Decker 1925). By 1929, Lundeberg (1929) himself a pioneer in the field, could list more than half a dozen projects.[2]

The most significant of these was the Bryn Mawr *Test of Ability to Understand Spoken French* (Rogers and Clarke 1933). Originally undertaken in 1926 by a committee of French teachers in the Philadelphia area (Clarke 1931), the test was expanded during the autumn of 1928 under the auspices of the Modern Foreign Language Study (Henmon 1929).[3] The technique adopted was to read a question in French (e.g. *Avec quoi écrit-on?*) to the pupil, who marked one of five words that answered the question. The written words were in English because this was to be a test of aural ability and the pupils might not know how to read French. The test was later standardized with the assistance of French teachers in six different New York high schools. The standardized form of the Bryn Mawr test consisted of eighty sentences, with the vocabulary selected from the *French Word Book* prepared by the Modern Language Study, and arranged in order of difficulty. Questions were no longer than eleven words or twenty syllables, to keep well within the attention span determined in the Binet-Simon Scale for a ten-year-old child repeating nonsense syllables in the mother tongue. The English answer words were restricted to the first thousand words of Thorndike and Lorge's *Teacher's Word Book of 30,000 Words*. (1944) The five-response multiple choice was intended to reduce guessing. All *qui* questions had at least two personal name answers; all *quand* questions had at least two answers with time references. Items which were assumed to be common mistakes were included.

Initial administrations showed correlations of about 0.80 between the two forms and seemed to agree with teachers' grades. Rogers concluded that 'The test can be criticized on the score that it departs from the real situation, but nevertheless it is useful in enabling the teacher to discover stumbling blocks in the way of achievement' (Rogers 1929: 248). By 1931, the audition test had been administered to 1,300 students in forty classes in six New York high schools (Clarke 1931). Mean scores showed progress over seven semesters.

Lundeberg himself, in collaboration with Tharp (1930), wrote a widely used audition test, the results of which correlated with general semester grades in classes at universities of Illinois, Wisconsin, and Ohio. While forms of the Lundeberg–Tharp test correlated highly with each other (about 0.84), the Lundeberg–Tharp test correlated poorly (about 0.47) with the subjective scores. Oral scores (subjective or objective) correlated poorly (about 0.35) with final semester grades, which seemed to be affected mainly by grammar. Another test, authored by Louise Seibert and Ben Wood (1930), also used multiple-choice written questions to test listening comprehension. In Part I, the examiner read a series of statements in French about three pictures and the candidate noted whether the statements were true or false. In Part II, the candidate had to answer yes or no to a series of questions read in French by the examiner. In Part III, the examiner read a passage in French, then directed the candidate to turn to a page in the test booklet where there were three multiple-choice questions in English. Part IV consisted of fifteen sentences for dictation. The vocabulary in the test was controlled.

Oral testing was considered especially important in Canada, where the emphasis on the spoken language had political motivation. Ferguson (1930) described tests developed for French classes in Ontario where the department of education required all initial training in French to be oral and aural. The tests covered the early stages (pronunciation, classroom commands, number to 100, first 20 exercises in grammar, first 11 pages of the reader). Students followed commands in French to perform actions, to underline words containing sounds pronounced, to write down numerals, to note homonyms, and to answer multiple-choice and true-false questions.

The Bryn Mawr test and the others mentioned were objective tests of aural comprehension, using new-type objective items to test the skills. A quite different tradition of oral testing, based on the scaling of integrative performance, was illustrated by the Spanish oral interviews at Yale that started in 1932. Hall (1936) recounted that a few years before, the staff of the Spanish department had been troubled by the finding of the Modern Foreign Language Study that, with a few exceptions, 'modern foreign languages were not being taught as living languages, and therefore not succeeding in developing oral and aural ability in the language'. Believing firmly that it was inconsistent to emphasize speech while only examining writing, they determined to create their own oral examinations. After a year's warning, Yale Spanish students were required in 1932 to take an oral as well as a written examination at the end of their first year. The results of the oral and written examinations for the conversation class were practically the same, so it was decided to use the oral examinations in future. The Yale oral examination took place in the presence of an examining board of all teachers of conversational Spanish, and averaged fifteen minutes per student. The idea of prepared questions was discussed but abandoned, but it was agreed that at least half of the questions should be based on work done during the year. Early questions were based on a list of useful phrases that the students had studied 'in order to counteract nervousness and set the student at ease' (ibid.: 463). For the first two years, students also prepared a 100-word talk on a topic that had interested them. All questions were in Spanish. Each of the examiners gave an estimate, on a five-point scale, of the student's ability under the four headings of pronunciation, grammar, content, and comprehension. The four marks were averaged, and the final grade was the average for all the examiners. By the fourth year, it was noted that the grades of individual instructors seldom varied by more than 2 per cent from the average, and consideration was being given to splitting the board of examiners into two parts.

The aural comprehension tests and the Yale oral examination were precursors of tests that were to be much better developed in later years. They represented both the discrete-psychometric and the integrative-scaled approaches to the problem that were to continue in competition.[4] There was not much other activity, and there was no further development of oral testing until the war.

Only two new studies concerned with the testing of aural and oral abilities are included in the analytical bibliography prepared by Coleman in 1938 (Coleman and King 1938). One is a description by a teacher, Lawrence Ross (1937), of a monthly pronunciation test he gave to his class, with a chart that showed progress in 'speed, smoothness, clearness, knowledge of sounds, linking and phrasing'. The second was a master's thesis (Evans 1937), written at Ohio State under the direction of Professor J. B. Tharp, that studied the Lundeberg–Tharp Audition Test in French to ask if it was possible to rely on an indirect objective measure like the phonetic accuracy section of the Lundeberg–Tharp test to give results that could be used in place of more elaborate judge-rated recordings of actual speech samples. Three expert judges rated and re-rated recorded samples of speech taken from 215 pupils, reading two paragraphs and pronouncing a word list. The ratings correlated between 0.82 and 0.93. The scores of the 215 pupils on the indirect test correlated about 0.80 with the ratings of their speech samples. The writer concluded that the direct and indirect tests were measuring the same thing, and that the test of phonetic accuracy gave a good approximation of the results that could be obtained by more expensive and elaborate direct testing.

One technical improvement in the pen-and-paper testing of French pronunciation was proposed by Kaulfers (1937). Students were to be presented with sets of five words, four of which were said to include the same vowel sound; their task was to write the word that did not have the vowel, and also write the phonetic symbol for the common sound.

Progress in language testing in the 1930s

Reviewing the work of the Modern Foreign Language Study, Henmon (1934a and b) argued that it had contributed usefully to answering the fundamental questions facing teachers of modern foreign languages, had provided useful leads on prognosis and the question of who should study foreign languages,[5] and had shown that adults can learn foreign languages better than or as well as children. Henmon (1934a: 203) reported a number of studies that showed advantages for adult learners over children. While acknowledging that different results might emerge had oral-aural skills been measured, he concluded that 'the widespread belief hitherto prevalent concerning the best time to learn a foreign language rests on an insecure foundation, to say the least.' (ibid.: 204). Henmon referred to a study by Thorndike, Bregman, Tilton, and Woodyard (1928), who, in a chapter of a book on the study of adult learning, reported an experiment in which two groups of university students from 20 to 57 years old had studied Esperanto for 20 hours, showing little difference in learning ability between ages of 22 and 40. A group of children from 9 to 18 with twice as much formal instruction as the over 35 group gained less than half as much. As Henmon pointed out, given the complexity of differences of objectives and methods in language learning, it was dangerous to over-generalize, but there seemed to be no support for the popular belief that only young children could learn a foreign language well. In spite of this, authors of articles written since then claiming superiority for older or adult learners continue to assume that they are the first to ever make this point.

The Study had also cast serious doubt on the notion that any worthwhile language skills could be developed in two years' formal course work. Its major recommendation (although Henmon insists 'not a major contribution') was to restate the primary objective proposed by the Committee of Twelve in 1898, namely, the ability to read with enjoyment.

A few years before, Henmon noted, when Ruch and Stoddard (1927) had reviewed the state of measurement in high school, they could fairly state that 'measurement in French and Spanish is in a state of flux' and remarked that tests available were 'few in number and rather narrow in scope'. Two years later things were very different. By 1928, there were more test batteries and specialized tests in modern languages than in any other school subject—four well-standardized batteries, and ten other special tests, and since 1928, more than half a dozen standardized tests had been added.

Henmon's claim for the quality of these tests remained modest:

> Granting that these tests fall short of giving perfect measurements, it has at any rate been pretty convincingly shown that they are more valid and

reliable than the subjective measurements they replace or are designed to replace. This is all that those of us who are interested in them would claim.
(Henmon 1934a: 197)

Tests in reading he thought to be reasonably good, those in writing were less satisfactory (though composition scales were an advance), and in spoken language progress had been even slower. 'So there is still much to be done, while the laborers are few.' New examination techniques, cheaper than the old methods, were slowly invading examination systems. Achievement levels rather than time spent in class were gradually being accepted as the definition of progress. Henmon (1934b) listed the most important gaps he saw in the testing programme.[6] The first were aural-oral tests, and in particular oral composition. A second gap was the absence of objective scales for scoring translations. A third was the need for objective classroom tests. In view of the multiplicity of standardized tests appearing, there was a need for comparative studies. More studies were also needed to show the greater reliability and efficiency of the new-type tests. The objective tests being used were producing interesting results, but had not solved all the problems.

While there was considerable progress in technology for objective language testing, the invasion of institutional examination systems was somewhat slower. Brinsmade (1928) complained about the strong weight still given to translation in the College Board examination and argued for using the new-type tests. Criticism of the College Board foreign language tests was not new. Wood (1928), arguing the greater technical reliability of the new-type tests, had directed his attack mainly at the New York Regents' Examination, but he did point out their relevance to the College Board tests. The new-type tests, he argued, would be not just more internally consistent but also cheaper.

Only a small step was taken in 1930, when a Preliminary Committee of five including Algernon Coleman and Robert Fife recommended to the College Board a revision of the foreign language requirements 'to bring them into line with the present position of the modern languages in the school curriculum' and to study the examinations used by the College Board 'with a view to closer adjustment to contemporary educational practice'. Such changes in the examinations, they believed, would help in the 'betterment of modern language instruction in all sections of the country' (College Entrance Examination Board 1930: 18). The committee still saw the role of the College Board examination as controlling the curriculum.

The double goal of the examination—the College Board's concern to maintain some control of the curriculum, conflicting with their need to find an objective way of measuring individuals—remained an issue that could be most easily seen with examinations in language: 'Few people realize that if the Board adopted immediately the best of the objective tests in modern languages, there would be no tests and therefore no requirement in controlled language composition—the translation of an English passage into a foreign language' (ibid.: 11). A commission of eleven members was duly set up to handle the task, and while its unanimous recommendations (College Entrance Examination Board 1931) had been influenced by the Modern Language Study, the College Board was not convinced by the proposal for a single examination covering all levels. They did not think that examinations should be allowed to become stereotyped, and assumed that the examiners would use any new methods developed. For the immediate future, however, they proposed a 'combination examination' divided into two parts: translation to and from the foreign language (to be offered at three levels), and a single level examination of vocabulary, idioms, functional grammar, comprehension, and free composition. They proposed a definition of requirements; at each level, reading was placed first. Responses[7] being favourable, the new proposals were approved by the College Board in 1932.

As the debate over new-type tests continued, Kaulfers (1931)[8] summarized fifty-one studies (including eight of his own) claiming that standardized scores correlated better with performance in other fields than did grades, and that achievement was a better predictor of prospective success than was intelligence or aptitude. Cheydleur (1937) also demonstrated again the unreliability of subjective tests by showing the disagreements between trained examiners when they graded subjective examinations at the University of Wisconsin. He showed the economies possible by using objective examinations in foreign languages for placement and to measure achievement.

The pressure for a single examination continued. Using an image that Brigham used, the notion that the College Board's goal was to provide 'a general admission ticket' to college was yielding to the idea that it should provide information for the successful placement of students. Foreign languages testing was considered the area most ready for this development (College Entrance Examination Board 1934a). The Board accepted a recommendation that the modern language examiners should start to move away from the unit concept (a unit being a year's work) and develop single placement examinations, at the same time reporting in such a way that colleges could make the old unit interpretation.

The College Board tests slowly added more new-type materials. After 1934, the reading test consisted of twenty short passages in French, followed by a question in French to be answered in English; in 1936, much of the test was new-type (reading and grammar items), but there were still two translation passages and a composition (Cole and Tharp 1937: 269).

The inclusion of new-type questions in the 1935 French examinations did not pass without criticism, which was answered in the annual report: 'Apparently many teachers failed to understand that at examinations of the newer types no candidate is expected to answer all the questions, that some of the questions are intended primarily to test the powers of the ablest candidates' (College Entrance Examination Board 1935: 17).

The concern about goals remained. James Conant (1934) urged that the only language requirement that should be kept was of a reading knowledge of French or German, dropping the provision for 'an elementary knowledge' of these languages or a reading knowledge of a classical language.[9] Moreover, he argued that the reading knowledge required for a specific subject, such as chemistry, might well be examined in that field.

The physical appearance of the 1936 French examinations marked a further step towards objectivization, eliminating the old answer books and leaving blank spaces on the question paper for the answers of the candidates. The readers who graded the papers reported they could work faster, and believed the change was good for the candidates too. Printing the papers this way cost $700 more, but reading cost 6 cents less per paper, a total saving of $366.

New techniques also brought scoring under tighter control. The readers were divided into groups, each group marking different parts of the examination. Sample essays were copied on the blackboard and discussed by the nine readers in the group until six levels of achievement (bad failure, failure, poor, average, superior, excellent)[10] were agreed on. Essays representative of each level were mimeographed and used as the norm (College Entrance Examination Board 1936: 16).

In 1936, the Board also accepted the notion earlier proposed by Carl Brigham of changing the scale from 0–100 (with its 'fictitious and fallacious "passing mark" of 60') to a new 800-point scale, with the average set at 500 and a standard deviation of 100. Henceforth, all College Board examinations, on whatever scale they had been marked, would be reported in this way.

For the first time in 1937, practically all examinations were marked in parts. A fraction of the papers were selected to be marked twice, and the inter-rater reliability was high (above 0.91, and often about 0.96) in most subjects; English, with 0.84 was the exception. The report was not over concerned, however, for the writer believed that 'the general problem of reliable reading of examinations has been overstressed. The index of genuine significance is that of validity, or the extent to which an examination actually measures what it purports to measure' (College Entrance Examination Board 1937: 31). Validity being hard to determine, and lack of reliability being one cause of lack of validity, the report presented its reliability results 'more to correct the fallacious notion that the Board's essay examinations are not read reliably than to further overstress the significance of reliability'. The 1937 report also includes the cost of reading per book: in most subjects, it was about a dollar (French was 91 cents, German $1.01, Spanish 95 cents); English, however, cost $2.01.

By 1939, the notion of combining short and extended answers in the language papers was well established, and both kinds of questions were considered 'important and significant' (College Entrance Examination Board 1939). Professor Joseph Jackson, who was chief examiner and chief reader in French, believed that:

> In general the objective test weighs a passive knowledge of French, the ability to recognize correct forms, to discriminate between various alternate forms. It does not really tap the student's active fund; that is, he is not called on to supply directly and independently from his store of information.
> (ibid.: 6)

But superior candidates had both passive and active knowledge, so that an objective test provided an accurate measure. The report noted that 'measures of ability from quite different forms of examination usually turn out to be highly related'.[11] But there was a danger that if the Board used a single form of examination, this would encourage 'a narrow and faulty type of preparation and inevitably distort the significance of the grade'. The Board should be on its guard against 'stereotyped methods of examining'. The 1939 report also expressed satisfaction with the combination achieved between the work of the subject matter specialists who were readers and examiners and the 'technicians trained in measurement' who co-operated with them.

There are further signs in 1940 of the gathering strength of the new-type examinations and of the movement towards industrialized testing. In that year, machines were used for the first time to report results, and although the experience included the usual technical problems, the mechanization and industrialization of testing was clearly under way. In the continuing debate over short versus extended answers, the economic argument was repeatedly made: 'the essay form of question is costly in the time required of both the candidate and Reader' (College Entrance Examination Board 1940: 31). It was coming to be accepted that objective questions were quite satisfactory in some subjects, including languages, mathematics, and the elementary sciences. Only in English was there a continuing struggle over extended answers, as the essay still held a firm grip.

New foreign language tests in Britain

In Britain, too, there was concern at the slowness of public examinations to incorporate new testing methods. Paralleling the criticism of essays by the Hartog committee,[12] A. M. Gibson (1934, 1935) complained about the over use of translation in modern language testing.

There were experiments under way in Britain to develop alternative questions for students following a direct-method programme. A subcommittee of the Modern Language Association (MLA) asked teachers to try out an experimental test that included the reproduction from memory of a passage after fifteen minutes' study and a comprehension test (Hedgcock 1933a and 1934b). Hedgcock (1934) said that the majority of the sixteen teachers who had been involved in the experiments thought it had classified their pupils satisfactorily . The examiners' opinions on its value were divided. The committee suggested including an alternative question based on this approach in the School Certificate examinations so as to continue to encourage direct-method teaching.

Continued disagreement about the nature of the French section of the First School Certificate examination led to the establishment of a subcommittee of the MLA to interview heads of French departments in secondary schools. The subcommittee reported (Libbish, Warne, and Wagstaffe 1935) that 500 out of 800 favoured dropping the written translation of French verse, the overwhelming majority opposed a proposal to make a foreign language an optional subject, and two-thirds thought that the high standard set for composition had led to unwonted neglect of oral French.

Non-pedagogical uses of language tests

In actual practice, the change to the new-type tests in American schools and universities was more deliberate and unhurried than the account of innovation suggests. A detailed survey of university comprehensive graduating examinations in the humanities carried out by Jones (1937) showed the wide range of question types used in modern language examinations in over a score of major institutions. Just under a fifth of the questions were essays; close to a half were 'directed discussion'; about 4 per cent called for summaries, 2 per cent for translation, and less than that for miscellaneous 'objective' items. More than 40 per cent of the questions in Romance languages were offered with choices, the highest percentage in the humanities, showing the wide range of reading allowed to students in the various schools. It would seem that none of these comprehensive examinations placed emphasis on productive control of the foreign language.

The uncertainty about goals continued to plague language testers. Frantz (1939), a teacher of German at Bucknell University, was disturbed that many universities and colleges exempted students from further language study if they could pass a test of reading knowledge. The lack of standardization, he said, produced a situation at his institution that was 'rather confusing and discouraging not only to our students but to us as instructors as well'. The standard of attainment was loosely defined, departmental examinations were subjective, and externally produced examinations were too difficult for students. He therefore determined to study the experiences of other universities. He summarized the thirty-nine responses he had received to a questionnaire that he had sent to fifty institutions. A bare majority (not including some major universities such as California, Minnesota, Pennsylvania, Princeton, and Stanford) did allow exemption to students who passed a special reading knowledge test. The tests employed 'were almost as various as the institutions replying'. Two allowed dictionaries. Five emphasized reading passages. One required translation to and from German. One included sight reading and prose composition. Another included oral and written exercises. Another required paraphrases. Four claimed their tests were standardized. Twelve prepared their own tests; four included externally prepared tests in the battery. The tests took between an hour and a half and three hours to administer. The pass mark and rate varied by institution, and within institutions, by field. The pass rate varied from about 50 per cent to about 90 per cent. Twelve institutions were satisfied with what they were doing; four were dissatisfied. Thirty institutions responded to a questionnaire asking for their definition of reading knowledge of a language, with widely disparate results. The main answers were: 'ability to read or translate with understanding or give the accurate rendering of a relatively difficult text or a reasonably correct translation of a typical text without the excessive use of a dictionary' (seven responses); 'ability to read and understand without using a dictionary a given passage ... of normal difficulty' (four responses); 'ability to get the sense of a moderately difficult passage ... to read a text of average difficulty at sight ... to get the main ideas of a paragraph with its essential connotations ... to read with understanding texts of both narratives and of content' (eight responses); 'ability to use a language as a tool' (three responses): 'ability to understand a text ... in *one's field*' (three responses, author's emphasis). Four institutions defined reading knowledge as determined by the amount of time of study; one response said it was a 'most elastic term' and one respondent confessed that he had no definition. Twenty of the respondents considered that the required standard could be reached in two years of work, ranging from three to five hours a week. Nine thought that it took longer. Frantz concluded that more satisfactory tests could only be developed when there was agreement on what was being measured.

Frantz's article was an important presentation of a key point that had been made regularly by earlier testers like Henmon: the development of valid tests depended on the clear definition of what was being measured. While many universities required their students to have some skills in a foreign language, few had thought through the precise specification of these abilities, leaving the question to language departments that had little knowledge of modern language testing.

A related issue of widespread concern was the use of placement examinations. Klemm (1942) found that half of the twenty Pennsylvania colleges and universities he surveyed did use tests. At the University of North Carolina, Giduz (1942) reported (as he had since 1935) on the use of the co-operative French test for this purpose, but the notion of measuring progress in years rather than by level of attainment was hard to change.

In practice, the first flush of enthusiasm for objective language had not been followed by widespread acceptance, and individual and institutional inertia, on the one hand, and the scepticism of humanistically trained language teachers towards scientific testing, on the other, seem to have maintained a wide gap between theoretical advances and practical policies.

Technological advances in language testing in the 1930s

Alongside these slow changes in the use of objective modern language tests, there continued to be proposals for improvement in the tests themselves. At the University of Chicago, there were studies of the testing of vocabulary, and of the value of contextualization. A four-hour comprehensive test was developed that included vocabulary in context, translation from French to English and vice versa, and knowledge of grammar and syntax (Haden and Stalnaker 1934). While the translation sections were the least reliable, the overall reliability was very high, and there was a pleasingly high correlation (0.83) reported with instructor's ratings. To study the hypothesis that objective tests for vocabulary should be contextualized, two Chicago scholars, Stalnaker and Kurath (1935), developed two tests, one with and one without context (see also Kurath and Stalnaker 1936). Very little difference was noted. The two tests correlated equally well with teachers' estimates, with IQ and with a comprehensive German language test, and with each other (about 0.95). A small majority of students preferred the contextual test.

The rising academic status of language testing was marked by its recognition as an appropriate topic for theses and dissertations. A doctoral dissertation at the University of Wisconsin by Ficken (1937) showed that the correlations between the various parts of the Cooperative French Test varied according to the kind of teaching programme: vocabulary and reading generally correlated about 0.80, but less than 0.70 when there was an oral emphasis and less also in schools that stressed reading, where the highest correlation for reading was with vocabulary. An MA study by Heim (1933) at Temple University found only a low correlation (about 0.45) between teachers' grades and objective scores for some 500 students in French, German, and Spanish tested in vocabulary and reading comprehension. A doctoral thesis written by Sammartino (1931) at New York University traced the steady improvement in French written comprehension and vocabulary scores of 547 high school pupils who were receiving bi-weekly tests.

Testing techniques were also studied. In a 'comprehension maturity test' developed by Feder and Cochran (1936), each of the four responses to a model choice test was differently valued: one was false, a second picked on an outstanding detail of the passage, a third was more complete, and the fourth was the correct summarizing statement. Hagboldt (1933) argued for better grading of reading comprehension passages, making use of a syntax count and a study of words and idioms in popular readers. He criticized a number of types of reading tests: true-false, a modified true-false requiring correcting each statement with a single English word, true-false with correction of the false, multiple choice, and definitions in German of English words. He was most favourable to the American Council Test, and noted the high correlations among the sections, evidence of the close connection between the various aspects of language teaching.

Seibert and Goddard (1935), both teaching at Goucher College, were concerned about the effect of translation tests, especially unsuitable in earlier stages, and agreed with Viëtor's remark fifty years earlier that translation was 'an art which has no place in the schoolroom'. Free composition was preferable, but scoring was a difficulty. Even the simplest of compositions involved a great deal beside language ability (such as imagination, clarity, organization) which compromised the 'purity of measurement' that a tester should aim at. Furthermore, there was so much variation in free compositions that comparison would be almost impossible. Their placement test included four objective parts (vocabulary, grammar, reading, and aural comprehension) and a composition, requiring the students to retell a story read in class. The most reliable kind of marking they found was to score by the density of errors, using a scale for seriousness of error of $\frac{1}{2}$, 1, and 2. They found that this density of error scores correlated satisfactorily (between 0.71 and 0.82) with subjective marking by 'a competent teacher' of the same papers. Using the retelling question and scoring for density of error, they achieved correlations between the composition and the objective section of the examination of about 0.85.

Another new technique proposed was a 'citation' exercise, where pupils were instructed to locate a word, phrase, significant character, figure of speech, etc. in a passage being read. Kaulfers (1933b)—who was at the time teaching at Long Beach Junior College—did not claim that this measured appreciation, but he thought it was a way to assess the necessary prerequisite, comprehension. In the area of literature, Koischwitz (1934) proposed the use of combined short-answer and essay-type questions, where pupils were required to list fifteen plays they had read (with author and date), and then answer a different question (the main characters, the setting, the author's philosophy) about each of them.

Smith and Campbell (1942) compared recall with recognition by giving the American Council of Education Cooperative French test and then a parallel recall test to 168 second-year students. The two tests had a high correlation (above 0.80), and seemed interchangeable to the authors of the study.

There was interest in scales at Columbia University, where Peter Sammartino (1938) published the Language Achievement Scale that his department used. Quite different from the absolute scale that his colleague from across campus, Professor Edward Thorndike, was talking about in Dinard in the same year, it was rather a listing of the abilities in each of seven areas (silent reading power, aural comprehension, civilization—but not literature—speaking, grammar, translation from French, and free composition) that made up the curriculum. It was simply stated (so that the student too could understand it), with each point labelled as a goal for general, minor, and major students. Teachers were expected to use comprehensive examinations (given each semester) and other tests to determine when the individual goals were achieved. The scale for speaking is given below. The first five entries apply to general students and minors, the sixth and seventh to majors.

1 Ability to pronounce all elementary sounds as found in simple words and read sentences with correct inflection, intonation, enunciation and pronunciation.
2 Ability to answer simple questions when there is no vocabulary or thought difficulty.
3 Ability to read extended prose and poetry in an intelligent and clear fashion.
4 Ability to give a five- or ten-minute talk (prepared) on a simple topic or about something heard or seen.
5 Ability to engage in normal, everyday conversation.
6 Ability to give in almost faultless French a prepared talk on a special topic in an advanced field such the style of Victor Hugo, the painting of Renoir, etc., and also be prepared to answer questions on the topic.
7 Ability to participate in a discussion with native Frenchmen on some definite topic such as literature, economics, politics, etc.
   (Sammartino 1938: 431)

There was obviously no attempt in this scale to arrive at the equal-unit intervals that Thorndike was calling for. Nor does it have the kind of occupational precision that made the Foreign Service Institute (FSI) scale (see Chapter 8) so useful. None the less, it must be recognized as a clear forerunner of the scales that were to prove so attractive to the language teaching profession such as the American Council on the Teaching of Foreign Languages Guidelines.

Two studies were made of test content. What is probably the first attempt at a standardized test of the non-linguistic content learnt in a modern language course (the term used for this was *realia*) was a master's thesis written at City College of New York by Buda (1931) which described a multiple-choice test, given in English, that consisted of 75 questions about French history, geography, literature, education, religion, culture, and arts. When it was administered to 80 college students and 200 high school students, the scores were generally low, but increased with length of study.

Ten years later, a master's thesis by Gerber (1940) written at the State College for Teachers, Albany, described the divergence in the requirements that different states set for prospective teachers, favouring the State of California requirement of one year's graduate work in the language to be taught. A study of examination papers used in New York from 1915 until 1939 showed poetry and literature to have been included only in earlier years. Translation from French to English was part of the examination after 1932, and from English to French after 1930; a separate comprehension passage had been included since 1937. Questions on cultural topics had been included since 1936. The form of the oral examination was not described.

This small but growing body of research in modern language testing during the decade that preceded World War II reflected the acceptance of the topic as suitable for theses and the slow growth, not yet characterizable as professionalization, of sophistication in test development. While the major proportion of language teaching was considered preparation for reading great literature, a small group interested in the teaching process found language testing to be a useful technique for studying language learning and for encouraging more focused teaching. At the same time, objectivization and technical reliability continued as the goals of institutional language testing. These interests were to be encouraged by a new care for the responsible use of tests.

Consumer protection and the Buros reviews

The mushrooming of an educational testing industry that took place between the two World Wars led to a concomitant apprehension for quality, driven first and foremost by the indefatigable pioneering work of Oscar Krisen Buros. As early as 1925, when he was a student at the University of Minnesota, Buros had written a paper called 'Common fallacies in the use of standardized testing'. He was stimulated shortly after by the founding of the consumer movement to think about a users' organization that would evaluate tests. Unable to find funds to support this, he lowered his goal to that of establishing a co-operative test reviewing service. In 1935, 1936, and 1937, he published bibliographies of tests that were in print, hoping all the time to find funds for an independent agency to review them, but failing in this, he published in 1938 his first co-operative reviewing volume. Published by the School of Education of Rutgers University, *The Nineteen Thirty-Eight Mental Measurements Yearbook* was the first of a series that would subject published tests to detailed scrutiny.[13] These reviews vary greatly in quality, often expressing the personal and unsupported views of the reviewer. They are not always, John Carroll reminded me (personal communication 1993), 'trustworthy or reliable', and are often as interesting for revealing the prejudice of the reviewer as for showing a weakness in the test. The time-lag between publication of test and its review also needs to be noted.

Ten language tests were reviewed in the 1938 yearbook, two of them for Latin. Some of them had just appeared. In 1937, the Committee on Foreign Languages of the American Council on Education announced the publication of a series of *Reading Tests in French and German* that had been prepared by the Cooperative Test Service of the Council (Fife 1937).[14] Nelson Brooks[15] was harsh in his review of the 1937 form of the *American Council on Education French Reading Test* (1: 984), which he found to have unfair questions, poorly chosen passages, questions that could be answered without the text, and implausible distractors. It would not test reading and thinking in French, but should none the less measure vocabulary, syntax, and ability to grasp the general meaning of a sentence or paragraph. Brooks responded slightly more favourably to the *Cooperative French Test (Advanced Form)* (1: 985), the methods of which he considered generally sound, but not altogether well worked out. He was disturbed by the limitations of multiple-choice questions, and happy to note 'one or two touches of humor amid the rattle and clatter of such [a] highly mechanized testing apparatus'.

A third French test, the *Cooperative French Test (Elementary Version)* (1: 986) was reviewed by Walter Kaulfers of Stanford, professor of secondary and comparative education at Stanford from 1936 until 1948, who, in spite of the weaknesses—overshort exercises, possibly invalidating use of cognate vocabulary, probably irrelevant proof-reading-type exercises—found this the best available test of French vocabulary, reading, and usage for pupils beginning their study before tenth grade.

Three German tests were reviewed by Curtis D. Vail of the University of Buffalo. He considered the *American Council on Education German Reading Test* (1: 999) that had just been published to have high validity for testing German reading knowledge and to have good internal consistency. He was also quite satisfied with the *Cooperative German Test (Advanced Form)* (1: 1000), especially with the multiple-choice comprehension items in Part I, and except for an unforgivable misprint, the multiple-choice grammar completion items in Part III. He was less pleased with the success of Part II, the vocabulary, where German was used both for the stem and for the distractor, leading to very easy or very difficult items. The longer forms of the *Cooperative German Test* (1: 1001), developed and regularly revised by the Cooperative Test Service, had the advantage that they could be used over again to check progress. The 90-minute forms were extremely reliable, the 40-minute forms less so, a result of course of the different number of items. He pointed out that while they measured what they covered with success, they did not include a number of important outcomes: speaking, translation, understanding speech, or writing in German. Finally, he noted the benefit of being able to use cheap machine scoring for the tests.

Walter Kaulfers also reviewed the two Spanish tests. He found the *Cooperative Spanish Test* (both the advanced and the elementary form) (1: 1156) to be satisfactory in taking into account vocabulary frequency; unfortunately, he noted, the syntax frequency list appeared too late to be used. The tests measured adequately a student's ability to understand short sentences, to recognize the English meaning of isolated Spanish words, and to proof-read for grammatical correctness. He was uncertain of the value of the third aim. The presentation was satisfactory, but some practice items might have helped.[16]

The Second Mental Measurements Yearbook (more correctly called *The Nineteen Forty Measurements Yearbook*) did not actually appear until 1941. It started with an effort to catch up on the reviewing of older tests, including reviews of the original 1924–7 American Council Alpha and Beta tests, discussed in Chapter 2, that were still available and being used a decade later.

C. E. Ficken and Warren Holmes each reviewed the *American Council Alpha French Test* (2: 1342) for grades 9–16. While Ficken considered this pioneering test to be one of the best on the market, Holmes thought that it had become somewhat dated. Nelson Brooks reviewed the aural comprehension test by Agnes Rogers and Frances Clarke and published in 1933 as the *American Council Alpha French Test: Aural Comprehension* (2: 1343). He thought the goal commendable, but seriously questioned the use of English answers to the French questions. He found the ordering of the questions a problem, and was worried about 'the dullness of many of the questions and the generally stuffy atmosphere'. Brooks concluded his review by suggesting that language testers as well as textbook writers should listen to Otto Jespersen's advice to the latter, 'that there might be a limit to the amount of rubbish that can be offered children under the pretext of teaching them grammar'. The *American Council French Grammar Test* (2: 1345) prepared in 1927 by Frederic Cheydleur was reviewed by Harry Heller, who thought it did its narrow job well enough, and by Charles Holzwarth, who was unhappy with the multiple-choice approach and thought the test needed considerable revision.

Holzwarth also reviewed the *American Council on Education French Reading Test* (2: 1346) that had been prepared by Cheydleur, Henmon, and Walker and had also been unfavourably reviewed in the 1938 yearbook by Nelson Brooks. He started with a strong attack; while the scoring of a test might be objective, its subject matter was necessarily subjective. 'Any competent classroom teacher can make up a test better suited to test the progress and the knowledge of his own particular classes', but of course such tests would not be standardized. He was also concerned about the use of 'recognition' items, being willing to be considered 'a conservative of the old school' for his belief that oral/aural mastery should be tested. He was afraid that tests like this were 'a guessing game', and analysed the strategy a candidate might go through to answer a question. Personally, he favoured translation testing.

The original 1926–7 *American Council Alpha German Test* (2: 1357) by Henmon and colleagues was reviewed by Professor C. H. Handschin,[17] who saw little value in a multiple-choice test where the candidates spent their time on the English distractors rather than on the German key, and would prefer to reverse the procedure. He considered the test 'adequate' but he had many criticisms. The 1926–8 *American Council Alpha Spanish Test* (2: 1371) was reviewed by Lawrence Andrus, examiner with the University of Chicago Board of Examinations, who thought that the vocabulary items were well selected, the grammar was good for its time,[18] the comprehension items were well chosen, but the composition was not objective. Andrus did not think that a marking scale could ever remedy the 'evils of purely subjective grading'. In a second review, Professor Christian Arndt of Northwestern University did think the more subjective parts were justified, but was concerned about validity: 'Until more information is at hand to show that such language tests are measuring what they purport to measure the results can only be accepted with considerable reservation.'

The 1940 yearbook also examined a number of the tests that had been developed by Ben Wood and his associates at the Columbia Research Bureau in the late 1920s. The *Columbia Research Bureau French Test* (2: 1348), written by A. A. Méras, Suzanne Roth, and Ben Wood in 1926, was reviewed by Joseph Jackson, who found that it fell short of its potential, and by Laura Johnson, who disagreed and considered it 'among the most satisfactory standardized French tests for high school students'. The *Columbia Research Bureau German Test* (2: 1359) written in 1926–7 by C. M. Purin and Ben Wood, was reviewed by Harold B. Dunkel, examiner with the Board of Examinations at the University of Chicago, who objected to the lack of context and the poor distractors in the vocabulary section, considered the true-false items used as comprehension to show 'all the faults of this form' so that it was 'nothing short of miraculous' that it reached an internal consistency of 0.80, and found the last section, grammar, also misnamed, being a test of active writing rather than of reading. He was very dubious about the current validity of the norms. His final comment brought home the point of being asked in 1940 to review a 1926 test:

> In the past thirteen years more progress has been made in testing than in automobile construction. To say that this test and a 1926 Ford appear odd to us is no reflection on the authors or Mr. Ford. Both the test and the car were good in their day; but that day has passed.
> (Buros 1975: 48)

It was to protect consumers with reviews like this that Buros started his venture, for the Purin–Wood test seems to have still been in print in 1939, published by the World Book Company. These early tests seemed to have had an admirable longevity: the Stanford Spanish tests, published in incomplete form in 1927, were still in active demand a quarter of a century later.

The *Columbia Research Bureau Spanish Test* (2: 1372), written by Frank Callcott and Ben Wood in 1926–7, was reviewed by Professor James Babcock of the University of Chicago, who thought that the selection of items had dated and did not like the comprehension sentences, and by Professor Harry Russell of Miami University, who found the format 'all that could be desired', but agreed that the comprehension section should be changed and more weight given to reading in a natural situation. The *Columbia Research Bureau Aural French Test* (2: 1347), which was the aural comprehension test developed in 1930 by Louise Seibert and Ben Wood, was found by Clarence E. Turner to be 'a sound and well-constructed test', but he was concerned that the candidates were at the mercy of the reading skill of the examiner, and that the style remained literary, and provided no measure of colloquial French.

Another early aural comprehension test, the *Lundeberg–Tharp Audition Test in French* (2: 1354), originally published in 1934, was reviewed in the 1940 yearbook by Nelson Brooks, who commended the naturalness of the language problems involved, and thought it was well presented.

The third major series of tests reviewed were those developed by the Cooperative Test Service, originally produced in the early 1930s, revised since then every year. Newer versions of the *Cooperative French Test (Advanced Form)* (2: 1349) were included in the reviews by C. E. Ficken, Heller, and Jackson. Ficken, professor of French at Macalester College, complained that he could provide only an 'armchair appraisal', lacking evidence of formal reliability or validation, but agreed that it was, with all its limitations, 'a far better measuring instrument than the traditional examination of yesterday'. Harry Heller, head of a New York high school French department, noted that while language tests generally continued to measure what was easily measurable, this test did its stated job better than most. Joseph Jackson, professor of French at the University of Illinois, thought the test was satisfactory but 'highly mechanized and narrowly limited'.

Both Warren Holmes and James B. Tharp thought that the *Cooperative French Test (Elementary Form)* (2: 1350)—revised forms up to 1940 were available—was an excellent test. Tharp described the careful research that had accompanied revisions of the test, and had high praise for 'mechanical and statistical features'. He thought, however, that there should be considerable revision still in the content.

Professor Handschin wrote the review of the *Cooperative German Test (Advanced Form)* (2: 1360), which he considered to be 'effective', and was only concerned at the lack of information on how the word frequency lists had been used. The *Cooperative Spanish Test (Advanced form)* (2: 1373) was reviewed by Lawrence Andrus, who found the reading section too easy, commended the vocabulary, found the distribution of syntactic items general suitable, and would have liked more information on norms. Harry Russell, associate professor of Romanic languages at Miami University, wrote a second review and found both the information in the test manual and many features of the test to be unsatisfactory. The *Cooperative Spanish Test (Elementary Form)* (2: 1374) was considered by Christian Arndt 'to meet the practical needs of all teachers who desire an accurate measuring device for the evaluation of progress in Spanish in secondary schools'.

The first collection of reviews edited by Oscar Buros (1938) was welcomed by Coleman *et al.* (1949) as of 'inestimable value' and a stimulus to the 'whole movement of test construction'. Reading the reviews written in 1939 and 1940 of the major tests of the 1920s, one can appreciate both the pioneering work and the growing sophistication of the field. It is clear from them that many professionals were still far from convinced by multiple-choice testing. At the same time, there were others who completely accepted the new psychometric principles and required full reliability data and norms to accompany any published test.

A very important point needs to be made here. The institutionalization of the tests—their norms and standards—made them very hard to change. It was not just that they were in print—new forms of the *Cooperative* tests were written every year—but that any major change in form would lose equivalence. Commercial tests take some years before they are accepted, and longer to reach their widest market, so that publishers are naturally reluctant to change them too much. As the test is used more, more data can be collected on its reliability and validity. It was this theoretically justified inertia that turned the giants into brontosaurs, for a fixed test form (which encourages cramming and narrow preparation) is necessarily stultifying. At the same time, the fact that the tests were being used by teachers and schools for their own purposes gave them the continued freedom of interpretation that avoided the potential hazards of institutional use.

The reviews in Buros demonstrate the rise of a consumer protection movement in testing, and give evidence of the growing level of sophistication shown in two decades of modern language testing, during which the main emphasis had been on objectivization and standardization. The pursuit of technical reliability was proving a harshly effective taskmaster.

Notes

1 See Chapter 2.
2 He mentioned tests by Ballif at Utah, by Rogers at Bryn Mawr, at the University of Illinois, the Seibert test, the Russell Spanish test, and the Stanford Spanish test.
3 The earliest form of the test was described in the volume published by the Study (Rogers 1929).
4 After 1932, the Bryn Mawr tests were published and continued to be used (Rogers and Clarke 1933). The Yale oral examination was still in use in 1936 (Hall 1936).
5 The work on prognosis will be discussed in Chapter 11.
6 In a second summary, written in the concluding volume of the work of the Committee on Modern Language Teaching, Henmon (1934a) characterized progress in recent developments in the 'construction, evaluation, and use of tests in the modern foreign language'. Education in the last two decades had been marked, he opened, by 'the development and application of psychological tests to measure human ability and achievement more accurately and objectively than had previously been done'. These tests were derived from Binet's 1905 scales, since when 'educational tests have multiplied by hundreds'. But standardized language tests had been late in the movement, only appearing in 1919. Since then, there had been great progress, but, though there remained areas untested, 'even the most Pyrrhonic of sceptics could not well deny' that important progress had been made.
7 Their report was printed, among other places, in the *Modern Language Journal*, where James Tharp (1932) commented on the stability and inertia brought to the field by the Board. The new revision, he thought, did make a step in the right direction, by incorporating new objectives.
8 Born in Germany, Walter Vincent Kaulfers received his BA from State Teachers College of San Diego in 1925, and an MA from Stanford University in 1929; his PhD from Stanford was earned by 1933. He joined the Stanford University faculty in 1936.
9 Interesting light was thrown on the non-functional approach of College Board French and German tests in a study carried out for the Social Science Research Council (Brigham 1935). To check their ability to read French and German, all candidates for SSRC first year graduate fellow-

ships were required to take the Level 3 tests; their results were poorer even than those achieved by applicants for college admission. The College Board test was formal and not adapted to reading ability; in fact, after a period self-study, all the applicants awarded fellowships were able to achieve a requisite level of reading ability. The Board was therefore planning to add to the examinations an objectively scorable section on reading comprehension, consisting of passages in ordinary prose to be translated into English.

10 Compare the eight-level grading used for the English essay at this time; see Chapter 4.

11 See Chapter 8 for a discussion of this important observation by Thibault.

12 See Chapter 4.

13 All references in this section and elsewhere to reviews in the various *Mental Measurements Yearbooks* will employ the reference system used in the monograph in which Buros (1975) collects the Foreign Language sections. The first number is that of the yearbook and the second that of the test in the yearbook.

14 The tests were offered for sale at $1.10 for a packet of 25 tests, including scoring stencils, manuals of instruction, norms, and report sheet. The French test had been prepared by F. F. Cheydleur and V. A. C. Henmon; the German by E. P. Appelt and V. A. C. Henmon.

15 He was at the time teaching at the Westbury School in Connecticut and was later to be involved in a central role in the post-war language testing development—see Chapter 9.

16 Kaulfers also reviewed a pioneering test of *realia*, the *Spanish Life and Culture* test (1: 1157) published by M. M. Miller in 1937, finding it an initiative to be commended in spite of weaknesses in the test itself.

17 In 1919, he had written and published what is considered the first modern language test, and in 1940 was professor of German and executive officer of graduate work at Miami University.

18 It was written long before the *Spanish Syntax List* edited by Hayward Keniston and published in 1937.

6 Language testing goes to war: 1940–1945

Oral language proficiency

Oral language testing was an important part of traditional (pre-scientific) testing, and is now a central feature of post-modern testing, but it presented special challenges for psychometric approaches, especially the establishment of technical reliability. Indeed, Raatz (1981) took the extreme view that no subjective (or even semi-subjective) test could meet the equal intervals requirement of psychometric theory, although his judgement would disallow attempts since Thorndike (1910) to do so.

In language testing history, pride of place for a direct measure of oral language proficiency is generally now granted to the oral interview created by the Foreign Service Institute (FSI) of the US State Department, developed originally between 1952 and 1956. The first published account (Rice 1959) gave only a brief description of the test. A fuller discussion of the nature and principles underlying the interview had to wait until the 1970s when papers by Wilds (1975) and Jones (1979) were commissioned, and a two-day conference was devoted to the topic (Clark 1978a).

The FSI testers understood the special problems of oral language testing as being to elicit a useful sample of speech, and then to arrive at a reliable and valid judgement of it. The developers considered themselves pioneers working in virgin territory. As Lowe (1988: 16) put it, ignoring like them all the earlier work recorded so far, 'Linguists at FSI would have gladly adopted or modified a system for ascertaining oral proficiency if one existed; the fact was that none did.' The tardiness of public and scholarly discussion—the twenty or so years between the start of their work and the first published papers dealing with it in any detail—also indicates that the developers of the test tended to believe that their problems were to be worked out in-house, and that they would have little appeal for scholarly debate.

On closer reading of earlier publications, it turns out to be the case, however, that most of the issues that the FSI linguists had to struggle with, especially those concerning reliability, had been anticipated and intelligently ventilated in both America and Britain. Two papers, written towards the end of World War II as a result of pressures to move language tests from school certification and control to practical issues of the world outside school, had already shown up the serious gap that had been allowed to remain in language testing. How testers in each country tried to deal with this vacuum is revealing of the different intellectual and institutional climates.

US language testing goes to war: 1943–1945

The exigencies of World War II exposed the major deficiency that had been left in American language teaching as well as testing by the decision of the Modern Language Study in 1924–8 to agree to the limitation to reading. When the US armed forces became cognizant of the shortage of soldiers who could speak, understand, and read the large number of languages required for military purposes, they quickly found how inadequate also was the ability of the current language teaching establishment to meet this demand and so found it necessary to develop a completely new approach.

The Army Specialized Training Program (ASTP) was created on 18 December 1942.[1] By 30 August 1943, some nineteen curricula had been established for language and area schools (Lind 1948). The first ASTP language courses began in April 1943, with 15,000 non-commissioned trainees[2] at fifty-five colleges and universities. The curriculum was based on the Intensive Language Program[3] of the American Council of Learned Societies, with the objective of developing control of the spoken variety of the target language. In principle, any methodology was acceptable, provided that the teaching was carried out in intensive conditions, which meant about fifteen contact hours a week.

One immediate result of the programme was a public controversy between the language teaching establishment and the linguists involved in the new development. In answering criticism of extravagant claims purportedly being made for the new programme, Cowan and Graves (1944) submitted a list of 'the modest "claims" which these advocates really do present'. The first was that the 'dribble' method of three hours a week, while it may have had other educational value, could not teach the 'practical speaking command' of the languages that the war situation demanded, which required a minimum of ten hours per week. Their guess was that about twenty-five hours per week for three months or more would be desirable. Such intensive teaching should be conducted ideally by a trained technical linguist who was bilingual and an inspired and inspiring teacher. While there was probably no new method, there were new materials needed for teaching spoken language, with grammar taught 'scientifically' as and when useful. The fact that many structural linguists were involved in the teaching of the uncommon languages led to a belief that they developed a new scientific method of language teaching. Cowan and Graves downplay this claim, which can still be found in such a recent treatment of the topic as Barnwell (1992). A wide range of teachers was possible (assuming they were scientifically trained).

The immodest and modest reports of the success of the new approach led to a call for more careful evaluation. At a meeting of the Commission on Trends in Education of the Modern Language Association of America in November 1943, Dr William Berrien (assistant director for humanities of the Rockefeller Foundation) passed on the suggestion of Elton Hocking of Northwestern University that a group of specialists should evaluate this new approach. With funds provided by the Rockefeller Foundation, an evaluation team began its work on 16 February 1944 but only just in time, for on 18 February, the War Department announced that by 1 April 1944, the ASTP would be suspended, as reinforcements for troops in Europe had a higher priority than language specialists.

In the next six weeks, the six members of the project staff[4] visited forty representative institutions across the country, saw 427 classes teaching sixteen different languages, met with programme directors, teachers, and trainees, and talked to college and university administrators and faculties. Their report (Agard, Clements, Hendrix, Hocking, Pitcher, van Ernden, and Doule 1944) concluded modestly that for trainees for whom this was the first exposure to the target language, the results 'while by no means miraculous, were definitely good, very satisfactory to the men in charge of the programme, and very generally gratifying to the trainees themselves' (ibid.: 25). Wherever the programme was well conducted (and they made no attempt to specify how many of the institutions met this criterion), a 'considerable percent' of the trainees developed ability to express themselves with fluency and a high level of ability to understand native speakers in normal conditions. As a result of their survey, in a cautious statement issued in May 1944, the Commission on Trends in Education of the Modern Language Association expressed 'deep satisfaction' in the results of the ASTP, which derived not from new methods but from well-tried practices, that had been achieved not under the 'direction of linguistic magicians' but by regular foreign language teachers. These results, they stressed, were due to no 'miraculous formula' but to the liberal time allowed and to the use of small groups. Foreign language teachers would be happy to continue to work in these conditions, which would permit the 'creation of a body of American citizens whose knowledge of other languages would be adequate for our international contacts in post-war days' (Commission on Trends in Education 1944).

In spite of this belated interest in evaluation, there is little evidence that any general attempt was made to assess the results of the programme. Most of the extensive debate, on one side or the other, depends on impressions and anecdotal evidence such as that recorded in Angiolillo (1947). In their report, the commission referred to the problem of examinations:

Army experts and other specialists are still trying to devise objective tests of aural comprehension and oral fluency. Until these are provided the

best tests have been found to be the standard devices: retelling or paraphrasing a spoken anecdote, situation, or description; impromptu
responses to questions of familiar subjects; dictation; and, for comprehension only, written responses (true-false or multiple-choice) to spoken
phrases. The success of sectioning, and indeed of the whole oral method,
rests upon regular and reliable testing procedure.
(Agard *et al.* 1944: 17)

Angiolillo (1947), in the fullest available but still incomplete account of
the programme, claimed that the Army desired tests and wanted the grading for them to be criterion-referenced[5] and that they required two levels
of positive achievement: expert and competent:

1 Trainees who have satisfied the institutional authorities that they can
   both comprehend and speak the language as well as a person with the
   same amount of formal schooling should speak his mother tongue,
   will be graduated from Term 6 and will be designated on availability
   reports as expert.
2 Trainees who have satisfied the institutional authorities that they can
   readily comprehend the language as spoken by one adult native to
   another and can speak the language well enough to be intelligible to
   natives on non-technical subjects of military importance, will be
   graduated from Term 6 and will be designated on availability results
   as competent.
   (ibid.)

The wording of these criteria is interesting, appealing to the native-speaker
comparison and setting up the distinction between the normal 'adult native'
and the educated native that was maintained later in the FSI scale. The
Army had two other grades: non-competent, and hopeless. In actual practice, however, institutions appear not to have used this system, but either
a three-level system (fair, good, excellent) or a percentage score (ibid.: 159).
  Angiolillo, on the basis of an interview with Anthony Tudisco, reported
one case of a more elaborate programme of testing, the work of Harry
Rivlin[6] at Queens College, who had recorded an elaborate oral examination, on phonograph discs, including vocabulary, idioms, sentences, paragraphs, conversations, and translator-situations. It used all of the devices
and techniques and materials employed in the teaching itself, including
cartoons, pictures, and spontaneous conversation. Moreover, other
mechanical devices (such as electric signals) were utilized to maximize the
potentialities of the phonograph as a test-giving and test-recording device.
The tests developed at Queens were very difficult, Antonio Tudisco told
Angiolillo, and they seemed to have been fashioned so as to 'trip or trick the
men'. The Queens' testing programme was indeed one of the most highly
developed in all of the ASTP. It attempted, by group and individual oral

testing, to measure all aspects of oral ability in the foreign language (ibid.). But this was an exceptional programme, 'not characteristic of the rest of ASTP'.

Some of the other programmes used standardized tests. At the University of North Carolina, three tests were given: the Cooperative French Test, both the Advanced Form and Form 19, and the Columbia Research Test Form A (Ghigo 1944). While the staff of the French section was 'fully cognizant of the fact that there is little correlation between oral and aural work, and written tests', they found that the men who did the best work on written tests also did best in oral and aural work. When the tests were repeated after three months, there was generally considerable improvement.

A set of tests for oral–aural skills in Russian and German was developed at Harvard by P. J. Rulon (1943, 1944a, 1944b, 1944c) under contract from the War Department. These tests, which Carroll (1954: 6) reported as existing on professionally produced phonograph records, were never used, as the ASTP programme for which they were prepared closed down before they were ready. While all these tests were limited in their use and influence, the Army experience did lead to some further thinking about the problem of testing oral ability.

A wartime proposal

The most interesting discussion of oral language testing arising out of this wartime experience is a programmatic article[7] by Walter Kaulfers (1944). Kaulfers[8] believed that if the 1925 survey of foreign language teachers (which led to the Coleman report discussed in Chapter 4) were to be repeated in 1944, the majority of teachers would not again put reading as the most important objective. Planes and radio having made the world smaller, there was a developing consensus that oral–aural abilities were more important than ever and these must become the primary goals of a curriculum driven by requirements outside the school.

This belief was strongest, Kaulfers believed, in the Army language and area schools for which he had been called on to plan progress tests for these programmes. The large number of trainees meant that any test specifications must be translatable 'into practical terms'; must be machine scorable as far as possible 'to minimize on labor costs'; must not require an elementary and intermediate level student to read and write the foreign language (for this would only be taught at higher levels); should provide 'evidence of the examinee's readiness to perform in a life-situation' where lack of such ability could be militarily damaging; should have items graded or scaled in difficulty to provide 'a kind of ladder'; must provide scores that could be interpreted in terms of 'performance norms', which would make clear 'what an examinee who reaches a certain point on the scale can be expected to do with the foreign language in real life communication situations'; should avoid the 'correlation fallacy'—the false notion invalidating 'practically all existing standardized tests' that a pen-and-pencil task correlates with the corresponding ability to speak and understand; and finally, must permit uniform, standardized administration, using, for example, recorded discs or tone-control talking machines. Kaulfers suggested some examples of techniques which might be suitable. In one, the examiner would read a question twice; the candidate would be required to mark answers to the question. In a second, the examiner would make a statement correctly and incorrectly; the candidate would mark which was the corrected.

The test would need to be normed with real life. Kaulfers proposed a performance scale[9] for measuring aural comprehension, as follows:

0   Cannot understand the spoken language.
1–5   Can catch a word here and there and occasionally guess the general meaning through inference.
6–10   Can understand the ordinary questions and answers relating to the routine transactions involved in independent travel abroad.
11–15   Can understand ordinary conversation on common non-technical topics, with the aid of occasional repetition or paraphrastic restatements.
16–20   Can understand popular radio talks, talking-pictures, ordinary telephone conversations, and minor dialectal variations without difficulty.
         (ibid.)

Its functionality is clear and obvious as it reflects probable needs of the soldier.[10] Some of the phrases that Kaulfers used in it turn up in the later FSI scale, showing the seminal importance of his work, and the techniques and approaches are very close to those that were later adopted.

Measuring oral fluency, Kaulfers believed, was unusually difficult. He argued against using pen-and-pencil tests: 'It simply cannot be taken for granted that ability to express oneself in writing is correlated with a like ability to speak the language extemporaneously' (ibid.: 140). Individual tests must be long enough to allow the candidate to show his ability, but short enough to be practical. The average test would be five minutes. By using the notion of 'plateaus'—groups of three items at each level, maximum efficiency would be reached. If an examinee failed three items in succession, the test stopped because his level had been reached. A modification of this technique is now used in computer-controlled tests. He added that the tests would be spaced over 4 to 5 days and forms would need to be equated. The fields tested must be functional and distinguish various areas of language fluency, e.g. ability to ask questions, to answer questions, to give directions. Within each field, the difficulty level would be varied by frequency of vocabulary tested and by difficulty of syntax. But items should first be written according to extra curricular uses and only after graded by difficulty. He proposed that norms should be established based on the performance of bilingual subjects.

Suitable examiners would be educated people who had lived abroad, whose standards must be based on normal and not on normative usage, and who must be trained, including trial rating of phonographic recordings. The test must be given privately in quiet but pleasant surroundings. The examiner should be 'cordial' but businesslike and informal. The test should begin with informal conversations to relax the examinee, followed by some practice items. These suggestions are very similar to those given to FSI oral interviewers.

With the graded approach that Kaulfers suggested, the examiner should start just below the point on the scale where he thought that the examinee would be most comfortable and stop after three zeros. Examiners should stick to the time-limit for each item, avoid coaching or comments on quality, but encourage if needed. They were not to write down rating where the examinee could see them. If the test were given by a 'recorded voice from a loudspeaker or tone-controlled talking machine', the examinee should face it and the examiner sit alongside or behind him. Complete recording he thought would be more reliable and paper discs were inexpensive. Otherwise, one examiner should administer the test and a concealed scorer should rate. The examinees should be told about the test in advance and given a practice session with parallel items.

Kaulfers presented a sample aural-oral proficiency test in Spanish and a rating scale. For oral fluency, a distinction was made between scope and quality; there were four levels for each. The items in Part 1 were to test the ability to secure services: the instruction was to 'imagine yourself talking to a native abroad'. How would you tell the native speaker to 'speak English, get a doctor, let you have a room with a bath, change a ten-dollar bill, find out how long ago the train left, look for someone who can speak German and French . . .'? Each had two similar items. Part 2 was concerned with asking for information, Part 3 with giving information. In Part 3, the questions were in Spanish. The test needed to be tried out on several hundred subjects, he concluded. He did not claim to have solved all the problems of oral testing, but 'to indicate possibilities and practical lines of approach to those who are interested in pioneering in a heretofore unexplored, but increasingly important field'. He hoped that teachers would try out his ideas, and that some reader would 'choose the construction of a valid and reliable oral fluency test, with norms, as a problem for a master's or doctor's thesis'.

Kaulfer's proposals, novel though they seem in this context, were clearly derived from his deep knowledge of pre-war modern language testing, and may be considered the logical continuation of it. The test that he proposed and the techniques that he recommended are remarkably close to those later adopted in the oral interviews. In 1944, though, his proposals generally seem to have fallen on deaf ears[11] and to have been left in the archives for future historians of the field to rediscover.[12]

Post-war impact of the Army Specialized Training Program

In spite of the failure of diffusion, the ASTP was influential in recalling American attention to oral foreign language teaching and testing. When Ralph W. Tyler, with support from the Rockefeller Foundation, conducted research at the University of Chicago called *The Investigation of the Teaching of a Second Language* on the effects of the new intensive programmes, there was no testing programme to measure the types and levels of skills that were objectives of the intensive instruction, so that in 1946 the project started to develop tests of oral and aural ability that would include among other techniques a talking film (Agard 1946).

The aural comprehension series of tests, aimed both for students after 90–130 hours (a year of three hours per week or an intensive semester of study) and for an advanced level of students with over 150 hours (in the second year of non-intensive or the second semester of intensive instruction) included material recorded on phonograph records by native speakers of Spanish and a booklet with multiple-choice response items. In each level, there were three parts. In the lower level, Part I consisted of twenty-five completion items: sentences to be completed by adding a word or phrase. The sentences were in Spanish, but the completion offered was in English, so as not to restrict the choices unduly. Part 2 consisted of twenty-five definitions in Spanish; the candidate marked the English word defined. Part 3 consisted of six short and humorous anecdotes in Spanish; the answer sheets had statements in English that summarized some aspect of the anecdote. In the upper level test, Part I consists of twenty-five definitions, Part 2 of six anecdotes, and Part 3 of a five-minute dialogue between a man and a woman speaker. The questions in Part 3 are of the same type as in Part 2. The dialogue was chosen from a Spanish play; the questions concentrated on the outline and not the details of the plot. In answer to criticism of the use of English in the test, Agard argued that 'it is useless to delude oneself into thinking that a first-year or second-year student has passed the stage where his thoughts first take shape in English'. Agard recognized that the ideal conditions that were desirable for the test—high quality phonographs, good needles, a room with good acoustics, a loudspeaker at ear-level in front of the room—were not uniformly achievable. In pilot presentations, there had been concern expressed about the speed of the speech, something that Agard attributed to the lack of experience with native speech. He did say, however, that 'in a few institutions the "oral method" was not distinguished from "hot air" and the results were dismal'.

One other war-related activity was a set of tests developed in the closing years by the examinations staff of the United States Armed Forces Institute, with assistance from the College Entrance Examination Board research and test construction staff in Princeton,[13] to assist colleges and universities in placing applicants who had taken courses while in the armed services and in granting them credit for this work. There were tests prepared in French, German, and Spanish grammar, reading comprehension, and vocabulary. In spite of the report that they were pre-tested and submitted to critics designated by professional associations, they appear to have been technically and theoretically weak: badly chosen distractors, incorrect language, inappropriate texts, trick questions, implausible contexts, inadequate norms, poor comprehension questions are among some of the criticisms. One innovation that does not seem to have met with acceptance by the reviewers was to supply distracters for the comprehension questions in the foreign language.

World War II might have been a critical period in the evolution of modern language tests in the United States, but, its effect was in fact limited, and as Barnwell (1992) concludes, 'no fundamental change in testing practices in high school or college grew out of the innovations brought about in the 1940s'. Barnwell (ibid.) does claim a direct line from the ASTP through Agard and Dunkel to modern practices, but deeper analysis suggests a more complex relationship.

The absence of a formal centralized assessment for the ASTP lessened the potential impact of the wartime developments, but the change in curricular emphasis from reading to speaking added new urgency to the long-standing challenge of finding an acceptable way to assess proficiency in the spoken language. The old tests were not wrong; they just seemed irrelevant.

Cambridge examinations in wartime[14]

In Britain, there was nothing like the drama of the American ASTP, but the teaching of English to foreigners, carried out by officers of the Education Corps, became an important aspect of the collaboration with Allied military forces stationed in Britain. The University of Cambridge Local Examinations Syndicate (UCLES), with its long experience of overseas testing and the testing of English for foreigners, became involved in testing these students.[15] This testing of soldiers became an important part of UCLES' work in English for foreigners. As a result of the war and the loss of access to overseas centres, in 1940 there had been only 326 candidates for the Certificate of Proficiency in English offered by the UCLES, and in

1941 only 276. However, in 1942 and 1943, the inclusion as candidates of members of the Allied forces (many of them stationed in Britain) led to an increase to 444 and 861. At the same time, the Lower Certificate started to grow; offered at first at overseas centres only, it attracted 144 candidates in 1939, 254 in 1940, 112 in 1941, and 242 in 1942. With the offering of this examination to members of the Allied forces at United Kingdom centres in 1943, the total jumped to 846. Thus, in 1943 the two examinations had 1,700 candidates, and in 1944 (including a Preliminary Test for Allied service personnel) nearly 4,000. This activity led to a study of the process of oral testing by John Roach[16] that is probably still one of the best treatments in print of the way that non-psychometric examiners attempted to ensure fairness in subjective traditional examinations, whether oral or written.

Roach (1945: 37) reported that the primary function of the examination for Allied service personnel was to encourage busy people in their study of English. English courses had to be fitted into a crowded timetable by students in a staff college or training wing; some of the pilots learning English came straight from operations to the examination room; many non-military foreign civilians were working in factories or hospitals or in the offices of governments in exile; others were British subjects in prisoner-of-war camps in Germany.[17] The examinations gave 'a stimulus and a focusing point for both teachers and taught'.

The paper by Roach dealt with the oral examination that had long been included in the Cambridge Certificate examinations. It opened with two basic practical questions: first, how closely could the standards of different oral examiners be co-ordinated by having them examine jointly, and, second, could standards be defined more precisely? The test was one in which the candidate read a passage of English aloud, but Roach mentioned the related issue of testing conversational ability. Because the Cambridge oral examinations were given overseas, conferences of examiners could not provide the standardization that was feasible with written papers marked in Britain. Even greater difficulties were produced by the fact that candidates came from so many different language backgrounds, each with their own typical errors.

Roach, as might have been expected of an institutional tester, accepted as a basic restriction the necessity to work within the existing testing system rather than devising a new one. Although, in an earlier paper responding to the Hartog committee, Roach (1936) had defended the efforts made in practice to achieve justice, he could still recognize the need for fundamental changes in the examination process as a whole. But he was dedicated to making the existing examinations work as well as humanly and organizationally possible. In this, he was reflecting the typical reluctance of the various examinations boards to tamper with examinations which served essentially as the syllabus for the many overseas schools which prepared students for them. The British boards were much slower than the American College Entrance Examination Board to give up on their power over the curriculum, and so took longer to accept arguments for psychometrically objective testing.[18] Changes did take place, but slowly and only after extensive consultation with the overseas schools and other agencies interested. This attitude to examinations and the importance of what is called backwash was commented on by Strevens (1989). The British examinations, he argued, were intended to control the instructional process rather than to assess proficiency. UCLES, Strevens was ready to concede in 1989, was 'exercising responsibility for bringing about changes in the teaching syllabus and in classroom methodology', while resisting any basic modification in the examination.

Roach's report[19] is written somewhat disjointedly, with the various parts overlapping and topics taken up cyclically. Drafted for internal use, it might strike a more formally trained modern language tester as somewhat tentative, almost amateurish. But the ideas in it show a fine grasp of the problems of testing oral proficiency and it presents an excellent picture of the transition from traditional examinations to modern language testing. Roach was equally concerned with the need for accurate and reliable decision making, and with the very personal and human considerations that made such decisions both difficult and important.

In the first experiment, twenty-four Polish air force officers and men in training in Britain,[20] candidates for the Cambridge Lower Certificate in English, had to read a passage in English aloud in front of a panel of three examiners and in the presence of the British education officers who were their English teachers. The examiners and the observing education officers, who knew nothing about their performance on other parts of the examination, awarded a numerical score to each candidate. The maximum was 20 marks, with the agreed standards set at 8 for a pass, 12 for good, and 16 for very good. How these standards were established and maintained was Roach's key concern.

The relevance of this issue is obvious. A central notion in what I have labelled the traditional period of (or approach to) testing (Spolsky 1977) is the ability of an examiner to arrive intuitively at a meaningful mark to award to a candidate's performance, whether in speech or in writing. When they do this, examiners are assumed to be able to rank the candidate's performance according to criteria established explicitly or implicitly by an examination board, and to determine into which of a predetermined set of clusters or classes the candidates should be placed. The most important of these categorizations is the division into pass or fail, although each of these broad categories may have a number of further subdivisions. Traditional examinations partition the issue of testing validity in two parts. First, the examination board must determine what should be tested, and how, and lay out its criteria in general terms, and second, the examiner's task is to interpret these standards and apply them in practice.

Roach was not convinced that the examiners in the first experiment had a clear idea of the absolute standards of the Certificate, but rather felt that they were applying a kind of relative standard: 'It is probably, at least to some extent, the candidates who tend to set the standard in any test which has no absolute criterion' (Roach 1945: 8). Over the years, standards in the Cambridge examination had maintained reasonable consistency, perhaps, he suggested, because of the homogeneity in the quality of the candidates as a whole. While examiners in written examinations could keep an eye on their general statistical pattern (noting how many marks they gave at the various levels), the pressure of time and the smallness of the sample tested by each examiner made this impossible in oral examinations.

Roach described his own experience[21] in becoming an examiner in German, noting that after a year or two he began to get a genuine 'feel' for the standard. He believed that the candidates taught him the standard; and that 'no doubt' his general experience accelerated the process (ibid.: 9).

From his experience, Roach concluded that 'Standards of impression marking cannot be defined beforehand merely by written instructions . . .' (ibid.: 5). Examiners learn their own standards, or bring them with them from previous experience, although some effort to set permanent standards may be made with gramophone recordings. He noted the general principle of moderation followed in British examinations:

> The general experience of examining bodies leads to the conclusion that an examiner as a member of team on a written paper is doing what is required of him if he is consistent and if he places the candidates in the right order of merit. The chief examiner will report whether any member is out of step with the standards and methods imposed by him on all his team, and whether any examiner is erratic. The examination machine will then decide by statistics whether the standards to which the chief examiner have worked are suitable in the light of past experience and general policy . . . However, in the case of oral examinations, the standards are not manipulated statistically, and each examiner carries his own notion of absolute standards.
> (ibid.: 13–4)

In the experiment, he had the opportunity to see seven candidates twice, on successive days, and his ranking agreed. Moreover, his marks agreed with the teacher's rating. In only one case did he note that he seemed to have given an extra point or two to one candidate to make sure he received an overall 'good'; this was because of the effect of the mark on the dictation.

Roach noted that there were a number of causes of contamination that threatened valid results. The candidates were reportedly anxious in the presence of an audience that included their officers, and the first seven candidates were in fact at a higher level than the Lower Certificate (which is why they were examined again the second day). The effect of this was that the first set of marks were too low and had to be raised. Another confounding effect was the dictation, the relevance of which was questionable, and which was independently set.[22] Roach felt that it would have been best to have all candidates go through the reading examination one after another, rather than having it taken at the same time as the conversation. However, if this were to be done, an examiner would quickly become aware of the content of the reading passage and so be less able to judge how well he would understand it had he not heard it before: a large number of short reading passages were therefore being prepared. Roach noted also the problem of the personality of the candidate. 'Charm (or the reverse) of manner or voice or appearance' or even 'good manners' may influence the judgement of the examiner. Males examining females and vice versa may perform differently than with members of their own sex.

In all his discussion of standards, it is striking how aware Roach was of the candidates as people. Traditional examinations and direct tests have, among their other advantages, the immediate personal involvement of the examiner with the candidate and his or her performance. The strength of this ethical perspective can be seen in Roach (1936), where he expressed his care for 'misfits and miscarriages of justice' especially at the borderline. He manifested concern that 'a career may often depend' on the application of a standard in a single examination, for the standard was 'hard to define and is almost certainly liable to error . . .' (ibid.: 115).

Given the existence of individual standards, the crucial question was whether 'standards can be communicated from one examiner to another by joint testing of "live" candidates, not recorded, and live discussion' (Roach 1945: 10). The issue here was not validity but inter-rater reliability, 'the possibility of reaching agreement among the examiners' (ibid.).[23] In the first experiment, the candidates' reading performances were marked by three examiners. In most cases, there was fairly close agreement (less than a three-point spread), although occasionally (because of the division into levels), these divergences straddled the pass mark. There were three cases of serious divergence. In one case, one examiner gave a fail, one a bare pass, and a third a good. These doubtful cases were given a second test the next day (a gramophone recording of one was scored later) and decisions reached.

This satisfied Roach 'that examiners could come together in matters of standards in an astonishingly short time'. Because errorless marking could not be expected, there was value in having a second examiner, or even using a teacher, who could quickly learn the standards of the examiner.

Gramophone recording of candidates at agreed levels might be used to establish this consistency further. While Roach saw little value in an average taken of the marks given by two examiners who regularly disagreed, he believed that the average of two examiners who were in general agreement was likely to contribute to standardization. If the expense of two examiners could not be justified, a similar purpose could be served by having the teacher join the visiting examiner, provided that they could establish standards together. He was more uncertain about the issue of using two examiners for testing conversation, noting a number of potential problems: unless they were trained to work together, they might interrupt each other. Another idea he considered worth trying was for one examiner to remain silent throughout the conversation. He concluded that 'the whole problem of conversation tests needs fuller investigation'.

Joint examining was tried in a second series of experiments, in which three examiners examined a group of fifty-three Proficiency candidates of various nationalities. In the reading test, the first three cases were discussed before a mark was given; after that, each examiner marked independently, but announced marks after the candidate had left. In forty out of fifty cases, there was agreement on category; in the other ten cases, two examiners always agreed, the third being one mark out in seven cases, two marks out in another, and three marks out in two cases. In the conversation test, five candidates were examined by the three examiners together and received an agreed score; after that, the remaining candidates were examined separately. Two of the examiners agreed on category for fifteen candidates they both tested; the new examiner agreed in six of twelve cases, but was a category higher or lower in the other six.

The experience raised, among a number of issues, the need to make clear what should be listened for:

> It is also clear that, while all marks in this kind of work must in the last resort depend upon an impression, it is desirable to tell examiners what they should chiefly be listening for, and what they should leave out of account. Thus, in the new 'unseen' reading test, what they will endeavour to assess is comprehensibility. The conversation tests fluency and correctness of speech, not the finer shades of pronunciation and intonation; indeed, errors of pronunciation ought perhaps only to affect the mark insofar as they make the candidate difficult to understand. Whether the examiner will succeed in isolating fluency from pronunciation is another matter.[24]

(Roach 1945: 31)

On another occasion, Roach used the local education officer as a joint examiner for four candidates in a Bomber Command station. Agreement was very close; the education officer was if anything more accurate in giving a mark to a sergeant, for while the visiting examiner also failed him, he gave a more generous mark out of respect for his rank and politeness. Roach therefore believed that subjective examinations could be made fair and standards could be communicated from one examiner to another.

The third section of the report described in some detail the gramophone recordings developed in connection with the experiments. The records contain sample readings of the dictation passages and special recordings made of some of the conversations.[25] These recorded examinations were played to a committee of nine examiners with various levels of experience. Their aggregate marks placed the six Proficiency candidates in the same order as had Examiner C. From the experience, Roach saw the value of recordings to make clear the standards of UCLES; such recordings, first discussed by a committee of examiners, might be sent from country to country. While the idea of using recordings had been proposed earlier in American language testing writing, the first extensive use there seems to have been during the war. In Britain, developments were slower. In a letter to me, Roach (personal communication, 28 February 1990) writes that 'Tape recorders were unknown even to the experts. With them, my idea of sending records around the world is now commonplace.'

The lack of contact between British and American testers is revealed by Roach's proposal of what he called semi-oral tests, a series of short answers to be written to oral questions. As has been noted, tests of aural comprehension more or less like this were first introduced in America in the late 1920s. The cultural and intellectual lag is intriguing, for items like this were to be incorporated into the Cambridge English examinations only in 1970, when objective testing had finally been accepted in Cambridge as a supplement to the traditional testing methods, and technological developments made it much easier to prepare and use recorded passages.

Roach (1945) concluded his paper with an invitation for advice from teachers and examiners 'who have at heart the improvement of oral examinations, whether in English or in other modern languages. We are still only at the beginning' (ibid.: 33).

Reading this report with the benefit of nearly fifty years of further experience and twenty years of discussion of tests of oral proficiency, one can see how Roach successfully identified some of the key problems. First, it must be stressed that he was working within constraints that he understood both of technology (recording in Britain was possible but much more difficult than in America) and institutional requirements (the conservatism of the examination syllabus, the expense of providing for joint examining). Second, he recognized the fundamental psychometric goals of inter-rater reliability and validity. For the former, he proposed examiner training, joint examining, and guidance in what to judge. Validity for him was mainly a matter of the need to find a way of applying in examinations with multiple examiners the common standards set by UCLES. Here again, joint examining, specific efforts by examiners to agree on standards, the use of recorded samples, and the correlation of the more subjective oral marks with more objective parts of the examination (including dictation), were the system he proposed. The paper's influence, however, appears to have been quite limited, even within UCLES, for Roach himself left its employ shortly after the report was completed. In 1963, when the executive committee in charge of UCLES' examinations in English for foreign students was considering a revision of the Proficiency syllabus, the issue of oral testing came up, but there was no reference to the Roach report; rather, a suggestion was made to ask John Trim to report on research in oral testing.

The lack of external impact can also be understood. First, the report was initially distributed only within UCLES and its examiners. While a second version was in fact offered for sale, and while there is some indication of wider circulation,[26] the lack of citation in language testing literature is evidence of its limited impact. None of the standard books on language testing, whether published in the United States or the United Kingdom, cite it or appear to be aware of Roach's pioneering work.

This is further evidence that language testing was not really an established field, with a collective memory, until the early 1950s. Until then (and effectively for some time after), scholars working in the field of language testing were trained in other fields, lacking any common professional core of experience or common body of knowledge. The want of wider publication and of integration into the published canon is to be regretted, for Roach (1945) is a report deserving of continued and careful study, not just for the fascinating historical light it casts on a stage in the development of modern language tests, but also for its posing of basic questions about validity and its proffering of sensible approaches to their solutions.

In both the United States and Britain, then, World War II had salutary side-effects in language testing by re-establishing the challenge of testing control of the spoken language and by reasserting the concern for non-academic language abilities.

Notes

1 It was under the jurisdiction of Lt. General Brehon B. Somervell, commanding general, Army Service Forces. The director of the Army Specialized Training Division was Col. Herman Beukema.

2 Trainees were selected on the basis of their performance on the Army General Classification test, their proficiency in foreign languages, and their having completed one year of college (Agard *et al.* 1944).

3 The Intensive Language Program of the American Council of Learned Societies, started in 1941 with two grants from the Rockefeller Foundation of $50,000 each, in order to begin teaching unusual languages,

under the directorship of J. Milton Cowan, secretary of the Lingustic Society of America.

4 Three of the field workers had experience in ASTP programmes; they spent two days preparing an outline of what they would look for.

5 The term 'criterion-referenced' was used, a reviewer reminds me, only sixteen years later, in an article by Glaser.

6 Born in 1904, Rivlin edited the *Encyclopedia of Education* in 1943, and later published on educational matters.

7 It was not cited by Angiolillo.

8 He was then associate professor of secondary and comparative education at Stanford University. During the war, Kaulfers also taught at the Stanford School of Military Government and was consultant to the Language School at the Presidio of Monterey (curriculum vitae).

9 It is revealing to compare this with Thorndike's dream (Thorndike 1938 in Monroe 1939) of an equal unit interval scale and the primitive unequal interval scale published by Sammartino (1938) in the same year that Thorndike spoke.

10 The notion of performance testing that Kaulfers clearly appreciated was sufficiently in advance of its time for it to have been chosen, nearly half a century later, as the theme for the 1993 Language Testing Research Colloquium.

11 In a comment dismissing Kaulfer's proposal, Myron (1944) saw no value in 'clinical testing methods', with the 'intricate set of scale values' and a 'recorded voice cavernously calling out the questions' and a grader 'concealed from the view of the palsied and petrified examinees'; he rather recommended the 'Army system, a normal cultural situation in which an examinee sits on one side of the table and talks to several examiners on the other'. He was also satisfied with the 'sane classifying system' used by the Army, of 'expert, competent, non-competent, and hopeless'.

12 The first in print is probably Barnwell (1992), whose paper was drawn to my attention after this section was almost complete.

13 The tests are reviewed in *The Third Mental Measurements Yearbook* (1949), as they had been published in 1944–5 by the American Council on Education and were available from the Cooperative Test Service and also from Science Research Associates. The reviews are almost without exception unfavourable.

14 An earlier version of the material in the rest of this chapter appeared in Spolsky (1990). A number of errors there have been corrected: the mistaken identification of John Roach with John O. Roach, and some misinterpretations of insular independent invention as originality.

15 Earlier work of UCLES with the English examinations for foreign students was reviewed in Chapter 4.

16 Written in 1944, it was printed and circulated internally among UCLES examiners. Another edition was for sale, price 1s 3d.

17 One of them Roach (1945: 37) reported, prepared for the English Life and Institutions paper from the 'combined memories' of other prisoners.

18 As late as the 1990s, a Board secretary was heard to say that it was enough for a test to be 'felt fair'.

19 The report is divided into seven parts. Part I deals with joint examining, Part II with testing standard, Part III with the use of gramophone records for training, Part IV with experimental marking of recorded examinations, Part V with joint examining again, Part VI with semi-oral test, and Part VII with more experiments in joint examining. An appendix provides a brief history of the Cambridge Examinations in English; there is an appended summary of conclusions, and four pages of tables.

20 One of the candidates, Roach (1983: 6) sadly recorded later, was shot in the great escape from Stalag Luft II. Roach also worked with the Czech Armoured Brigade.

21 He writes of himself in the third person as Examiner C.

22 In passages quoted from 'Examiner C', Roach narrated the problems he had faced in those cases where his judgement and the results of the dictation were in conflict: in three cases at least, he gave total marks that went against the direction imposed by the dictation; in only one was he willing to concede that the dictation might perhaps have proved 'a surer guardian of the Syndicate's standards' (Roach 1945: 16). His conclusion from this possible conflict was that dictation should be removed from the oral mark and reported separately.

23 The topic of reliability was one on which Roach had already published a paper, some 'unofficial notes' written in response to the appearance of the classic study of the unreliability of traditional examinations written by Hartog and Rhodes (1935). See Chapter 4.

24 It is intriguing to compare this last point with the original scoring guides developed by the FSI, in which pronunciation was given minimal weight (Rice 1959, Wilds 1975).

25 The recordings were made by the Post Office Research Station, and played at Cambridge in the next experiment through special equipment. Roach has written to me (personal communication, 28 February 1990): 'This was clearly a pioneer experiment for the Post Office in outside broadcasting. They sent the vans and apparatus with which we are now familiar free of charge. I still have them but can't play them because the hole in the middle is too small for present record players.'

26 Roach (1983) does claim that 'That Report was in demand round the world for years: the inspectors of the Ministry of Education even sought it after I had joined there in 1954.'

7 Prognostication and aptitude: 1925–1960

Some early tests of prognosis

The achievement test or examination served as a powerful tool for control over the language teaching process, and the proficiency test or examination was an equally effective way to maintain authority over the language qualifications of applicants for admission to universities or countries. Between the World Wars, these tests evolved steadily, with the progress towards objectivization that has been recounted so far. There remained another area of worry, the control of admission to the language learning class itself, and it is to this parallel development that this chapter turns. Motivated by what Michel (1936) referred to as 'the deplorable mortality in foreign language classes', language testers set out to build prognosis (or aptitude) tests. A prognosis test, it was hoped, could provide information about how well someone would perform in a language learning situation, or more precisely, about how to keep prospective failures out of classes.

Work on prognosis tests has had both theoretical and practical outcomes. The theoretical issue of greatest interest has been the nature of language learning ability. Is it unitary, or can it be broken into smaller identifiable (and testable) abilities? While there has not yet been a final answer to this question,[1] research into aptitude has made major contributions to understanding second language learning. The practical effect has been to provide administrators with a seemingly objective and fair excuse for refusing admission to language programmes to students with a low likelihood of succeeding.

The genesis of prognosis tests was strictly practical or even political, rather than theoretical. Once it had become accepted in the United States in the early 1920s that general intelligence tests could be used with some effect to forecast how well a student would do at school, it was inevitable that some people would start to ask about the possibility of predicting success in specific subjects, including language study. This could then be used to alleviate the problems of teachers who felt themselves required to deal with students they believed unqualified for language study and who had been admitted to their classes through a policy of mass education.

This concern was highlighted in a paper entitled 'Mortality of modern languages students' by Cheydleur (1932), reporting a long-term study of drop-outs and failures in classes at the University of Wisconsin. After painting a picture of language departments agonizing over the numbers of their students who dropped out or failed their courses, Cheydleur argued for the

value of intelligence, placement, and advancement tests in order to control
student access and progress.

Three prognosis tests for school use were prepared between 1925 and
1930 and stayed on the market for some years. All of them included various
combinations of verbal intelligence items and mini-lessons in an artificial
or foreign language. One of the earliest was written by Stoddard and
Vander Beke (1925).[2] A second was the *Language Aptitude Test* prepared
by a team at George Washington University (Hunt *et al.* 1929). It consisted
of ten subtests and 200 items. Four of the subtests involved learning elements of an artificial language: prepositions, memory, affixes, and using
rules. Other subtests were comprehension, vocabulary, English grammar,
following directions, sound recognition, and accent knowledge.[3] A third
was the *Luria–Orleans Modern Language Prognosis Test* (Luria and Orleans 1928). The test, which took eighty-five minutes, contained a language
learning trial, consisting of vocabulary exercises (cognates and
memorization) and eight grammar translation lessons in French and
Spanish.[4]

The Modern Foreign Language Study and the Canadian Committee on
Modern Languages were ardent supporters of prognosis:

> This Committee felt that no part of its experimental program would be
> more welcome to its colleagues as likely to throw light on their problems
> and bring relief from the difficult and often hopeless situation created
> by the numbers and unfitness of students, and it arranged, therefore, as
> soon as the foreign language achievement tests were well under way, to
> sponsor experimental undertakings in the field of prognosis.
> (Henmon 1929: v)

The motivation was fundamentally economic, the goal being to replace
'wasteful methods of trial and error' with more efficient selection of students and their assignment 'to the work for which they are best fitted'
(ibid.: 3). The problems studied by the eight researchers whose work was
supported and reported by the committees turned out in the event, however, to be extremely resistant to solution and their studies were discourag-
ingly inconclusive, and failed to 'bring evidence that any test has yet been
devised which can be counted on to reveal linguistic incapacity or to show
itself as a reliable instrument for selecting successful students of foreign
languages. The question of language prognosis is far too complex for such
a categorical answer' (ibid.: vi).

The question underlying the design of a selection technique was whether
the mind should be conceived of as a 'host of highly specialized capacities
which may vary independently' or as 'a unitary affair' with the various
parts correlated and forming 'a common factor of general intelligence'.
American educational psychology, Henmon noted, was inclined to the
belief in a high degree of specialization, which was why the search for

specific abilities was being so enthusiastically pursued. Both views were, however, now being challenged by the 'extraordinary pronouncement' of the first of the behaviourists, Watson, who did not accept the inheritance of mental traits but thought, rather, that complete environmental control of human behaviour was possible. Henmon believed the extreme behaviourist view to be untenable; indeed, he saw the task as being to determine the relative contributions of general intelligence and special aptitudes to predictions about student performance.

The belief in the importance of special aptitude was well entrenched in the profession. Two-thirds of the modern language teachers questioned in a 1926 survey had found cases of students with 'linguistic disability or incapacity not accompanied by low general intelligence'. The issue continues to be a live one in colleges with foreign language requirements, as teachers ask at what stage a student can be considered to be disabled for language learning.

Intelligence was believed to be a factor. Henmon saw it as the task of his research group to answer four basic questions: Is there a minimal IQ level for successful modern language study? Is there a minimal general scholarship level for successful modern language study? Can special language learning abilities be recognized, tested, and used for prediction of success? Can one semester's results be used to predict future success?

Henmon *et al.* (1929) summarized recent work looking at correlations of intelligence quotients and scores with school marks or objective test scores in modern languages. Most of the studies had showed a low positive correlation, ranging from 0.20 to 0.60, not much use for practical decision making. The 'variability, inaccuracy and subjectivity of school marks' was so well established that they could not be expected to help much. There were, none the less, some studies showing that high school averages in all subjects were better predictors of freshman marks in languages than IQ or high school marks in the language. These results encouraged Henmon in the continued search for special language abilities.

Part of this search was described in other chapters of Henmon *et al.* (ibid.). John Bohan looked at the relation between scores on intelligence tests given to entering students at the University of Minnesota between 1921 and 1925 and their later grades in English and foreign languages, finding correlations between 0.15 and 0.50.

Carl Brigham, now teaching at Princeton University and already associated with the College Entrance Examination Board, studied the Princeton artificial language test invented by Stuart Dodd, which had been shown to have high diagnostic validity as a general intelligence test but the prognostic adequacy of which was limited. The test presented ten vocabulary items and six grammatical rules of an artificial language, and then gave translation tasks. Brigham analysed various correlations in the case of 236 men for whom there was full enough data. The best predictor of college French marks was the average of College Board Entrance Examinations in French, English, and Latin (0.480); neither the intelligence test (0.276) nor the language test (0.269) were nearly as useful predictors, nor did the latter two tests add much to the prediction of the examinations (0.533).

L. Thomas Hopkins, at the University of Colorado, found the Wilkins Prognosis Test and the Wilkins Elimination Test to be 'a reliable measure of some kind of ability or particular type of function', but not of the ability to succeed in foreign languages. George Rice, at the University of California, gave a test written by May Barry which taught some Spanish grammar items and vocabulary to 100 pupils as a trial experience in language learning. The test correlated with intelligence quotient (0.79), and with teacher's marks at the end of the year (0.60) better than the intelligence score did (0.53).

Percival Symonds, teaching at Teachers College, Columbia University, whose test was later used in a number of studies and must have been widely accepted, pointed out the problem of determining the value of a prognostic test. Even if such a test could measure aptitude, it was judged by its correlation with achievement, which was the combined result of aptitude, 'and of the forces of instruction, including interest and interest of the learner, organization of the material, skill of the teacher, etc.'.[5] This made the validation of a prognosis test doubly difficult: first, it would have been used to limit the students tested in the later study, and second, it was known to measure only part of the assumed causes of later variation. In spite of this problem, Symonds believed that three types of aptitude tests made sense: measures of general intelligence, tests of ability in the student's native language, and 'quick-learning tests in the new language'. He gave pupils in four schools a set of intelligence tests compiled by E. L. Thorndike, four quick-learning tests (two by Dodd and two using Esperanto by Symonds himself), and the Iowa Placement Examination (Foreign Language Aptitude). Those pupils who lasted the semester then took the American Council Beta French and Spanish tests. While various problems with the skewing of some of the tests meant that the regression weights could not be relied on, the correlations suggested that those tests which included elements of translation ability (grammatical knowledge in particular) were likely to be good predictors of success in the classes.

In a study that foreshadowed later research, John Todd, a psychologist at the University of California, included in a test items based on a psychological analysis of the language learning process: a general questionnaire, a test of immediate auditory memory span for isolated digits, and tests of the extent of native vocabulary and range of information. Later, the memory test was replaced by logical memory, and comprehension items were added. A number of studies were carried out. IQ was found to correlate well with school marks in languages. IQ tests also correlated well with Todd's linguistic test. There was some evidence of the usefulness of the memory span test as a predictor. Comprehension did not correlate as well as anticipated with school marks. Todd was satisfied that he had not found evidence of a special language aptitude: 'Whatever our tests may have measured it plainly was not a linguistic "talent" or special aptitude. If linguistic special aptitude is a reality, some other distinct type of test must be invented for the purpose of measuring it' (ibid.: 161). Todd's negative findings must have had a temporarily dampening effect on what ultimately proved to be the most useful avenue of research, namely the testing of much more specific abilities.

With the publication of the collection of papers by Henmon *et al.* (ibid.), then, the place of prognosis as a central topic in language testing research had been established, but there had been no widely accepted answers to the questions that had been raised.

The Symonds' tests of prognosis

Over the next decade, research on prognosis continued. Symonds continued his research with the aptitude test that he had designed (1930a), reporting in a study (1930b) a correlation of 0.71 between the prognosis test and an achievement test. The Symonds' test was advertised as intended for grades 8–9. Form A had four parts: English inflection, word translation from English to Esperanto, sentence translation from Esperanto to English, and related words; in Form B, inflection was replaced by parts of speech and related words by an artificial language subtest; the use of both parts was recommended.

The effectiveness of the Symonds' Foreign Language Prognosis tests was examined in a number of studies over the next few years. Richardson (1933) administered them to 242 high school freshmen planning to take foreign languages, finding a correlation of about 0.60 with first semester scores. The fact that IQ scores added little to the prediction, he believed, supported the claim of special linguistic abilities.[6] Richardson did find the prognosis tests gave better predictions than intelligence tests with two cohorts of 120 high school students. In research for an MA thesis at the University of Chicago, Lau (1933) administered the test to eighty pupils in three Michigan high schools on their first day of class, and found a 0.60 correlation with the American Council Alpha tests at the end of the semester. The weakest correlation was with vocabulary and the strongest with grammar.

An elaborate study using both the Symonds' and the Iowa Foreign Language Aptitude tests was undertaken as a master's thesis at the University of Minnesota, by Sister Virgil Michel (1934, 1936), a teacher at the Saint Joseph's Academy. She acknowledged her inspiration to the statement by Symonds that 'prognostic testing is the romantic chapter in the history of educational measurement', and agreed also with the platitude that failing students should have been guided into easier classes, but noted that educational prognosis was 'still in its infancy' (1936: 275). Her review of earlier research found that IQ scores were not good enough predictors alone, that previous school achievement was a little better, that some special aptitude tests were even better, but that not enough multiple correlation studies were available to show the best combination. She therefore administered the Symonds' Foreign Language Prognosis Test to a group of high school students and the Iowa Foreign Language Aptitude Test to a smaller group of beginning college German students at the college level, and to both, a newly devised German prognosis test that she had constructed with the assistance of Oscar Burkhard, professor of German at the University of Minnesota. It consisted of a memory test of short German sentences with their English translations, an analogies test of words that were cognate in German and English, and a series of German grammar rules and exercises, and was reliable (0.917 Spearman-Brown split half). For the high school students, none of these tests gave useful correlations with the Columbia Research Bureau German Test or with teachers' marks at the end of the first semester. Multiple correlations combining the tests did not help much. She concluded that the Symonds' test using Esperanto seemed to have not done as well with German as with French and Spanish. For the university students, combinations of the Iowa test (which also used Esperanto) and the German prognosis tests did achieve correlations with the end of semester marks, but not much better than did the high school average. The College Aptitude Test was not a predictor of German achievement. Her thesis concludes somewhat pessimistically:

> In general, the experiment corroborates the findings of the majority of investigators in foreign language prognosis in so far as the correlations are rather low, in so far as predicting success in any one subject is much more difficult than prognosis of success in all subjects in high school or university, and in so far as it points with increasing insistence to the need for further research in order to secure more efficient predictive measures than those that exist at present.
> (Coleman and King 1938: 435)

'Romantic' as the topic may have been, there were no signs of a happy ending yet, but the Symonds' test continued to produce useful results for French high school classes. A study of 170 high school pupils in Massachusetts by Maronpot (1939) found the Symonds' Foreign Language Prognosis test to correlate 0.70 with teachers' final yearly grades, better than the general scholastic average (0.51) and IQ (0.27). In this case, the test results were not used to exclude students identified as 'modern language risks', but to 'salvage' them by grouping. For democratic reasons, low-aptitude students were permitted to study French, but in a special class which made lower linguistic demands.

Kaulfers on prognosis

If these correlations seem low, an even more pessimistic picture emerged from the work of the California foreign language education researcher, Walter Kaulfers (1931), who found IQ scores or English marks to be better predictors than standardized foreign language aptitude tests. Kaulfers' work on prognosis formed the basis of his PhD dissertation written at Stanford University (1933a). Reviewing over 650 correlations, published since 1901 by nearly fifty researchers, between foreign language achievement and nearly seventy other factors, he found large variability. The medians for the most common factors were prognosis tests (0.60), English ability (0.46), general language ability (0.44), and mental ability (0.35). In his own study of 461 eighth grade and 209 ninth grade beginning Spanish pupils, using fifteen different measures to predict an achievement measure based on five criteria, he discovered that the best predictors were the Luria-Orleans prognosis tests, the Stanford word meaning scores, the Terman IQ scores, and the Stanford paragraph meaning and dictation spelling scores. This work left Kaulfers unconvinced that there was a special language aptitude, with the result that he considered the prognosis tests to be weighted intelligence tests. Because of the unstandardized conditions in junior high school Spanish classes, he saw little likelihood of getting predictive efficiency of much higher than 20–30 per cent. He none the less thought that students should have an IQ of about 111 to have a 4 to 1 chance of passing first semester of junior high school Spanish with at least a D. Coleman and King (1938) observe that part of the problem was the attempt to forecast junior high school performance, which meant correlating test results with unreliable class marks.

Kaulfers continued to think about prognosis. In a paper published in 1939, he again expressed a fundamentally pessimistic view, and concluded that 'prognosis as a panacean solution to foreign-language problems is destined long to remain in the limbo of wishful thinking'. The fundamental problem as he saw it was the proliferation of approaches to teaching: 'it is inconceivable that any one test, however comprehensive, could predict achievement in a field in which such a variety of methods, materials, and objectives abound'. In the same year, Kaulfers wrote reviews of the Symonds' *Foreign Language Prognosis Test* (2: 1340)[7] and the *Luria–Orleans Modern Language Test* (2: 1341). The former he considered to be no more than 'a linguistically weighted intelligence test', lacking any validity data and achieving too low a prediction correlation to warrant its use to reject a student. In any case, its usefulness would be limited to grammar-translation courses, and it would be too difficult for any student below eighth grade level. The second test also appeared designed to predict achievement in 'the traditional grammar-translation type of course of a decade or more ago'. He had found its validity to be low, not enough to have any advantage over more easily available measures like a twelve-minute test of English vocabulary.

Kaulfers had put his finger on a key issue: a prognosis test measured not so much a general (or even a general special) ability so much as a number of abilities that would be of benefit in various language learning situations. To the extent that a foreign language teaching method was focused on the same skills as were being used in other subjects, a simple native language vocabulary test would be as good as anything else as a predictor.

Other studies of prognosis

The study of language aptitude and of the possibility of predicting achievement in language learning continued to be a matter of considerable interest for the decade after the publication of Henmon *et al.* (1929).[8] It was a popular topic for theses[9] and articles,[10] but there was no breakthrough. Other possible predictors were investigated. Finch and Floyd (1935), studying superior students at the University of Minnesota University High School, found that chronological age had virtually no predictive power but mental age correlated with language grades between 0.3 and 0.4. In other studies of the superior student at the University of Buffalo, Wagner (1934) and Wagner and Strabel (1935) found that neither the American Council intelligence tests nor the Iowa High School content examinations were of much predictive value, but the Regents' examinations in languages and high school grades in languages were good predictors of overall achievement in all subjects in the first two years at college, and equally good predictors of grades in languages.

Studying the effect of attitude, Jones (1934) asked second-semester Spanish students at Miami University whether their goal was talking, reading, or culture, and found the best students to be those who were 'talkers' or 'readers' while the 'culture-seekers' generally had low grades. Personality, too, was considered a possible factor. In a first article based on a dissertation he wrote at the University of Minnesota, Nemzek (1938) reported that he had found no evidence that any of the personality traits (such as neurotic tendency, dominance, self-sufficiency) measured by the Bernreuter Personality Inventory contributed in any significant way to high school achievement or predicted differences of achievement between mathematics and languages. In a second article, Nemzek (1939) reported the finding that intelligence tests that predicted overall high school achievement for 350 Minnesota University High School graduates did not differentiate by subject. He concluded that 'undoubtedly, the mental functions measured by honor-point averages[11] in mathematics, science, history and social sciences, and languages have a high degree of community of function'. Socio-economic variables (such as education and occupation of parents), however, did not predict grades.

In Britain, there were some beginnings of interest in prognosis in the Scottish Council for Research in Education Examination Inquiry (1934)[12] that showed that, in French, university class marks were slightly better predictors (0.69) of degree marks than were secondary school teachers' estimates of the Leaving Certificate Examination administered by the school (0.55). In a later study of two groups of about 180 pupils each who took secondary school entrance examinations in 1930 and 1931, and the School Certificate examinations five years later, Stubbins (1940) found that the English entrance examination was a better predictor of French and German marks (from 0.31 to 0.36) than was the IQ test (from 0.03 to 0.24); IQ scores were a better predictor of success in mathematics and physics.

In the United States just before World War II, more analytical general intelligence tests were being developed, following the splitting of the Junior Scholastic Aptitude Test into verbal and numerical scores,[13] and a study by Traxler (1941) showed that the verbal score correlated 0.54 with French marks, while the numerical score correlated only 0.36.

One paper that appeared in 1939 looked ahead to much of the work that was to come. Spoerl (1939) asked what in fact constituted language learning ability? Was it intelligence, or courage, or form-colour preference, or memory? She tested thirty-eight advanced German students at the American International College in Springfield, Massachusetts, on the Henmon-Nelson test of mental ability, the Allport Ascendance-Submission Reaction Study (to test attitude and openness to suggestions in the new foreign language situation), and the Revised Minnesota Paper Form Board Test (to see if form recognition was relevant), and also gave them the Cooperative German Test. Major differences emerged between men and women: the correlation between class grade and Cooperative test score was 0.35 for men and 0.73 for women; similarly, the correlation between the intelligence measure and the grade was 0.63 for women and 0.123 for men. Neither the test of forms nor the ascendance-submission test had significance relation to the German scores. Her conclusion was that while intelligence was significant for women, it was not for men.[14]

Looking back over the first decade's work in prognosis testing, it is evident that Henmon's earlier expectation had not been met. An article by Tallent (1938) was recorded by Kaulfers as the sixtieth article published since 1901 showing that 'prognostic testing cannot be depended upon to solve foreign language problems'. Prophesy, it seemed, was dead.

A more dispassionate reconsideration suggests that the researchers of the period had helped clarify the issue enormously, and recognized the limitations of their task when they were asked to predict a more or less immeasurable attainment in uncontrolled and variegated learning situations. They were aware of the problems caused by the variation in goals and methods of teaching contexts, cognizant of the need for multiple rather than single predictors, open to the complexity resulting from the fact that aptitude (however measured) was only one of a number of factors accounting for achievement. The tests they had developed, which were either slightly modified intelligence tests or mini-lessons in language, did, together with other available data, permit a wise counsellor to give useful advice to students identified as unlikely to succeed in formal language learning classes, and did permit responsible schools to make special provision for pupils who would be unlikely to benefit from such classes. Their tests were, as Carroll (1960) concluded when he started his own major work, 'reasonably effective in predicting success' in classes whose main objective was teaching the ability to read and translate a foreign language. They were to prove much less effective in predicting performance on more communicatively oriented programmes, a challenge that was to be met by Carroll and others a quarter of a century later.

The Army UCLA aptitude study

The issue of prognosis was not allowed to die. During the war, admission to intensive language training courses in the military forces was based mainly on previous education. Frith (1953) reported at the 1953 Georgetown Round Table that the Air Force used scores on general intelligence and technical aptitude tests, possession of a high school diploma, and a desire to study the language as the criteria for starting the study of Mandarin Chinese. With the peacetime need for more economically sound approaches, the issue of which people to train became significant. Frith (ibid.) described trial courses conducted as screening devices at the Air Force Institute of Technology. Morgan (1953) reported that another government agency used the same approach, but Morgan himself believed and claimed to have demonstrated that an hour's careful study by a clinical psychologist of material collected with a battery of tests, including a projective 'written interview questionnaire' and a personality inventory, would produce equally valid predictions.

As language training developed in the post-war years at the Army Language Training School in the Presidio of Monterey, the possibility of saving wasted time and effort persuaded the Army to fund the construction and validation of foreign language aptitude tests. The contract for the study went to three psychologists at the University of California, Los Angeles. The project, led by Roy M. Dorcus assisted by George E. Mount and Margaret H. Jones (1953),[15] lasted from June 1950 to May 1953 and dealt with six languages, Russian, Hungarian, Serbo-Croat, Arabic, Japanese, and Mandarin Chinese.

A preliminary search of the literature produced 'no studies of value in the design of language aptitude tests for the selection of language trainees', apart from some results of the language portions of the West Point Qualifying Examination. The report did not discuss any of the large body of pre-war work on foreign language prognosis described earlier in this chapter, and it is not clear whether the authors knew of its existence and considered it irrelevant, or whether as psychologists they were unaware of foreign language testing literature. Analysis of data routinely collected at the Army Language School revealed that only pitch[16] correlated significantly[17] with any of the language proficiency scores, and that only for the first written and the first course oral examinations.

None the less, encouraged by the high correlation between early and late language scores to believe that there must be measurable aptitude facts that could help predict later results, the team developed a list of ten 'major aptitude skills' which could be measured with a group pencil-and-paper test; this latter limitation prevented the testing of oral manipulation skills. The ten skills were: word assimilation (measured by synonyms test); symbol manipulation (scrambled word test); verbal persistence (reading with confused punctuation); personality factors (interests); span of apprehension (digit memory test); associative learning (code learning of nonsense syllables test); recall (recall of code learning); field independence (recognizing speech with multiple speech background); understanding distorted speech; and discriminating minimal speech distinctions. The items chosen show a psychologist's rather than a linguist's view of the process of language learning.[18]

The test battery, different for each language, was administered to 150 incoming trainees in 1950 and scored at the University of California, Los Angeles, with the results kept away from instructors. A complete battery of language proficiency tests was also constructed by Army Language School staff for the study, and reviewed and modified by the project staff. The proficiency battery had nine parts: there were five written tests (translation to and from English, morphology and syntax, idioms, and vocabulary) and four aural-oral (aural comprehension, question and answer, oral description of picture, oral interpretation). In addition, rating forms (using a seven-point scale) were prepared for scoring the tests and for recording instructor ratings for course performance. They were given at the end of training, generally by having two instructors rate the performance independently. Some of the languages were also independently rated by foreign language instructors from the University of California, Los Angeles; the correlations between the two sets of ratings were satisfactorily high (0.83). After discussion with the Army Language School, a general proficiency measure was calculated, giving equal weight to written and spoken scores.

The results of the study were disappointing. The West Point Qualifying

Examination continued to be the best predictor of the outcome of training, about 5–10 per cent above chance. Adding the selection tests did not improve the predictive power much. While there continued to be evidence of aptitude in the high correlation of early and late scores, the various aspects measured appeared 'to include a relatively small part of the aptitude and skill required in the learning of a language'. While still convinced of the existence of language aptitude, the researchers had failed to find a way to measure it.

The prediction of success in intensive foreign language training

A more systematic attack on the problem of language aptitude was made by John Carroll, in some years of research funded by the Carnegie Foundation and conducted at the Laboratory for Research in Instruction, Graduate School of Education, Harvard University.[19] Carroll acknowledged the economic basis for the concern, because of the expense of the intensive language programmes which required eight to twelve months of full-time study and which were being offered in programmes such as that of the Army Language School at the Presidio of Monterey.[20] An accurate measurement of foreign language learning aptitude should be able to provide a valuable screening device for costly governmental programmes and minimize training failures, which ran as high as 80 per cent in one Japanese programme that had been studied by Williams and Leavitt (1947).

Carroll premised his investigation on two 'propositions'. The first was that the facility to learn to speak a foreign language is 'a fairly specialized talent (or group of talents)' independent of the traits included under 'intelligence'. The second was that it is rare enough in the general population to make it worthwhile to be selective in choosing people for expensive intensive programmes. Intelligence tests, he pointed out, had been relatively unsuccessful in screening people for language training. Even with groups carefully selected for general intelligence, Frith (1953) had found that trial courses led to the rejection of as many as 75 per cent of the students. The prognosis tests tried in the 1920s and 1930s had generally been limited, Carroll noted, to pencil-and-paper testing of English language ability or work-sampling of short lessons in cognitive, intellectual aspects of formal language learning. These tests, which generally correlated quite highly with intelligence tests, were often reasonable predictors of learning to read and translate but they had less relevance to learning to speak a language in an intensive course.[21] Dorcus and colleagues, Carroll believed, had 'just missed' measuring the crucial abilities, in that their tests failed to tap the relevant abilities. Memory for digits, for instance, which they tested, was not relevant to language learning, while memory for sound, which they did not test, probably was significant.

Carroll started with an initial battery that contained twenty separate tests, each intended to check one of five factors of verbal ability that had been proposed by French (1951): verbal knowledge; word fluency (knowledge of orthographic habits); fluency of expression; associative memory; and naming. Another type of item in the test was the 'grammatical analogy' in which the subject was to say which word in a sentence had the same function in the sentence as an underlined word. Also included was a phonetic discrimination task developed by Stanley Sapon[22] that asked the subject to identify the odd sound out in a triad.[23]

Carroll tried several kinds of work-sample tests. One was an artificial language test in which subjects learnt the names of a simple foreign language number system. Another was a tape recording with accompanying film strip which taught a simple artificial language. A third presented a more formal artificial language through grammar lessons.[24] Carroll was working, it seems, on a double strategy. If he could, he wanted to find tests that tapped the most basic abilities in language learning, the discrete primary skills. Failing this, he sought to find the smallest trial learning situation that would predict performance in a full course.

The new tests were tried in a number of situations. In February 1954, 111 men pre-screened for admission to an eight-month intensive course offered for the US Air Force at Yale University took a four-hour battery of tests. They then went into a three-day preliminary training period, during or after which thirty-one withdrew voluntarily. The validity analysis was based on the remaining eighty, only thirty-three of whom were selected for the full course. Using as the criterion measure either grades given by instructors or the selection decision, a large number of test variables showed significant correlations. The summed results of four tests (artificial language learning, phonetic association, words in sentences, and paired associates) produced a multiple correlation of 0.74. The prediction test and the trial course had agreed in sixty-six out of eighty cases.

A second trial was carried out in June 1954, using some new types of items. Once again, validity coefficients were remarkably high, a multiple correlation of 0.77—and, using some of the new tests, 0.839. On the basis of these successes, the *Psi–Lambda*[25] Foreign Language Aptitude Battery was made available to the Air Force in 1955 for further testing, with generally satisfactory results. The screening policy finally adopted by the Air Force was to use the result of the battery as a criterion for admission to the trial course, and make a further cut after that.

Two series of tests were conducted to check the relevance of the battery for different types of languages. While the correlation in one sample was lowest in predicting success in learning languages with characters (Japanese, Chinese, Korean), this did not show up in a second sample. This result and other analyses supported the hypothesis of the non-specificity of language aptitude. The battery seemed to predict oral and written skills equally well, depending on the instructional approach.

Experimental testing was also conducted at the Foreign Service Institute (FSI) of the US Department of State. Good correlations (about 0.70) were found with instructor grades in six-month long courses in twelve different languages. In another test, eighty-three trainees at the FSI were given the battery, which achieved a multiple correlation of 0.778 with performance at the end of a six-month course. The test was much better than the prediction based on a fifteen-minute 'diagnostic interview' given to the candidates by the chairman of the language department in which he was to study. The results of this study also produced evidence of the effect of age; while the subjects' age showed a slightly negative linear correlation with their success in language learning, the fact that adding the age variable to the aptitude test did not improve the prediction showed that the aptitude test measured whatever in the age variable was relevant to success in language learning; it further contradicted the notion that older people cannot learn foreign languages successfully.

The Modern Language Aptitude Test

Given the general success of the battery,[26] a commercial form of the Carroll and Sapon test was published in 1959 by the Psychological Corporation under the name, *Modern Language Aptitude Test*. In this form, it was tried out in the summers of 1958 and 1959 with students in intensive eight-week summer courses in Arabic, Persian, Turkish, or Modern Hebrew, producing correlations of about 0.5 with final grades.

In a major paper reviewing his work in developing successful aptitude measures, Carroll (1960) raised a more fundamental question. His studies to date had assumed that success was a direct function of measured aptitude. Such a model was 'oversimplified, if not downright wrong'. A better model would take into account other relevant factors, such as motivation and instructional variables. He proposed a model that included at least two instructional variables (adequacy of presentation and the time allowed for learning) and three individual variables (verbal intelligence, aptitude—or the amount of time needed to learn—and motivation—or the amount of time the learner would apply himself to the task). Using the resulting model, Carroll was able to demonstrate how variation in the conditions of the various courses accounted for variation in the predictive ability of the aptitude battery. Because aptitude is not the only variable accounting for success in language learning, its validity can only be shown when the other factors are taken into account.

In summing up his major study, Carroll concluded that language aptitude consisted of the four distinct and measurable abilities: phonetic coding[27] (the ability to code an auditory phonetic signal so that it could be remembered for more than a few seconds); grammar handling[28] (the ability to recognize functions of words in sentences); rote memorization (the ability to recall a large number of foreign language items);[29] and inductive language learning ability.[30] With the completion of this body of research, then, Carroll could feel reasonably confident that he had managed to identify and measure the chief factors involved in aptitude for learning to speak a foreign language. His tests were able to account for most of the variation that could reasonably be attributed to aptitude.

The *Modern Language Aptitude Test* was reviewed in *The Sixth Mental Measurements Yearbook* (Buros 6: 357) and in a number of other places. In the *Yearbook*, Wayne Fisher (an assistant professor of education in Russian) and Bertram Masia (an assistant professor of education), both at the University of Chicago, reminded readers that prognosis tests 'inevitably' reflected two weaknesses: a failure to be rooted in 'psychological studies of language', and a failure to specify kinds of language learning objectives. Believing this, and believing also that language learning abilities could not be isolated, they did not expect to find this test to be much good for measuring language aptitude but more likely to predict English. In a more favourable review, Marion Shaycroft, senior research scientist with the American Institute for Research, thought the test to be 'quite novel' and 'an ingenious attack' on the problem. Larger norming samples would be useful. Its few weak points were far outweighed by its many merits. Other reviews appeared. Harold Dunkel (1960) thought the test had many excellent features, but how useful it would be would no doubt depend on the kind of course for which it was expected to predict. Herschel Manuel (1960) found the new test very promising and 'a significant contribution'. He would like to see further study of this very important topic.

While Carroll and Sapon's work did include validation of the use of the test in high school situations,[31] the main goal of their test was to predict success in intensive courses of the kind more likely to be used at university level or for adults. A study of its usefulness in regular courses conducted at the University of California, Los Angeles, Pimsleur, Stockwell, and Comrey (1962) looked at two groups of about 200 students who were studying in second semester French courses. Data were collected on twenty-three variables, including four parts of the Modern Language Aptitude Test. Analysis of the results confirmed the usefulness of the tests. A seven-test battery produced a multiple correlation of 0.43 with French grades. The battery consisted of: number learning (MLAT I); words in sentences (MLAT IV); letter series (predicting the next letter in a series like D E F D E F . . .); reading aloud I (speed of reading an English passage); paraphrase (number of paraphrases of an English word or phrase in four minutes); linguistic analysis II (a morphological exercise with words from an unknown language), age, and high school mathematics and science grades.

Spelling clues (MLAT III) could be substituted for number learning (MLAT I) without changing the results.

Using scores on a French-speaking test rather than teacher grades as a criterion, only five tests had to be included in the battery. These were: spelling clues, letter series, reading aloud II (accuracy of reading an English passage), verbal comprehension (a test of English vocabulary), and bilingualism (a native language other than English, or another language spoken regularly in the home). Considering the unreliability of the criterion of teacher grades and the relative homogeneity of the group, the predictions were good. It should be noted that the test went beyond aptitude, including some of the other individual characteristics that Carroll had allowed for in his own extended model.

A second study added some new variables and dropped ones that had been insignificant.[32] Three criterion measures were used, the Cooperative French Test for reading and writing, a grade given for oral ability based on semester work and a final test, and a pictorial auditory comprehension test. Again, there were about 200 students, tested at the beginning and end of a semester course. The best prediction was achieved by a six-test battery predicting the Cooperative French Test scores. The components of the battery were: verbal comprehension, Chinese pitch (recognizing three Chinese words with different pitch embedded in sentences), interest I (number of reasons for being interested in learning French), interest II (strength of interest), sex (male), and high school language grades. The level of prediction was a multiple correlation of 0.652. For the oral grade, a five test battery produced a multiple correlation of 0.41: the relevant tests were: verbal comprehension, interest II, bilingualism, high school language grades, and high school mathematics and science grades. For auditory comprehension, a somewhat different five-test battery achieved a multiple correlation of 0.405. Its constituents were: verbal comprehension, linguistic analysis I (the mini-language exercise), Chinese pitch, and seashore timbre (recognizing chords as same or different). The lower predictions for the second two were assumed to be affected by the low reliability of the criteria. The results of their study were consistent with Carroll's views. Performance in traditional non-intensive language programmes could be largely predicted by general intellectual measures. Motivation should also be included to make the prediction more valid. Aptitude factors of the kind that Carroll had identified were more significant in learning to speak.

A number of years later, Paul Pimsleur translated his findings into a published test battery, The *Pimsleur Language Aptitude Battery*. Published by Harcourt Brace Jovanovich in 1967 (Buros 7: 256), the battery had six parts: grade point average for all school subjects, interest (a single scale), vocabulary (English), language analysis (as described above), sound discrimination (pitch and timbre), and sound-symbol association. A review in *The Seventh Mental Measurements Yearbook* by A. Ralph Hakstian raised doubts about the first two parts, and concluded that reliability and validity data that were as yet incomplete might show the test to be useful. Another review by Donald C. Ryberg (1968) similarly counselled caution in use of the battery.

The state of prophecy

When the Temple was destroyed, the Talmud says, prophecy was taken from prophets and given to fools and children.[33] Henmon and his colleagues' hope of achieving close to perfect prognosis was, it is now clear, over-optimistic. But they managed to show, and Pimsleur confirmed, that verbal intelligence tests do a good job in predicting not just how well a student will do at school, but how well he or she will do in typical foreign language classes, making it possible for schools to exclude students who are probably going to fail.

John Carroll added three vitally important dimensions. Firstly, more successfully than anyone, he developed tests that measured, as well as anything can, some of the components of individual variation in ability to learn to speak a foreign language. The items in the *Modern Language Aptitude Test* continue to show up as robust factors in studies of second language learning.[34] Secondly, he pointed out the way that measurable abilities interact with goals and methods. Thirdly, his extended model made the whole issue clearer, by showing that aptitude was only one of the factors involved in what I have called a general theory of second language learning (Spolsky 1989a). Ultimately, then, the work on prognosis and language aptitude produced tests that could be used cautiously for selecting promising language students, and it provided, perhaps more important, an improved understanding of the nature of second language learning.[35]

Notes

1 But, see Carroll (1993: 171–4, 176–7).
2 It was prepared for the Bureau of Educational Research and Service at the State University of Iowa under the supervision of Professors Seashore and Ruch. The first version included six subtests, three involving English grammatical skills—singulars and plurals, tense, nominalization, and three to do with guessing Esperanto words, applying Esperanto grammatical rules, and translating Esperanto sentences into English. The test was still in print in 1949 when a revised form was reviewed in Buros.
3 This test and its revised forms were also reviewed in Buros (1949).
4 This test was reviewed by Kaulfers in Buros (1940).
5 This model was later set out formally by Carroll (1960, 1962).

6 Alastair Pollitt (personal communication) has pointed out that his logic was faulty: if IQ added nothing, it suggests that both were measuring much the same thing. This, he notes, would confirm Kaulfers' view that the Symonds' test is a 'linguistically weighted IQ test' as noted later in this chapter.

7 References are to Buros (1975).

8 The second volume of the *Analytical Bibliography* listed seventeen items dealing with prognosis, including Walter Kaulfers' doctoral dissertation discussed above, and the third volume, covering the years 1937–42 but its publication delayed until after the war (Coleman *et al.* 1949), listed twenty-five items.

9 For instance, Brock (1933), in a thesis written at the University of Southern California, studied 250 first-year students, and looked for any evidence that mental or chronological age or scores on a number of English tests would predict Spanish scores; there was none. Canty (1935) at New Jersey State Teachers College looked at twenty-five pupils, and found the only common factor predicting success to be 'imagination'. When Josephine Young (1933) at the University of Pittsburgh studied 100 high school French students she found that English marks and IQ scores gave some degree of prediction of marks in French, as did the teacher's rating of pupils on six personality traits (habits of work, accuracy, initiative, quickness, memory, and attentiveness), but that they were not as good as predictors of scores on the American Council Alpha and Beta tests. At San Francisco Junior College, Gabbert (1941) developed a prognosis test, based on the Buchanan and the Keniston word and idiom lists, that, given at the beginning of a semester, predicted (with a correlation of 0.69) the student's grades in a final examination (which included vocabulary and idioms). He proposed thus to be able to warn students at the beginning of a semester that they were likely to fail the course. The issue of the relevance of IQ to formal foreign language study was also the topic of a doctoral thesis at New York University by Jacob Greenberg (1938). Greenberg looked at data on 8,423 pupils in their last semester of junior high school; the data included IQ scores, teachers' term marks, Metropolitan Achievement English reading scores, and scores on the Uniform Foreign Language Test (not standarized, and covering grammar, reading, and realia). The correlations between IQ and language scores were positive but quite low (about 0.24), too low to be useful for guidance purposes; in contrast to Kaulfers, he thought that a student with an IQ of 80 could still benefit from foreign language instruction.

At the University of Illinois, a study by Larsen, Wittenborn, and Giesecke (1942) of 130 students of German looked at the correlation of various mental ability measures (the Otis Quick Scoring Mental Ability Test and selected tests of memory, reading, attention, and perception) with scores on the Cooperative German Test (Form O). The mental measures generally failed to distinguish high and low achievers in German; somewhat better prediction was provided by an English Training Test which seems to have focused on grammar. In a study at the Virginia State College, Matheus (1937) reported on 100 students in three different languages. The George Washington University Series Language Aptitude Test (prepared by Hunt and others) correlated 0.66 with the ACE Psychological Examination; the two tests correlated about 0.41 with semester grades in French, German, and Spanish. One of the students who had worked on the George Washington University Language Aptitude Test had made her own study of prediction. Schwartz (1937) studied 200 pupils beginning French in eighth grade at the John Q. Adams School in Washington DC in successive semesters in 1934 and 1935, using the French grades for the criterion and IQ ratings, and English grades and grade point average for major subjects in the seventh grade as predictors. Seventh-grade point average was the best predictor (0.77), confirming that one semester's performance is a good predictor of the next, for any subject. English grades in one semester were a better predictor of French grades the next (0.67) than was IQ (0.53). The minimum IQ recommended for studying French in eighth grade was set at 89.

10 In a study that built on Kaulfers' earlier view (1931) but not his later original study for the dissertation (1933a), Seagoe (1938) followed a group of 120 junior high school pupils over a three-year period. The pupils received a number of intelligence and aptitude tests, including the Luria–Orleans Modern Language Prognosis Test. The tests were then used in guidance. The various mental tests were judged to be useful in this, and to have achieved a high prognosis for foreign language (about 0.71), but the Luria–Orleans test did not do as well as the general intelligence measures. Two studies at the University of Tennessee studied a random sampling of 184 (out of 845) students of French, German, and Spanish. Tallent (1937, 1938) reported that IQ scores had only a low correlation (0.211) with modern language grades; English placement test grades were stronger (0.487). She surmised that the low correlations could come from the lack of validity of both the IQ tests and the modern language grades. Looking at students at the University of Tennessee somewhat earlier, Teague (1931) had reported slightly stronger correlations, about 0.38, for 664 students for IQ and college foreign language grades.

11 Honor-point or grade-point averages are on a four-point scale, with 4.0 for A, 3.0 for B, and 2.0 for C. A student with a 4.0 average is also one with straight As.

12 It was funded by the International Examination Enquiry described in Chapter 4.

13 Carl Brigham led the work in developing this major testing instrument.

14 This intriguing result no doubt deserves more careful analysis. Might it perhaps have reflected a greater tendency to award scores to men on the basis of non-scholastic criteria?

15 The title page of the report bears the date 30 June 1952, but the text says that the study continued until 1953, and the stamped approval by the acting chief of the Personnel Research Section is dated 6 November 1953.

16 One of the three Seashore Music Tests (of Tonal Memory, Timbre, and Pitch) given to trainees.

17 The Army General Classification Test (a general intelligence test) and the West Point Qualifying Test also had low but significant correlations with some of the language proficiency tests.

18 Perhaps if Harvard had been closer to Monterey, a more qualified research team might have been selected; it was on the grounds of distance that John Carroll's bid for the contract was turned down (Carroll, personal communication, 19 October 1993).

19 Carroll's work started about 1952, and was reported in a final report presented in 1960 at a University of Pittsburgh Symposium on Training Research.

20 There were similar programmes operated by the Air Force, the Navy, and the FSI.

21 Some tests had been suggested by Bottke and Milligan (1945), but no results of their use published. In another reported study, Williams and Leavitt (1947) found measures of verbal intelligence to provide reasonably good prediction (with biserial rs of 0.70), but this is not true everywhere.

22 Between 1953 and 1955, Carroll was assisted by Stanley Sapon of Ohio State University.

23 These items turned out to be too easy, and finally not to be relevant.

24 These last two types turned out to be too complex to include in the final battery.

25 An abbreviation, Carroll noted, for psycholingustic.

26 Carroll (1960) reported two situations in which the aptitude battery failed to make significant predictions. Sixty-two persons in six-month courses conducted by the National Security Agency were given a battery of tests before they began courses (typically six months long); the tests failed to predict their grades in these courses, which were concerned with the use of foreign language skills in 'cryptanalysis and related matters'. Carroll explained this as a result of the criterion being 'poorly defined' or 'irrelevant'. (It is likely that Carroll was given no further details of the course or of the criterion tests. The National Security Agency tended to be security conscious; as I recall, its linguists used to pretend to be working for the CIA.) In the second case of failure that he

reported, the battery was given to two classes of US Air Force personnel learning Russian in an intensive programme in a charitably unnamed American university. Carroll attributed the lack of correlation between the battery and the criterion grades to the inconsistency of the latter scores, as well as to such associated matters as 'the quality of the teaching, the quality of the text materials, and the reliability of the grading'. From all these studies, Carroll was satisfied that he had good evidence that the tests in the battery were 'generally speaking, highly valid'.

27 The phonetic coding factor, Carroll (1993: 171) notes, may be identical to the spelling cluster of abilities.

28 It is still not clear, Carroll (1993: 176) remarks, if the grammatical sensitivity factors represent a learned ability.

29 The memory factors identified in the aptitude studies appear to be special. See Carroll (1993: 297–8).

30 A more general foreign language ability factor may emerge, Carroll (1993: 176–7) now says, if the test battery does not permit the grammatical sensitivity and the phonetic coding factors to emerge.

31 Carroll and Sapon continued with their development work, publishing in 1967 a version for grades three to six, called the *Modern Language Aptitude Test: Elementary* or *EMLAT*. Three parts of the test were in the older battery; an innovation was a section asking the subject to identify words that rhymed. Reliabilities were reported to be high. Validity correlations with groups of various sizes and languages were reported to be high. In a review of this test (Buros 7: 255), A. Ralph Hakstian, an associate professor of educational psychology at the University of Alberta, considered it to be 'a carefully constructed and useful instrument'.

32 All the Modern Language Aptitude Test items were dropped because they were copyright.

33 Babylonian Talmud, *Baba Bathra*, 12B.

34 For example, in a study of language gains by 658 American students in four-month study-abroad programmes in Russia, Ginsberg (1992) found two MLAT tests show up as significant predictors for gains in listening and reading. Carroll (1993) provides a reanalysis of early studies. The *Modern Language Aptitude Test* is still, at this writing, in print and use.

35 More recent studies by Skehan (1986, 1989) have rounded out the picture. A new study has just been started (June 1993) by the Center for Applied Linguistics for the FSI.

8 Language testing in the national interest

Intensity and the Cold War

The dramatic success believed to have been achieved by the Army language schools during World War II led modern foreign language teachers in the United States to reassess both their goals and the organization of their teaching programmes. When war began, the needs of the armed forces for soldiers fluent in the spoken languages of enemies and allies had showed up the major gap left by the decision of American schools and colleges in general to go along with the Modern Language Study's proposal (Coleman 1929), that the main objective should be the ability to read the language, effectively wiping out the earlier direct method interest in speech.[1] This literary goal was reinforced by the fact that language teachers in US colleges and universities were on the whole trained in, and carried out their own research on, the literature of the language they taught.

When the Army programmes started, there was no teaching material at all for many languages; for most others, the emphasis was teaching the literary language. The first gap was filled in large measure by the Intensive Language Program of the American Council of Learned Societies, which, from 1941 on, developed courses for teaching spoken languages such as Arabic, Korean, Japanese, and Russian. The second was addressed when the Army started its language and area schools in the 1944, where the stress moved from the cultural value of the foreign literature to the 'practical speaking command' (Cowan and Graves 1944) of the foreign language. The directive for the Army Specialized Training Program (ASTP) stated clearly: 'The objective of the language instruction is to impart to the trainees a command of the colloquial spoken form of the language.' The organization of instruction changed from what Cowan and Graves characterized as the 'dribble' approach of three hours a week, to intensive instruction of at least fifteen hours per week. The Army directive differentiated between this and a putative 'intensive method', stating that any method was permissible that would achieve the stated objective. For the previously untaught languages, the materials developed and the division of activity between a linguist and a native-speaking drill-master led to the aural-oral method, which itself became a matter of considerable controversy, but intensity was the key innovative feature recognized by the review of experts appointed by the Modern Language Association (MLA) (Agard, Clements, Hendrix, Hocking, Pitcher, van Ernden, and Doule 1944).

After the war was over, in the lingering enthusiasm engendered by the experience, a number of US universities launched a programme to reform their language instruction. One well-described case is Yale University, where a committee recommended semi-intensive language classes meeting ten hours a week for all beginning language students, who would be encouraged to continue their studies and use the language skills obtained in courses in literature or other fields. At the beginning of 1944, a group of ten linguists at Yale (including Leonard Bloomfield, Bernard Bloch, William Moulton, and Edward Hall) wrote to the President of the University proposing that Yale adopt the ASTP methods for its elementary language classes (Pottle, Buck, DeVane, and Hubbell 1944).

During the next decade, debate continued. The renewed public interest was demonstrated by a statement by John Foster Dulles on 1 May 1952 (cited by Parker 1954: iv) that 'It is important that Americans should get more familiar with foreign language.' With its growing international responsibilities, the United States was at a disadvantage 'because of the difficulty of finding persons who can deal with the foreign language problem'. Starting in 1952, the Foreign Language Program of the Modern Language Association of America, worked to respond to this 'national urgency with regard to foreign languages' (Starr 1962: 31). Parker (1961: 8) notes that 'Beginning in 1952 the profession of modern foreign language teachers in the United States organized itself to discover and to meet its new responsibilities to American society, and this constructive move coincided, providentially, with a growing public awareness that language study was being tragically neglected in American education.'

One major problem recognized was the credentials of teachers. Language teachers, Parker said, were 'fixing blame' for the 'widely publicized failures' on 'instructors who are inadequately prepared to teach languages' (ibid.: 155). Teachers in some states, he pointed out, were required to have had only a total of 225 contact hours of instruction, compared with the 612 or more hours in the wartime intensive language programmes (ibid.: 112). The Program formulated in 1955 a statement of the ideal 'Qualifications for Secondary School Teachers of Modern Foreign Languages',[2] which proposed three levels of proficiency (minimal, good, and superior) for the seven areas in which a foreign language teacher should be competent, namely: aural understanding, speaking, reading, writing, language analysis, culture, and professional preparation.

The original qualifications for speaking gives some notion of how these appeared:

2 Speaking
Minimal: The ability to talk on prepared topics (e.g., for classroom situations) without obvious faltering, and to use the common expressions

needed for getting around in the foreign country, speaking with a pronunciation readily understandable to a native.
Good: The ability to talk with a native without making glaring mistakes,
and with a command of vocabulary and syntax sufficient to express one's
thoughts in sustained conversation. This implies speech at normal speed
with good pronunciation and intonation.
Superior: The ability to approximate native speech in vocabulary, intonation, and pronunciation (e.g., the ability to exchange ideas and to be at
ease in social situations).
(ibid.: 156)

A formal method of testing and certifying candidates was needed if these
guidelines were not to remain an idealized blueprint. The tests that were
subsequently developed were intended to serve the double purpose of controlling curriculum and determining qualifications, so that their limited
impact should not be surprising.

Modern language testing at the end of the 1940s

The need to develop new tests for these purposes is apparent if one con-
siders what was available at the time. For the first time in 1953, *The Fourth
Mental Measurements Yearbook* published detailed reviews of the College
Entrance Examination Board tests[3] now being administered by the Educational Testing Service (ETS) which had come into existence in 1949.[4]
Walter Kaulfers[5] considered the *Achievement Test in French Reading* (4:
237)[6] to be 'probably as scientifically efficient per unit of testing time as
any standardized tests in any field of subject matter', conforming strictly
'to the best in current statistical theory and practice', and 'technically about
all that can be desired'.[7] His objection was that the tests were confused as
to purpose. They included excellent *diagnostic* recognition tests of difficulty
with integrative[8] tasks of reading, but by adding vocabulary and grammar
scores to the reading scores, they confused two purposes. He was also
deeply disturbed by their failure to recognize in any way a student's ability
to speak. The test, he argued, was not really an *achievement* test, but rather
a specialized *placement* test for institutions that offer 'reading courses
stressing belles lettres and conducted primarily in French'. Within these
limitations, Kaulfers found the tests to be 'superior to most standardized
foreign language tests in scientific excellence'. He found the scaling, with
460 as the average for students who had studied for two years, 520 for
three, and 580 for four, to be very convenient. He did propose, however,
some major changes. First and foremost, he would like to see added a test
of ability to understand spoken French (which should be easy, he thought,
with the recent improvement in recording devices). His comment here drew
attention to the still undeveloped area of tests of the spoken language.

Second, he would like to see profile reporting rather than a single score for the various parts. Third, he would move the emphasis from achievement to placement.

Herbert Schueler, associate professor of education at Queens College, who reviewed the College Entrance Examination Board *Achievement Test in German Reading* (4: 244), which were also in multiple-choice format, would have preferred a greater number of reading comprehension passages, in order to avoid topical bias. Reliability was equally high (0.97). The difficulty of the test meant that it was less useful at the lower levels, but it discriminated well in the upper ranges.

By 1953, the Cooperative Test Service had become the Cooperative Test Division of Educational Testing Service, and new forms of its tests continued to appear. Elton Hocking, professor of modern languages at Purdue University, reviewed the *Cooperative French Test: Lower and Higher Levels* (4: 239), which included a number of innovations. Part I (comprehension) had been expanded by increasing the number of vocabulary items, adding sentences, and including more material in the eight to ten prose passages. Hocking was unhappy with the 'butchery' in Part II (grammar), which included items which required selection only of single words or even endings. He also pointed out that scores on this kind of test item were known not to correlate with functional skills. Another innovation was Part III (civilization), a fifty-item test of French culture. This knowledge would of course be the by-product of the reading of a cultivated person, but once it was incorporated in a test, the result, he feared, would be to impel students 'to cram the answers by conning guidebooks and outline manuals'.

Herbert Schueler found the *Cooperative German Test: Advanced Form* (4: 245) useful and improving with each new form. Part I (reading comprehension) contained a large number of reading comprehension passages, some as short as a single sentence, with multiple-choice questions; this covered a wide range of vocabulary and avoided topical bias. Part II (vocabulary) gave single word stems; he would prefer vocabulary to be tested in context, as in the United States Armed Forces Institute foreign language tests. Part III (grammar) included two sections. Schueler was unhappy with the second, which provided not just a choice of grammatically correct sentence completions but also what he considered unnecessary English translations. James Tharp[9] praised the *Cooperative Spanish Test: Lower and Higher Levels* (4: 269) for its 'careful selection' of items and 'skillful execution', and for its continued innovations. The vocabulary items were based on frequency lists and included a section where idioms were paraphrased in Spanish sentences. The passages were ordered by difficulty and this ordering was supported when he applied a readability formula that had been proposed by Spaulding (1951). The grammar section required the candidate to select correct sentences. Tharp did not accept the widespread objection to items which presented incorrect sentences, and considered that 'proof-reading' was a valid testing technique, provided that the students realized that the language was not to be imitated. He did not share Hocking's disapproval of the civilization section, which he found a welcome feature.

Not everything was praised. Hocking found *French I and II: Achievement Examinations for Secondary Schools* (4: 239) prepared by a curriculum committee of high school teachers for use in the Minnesota State Board Achievement Examinations Program, to be unusable 'in any circumstances', the 'product of persons who have little competence in test construction, in French, or even in English'. Techniques used were faulty; layout was bad; instructions were unclear; portions were cribbed without acknowledgment from the University of Chicago (Agard and Dunkel) tests. Clarence Turner, professor of Romance languages at Rutgers University, considered the purpose of the *French Recognition Vocabulary Test: State High School Tests for Indiana* (4: 240) published in 1948 by Einar Ryden and discussed in his dissertation (1947), to be a result of the 'tragic confusion' of those who believed that passive recognition of vocabulary items was a desirable objective.

The 1953 yearbook also included a review of a 25-year-old test battery, *The Stanford Spanish Tests* (4: 266) written by Aurelio Espinosa and Truman Kelley and in print since their publication in 1927. Only the first three parts—grammar, vocabulary, and paragraph meaning—had appeared. Tharp concluded his review by pointing to their obvious popularity and long service. The vocabulary seemed to be all right; the comprehension did not show a balance of difficulty; and the grammar was not confusing.

Non-American tests were also reviewed. A test written in 1945 by S. W. Cohen for the Australian Council for Educational Research, the *Cohen French Test* (4: 236), contained four sections: vocabulary in sentence context, silent reading (four paragraphs), grammar, and aural comprehension. The reviewer, Mary Turnbull, former head of test production at ETS, found it a useful test but flawed by poorly written items and poor proof-reading. Nelson Brooks, reviewing *A Standardized French Grammar Test* (4: 242) written by T. S. Percival (1950),[10] remarked on differences in English usage[11] but felt the test covered the appropriate points. He was less happy with *A Standardized French Vocabulary Test* (4: 243) by the same author, which consisted of a list of French words followed by five English equivalents. Many of the distractors were not plausible, the correct answer should have been distributed among the five positions, there should only have been one correct answer per item, there should not have been repetitions of words, and the absence of context was a problem. But all in all, he considered it a good test that just needed careful editing. Donald Burns, lecturer in education at the University of Leeds, pointed out that these were the first standardized tests in the area published in England for many years.

While most of the standard tests ignored the spoken language, aural comprehension testing was the topic of a doctoral thesis by Jesse Villaréal (1947).[12] In the test he developed, subjects listened to ten passages and five dialogues recorded on twelve-inch phonograph records, then answered seventy-five multiple-choice questions, written in English (for English-speaking students) and in Spanish (for Spanish speakers). Villaréal reported 0.80 internal consistency, and a correlation with the judgement of 'qualified observers' of 0.78, and with subjects' self-ratings of 0.31.[13]

By 1950, then, American testers were capable of writing reliable and professional tests of vocabulary, grammar, and reading comprehension, but the testing of aural comprehension was in an early stage and testing of productive speaking and writing remained to be tackled. Linguistic items that could be listed could most easily and satisfactorily be employed to produce multiple-choice tests. In fact, psychometrists were happy with the growing willingness of language teachers (and the newly involved structural linguists) to concentrate on linguistic items and their arrangements. But this was of little use, it seemed, in producing tests of what were to become identified as productive functional skills, such as speaking and writing. These were to be the major challenges for the new modern language tests. A test of English for foreigners provided a chance to explore these problems.

The 1947 English Examination for Foreign Students

American testing of English for non-native speakers began to develop a more or less independent life of its own only in the 1950s, but there were two earlier ventures that remain of considerable interest. The first venture, the test developed by the College Entrance Examination Board in 1930–1 and in active use until 1936, has been described earlier.[14] The 1930 test was never reused, but in the immediate post-war days, the need for a test like it was once again noticed. This time, the initiative came directly from the Department of State, who felt such a test would be helpful 'in eliminating at the source foreign students desirous of federal or other support for study in this country, whose command of English is inadequate' (College Entrance Examination Board 1946).

Responding to this interest, in October 1945, the associate secretary of the College Board, Henry Chauncey, asked William Turnbull, the head of test construction, to develop a new test which would also include a recorded test of aural comprehension (Saretsky 1984: 4). When the executive secretary of the College Board, George W. Mullins, wrote to the Department of State asking for financial support, the Department expressed willingness to co-operate in the development and administration of the test and 'to provide a substantial part of the financial support required for a first-rate instrument to measure reading, writing and aural abilities'. An advisory committee of people with experience in the field was set up which met first on 1 July 1946.[15]

The committee proposed two forms of the test, one for use by member colleges, and one to be administered, through the Department of State, at cultural centres overseas, and other foreign centres. The experimental forms of the new examination, planned to be ready by spring 1947,[16] included a number of paragraphs on historical and cultural topics recorded on gramophone records with multiple-choice questions in a booklet. Originally, quite long texts were proposed, but Fries and Lado argued for shorter passages. The battery of tests[17] provided seven separate scores. Scores were to be reported for: reading comprehension (short passages like those found in first-year college social science, history, and literature textbooks, and sentences for recognizing correct and incorrect grammatical forms); pronunciation (tested through a pencil-and-paper test calling for recognition of rhymes and marking of stressed syllables); vocabulary; a separate section of scientific vocabulary; auditory comprehension; English composition; and non-verbal reasoning. Auditory comprehension was tested by written multiple-choice questions based on sixteen short passages (ranging from a quarter of a minute to two minutes long) spoken by a man and a woman on phonograph records. Forty minutes were allowed for the composition. A non-verbal section was included to help relate English proficiency scores to general intelligence levels. A practice book was provided. Full score reporting was provided: there were scores for English proficiency, non-verbal reasoning, and scientific vocabulary, all on a standard scale with a median of 50 and a standard deviation of 10. Percentiles and norms were reported.[18]

As only one form of the test had been prepared,[19] test users were urged to maintain security. Because the shortage of available finance in many countries was already limiting the capacity of the Department of State to co-operate, and would restrict the number of foreign testing centres, American embassies had been asked to identify qualified supervisors, and a number of centres had been selected in Europe, the Middle East, and Puerto Rico, where a fee of $10[20] was to be charged and tests were to start in November 1947. Department of State Cultural Centers in Latin America would start testing early in February 1948. Because of the co-operation of these centres, the fee in them would be only $5. Any US institution which wished to administer the test could do so for $2 per student, provided it guaranteed security and handled the administration.

In practice, there were problems caused by lack of co-operation from the State Department, so that Richard Sullivan, the assistant director of the College Board, later complained that the 'bad faith in keeping to the agreements' made the whole effort 'a real headache and very time consuming' (Saretsky 1984: 7). The problems were compounded by the organizational changes. By 1948, the College Board had undergone a major change, with the establishment of ETS, to whom the College Board passed all its Princeton plant, all its test construction, and most of its research. In January 1948, the English for foreign students test was one of those that was handed over to ETS.

The economics of the new test did not look good.[21] By the end of February, only 215 candidates had been tested, 166 of them in the United States. The strength of the US dollar made the cost very high for foreign students. In February 1948, the US Office of Education offered to pay up to $4,000 for 400 needy students in the Western Hemisphere to take the test, but only fifty-two took advantage of the offer before it ran out at the end of June. In April, the use of the test in Europe and Asia was suspended because of currency problems. Small numbers of students continued to be tested, many at Columbia University where the test was used for placement. In June 1949, the US Army ordered a thousand copies of the test for selecting Japanese students to be trained in the United States, to the amazed joy of the ETS developers. Another 500 tests were ordered for Puerto Rico in 1950. In 1951, ETS stopped rental and made the test available only for outright purchase.

The *English Examination for Foreign Students: Including a Test of Non-Verbal Reasoning* was listed in *The Fourth Mental Measurements Yearbook* (1953) as 4: 233, and reviewed for the first time in *The Fifth Mental Measurements Yearbook* (1959) (5: 256).[22] There were three reviewers. Ralph Bedell, specialist for higher education programmes with the United States Office of Education, remarked on the fact that the large number of foreign students on (or planning to be on) US campuses presented a challenge in understanding the special problems of English for those for whom it was a foreign language. Since World War II, he noted, English was becoming critical for those who wished to keep informed about modern technology. Many students were seeking to study in American colleges. This test should help in determining who was qualified, and it should also help teachers of English as a foreign language adjust their instruction. His detailed description of the test was generally positive, although he acknowledged that the pronunciation section would not do the job fully. He agreed with the need for candidates to have the practice book to study for a week before the examination, recognizing in this that for many of them it must have been their first experience of modern objective multiple-choice tests. The norms, he noted, were based on 507 students already at American colleges. No reliability or validity data were available, nor should the test be used for individual counselling. The test had been used since 1947 in colleges and universities, by some divisions of the armed services, and by foreign affiliates of industrial corporations. He was sorry that such a necessary and well-constructed test had not been validated and standardized. John Cox, Jr., research psychologist at the Personnel Laboratory at Lackland Air Force Base, and author of the Mutual Defense Assistance Pact English Proficiency Examination used there since 1955, also agreed that it was a well-constructed test; he too regretted the absence of statistical data, but commended the fact that the manual made clear that users would need to do their own validation.

A much more negative view of the examination was expressed by Charles Langmuir, director of Special Projects with The Psychological Corporation (a test publishing firm in competition with ETS). He described scornfully the unforgettable experience for foreign student and adviser that must precede a decision—a week of studying the practice book, five hours of testing time in two sessions for the student, a long laborious scoring procedure for the adviser, with complex instruction on how to get the converted scores to be compared to the limited norms. The scoring keys were badly made, the answer sheets non-standard, the essay unscorable, the norms on the non-verbal reasoning vague and not explained. No support was provided for the powerful validity claims, such as that 'Scores of less than 40 on Reading Comprehension, Aural Comprehension, or Pronunciation suggest the need for special work in these areas' and that 'Candidates with (composite) scores above 50 will probably not be handicapped in their college work because of an English deficiency.' He decried the absence of normative or validity studies.[23]

In 1961, when Kay Salter tried to find out more about what had happened to the test, William Bretnall (1961), who was responsible for College Board programmes at ETS, reported to her that current operations were 'as minimal as anything can be'. He thought that William Angoff, a psychometrist at ETS, might be able to answer the question 'Why aren't there any norms to speak of?'

The sad end to this second brave and promising attempt by the College Board to develop a test of English as a second language might well have resulted in a later reluctance to become involved with TOEFL. Saretsky (1984) surmises that, on the contrary, it gave some of those involved a realization of the value of such a test, citing a 1949 prediction by a tester at ETS, Edith Huddleston, that 'it should provide a valuable nest egg when the time is ripe'. Whichever view is correct, the test showed what could be produced, given the state of the art in the immediate post-war period. Modern language testing was ready to go professional.

Professionalization

To be considered a profession, a calling needs to have a number of attributes, such as professional associations, textbooks, training programmes, journals, conferences, and certification. While language testing is still not a distinct profession in these terms,[24] there were already signs of its emerging status at the end of the 1940s. Up until this time, language testing had been the work of people trained either as testers or as language scholars. The PhD dissertation completed by Villaréal in 1947 is probably the first in which someone was trained to bridge the disciplines.[25] This incipient professionalization became even more in evidence with the writing of a second dissertation, three years later, by Robert Lado, who, in another decade, was to make an equally crucial contribution to the process by publishing the first textbook in the field.

Lado had earned an MA degree at the University of Texas, where Professor Herschel T. Manuel[26] had introduced him to testing.[27] His MA completed,[28] Lado went to Michigan in 1945, where, under the direction of Professor Charles Fries, his interest in language testing continued to grow, leading to the development of three forms of the *Test of Aural Comprehension in English as a Foreign Language* (Lado 1946), published by the English Language Institute at the University of Michigan in 1946–7 (Buros 4: 235).

Following the philosophy that Lado enunciated in his thesis (1949) and developed in a later book (1957), the items in the test had been chosen on the basis of contrastive analysis to include features that would give special difficulty to foreign learners. The test covered pronunciation (*sinking* versus *singing*), word order (*chocolate milk* versus *milk chocolate*), progressive tenses, contractions, auxiliaries, negation, subordination, counterfactuals, two-word verbs, and inflection. The test was made up of sixty three-choice items, each consisting of a sentence (occasionally two or more sentences) to be read aloud by the examiner. An example of an item is quoted in the Buros review:

Examiner: Had John been sincere he would have told the truth.
Student's choices: a.   John was sincere.
                     b.   John told the truth.
                     c.   John did not tell the truth.

This test was still in demand ten years later, when a manual for use was printed. It was reviewed in *The Fifth Mental Measurements Yearbook* (1959) (5: 261) by Lado's former teacher, Herschel T. Manuel, who pointed how it differed from the test with a similar goal by A. L. Davis (see below), who had chosen to concentrate his attention on idioms. Manuel wondered how Lado's test, which he judged to be based on a good approach, would correlate with other tests of comprehension. He found the format good and the scoring straightforward. The internal reliabilities of 0.87 were satisfactory, but low enough to suggest that more than one form should be used before making decisions in the case of individual students. The 0.85 correlation with teacher judgements at the English Language Institute was also satisfactory, but data on use elsewhere would help. In fact, he called for more detailed (and independent) evaluation of this significant test. He hoped that Lado himself would go on to develop more tests.

The second review was written by Clarence Turner (professor of Romance languages at Rutgers), who noted a number of minor inconsistencies and problems, but was generally fascinated by all the linguistic riches in the test. Two of the next tests that Lado wrote focused on contrastive problems in phonology.[29]

While working on these practical tests,[30] Lado was also preparing the dissertation which set out the theoretical background to his work. In it, Lado (1949)[31] reviewed the few attempts that had been made to test aural comprehension and oral production. While he rejected some of them for their lumping all learners of English into a single undifferentiated set, he found points of interest in many. One that he singled out as containing the 'germ of progress in tests of language' was the test used by Marie M. Hughes (1935) in her MA thesis from the University of Chicago.[32] The *Hughes Picture Test of Vocabulary for Spanish-speaking Children* was noteworthy, Lado said, for its concern with oral-aural testing, for its selection of vocabulary from established lists, and for its use of pictures. While Hughes apologized for her test, it seems to have been as reliable as the more elaborate *Test of Aural Comprehension* developed as part of the Chicago investigation. These other Chicago tests, Lado thought, were undifferentiated as to target, and their questions could often be answered without listening to the passages. They had, in his opinion, a linguistically unsophisticated view of the nature of comprehension. He was similarly disturbed by the subjectivity of the Chicago *Test of Oral Production*.

Lado's starting-point in test construction was structural phonological theory, as he sought the minimal significant problems a foreign learner would face. His task was not to test the aural comprehension of a native speaker, but of a learner. If a native speaker did not score 100 per cent on the test, then something outside its scope was being measured. As the basis for his work in language testing, Lado followed the classic definition by his teacher, Charles Fries that

> A person has 'learned' a foreign language when he has thus first, *within a limited vocabulary*, mastered the sound system (that is when he can understand the stream of speech and achieve an understandable production of it) and has second, made the structural devices (that is, the basic arrangements of utterances) matters of automatic habit.
> (Fries 1945: 3)

Lado concentrated on testing the sounds[33] and the structures. Each item in a test, he argued, must measure one thing at a time; items of high frequency were preferable. Aural comprehension passages should be complete utterances. Pictures were useful stimuli. Responses should be multiple choice. The *English Language Test for Foreign Students* (Buros 4: 234, 5: 257) (usually called the Lado test) was published in 1951, and consisted of 134 items, 54 of them concerned essentially with phonemic contrast. The student was required to match the identical sounds in words spelled in different ways (e.g. *build, reindeer, kicked*). Both the pronunciation and structure sections concentrated on such phonemic problems, with items provided for various linguistic contrasts (e.g. /l/ and /r/ for Japanese, /b/ and /v/ for Spanish speakers). The third section covered vocabulary, with several cases of two-word verbs.

The Lado test was reviewed in *The Fourth Mental Measurements Yearbook (1953)* by Clarence Turner and in *The Fifth Mental Measurements Yearbook* (1959) by John Cox. Turner remarked that considerable 'careful linguistic analysis and testing ingenuity' had gone into the test, which he thought to be useful and easily administered, requiring no special equipment. While he was uncomfortable with some items, he thought the test as a whole to be 'an unusually sound and practical one'. Cox was not so easily charmed. While on the face of it, it appeared to be 'a satisfactory instrument for measuring proficiency in the comprehension of written English', he was unforgiving about the absence of reliability and validity data and norms. He refused to be reassured by the author's claim to have pre-tested until he saw the results of these pre-tests.

In retrospect, Lado's significant contribution in this work was to attempt to combine a theoretically based structural linguistics and a psychometrically based testing method in the process of constructing language tests. He was one of the first to claim that each of these disciplines should have its say in the development of tests. While there were later arguments both with the theories themselves[34] and with Lado's implementations, his explicit appeal to theory was a crucial step in the professionalization of the field. The structuralist-psychometric test that Lado constructed was a model for finding an objective method of measuring aspects of human language proficiency. With Lado, and with the students and colleagues he gathered at Michigan like Harris and Palmer, the language testing profession had taken a major first step.

Notes

1 See Chapter 6.
2 This statement was subsequently endorsed by the Modern Language Association and by a large number of other professional organizations, including those concerned with the teaching of French, German, Italian, Spanish, and Portuguese, Slavic and East European language, and regional and national modern language associations.
3 Nelson Brooks had published an earlier review in a journal.

4 There was no review of the College Board Entrance Examination *Achievement Test in Spanish Reading* in Buros (1953) but one was published by Donald Walsh in *Hispania* in 1951.

5 In 1948 Kaulfers had moved to the Midwest from California, where he was associated with so much pioneering work in testing before and during the war, when he was hired as professor of education at the University of Illinois as part of a major expansion of the College. Betty Richards, who was administrative aid to the dean of the College at the time, recalls his appointment along with such other major scholars as Lee Cronbach (personal communication, 8 February 1994). Kaulfers travelled extensively, visiting 'schools in 50 countries and territories on four trips to Europe, twelve trips to Latin America, a flight around the globe, and a . . . visit to seven countries of Africa'; this included visits to Nazi Germany in 1936 and the Soviet Union in 1948. He wrote twelve books and about 300 articles (curriculum vitae). Kaulfers retired in 1978; when he died in 1990, he left his entire estate (estimated at over $1 million) to the retirement community where he had lived the last years of his life 'in the smallest apartment available' (*News-Gazette*, 20 February 1992).

6 All references to reviews are to Buros (1975), the monograph collecting reviews of foreign language tests. The references give the original *Mental Measurements Yearbook* volume number and the test number in that volume; thus 4: 237 is test number 237 in *The Fourth Mental Measurements Yearbook* which was published in 1953. *The Fifth Mental Measurements Yearbook* was published in 1959.

7 It reported an internal reliability of 0.97!

8 He used the term *synthetic*.

9 He had been active in language testing since 1927 and was now professor of foreign language education at Ohio State University.

10 As part of his MA at Durham University and published in 1951 by University of London Press.

11 He noted *turning over* rather than *turning* a page, *working* rather than *taking* a test, being classified by *form* rather than *grade* or *year*.

12 While the dissertation was awarded by Northwestern University, Lado (1949: 21) recorded that the work was done at the University of Texas.

13 The 100 native speakers taking the test ranged in scores from 164 to 207 (the possible was 212), suggesting that the test measured more than just knowledge of English (Lado 1949: 23a).

14 See Chapter 4.

15 Members of the committee were Dr Leo Rockwell (Colgate University), M. Gordon Brown (US Office of Education), George Butler (International Training Administration), Dr J. Milton Cowan (Cornell University and ACLS), Dr H. Crain (Colorado School of Mines), Dr

Edgar Fisher (Institute of International Education), Dr Charles C. Fries (University of Michigan), Dr A. C. Howell (University of North Carolina), Dr William Jansen (Indiana University), H. H. Pierson (Department of State), Professor Carl Roehm (Wellesley College), Dr Carl A. Sauer (Department of State), Dr Hugh Walpole (University of Chicago), and Benjamin Woodbridge, Jr. (University of Texas).

16 The amount granted for the work, Lado (1949: 19) recorded, was $8,000, to be matched by $4,000 from the College Board's own funds. At the July meeting, Fries and Lado gave details of the University of Michigan's use of aural and oral tests. The test was developed under the direction of William Turnbull, later president of ETS.

17 There was some delay in finding suitable pre-test populations, but the experimental version was administered to foreign students at Queens College (New York) and to English students in Bogota, Stockholm, Ankara, Istanbul, and Shanghai (Saretsky 1984: 5). A second meeting of the Advisory Committee, chaired again by Dr Rockwell, on 27 June 1947 (College Entrance Examination Board 1947) reviewed proposed items, and on the basis of their suggestions a six-hour long first final form was prepared, ready for administration during the coming year.

18 The statistical analysis was carried out by Richard Pearson, later to be president of the College Board (Saretsky 1984: 6).

19 There was a second form of the composition test.

20 This was the cost of the 1930 test, and was to be the cost of the TOEFL in its early years.

21 For the information in this paragraph, I am grateful to the history of the test by Saretsky (1984).

22 The test was listed as published in 1947 by ETS for the College Entrance Examination Board, with norms published in 1951 and a manual in 1956.

23 From his review, it appears that the sale of the test started in 1951, but that the materials on sale were in fact remainders from the original stock; the test booklets he received were poorly printed and reduced, the record discs were, he judged, in substandard condition.

24 The first association specifically for language testers (the International Language Testing Association) was founded only in 1992, and there are still no certification or formal training programmes expressly for language testers.

25 There were earlier doctoral dissertations on language testing. The earliest (on prognosis) was Kaulfers (1933a). Another early one was Ficken (1937).

26 Herschel Truman Manuel was professor of educational psychology at the University of Texas in 1930, when, in a book on the problems of the education of Spanish-speaking children in Texas, he called attention to their linguistic problems and to the need for measures of their intelli-

gence that would reflect this. His standing is shown by the fact that he was a regional director for the Army-Navy Qualifying Tests in 1944. He argued strongly over the years for tests which would be 'fair' (Manuel 1965: 70), and led the team which constructed the Inter-American Series of *Tests of General Ability* and *Tests of Reading* (with parallel Spanish versions) that were published by ETS in 1950 and by Guidance Testing Associates in 1962.

27 Lado dedicated his book on language testing to him. Another of Manuel's students was Sydney Sako.

28 Lado's MA thesis, he recalls (personal communication) involved looking at aspects of the Inter-American tests of Spanish and English written by Manuel and used in Texas, Puerto Rico, and Latin America.

29 The *Test of Aural Perception in English for Latin American Students* (Buros 5: 262) by Robert Lado, was prepared in 1947 and revised in 1957. It was distributed by George Wahr Publishing. The *Test of Aural Perception in English for Japanese Students* (Buros 6: 362) written by Robert Lado and R. D. Andrade, appeared in 1950. Though originally intended for research use only, it was distributed through Follett's Book Store.

30 Another test constructed at this time under Lado's leadership was the *Examination in Structure (English as a Foreign Language)* (Buros 5: 260). Available in three forms in 1947, it was developed by the English Language Institute of the University of Michigan and distributed by Wahr's Book Store.

31 The cover page has the date 1949, and so does University Microfilms, but the copyright page gives the year 1950.

32 Though her training was in the Midwest, most of Marie Hughes' long and valuable career in early childhood education was in the Southwest. She taught for many years at the University of Arizona, and, after retirement, conducted a doctoral programme to train teacher trainers at the University of New Mexico, where I had the privilege of working with her, and both my children had the good fortune to be taught by teachers trained by her in the 'professional' approach.

33 In assessing aural perception, some of his early tests used a phonemic alphabet. The difficulties caused by this approach were overcome when he adopted a suggestion that he credited to Lloyd Swift, one of his colleagues at the English Language Institute. Swift proposed a technique of reading two words or sentences to the candidate and having him (or her) indicate whether the two were the same or different. This, it will be noted, was the technique proposed by structural linguists to identify phonemic differences in a language: in other words, the language learner was being asked to do what a native speaker is assumed to be able to do.

34 See, for instance, Upshur (1962).

9 Testing goes professional

The incorporation of language testing

A second important event in the development of the testing profession, and one that was to have repercussions for language testing too, was the founding of the Educational Testing Service (ETS) in 1948, which constituted a decisive stage in the march towards industrialized testing.

The work of the College Entrance Examination Board had been growing more and more complex. In the early 1930s, it was persuaded to add an interest in research to its work in test development. It was a decade later, however, after Brigham's death in 1943, that the burst of testing activities for the Government started to put serious pressure on the existing College Board structure.

Stalnaker, Brigham's successor as associate director of the College Board, with assistance from numbers of psychologists and testers on leave from their institutions, had became active in a major war programme that included development and administration of tests for the armed forces. For example, in 1944, the College Board reported, 564,000 young men had taken the Army-Navy Qualifying Test; 88,000 the comprehensive achievement tests for the College Board V-12 Program, and 133 different tests had been made available to the Bureau of Naval Personnel for qualifications for 100 service jobs.

When Stalnaker left the College Board to become professor of psychology and dean of students at Stanford University,[1] he noted in its annual report (1945), that the College Board's role and status had increased during the nine years that he had been working for it, bolstered most recently by its 'active and aggressive' role in the war effort. The College Board, he said, 'has finally developed a large, competent technical staff' which would be expensive to retain, but basic research should remain an 'integral part' of College Board activities.[2]

By 1946, the College Board's offices in Princeton, though expanded by the construction of an additional storey, were sorely pressed by the increase, not just in the 325 temporary staff needed to score the objective tests and read the English test, but also by the growth of regular salaried staff from sixty-nine to over a hundred (College Entrance Examination Board 1946).[3] The operation and its many 'extracurricular' activities (the term used in the 1947 College Board report) were clearly becoming massive and potentially too unwieldy to be managed by what had started as a group of Eastern college professors uniting to maintain admission standards.

The first tentative steps in this direction, an ETS brochure by Nargil (1992) reports, had been taken as early as 1937, when a speech by Conant at the Educational Research Board suggesting a unified testing agency set off a major debate. James B. Conant, then president of Harvard, to whom the notion of forming a single testing organization was widely attributed, responded that his promotion of the idea came from his enthusiasm for the Scholastic Aptitude Test; he denied, however, having originated the idea. Another early supporter of the notion was Ben D. Wood, one of the first proponents of multiple-choice new-type testing, and in 1938 director of the Educational Research Board. Wood had established (in 1930) the Cooperative Test Service of the American Council of Education, had done the basic work behind the Graduate Record Examination that the Carnegie Foundation began in 1937, had developed the first test-scoring machine in 1936, and was at work on National Teacher Examinations. There was one strong negative reaction among all the positive ones, when Carl Brigham wrote an article in *School and Society* and sent letters to Conant opposing the move:

> One of my complaints about the proposed organization is that although the word *research* will be mentioned many times in its charter, the very creation of powerful machinery to do more widely those things that are now being done badly will stifle research, discourage new developments, and establish existing methods and even existing tests, as the correct ones.
> (From a letter dated 3 January 1937 to Conant, in Nargil 1992)

Brigham's opposition seems to have blocked further discussion, Nargil concludes, until after his death in 1943.

The issue of an independent testing agency was reopened by the Carnegie Foundation, whose interest in testing has been noted earlier (Chapter 4). In October 1945, Devereux C. Josephs, president of the Foundation, wrote to Chauncey, newly appointed director of the College Board's Princeton office, raising the issue of the problem caused by the pending retirement of William Learned from the direction of the Graduate Record Examination. Chauncey took the question to the College Board secretary, George Mullins, who sent him notes he had made during the 1937 merger discussions. In February 1946, Chauncey and Mullins visited Josephs at Carnegie, and were intrigued to hear a proposal to move the Graduate Record Examination and another Carnegie testing programme, the Pre-Engineering Inventory, to the College Board as a step towards a new unified testing agency. The complications turned out to be considerable. As the College Board was small and Ivy League-based, the American Council of Education was unhappy at the idea. Carnegie was persuaded it was unwise to proceed in the face of dissension, and chose another path. In May 1946, O. C. Carmichael, president of Carnegie, asked the president of Harvard University,

James B. Conant, to chair a committee to look at the issue (Nargil 1992).

In October 1946, a Committee on Testing proposed the merger of all existing non-profit testing agencies to provide leadership for the 'scientific development of testing'. A single testing agency could better provide for the expansion of testing, for the conduct of good research, and for the development of better tests. After considerable negotiation, an agreement was reached and the ETS was created. When Conant presented the committee report to the autumn 1946 meeting of the College Board, there was some agreement in principle, but general opposition to the type of organization suggested. The Board therefore appointed a seven-man special committee, which reported to the April 1947 meeting of the Board, emphasizing that the new agency should be 'autonomous, financially independent' but remain 'constantly sensitive to the needs and desires of its clientele'. The College Board should continue to exist and be responsible for the admission programmes, but have a special relationship with a new agency which would prepare the tests and carry out the College Board's direction much as the Princeton office had in the past. The Board could then concentrate its attention on the issues of college admission, and leave the other 'extra-curricular' activities to the new agency and others. The Board unanimously adopted the report, which then became the basis for 'protracted' negotiations with the American Council of Education and the Carnegie Foundation for the Advancement of Teaching.

At its autumn meeting in 1947, the College Board approved the 'Agreement' resulting from this bargaining. In 'an altruistic action almost unparalleled in educational history', the College Board handed over to the new agency its Princeton office, tests worth hundreds of thousands of dollars, and a portion of its capital (College Entrance Examination Board 1947). One matter for long debate, Nargil (1992) reported, was the make-up of the board of trustees; the twelve members selected were acceptable to the three founding organizations, each of which had a veto right over all nominees.

ETS was established as a 'non-profit, non-stock corporation without members', its officers and trustees acting as agents for the memberless corporation. This absence of stock has protected it from take-overs, such as those suffered by the Psychological Corporation (taken over by Harcourt Brace Jovanovich), and the California Test Bureau (swallowed by McGraw-Hill) (Nairn 1980: 299). The governing board was to elect its own successors. Chartered from the New York State Board of Regents as a non-profit body, it was exempted from federal income tax under section 501(c)(3) of the Internal Revenue Code (ibid.: 299).

On establishment, ETS received a $750,000 grant from Carnegie, all of the American Council on Education's testing assets in excess of $185,000, and all of the College Entrance Examination Board's assets in excess of $300,000. The College Board kept only its New York office, and handed over also all contracts not directly concerned with college entrance (College Entrance Examination Board 1948: 2).

The new organization operated as the agent of client boards. The initial five-year arrangement with the College Board (ibid.) was the model for later contracts. ETS was responsible for preparing, distributing, administering, scoring, and reporting the results of tests. The College Board retained responsibility for the content of the examinations, the form of the examination programme, and its financial viability. ETS was paid on an expenses plus 15 per cent fee basis.

As it turned out, with the notable exception of the College Entrance Examination Board, almost all the other 'client' boards were *ad hoc* boards created by ETS. Following this procedure, the National Teachers Examinations advisory committee was created in 1949, the Graduate Record Examination Board in 1966, and the TOEFL Policy Council in 1973. Generally, members of these *ad hoc* boards were appointed to serve for three-year terms, and they met twice a year to lay down policy and approve budgets and other matters raised by ETS staff members assigned to them.

ETS also owned the tests. The result of this brilliant arrangement was to create the powerful and effective corporation that has come to dominate American testing. It has its critics—the Ralph Nader report (Nairn 1980) is voluminous, trenchant, but ultimately almost despairing in its impotence before the mighty power of ETS and the ingenuity of its constitution. There remain some fundamental questions about its underlying effects—and there are a number of people who feel that Brigham's fears were realized—but no one can deny that it led to a testing agency that has offered admirable industrial efficiency alongside sound fundamental research in psychometrics. Its creation gave the testing profession a natural centre, and the language testers who have spent part of their careers there, like John Carroll, John Clark, David Harris, and, more recently, Grant Henning, are among the leading professionals in the field.

Meeting at meetings

A third vital factor in the growth of the language testing profession was the provision of regular opportunities for personal contacts between testers. When Carroll (1961) opened the 1961 Washington conference with the words 'This is not the first conference ever called on language testing, nor will it be the last one', he was probably referring to a second meeting he had been invited to that same month on foreign language testing, but he could also have been recalling the session on language testing that he had chaired at the 1953 Georgetown Round Table (see below).

There had also been brief but significant references to language testing at an earlier meeting concerned with psycholinguistics. Carroll (1951) chaired the Cornell seminar[4] at which there were three linguists,[5] three psychologists,[6] and two graduate students.[7] A presentation on second language learning by Agard discussed the work of the Investigation of the Teaching of a Second Language at Chicago,[8] which had revealed the need for psychological experimental study of language learning. In discussion, three categories of research looked worthwhile. First, was the development and testing of measures of individual aptitude for second language learning.[9] Second, was controlled experimental testing, in laboratory conditions, of the various methodological approaches. The third was language proficiency, Carroll's special interest at the time. The report says:

> Objective tests of auditory comprehension, reading ability and grammar exist at present, but we are not certain that each constitutes a valid measure of the particular skill involved. We have no data on the reliability of the (as yet unstandardized) auditory comprehension tests which are now in use, and we have no objective tests of oral production at all. It seems probable, however, that only in the light of long experience gained in the measurement of second-language aptitude and in the experimental evaluation of instructional methods, can we expect to succeed in devising proficiency tests of proven validity and reliability for all the skills. (ibid.: 42–3)

While the main focus of the seminar was elsewhere, one of its results was to establish language testing as a relevant concern for psycholinguists and applied linguists, and to move it out of the unchallenged domain of psychometrists and language teachers working alone or in tandem. This was an important step in the burgeoning semi-independence of the field of language testing.

The territorialization was confirmed at the fourth annual Georgetown Round Table on languages and linguistics in 1953, organized by Archibald Hill (1953).[10] While there had been many earlier practical meetings,[11] and even some more theoretically inclined ones,[12] the 1953 Georgetown Round Table seems to have been one of the first with a session devoted specifically to language testing.[13] The session, chaired by John Carroll (then at Harvard)[14] consisted of five papers. Carroll (1953) himself opened by noting that language testing brought together two groups of people: 'psychometricians' and 'linguisticians', although he preferred the terms applied psychologists and applied linguists. Language teaching, he said, involved interesting problems of testing and measuring both aptitude and achievement, which were closely related, for the traits that were characteristic of a speaker were carried from one language to another. In a first language, there were a number of 'fundamentally independent dimensions of individual differences' that would show up in different performances, or as 'factors' in tests. One was vocabulary, probably including 'grammar' (though Carroll suspected that putting sentences together grammatically

was separate). Other factors that he identified[15] covered skill in doing ana-
grams, in making free associations, and in naming colours. There were
differences to be found, too, in 'the ability to emit language spontaneously
and effectively in various situations', and in speech rate and care of articulation. While Carroll expected that these same dimensions would be found
in second language achievement, he cautioned against 'clever' methods of
language testing that might turn out to measure unimportant traits. In this
remark, he foreshadowed his later suspicions about the cloze technique
(Carroll, Carton, and Wilds 1959).

Believing as he did that second language performance was based on first
language competence—a person who could not carry on a conversation in
his first language would be unlikely to be able to do so in a second—Carroll
argued that among the best predictors of success in learning a second language would be measures of proficiency in the first.[16] Finally, he noted
that the work of Henmon *et al.* (1929) showing that measures of general
intelligence, reasoning, and inductive capacity were the best predictors for
learning a second language in the grammar-translation method, but he
believed that for an approach emphasizing aural-oral skills, different traits
might be relevant. He mentioned one technique that he later tried out in
the Modern Language Aptitude Test, namely, the ability to imitate the
phonetic or phonemic structure of an utterance. But what these traits were,
he was unwilling at that time to list.[17]

The next two papers in the session also focused on studies of prediction
and prognosis. James Frith (1953), then with the US Air Force Institute of
Technology,[18] described trial courses used by the Air Force before sending
airmen to study languages. Earlier, on the basis of scores on general intelligence and technical aptitude tests, possession of a high school diploma and
a desire to study the language, airmen had been sent to university to learn
Mandarin Chinese. Because half of the candidates dropped out by the end
of the first three weeks, a trial course was set up that used the materials
from the first few days of the regular training course, was taught by the
same instructors, and met for six hours a day (four hours with live
instructors and two hours of drill). The trial course started in high gear,
with no time for review, and with frequent tests. After an initial trial run
of eight days, it was reduced to four. It turned out, Frith reported, that 70
per cent of the decisions could be made in two days, but for the rest the
extra two were needed. As a result of using the trial courses, the attrition
rate in training course dropped from 50 per cent to 14 per cent, each run
of the trial thus saving the Air Force over $10,000.

William J. Morgan (1953), a psychologist, also described aptitude testing
he had done for an unnamed government agency[19] to select students for a
course in Russian. He persuaded his fellow consultant, L. E. Dostert, director of the Institute for Languages and Linguistics at Georgetown University, who had proposed a two-week trial course, like the one described by

Frith, also to give the first batch of thirteen students a battery of tests, including a projective 'written interview questionnaire' and a personality inventory. After careful study (at least an hour in each case) of these data, Morgan made his own predictions of the rank ordering of the students in their course, which proved to be correct in all but one case. The various tests did have some predictive power[20]but only the clinical approach could consider the extra traits—attitudes, motivation, age, energy, perseverance, adaptability, or rigidity—which predicted language learning success. He was not convinced that there was such a thing as 'language aptitude'; rather, there were 'intellectual and personality traits and work habits' that in certain circumstances make it possible for individuals to learn a new language. To understand this better, it would make sense to 'breed' a new kind of psychologist 'equipped to work in the field of linguistic science'. In answer to a question by Frith, Morgan said that the Army was experimenting with pencil-and-paper tests of pronunciation,[21] but standardization had not been achieved because of many complex variables. He reported also that Dostert had suggested using tape stimuli and recording student responses, but this had not yet been done.

Dostert expanded on Morgan's report, saying that the Institute of Languages and Linguistics had prepared four Language Achievement Tests for the Army, and was engaged in testing employees of the World Health Organization for proficiency in English and Spanish. These tests included oral as well as written skills, but had not been systematized. He also pointed out the potential of using a tape recorder with a double recording head to develop imitation tests.

In the discussion that followed, Henry Lee Smith, Jr., then at the Foreign Service Institute of the Department of State, raised questions about Morgan's presentation, by recounting a wartime experience. He and William Moulton (later at Princeton) were given an afternoon to devise a test to grade a group of German prisoners of war who were about to start an intensive course in English. The test that they developed consisted of true-false questions in English based on passages taken from the Army Manual of Spoken German and two anecdotes in English. The results of these tests, which took only half an hour to administer, correlated very highly with a skilled interviewer's judgement in dividing students into four groups. They were followed by interviews. In grading 450 men, there was only one occasion when a grade had to be changed. The predictions of the test were also valid for success in non-linguistic parts of the test and in subsequent employment of the individual in military government. Smith asked why a test of half an hour and a five-minute interview worked so well. Carroll, who responded, linked his answer to Morgan's: 'Competency in language and in learning languages is a very central part of the G factor, or general intelligence. What you were really testing was this factor, measured by how much English the prisoners had learned in their previous experience' (1953: 38).

The next two papers dealt with achievement tests. The first was a seldom cited but very significant report by Paula Thibault (1953), a tester at ETS, who raised a question that Stevenson (1981) and others would ask about language tests a quarter of a century later: why is there such high correlation between different tests? Thibault wanted to sum up 'a few of the things that the Educational Testing Service has learned about foreign language testing'. Her summary included all tests for language administered by ETS, but the College Board modern language tests provided the clearest evidence.

Thibault noted that 'we seem to know how to put together impeccable tests . . . but we do not know why it is that they work' (1953: 22). Rather than setting out the results of studies that had been published or describing the 'common sense' basis for the 'knack' of item-writing, she planned to present some questions to which answers were not known. The first of these questions concerned the homogeneity of items in language tests. Language tests, she reported, produced biserial *r*s 'that are the envy and admiration of my colleagues in other subject-matter areas' (ibid.). The good side of this was the absence of the ambiguities in the items that produced low *r*s. But there was a puzzle to be solved in the implication that 'people who can do one kind of linguistic task can do other kinds as well' (ibid.: 23). Thibault found this hard to believe. She remarked that even when the proportion of vocabulary was reduced, or when items using more colloquial language were introduced, the measures of internal consistency remained high. Changes in comprehension items from word to sentence-level items produced no change, and English-to-foreign vocabulary items provided the same information as foreign-to-English items, and both were much the same as the grammar and reading sections.

The main business of the College Board's language committees at the time[22] was developing ways to assess oral-aural achievement. For practical reasons, it was not possible to add spoken tests to the batteries. In the meantime, she could be satisfied by finding items that looked like the skills taught in oral-aural skills, but that did not have the normal high correlations with reading skills. But there seemed to be no way to achieve this:

> The trouble must be, since one can not believe the apparent implications of those high biserial *r*'s, that our statistical techniques are too crude to allow us to draw any conclusion other than that we have highly homogeneous tests. What seems to be needed before we can make significant improvements in our tests in the way of weighting various aspects of language learning in an equitable way, is a series of detailed factorial studies that would tell us what aspects are differentiable, and would give us a clearer idea of the common factor that obscures everything by bringing about uniformly high *r*'s.
> (Thibault 1953: 25)

Lacking a solution to this problem,[23] Thibault went on to discuss other issues more amenable to solution, such as better face validity and better methods of selecting distractors. Commenting on Thibault's paper, Morgan wondered if the high *r*s might not correlate the 'rather mysterious entity' of 'abstract intelligence' referred to in British psychological literature.[24] 'If language-aptitude testing is to be significantly improved, it will have to go beyond paper-and-pencil tests, beyond personality tests, and be based on a systematization of the findings of linguistic scientists and language teachers' (ibid.: 33). Thibault expressed some concern about the use of isolated words in the pronunciation test.

A quite different approach was taken by Robert Lado (1953), who presented a strong claim for the objectivity that could be achieved by what he called testing the language, independently of the situations in which it occurred. He supported this claim which he based on Bloomfield's (1933) distinction between the finite language system and the infinite situations preceding and following speech, by pointing out the problem in the opposite (functional or situational) approach; 'it is often possible to by-pass language in grasping a situation' (Lado 1953: 30).[25] Applying this principle permitted him to answer a good proportion (from 54 per cent to 80 per cent) of the items in the English test for the Investigation of the Teaching of a Second Language (Agard and Dunkel 1948) without listening to the four long aural comprehension passages on which they were based. He attacked other aspects of the 'situation' approach: its failure to be specific, its preoccupation with voices rather than phonemes, its concentration on content to the detriment of form.

Lado's technique to test pronunciation on a pencil-and-paper test was not the essential part of his work in developing the Test of Aural Comprehension in English; what was important was the fact that he was testing 'the structural elements of the language' and, in particular, those elements which contrastive analysis had shown would be most difficult.[26] His paper concluded with the perhaps over-enthusiastic claim that 'Pronunciation, which seemed the most difficult of the linguistic situations to test, is now perhaps the simplest' (Lado 1953: 32).

The discussions at the Round Table session on testing showed a high standard of sophistication, with the interchange between psycholinguists, psychometricians, applied linguists, and language teachers that was to come to define the burgeoning professional field of language testing. By the 1950s, then, modern language testing was a well-developed field, capable of tackling practical problems in a principled way. These technological skills were to continue to be called on by governmental and educational agencies to deal with practical problems they faced.

The state of the art in 1954

A year after the Georgetown meeting, Carroll completed a fifty-page paper which he titled 'Notes on the measurement of achievement in foreign lan-

guages' (Carroll 1954).[27] The 'memorandum', as Carroll characterized it
in the introduction, set out to sketch the history of foreign language testing,
to survey approaches, and to outline procedures for building achievement
tests for different circumstances.

Carroll agreed with Thibault (1953) that 'the techniques of constructing
paper-and-pencil foreign language tests of vocabulary, reading and grammar are highly perfected at the present time' (1954: 4). Tests of aural and
oral skills had been slower to develop, partly because of lack of special
equipment and partly because of lack of interest, but mainly because no
effort had been expended on the issue. Carroll noted some early efforts, and
referred in particular to the English competence examination for foreign
nationals hoping to study in the United States, developed by College
Entrance Examination Board in 1930, that included measures of aural and
oral skills, and was intended for overseas administration.

Carroll referred also to aural-oral tests previously developed by Sandri
and Kaulfers (1945, 1946) in Italian and by Kaulfers (1944) in Spanish,
which he considered to be well designed and better than many later tests,
and to the auditory comprehension tests developed by Agard and Dunkel
(1948) and still available. In addition, he gave brief details of two series of
tests developed by the War Department,[28] and of some proficiency testing
in Russian, Japanese, Hungarian, Serbo-Croat, Arabic, and Mandarin
Chinese used by Dorcus, Mount, and Jones (1953) in a study of foreign
language aptitude for the US Army. Carroll completed his historical survey
with reference to the English as a foreign language tests under development
at Michigan by Robert Lado, to some work of Bovée (1947, 1948) with
French, and to the work of the committee on tests of the Northeast
Conference.

After this historical review, Carroll presented a model of foreign language achievement, in which he postulated three dimensions: mastery of
type of behaviour (auditory comprehension, oral production, reading, and
writing), mastery of linguistic structure (phonology, grammar, syntax) or
lexicon, and level. While linguistic structure might be more important, it
could only be measured using lexicon, which must therefore be controlled.
'It is very probable that most tests of language proficiency, regardless of
which aspect they measure, are difficult for the examinee in proportion as
the lexicon is difficult' (Carroll 1954: 10).

Carroll surmised that one reason for high correlations between tests of
the various behaviours might in fact be the common lexicon required,[29]
but one would expect lower correlations between two abilities, one of
which was emphasized in a course and the other not. 'By controlling the
type of training and the types of test performances, one could probably
produce any factorial structure that one might desire in a battery of foreign
language achievement tests' (ibid.: 10–11).

This led Carroll to the issue of the factorial composition of language tests. He pointed out the contamination of factors other than language knowledge, such as 'ideational fluency' and 'fluency of expression' that would intrude when, for instance, the candidate was asked to think up ideas as well as express them in the foreign language. Thus, it would be difficult to achieve the kind of purity of measure that Thorndike (Monroe 1939) had considered optimal. But he made a virtue of this weakness and pointed out the practical value of the high correlations. He cited the high correlations that Lado reported for his pencil-and-paper pronunciation tests with aural comprehension tests, or the correlations that Evans (1937) reported between a pencil-and-paper test and ratings of recorded samples of pronunciation. Carroll suggested caution, however, in acting too fast to cut out overlapping tests. Tests which were less practicable or reliable should only be dropped when it was certain that the dimensions they measured could be adequately tested with more practicable and reliable measures.

The fact that under many conditions different kinds of language achievement were highly correlated would often make it possible to rely heavily on the more easily constructed and reliable tests, with less stress on tests of such abilities as oral production, which seemed to be more difficult to construct or to administer (ibid.: 11). It was, however, likely to be the case that beyond a certain level, foreign language acquisition was almost solely the acquisition of new lexicon. Vocabulary must therefore be kept separate.

In the fourth section of his report, Carroll looked at each of the four linguistic skills in turn. Tests of reading required responses to written or printed material, and could be administered as pencil-and-paper tests given to groups. If the stimulus were one word long, one was dealing with a vocabulary test; if longer, it was a reading comprehension test.

Vocabulary tests might require recognition or recall. Many studies since Henmon (1929) had shown these to be closely related. Carroll listed six possible kinds of items for testing knowledge of lexicon: a word in the foreign language to be matched with one of a number of words in the native language; a word in the native language to be matched with one of a number of words in the foreign language; from a number of foreign words, synonyms or words that do not fit must be recognized; a word or phrase in the foreign language must be matched with another word or phrase in the foreign language; a foreign language word must be matched with a picture; or a picture must be matched with a foreign word. The first was probably the commonest; the last two were cumbersome but had advantages. The third and fourth raised problems in deciding what was the cause of the error. Testing vocabulary in context, he argued, probably involved a different ability, the ability to infer meanings of missing words. He cited two studies, Gibbons (1940) and Werner and Kaplan (1950), that showed that this ability was specific. The only reason he could see for context, then, was to make clear the specific meaning of the foreign word by giving it in a disambiguating context, but it had already been shown by Stalnaker and Kurath (1935) that this kind of test correlated very highly with multiple-choice tests of vocabulary.

Reading comprehension tests, where the text is a sentence or longer, also depended to a large extent on lexical knowledge, because not knowing a single lexical item could lead to misunderstanding even when all the other words and the grammatical structure were known. For this reason, lexical control was essential. Carroll described a number of techniques used for testing reading comprehension. One common technique was to give a sentence in the foreign language to be marked as true or false (one must of course then be careful that the candidates could be expected to know the correctness of the facts). Another possibility was to give multiple-choice, true-false, or completion items in the foreign or the native language after one or more sentences in the foreign language. There was also what Henmon (1929: 301) referred to as the Van Wegenen technique, where the candidate decided if a statement (in the foreign or native language) was consistent with the foreign language passage. It had been established in the Modern Language Study (Henmon 1929; Ruch and Stoddard 1927) that true-false statements based on a passage gave the most reliable tests. Carroll mentioned the need to make sure that the questions could not be answered as well by someone who had not read the passage.

Direct tests of 'writing skill', the ability to 'put one's thoughts on paper' in the foreign language, had two kinds of problem: the difficulty of getting a reliable rating, and the very openness of the task, its lack of control or structure. One way of dealing with the first problem was provided by the quality scales for some languages reported by Henmon (1929), but the multi-dimensionality of the items to be rated (what weight to give to spelling, what to originality) made this difficult. To control the second, the 'thoughts' should be provided by outline in the native language or by carefully selected pictures. Free composition, then, was a problematic kind of test, but there were many objective ways of testing language structure, with high correlation between recall and recognition. Among the newer items possible, he cited the 'interlinear exercise' developed in 1944 by College Entrance Examinations Board for measuring English composition ability, where candidates were required to revise a passage by correcting errors and improving expression; this might be useful for advanced tests of foreign language skill. He gave a number of examples from Lado's tests.

Tests of auditory comprehension were no more difficult than tests of reading comprehension, and must of course be given with good recordings and in good acoustical conditions, preceded by a 'warm-up'. There was a wide range of types of item possible: dictation, translation from spoken utterance, following directions, deciding on the truth or falsity of a spoken statement, answering questions, multiple choice (translation, answering questions, choosing associations or pictures, dictation), correct usage. All had used short (one sentence) foreign language stimuli, because foreign language learners seemed to have difficulty keeping up with normal rates of speech. Tests with longer discourse were likely to prove difficult to construct. He thought it desirable to have written questions in an aural comprehension test in the native language. Carroll recorded that a number of auditory comprehension paragraph tests had already been described in the literature: Sandri and Kaulfers (1946) for Italian; Agard and Dunkel (1948) for French, German, Spanish, and Russian; Villaréal (1947) for Spanish speakers of English; the Barnard-Yale aural test in French (Kellenberger 1954). Agard and Dunkel presented 'old-world literary' anecdotes (about $1\frac{1}{4}$ minutes long) followed by multiple-choice questions in English in some tests; in upper levels, they presented a five-minute dialogue between a man and a woman, recorded on a 12 inch 78 r.p.m. phonograph recording, with 15 multiple-choice questions in a printed booklet. No attempts had been reported, he said, to try in foreign languages the response latency tests that psychologists used in the first language. Most attention in pronunciation tests had been focused on accuracy of pronunciation. Evans (1937) thought it was enough to test single words. Lado had set up a pen-and-paper task, which appears not unlike Kaulfers (1937). Carroll noted the similarity to a task used by Thurstone with native speakers that found considerable variation in this ability.

There were some special problems. How could an achievement test in vocabulary or lexicon not be seriously influenced by the specific training that the students had received? Frequency counts would seem to be the best way to control lexicon, but they tended to be based on literary texts. Perhaps a semantically- or conceptually-based frequency count would be the answer, or using a count of the frequency of topics dealt with in elementary textbooks.

After a discussion of scales, Carroll's notes concluded with brief specifications for foreign language achievement tests. One form to be used with native speakers of English,[30] should have four sections, with subsections:

1 Tests of reading comprehension and speed. Vocabulary would be 100 multiple-choice items, reading comprehension 100 true-false items, and there should be a reading speed test in which the candidate would be required to cross out nonsense words in a continuous text.
2 Tests of writing and grammar should consist of a 50 item multiple-choice test and an editing 'interlinear' exercise.
3 For auditory comprehension, 50 true-false sentences; multiple-choice pictures or English words to be associated with a spoken stimulus; and a 'following directions' item.
4 For oral production, a controlled conversation of the kind proposed by Kaulfers and a list of words to be read to test pronunciation.

Though regrettably unpublished,[31] Carroll (1954) remains an excellent survey of the state of the art in modern language testing just as the major post-war activities were starting to get under way. Carroll's central role in the field of language testing would have been even more indisputable had this report been printed. Fortunately, his involvement as a consultant in test development meant that the ideas in the report were well disseminated. From the paper, we can see how his knowledge helped bridge the gap between earlier and later language testers and between testing theory and practice, just as his later research and writings have made the link between psychology and linguistics and between psychometricians and language testers.

Notes

1 He was replaced as associate secretary by Henry Chauncey, formerly assistant to the dean of the faculty of arts and sciences at Harvard University. At the same time, Dr Harold O. Gulliksen, professor of psychology at Princeton University, was appointed research secretary to the board.

2 He also cited Brigham's emphasis on tests as a method of measuring pupils with as small an error as possible, rather than of controlling the curriculum.

3 There were three technical departments: research, directed by Professor Gulliksen; test construction, directed by Dr William Turnbull (who, at the time of the events related in Part II of this book, was executive vice-president of ETS, and later became its president); and statistical analysis, directed by Ledyard Tucker. In addition, there were three service-oriented departments: test administration, office administration, and purchasing and accounts.

4 The 1951 summer seminar in psychology and linguistics at Cornell University had a wider scope than just testing, its outcome being the formal creation of the new field of psycholinguistics. The seminar discussed the role of psycholinguistics in communication theory, the encoding and decoding processes, units for linguistic analysis, the mutual implications of psychology and linguistics, content analysis and meaning, exolinguistics, and a final section dealt with psychological research in second language learning. The seminar met again the following year, but it was the third meeting that led to the major published report edited by Osgood (1954).

5 Frederick Agard from Cornell University, Stanley Newman from the University of New Mexico, and Thomas Sebeok from Indiana University.

6 Carroll and Richard Solomon from Harvard University, and Charles Osgood from the University of Illinois.

7 Don Dulany, a psychology student from the University of Michigan, and Leonard Newmark, a linguistics student from Indiana.
8 See Chapter 6.
9 This was later undertaken by Carroll, as detailed in Chapter 7.
10 He was at that time vice-director of the Institute of Languages and Linguistics at Georgetown. He later moved to the University of Texas, and was for many years secretary-treasurer of the Linguistic Society of America. Hill organized a day-and-a-half programme that brought together an interesting amalgam of theoretical and applied linguists. The luncheon speaker on the first day was Bernard Bloch, who presented in a brief talk his view of a unified theory of linguistic structure and linguistic analysis. On the second day, it was Norman Torrey who presented a number of anecdotes adding up to an argument for foreign language learning.
11 Starting with the 1913 committee and including the work of the Modern Language Study (Chapter 3).
12 The discussion of Thorndike's paper in the 1938 International Enquiry meeting in Dinard (Chapter 4) has good claims for forming part of the tradition.
13 The discussion there clearly was a continuation of ideas canvassed at the earlier 1951 seminar. The next major language testing meeting after Georgetown with published results was the 1961 Center for Applied Linguistics meeting. A broken series commenced in 1967 at the National Association for Foreign Student Affairs annual meeting (Wigglesworth 1967), followed by a meeting at Ann Arbor, Michigan (Upshur and Fata 1968), Idlewild (Brière 1969), and at Hasselt in Belgium in 1973, and at the TESOL Conference in Puerto Rico in 1973 (Palmer and Spolsky 1975). A third meeting in 1973 was the Washington Language Testing Symposium, held at the Georgetown Round Table (Jones and Spolsky 1975). Out of these meetings later grew the Language Testing Research Colloquium. In spite of the title of the collection, Davies (1968) was not based on papers given at the meeting.
14 The second session, chaired by George Boglum (Wayne State), dealt with technological aids; and the third, chaired by Albert Marckwardt (then at Michigan), was entitled 'Linguistics and the humanities'.
15 Carroll's life's work has been focused on this issue of isolating, as far as scientifically possible, the primary factors that make up human cognitive abilities; his book, with that title, appeared in 1993.
16 This was confirmed by Skehan (1989).
17 For fuller discussion of Carroll's work on aptitude, see Chapter 7.
18 He was later dean of the school of languages at the Foreign Service Institute.
19 One can surmise it was the Central Intelligence Agency, referred to in the linguistic literature of the day as the Department of Agriculture—

note the listing for Jacob Ornstein in the register for the Fourth Round Table (Hill 1953: 112).

20 The Iowa Foreign Language Aptitude Examination could have made a pass-fail prediction for 80 per cent of the students, while his own clinical predictions were about 0.92.

21 These may have been like the phonetic discrimination items used by Robert Lado.

22 See Chapter 8.

23 It is one that continues to plague the field, leading to the controversies over factors that involved the unitary language hypothesis (Oller 1979; Hughes and Porter 1983; Spolsky 1983; Carroll 1993) and the concern about unidimensionality expressed by Spolsky (1989b), and the work of Davidson (1988), Swain (1990), and, most recently, Henning (1992).

24 Presumably he means *g*.

25 The example Bloomfield gave was an interesting one. Two people were walking down a lane. One of them, Jill, who was hungry, saw an apple and said something. The other, Jack, fetched the apple. What Lado pointed out (recognizing the Gricean principle) was that Jack would have been right in his action even if Jill had said something like 'It's a beautiful day, isn't it?'

26 He went on to present some of the results of the use of the test, which he said correlated highly with teacher's judgements. It produces a good range of results. It correlated well (0.85) with a test of actual pronunciation. It also correlated highly with other English tests, including direct listening tests.

27 The document was 'circulated informally among a number of colleagues'. In October 1955, Carroll offered to expand and modify it for publication in the Georgetown Monograph Series, and Leon Dostert, director of the Institute of Language and Linguistics, said he would take the proposal to his committee on publications. When Carroll saw him some time later, Dostert told him they had decided not to publish, but gave no reason. Carroll (personal communication, 31 January 1992) surmises it was a problem of funding.

28 In 1948–9, proficiency examinations were developed in 20–25 languages, in order to locate Army personnel with language qualifications. Each test consisted of true-false statements and questions recorded on a phonograph record, with multiple-choice answers in English. There was a third part which Carroll did not recall.

29 The lexical component would probably explain some reported research such as Ficken (1937); Kamman (1953); Larsen, Wittenborn, and Giesecke (1942); and Wittenborn and Larsen (1944).

30 A second form would include changes in the above test that would be needed for candidates who could not read English.

31 There is a copy in Georgetown University Library that came there from the Center for Applied Linguistics; I have heard of another copy in the University of California, Los Angeles Library.

10   Language testing triumphant: 1954–1965

Maturity

If the decade 1929–39 was one of youthful exploration of the problems of objective and standardized language testing, the decade 1954–65 appears rather as a time of mature grappling with practical and theoretical issues. It was a period when an effective method of oral testing and elaborate and usable batteries of proficiency tests were developed, and the industrialization of language testing started to take firm hold. This chapter will look at the advances made in oral and proficiency tests, and note some continuing concerns about writing tests, forming a conclusion to Part One of the book and its history of the development of the objective language test. Against this background, the focus will turn to post-war tests of English as a foreign language and the associated rise of industrialized testing. Part Two, then, will describe in some detail the clash of theoretical and institutional demands that marked the origin and early years of the Test of English as a Foreign Language (TOEFL), and trace the subsequent history of that test and some parallel tests on the other side of the Atlantic. First, this chapter discusses the solution to the problem of how to reduce subjectivity in oral testing.

Speaking functionally at Foggy Bottom[1]

What is now officially known (to those who are being cautiously bureaucratic) as the *Federal Interagency Language Roundtable scale* is more familiar as the *FSI scale*, in recognition of its creation by the Foreign Service Institute[2] of the United States Department of State in 1957. The scale's genesis was the intensification of the Cold War in 1952, leading to concern over the language proficiency of government officials. Although the first attempt to use a test to encourage civil service knowledge of foreign languages failed, a beginning was made on specifying criteria for such a test. Sollenberger (1978:3), who was 'present at the creation', reported that in 1952 the Civil Service Commission was instructed, in accordance with the National Mobilization and Manpower Act, to establish a register of government officials with skills or background knowledge and experience in foreign areas and languages. As a member of an inter-agency committee charged with devising procedures for this, Henry Lee Smith, argued for differentiating between levels of knowledge, rather than just labelling people as 'fair/good/fluent/bilingual'. Smith and Sollenberger proposed the use of a test, but in the face of what some people thought was interference with the affairs of the agencies and a threat to individuals who had reported themselves on job applications as 'fluent', the committee agreed to allow each agency to conduct its own survey, using common criteria (but not testing procedures). With the ending of the Korean war and the change of administrations, the Civil Service Commission lost interest in the whole matter. The FSI, however, continued to work on developing both the scale and a related method of structured oral interview testing.

The matter was not allowed to drop, and in 1955 Loy Henderson, then Deputy Undersecretary, decided that a survey should be conducted of language skills in Foreign Service employees and insisted, in the face of opposition, that the survey be supported by testing. Foreign language proficiency would become a criterion for promotion in the Foreign Service, and the FSI, where US diplomats received their training, was instructed to design and conduct the requisite tests.

As Sollenberger (ibid.:7) remarked, this made the whole process 'serious business' for Foreign Service officials and for the Institute. Some two hundred officers were immediately tested and graded in accordance with the 1952 L1-L6 scale, but it became clear that differentiation between speaking (L) and reading was needed. Over 4,000 officers received a self-report scale to complete, but fewer than half reported themselves to be at or above the L-4 or R-3 level in French, German, or Spanish, which was then considered the level of proficiency that was 'useful to the service'. This minimum working level required that the officer have

> sufficient control of the structure of the language, and adequate vocabulary, to handle routine representation requirements and professional discussions within one or more special fields, and—with the exception of such languages as Chinese, Japanese, Arabic, etc.—the ability to read non-technical news or technical writing in a special field.
> (ibid.: 8)

Upset by these results, the Secretary of State announced on 2 November 1956 a new language policy, which stated that, because language proficiency was an essential skill for foreign affairs, every Foreign Service officer would be

> encouraged to acquire a 'useful' knowledge of two (2) foreign languages, as well as sufficient command of the language of each post of assignment to be able to use greetings, ordinary social expressions and numbers; to ask simple questions and give simple directions; and to recognize proper names, street signs and office and shop designations.

The officer's level of proficiency was to be determined by tests conducted by the FSI.

In a detailed account of the procedure published nearly two decades later,[3] Claudia Wilds (1975) listed the five unique problems faced by the FSI in devising tests for this purpose, most of them, it will be noted, practical or institutional rather than theoretical constraints. First, given that the people being tested were busy Foreign Service officers, the test of speaking and reading proficiency could take no longer than an hour. Second, the test needed to cover a wide range of ability, from that gained by 100 hours of language training or a month spent overseas to the educated native-like facility of an officer with years of experience using a language. Third, it had to be given to a wide variety of people of different ages and backgrounds. Fourth, it must apply to any language, and be easily interpretable by all involved, candidates as well as their supervisors. Fifth, it must seem valid (be felt fair) and be as reliable as possible.

The development work on the oral interview and accompanying scale took place within the FSI but in consultation with John B. Carroll.[4] While we do not know exactly what advice Carroll gave, we can get some idea from some notes that he wrote a year before, a section of which deals with scaling. The scales that did exist, were normed only in terms of percentiles; none of the standardized tests offered 'any information that would help in gauging what kinds of scores would signify near-native proficiency, what scores would signify minimal ability to conduct routine affairs in a foreign country, etc.' (Carroll 1954: 45).

Carroll was clearly starting to think about the need for absolute language scales ('quasi-absolute' was his term) of the sort that the FSI was to develop. He cited the scale proposed by Sandri and Kaulfers (1945)—the same scale had been presented in Kaulfers (1944)—favourably as 'a step in the right direction'.

There were a number of possible approaches to the scaling problem. Carroll (1954) first pointed out that the percentile scales of standardized achievement tests tell nothing about what a score means. 'For none of these standardized tests have I ever seen any information which would help in gauging what kind of scores would signify near-native proficiency, what scores would signify minimal ability to conduct routine affairs in a foreign country, etc.' (ibid.: 45). With the exception of the thesis by Villaréal (1947) none of the foreign language tests had been administered to native speakers of the language. There had been attempts at absolute measurement of vocabulary. Besides this, Sandri and Kaulfers (1946) had offered an interpretive scale for their Italian auditory comprehension test, ranging from 'Cannot understand the spoken language' through three other levels to 'Can understand popular talks, talking-pictures, ordinary telephone conversations, and minor dialectual (sic) variations without obvious difficulty as well as detect departures from normal usage.'

It is noteworthy that the centre-point on the Sandri and Kaulfers scale refers to 'routine transactions involved in independent travel abroad'.

Carroll, perhaps a little unfairly, criticized Sandri and Kaulfers for assuming that foreign language achievement is a 'unitary trait', arguing that there was need for separate scales for the different aspects. He described two methods of developing quasi-absolute scales. One would be to establish a difficulty scale (like the mental maturity scale of the Binet intelligence test) and seek expert interpretation of the meaning of the points. Another would be to norm the test on native speakers, so that one might say that a certain score is equivalent to the average achievement of third grade native children. For oral production, he recommended developing a 'controlled conversation' modelled along the lines of Sandri and Kaulfers (1945), where examinees were instructed in English to tell an Italian to do something.

In the course of conversations with Carroll, the FSI scale was modified. The symbol L was changed to S, for speaking; R remained the symbol for the reading scale, and each scale was divided into six levels, from 0 to 5. This system quickly became part of the FSI practice and jargon, since for the first time it furnished 'officially approved performance and criterion-based definitions' for teachers, testers, and test users.

The new system, Wilds believed, was usable by 1956. Sollenberger (1978) listed some of the growing pains. There was fear that standards varied from language to language—it was said to be harder to obtain an S-3 in French than in less common languages. Raters were believed to favour their own students, and to be influenced by the rank and age of the person into giving a 'compassionate' S-3. There was also concern about the influence of personality, an interesting echo of Roach's problems described earlier, his work evidently quite unknown to the American testers.

To overcome problems remaining before mandatory testing began in 1957, Frank A. Rice was appointed to head an independent testing unit,[5] which quickly developed a checklist for the S rating, consisting of five 'performance factors'— accent, grammar, vocabulary, fluency, and comprehension—each subdivided into a six-point scale labelled with two appropriate polar terms (accent from *foreign* to *native*, comprehension from *incomplete* to *complete*). In the first published description of the oral interview, Rice (1959) explained that the checklist was intended to 'counterbalance the inherent subjectivity of the testing procedure'. Wilds (1975) said that it was also intended to make sure that examiners considered each of the factors. Rice believed it also permitted showing the high degree of statistical consistency of the judges.

After she became head of the testing unit in 1953, Wilds developed a weighted scoring, which was derived by multiple correlation with the overall scoring (Wilds 1961b). In fact, as Wilds (1975: 32) says, judges were required to complete the checklist, but not to compute its results, because many of the teachers of less commonly taught languages felt suspicious of the weighting scores which had been set with Indo-European languages.

Having the checklists available did make it possible to verify that cross-language scores were more or less similar. She believed that the ratings were holistic, based on the judge's interpretation of the full definitions rather than on the statistical computation of the checklist. When the CIA adapted the technique some years later, the rating system was different. Each examiner independently made a mark on a segmented five-inch line; the lengths were measured and the rating based on the average.

The wording of definitions continued to be modified and interpreted. The issue of the + ratings led to a set of unofficial criteria (Wilds 1961a) intended to help linguists and instructors in deciding when to give a +. An S-1+, for instance, was to be given for extra ability in vocabulary, with corresponding ability to handle more complex travel and courtesy requirements, but with low knowledge of grammar making social conversation hard to deal with. Similarly, an S-2+ would be an S-3 with blatant interference from grammatical or vocabulary errors. Grammatical errors also would limit someone to an S-3+. When awarding an S-4+, examiners were to be able to cite a specific weakness; native-born and educated Americans could 'conceivably' attain S-5, and performance on the test (not biography) was to be the determinant. The checklist and the definitions served as part of the training process. As Wilds put it, 'It might be said here that successful interpretation [of the scale] depends not only on the perceptiveness of the examiner but at least as much on the thoroughness of his training and the degree to which he accepts the traditional meaning of every part of the definition' (1975: 32).

Wilds' notions of how standards were to be developed were very close to those of Roach as described in Chapter 6. She noted that examining teams varied in their practice. In some teams, only one member gave a rating and the second agreed or disagreed; in others, each voted separately; in others, further testing followed disagreement on a preliminary vote. In all cases of lack of final consensus, the rule at the FSI was for the lower rating to stand, it being felt that overrating had more serious consequences for the service.

The system was quickly accepted at the FSI for personnel decisions. The salary increases paid as 'language incentives' were no doubt influential. Even when occupying a position without a language requirement attached, a State Department officer received a two-step salary increase for each S-3 R-3 rating (or for a S-2 R-2 rating in a more difficult language), and a four-step increase for an S-3 R-3 rating in a more difficult language (Department of State 1967). One interesting problem, resolved in 1961, was the issue of establishing the proficiency of officers who were native speakers of language other than English. A memorandum by Wilds (1961b) established that all employees who rated themselves S-5 R-5 should be asked if they had had six or more years of education 'in and through the language' and six or more years living, between the ages of eight and twenty, in an area where the language was a primary one; in such cases, their grade would be certified without testing.

As the problems were worked out, the number of complaints about the system declined, Sollenberger (1978) reported. The complaints were effective, Wilds noted:

> Most of the troublesome elements have by now been removed or made tolerable by the necessity of facing them repeatedly. The articulate anger of a Foreign Service Officer who feels his career threatened by a low rating is enough to make those who give such a rating aware that they must be able to defend it, and the occasional but vigorous complaints especially in the early years, have done much to shape and refine the product.
> (Wilds 1975: 33)

It was a unique feature of the FSI Oral Interview that it was a test administered to examinees who were aware that their own rank and status in the bureaucratic structure were higher than those of their examiners. It reminds me of my own feeling, as an army private, called on to supervise an examination being taken by a class of officers: I was aware as never before of dependence on the 'consent of the governed'. In more typical examinations, of course, the examinee is completely at the mercy of the examiner.

There remained problems: the issue of acceptability of social dialects other than the standard, the problem of varying standards among examiners, the problem of obtaining a good sample of the examinee's proficiency. To deal with these problems, more elaborate training procedures, with libraries of typical testing interviews, were developed (ibid.: 34), and statistical analyses of actual testing results were carried out from time to time. In 1983, for instance, a number of changes were made in the FSI Oral Interview, that included revising the evaluation criteria (e.g. *discourse competence* was added and 'accent' and 'grammar' grouped together as *structural precision*) and performance standards were defined (e.g. imperfections could be rated as *blocking, dysfunctional, intrusive,* or *acceptable*) and the test format was revised to consist of three parts, a conversation, an interview (with the examinee as interviewer), and a five-minute briefing (Crawford, Argoff, and Adams 1983).

The FSI interview spread to other government agencies concerned with language teaching[6] and played a significant role in the Cold War. By 1968, when an interagency *ad hoc* committee met to standardize procedures, there were five agencies involved: the FSI, the Defense Language Institute, the National Security Agency, the CIA, and the Civil Service Commission (Jones 1975: 1). Use in the Peace Corps (Clark 1978b) and in schools led ultimately to its adoption by the American language teaching profession as a model for the dual purposes of curriculum control and testing (American Council on the Teaching of Foreign Languages 1982, 1986).

For all the debate and controversy that was to follow, it is worth noting that by the early 1960s there was an efficient, workable, and reliable (if expensive[7]) direct method of assessing speaking ability. With the higher motivation provided by the professional demands of government agencies, the cost was not a matter of first concern. In the less demanding domain of public education, where the deification of reliability had led to the triumph of the multiple-choice test, cheaper methods continued to hold sway.

The College Board tests in 1954: objectivity triumphant

By 1954, objectivity seemed to rule in the educational testing of modern language ability and the 'new-type' tests were now the established practice. These pen-and-paper tests were 'highly perfected', remarked Carroll (1954: 4), but there was still some public disquietude. In a continuing attempt 'to walk a tightrope between offering too little and too much information about its tests', the College Board issued a series of pamphlets in 1954 describing and illustrating their tests, but not giving 'detailed definitions of requirements' nor publishing old copies of tests, hoping to give enough detail to satisfy 'legitimate curiosity' without restricting teaching by too much specification.

One such volume described the foreign language tests (College Entrance Examination Board 1954). All the Board's language tests in 1954, it said, were objective and used multiple-choice items exclusively. In line with the recommendations of the 1927–30 Modern Language Study, testing was restricted to ability to read the foreign language. The tests were intended to measure the achievements of students who had studied the language at high school for two, three, or four years or at college for the same number of semesters. This also followed a recommendation of the Modern Language Study that the number of years of learning should not be used as a measure of language proficiency, but that proficiency must be tested. The Cooperative Tests were scaled so that the average score for two-year students (on the College Board 200–800 scale) was 460, for three-year students 520, and for four-year students 580.

The College Board recognized that many colleges would be interested in knowing about speaking and writing ability, or understanding of speech, or culture, but the restrictions imposed by a one-hour test precluded testing these aspects of achievement. Reading proficiency was, however, assumed to come closest to being a 'common core'.

The College Board had established an efficient test-writing system. For each language, committees of three college and two high school teachers, chosen to represent different areas of the United States, handled the writing and editing. All test items were carefully written and revised, and for many years had been pre-tested on sample populations. The College Board discontinued pre-testing once the testing committees found that their own estimates of difficulty were close enough to the results of trial runs. However, each test continued to be analysed and results of the analysis incorporated in new tests. About a half or a third of items were chosen for use by unanimous vote. Every test also included items repeated from previous years to keep the scoring standard level.

The test had a one-hour time-limit, and consisted of from 100 to 150 items. Candidates were warned that guessing would not help. In each of the sections, some items were easy enough for second-year students, but some were likely to be difficult even for four-year students. All tests included sections on vocabulary, 'grammar and syntax', and reading comprehension, using longish passages.

The booklet gave examples of item types. In vocabulary, candidates selected one of five English equivalents for a foreign word or phrase, the more difficult items being those that offered attractively misleading distractors. In other items, the candidate had to select a foreign equivalent for an English word. The examiners were experimenting with new types of item, such as recognizing synonyms in a set of foreign words, or selecting a word to complete a foreign sentence. For grammar and syntax, the item types included multiple-choice sentence completion, or identifying which sentence was a correct translation. Some of the reading comprehension items involved selecting an appropriate foreign sentence for a situation described in the foreign language. More usually, they consisted of questions based on texts of 100–150 words. Finally, the booklet advised students not to bother much with special preparation ('practice with objective tests is only helpful in acquainting the students with the kind of items that are used . . .') but told them that success depended on the knowledge and skills acquired in the classroom and elsewhere.

The smugness evident in this pamphlet indicates the self-confidence of the 1954 testing establishment. The tests were fair, and the examiners were so skilled that their items were always the best. What could be measured fairly (reading) was being measured fairly, and this should be enough. The testing did not interfere with the independence of teachers. Curricular experts were taking care of all problems. Any difficulties were minor and quickly brushed aside: the time-limit, the lack of pre-testing, the restriction to reading and to recognition skills. The objection to this complacency was to come not from language testers, but from the language teaching profession, especially as a result of the restoration of emphasis on teaching the spoken language that came out of changed wartime and post-war realities.

The Northeast conference: aural and oral testing

In the decade from 1954 to 1965, the progress that had been made in government-related language testing finally started to have an effect on school-related work. Following in the steps of the 1913 committee and the 1929 Modern Language Study, the work was done by committees of language teachers. The first task concerned the possibilities of testing oral–aural ability.

When, in 1954, the first published report of the Committee of Tests of the Northeast Conference on the Teaching of Foreign Languages appeared, in a paper written by the chairman, Nelson Brooks (1954), the group, carrying on the initiative of a Barnard–Yale group, had already been working on an aural test for some years. At the end of the 1952–3 school year, the committee had prepared two aural tests and tried them out in a number of schools. They showed the tests to the College Entrance Examination Board, who were 'favourably impressed' and agreed to help with statistical evaluation. One hundred items were analysed, and fifty were used in *Aural Test Form A*. Copies for proctors and students were prepared at Yale for presentation by live voice or tape recorder, and 2,000 copies of the test were distributed to ten colleges. The College Board agreed (on 23 November 1953) to include the aural test in its placement series and to start work on a similar test in German and Spanish. Sample forms were available. The sample consisted of a short conversational exchange between two people; each made four utterances. The passage was to be read aloud, followed by five questions. At a second reading, the readers paused to allow the student to check an appropriate answer on a multiple-choice form, without having seen the passage or the questions.

The new College Board test in the aural comprehension of French was described in detail in an article by Henry Dyer (1954).[8] He traced the development of the initiative, the work essentially of Nelson Brooks, from the Barnard–Yale Conference in the Teaching of French to the Northeast Conference on the Teaching of Foreign Languages. The committee's early tests were analysed, and an experimental form (Barnard–Yale *Aural Test Form A*) was put together, consisting of a script to be taped or read by an examiner, and test booklets. As a result of College Board interest, the test had been 'passed into the hand of the Board's committee of examiners in French' who might 'tinker with it with an eye to improvement' or decide to ' leave well enough alone'. The try-out as a College Board placement test would show whether administrative problems could be overcome.

In an early comment, Carroll (1954: 8) found them to have no new features and to be quite similar to the 1934 Lundeberg–Tharp audition test of French. He believed, however, that they would have a more lasting place than the tests that had been proposed for the same purpose as early as 1919.[9] Part of this optimism presumably came from the greater ease of standardization through tape recording; part from the re-established importance of teaching (and therefore testing) aural competence in foreign languages.

In 1954, the committee started work also on an oral test. It had the student read a few lines of prose (at sight and after preparation), repeat (without seeing them) a few sentences, say certain things and ask certain questions, answer some questions in the negative, and answer in sentences a few open-ended questions. The test was to be given by live voice, and answers were to be recorded. Two qualified judges were being used to rate the tape. The committee thought the test was working and seemed to be enjoyable. Finally, the committee was concerned about testing written composition: 'high on our list of desirable tests is one that will measure the student's ability to write a page of prose in the foreign tongue' (Brooks 1954: 51).

The following year, Brooks (1955) was able to report continued progress. During the year, the College Board had made extensive use of the listening comprehension test. The 1955 versions of the test were reviewed in *The Fifth Mental Measurements Yearbook*, which appeared in 1959. Walter Kaulfers, in his review of the *Cooperative French Listening Comprehension Test* (Buros 5: 265), written by Nelson Brooks and published by the Cooperative Test Division of the Educational Testing Service (ETS), was surprisingly unenthusiastic about a test that he admitted came 'much closer to being a real-life performance test than most achievement examinations produced to date'. The test was, he thought, too difficult for the large proportion of students who had had only two years of high school French, and would be better with norms based on native-speaker testing. A much warmer welcome came in a second review, this one by Kathleen Perret, an interpreter with the United Nations, who felt it to be 'a breath of fresh air' and 'a major breakthrough in the field of testing aural comprehension'. The committee had prepared a second test of this kind for placement use. The needs of younger learners had not been ignored, and Brooks (1955) reported that a language achievement test, for third-grade pupils had been prepared in conjunction with another Northeast Conference working committee, the Foreign Languages in Elementary Schools (FLES) committee. There was no reading or writing in the test, but pupils were required to respond to oral stimuli by marking pictures or drawings. The focus of the test was not on individual but on class progress. German and Spanish forms had also been prepared. With the success of the test, the Cooperative Test Division of ETS had become interested and proposed to develop the Sample Listening Comprehension test. More items had been added and pre-tested, and the test would be ready for distribution the following autumn.

Work on the speaking test continued. In such a test, each individual must perform, even if in response to a taped stimulus. Brooks recognized that this could be no amateur effort, but required major resources. 'To be effective, the speaking test must have the backing of a large testing agency, and many answers must still be found to the problem of administering and evaluating such a test . . .' (Brooks 1955: 66). By 1956, the committee felt that its work with the auditory test was complete, and it began to concentrate on the question of speaking tests.

As chairman of the committee that year, Sapon (1956) recounted exploratory work on developing 'objective measurement of oral achievement'. First, a 'philosophy' or rationale was proposed. Individual sub-tests must be pure and not be contaminated by non-oral skills. Responses must be controlled so as to be comparable. Objective scoring of responses was considered most difficult, perhaps even undesirable (taking into account the importance of the overall effect of speech), but reliability and confidence were important. A good oral test should be broad in range of applicability and sensitivity. It must represent valued goals. The language material should be 'lifelike'. It should focus on no one skill but sample a set of representative skills. English should not be used in the test, to avoid contamination or transfer effects.

Within the terms of this rationale, the test should include a number of dimensions: phonetic accuracy, at sound, word, and phrase level, and also, intonation, stress, liaison; control of structure (morphology and syntax); style (the control of idioms and nuances); and fluency (defined as continuity, absence of inappropriate pauses, absence of false starts).

A number of techniques were proposed for eliciting natural but controlled samples, including imitating or repeating a phrase or sentence, responding to commands of the sort *dites-moi, demandez- moi* and to commands to relay information, answering simple questions, and describing pictures or flash card drawings.The evaluation and assessment of responses remained a key problem, because replaying recorded answer tapes took a great deal of time. Training judges would be a major challenge too: 'While we know that trained judges can perform with relatively high reliability, the task of training all our F[oreign] L[anguage] teachers as test judges is an overwhelming one' (ibid.: 37). The answer perhaps would be local administration of the tests and central scoring by a testing agency.

The following year, the committee reported (Brooks and Sapon 1957) that the work on oral production tests had continued, and two years later, Brooks (1959) reported that the College Entrance Examinations Board would include a listening comprehension test of the type developed by the committee in its examinations starting in March 1960. The committee called for involvement of language teachers in test development: 'Test construction experts should consult more frequently and fully with language teachers concerning the forms and contents of the items they propose, and especially about the effect of the tests upon the learner' (ibid.: 56).

Brooks had a chance to put this policy into practice when in 1960 he was appointed director of a half-million dollar project under the auspices of the Modern Language Association (MLA) and funded by a contract from the United States Office of Education under Title VI of the National Defense Education Act (Bryan 1966). The purpose of the tests was to measure the language skills taught by the audio-lingual approach: separate tests were proposed for listening, speaking, reading, and writing in five languages (French, German, Italian, Russian, and Spanish), and at two levels, one corresponding to the first and second year of high school (or the first and second semester of college), and the other to the third or fourth years (or semesters). Twenty test-writing committees were formed, one for each skill in each language; each committee consisted of a college teacher, a public school teacher, and a private school teacher, with one of them a native speaker. The committees were also advised by foreign language specialists from the ETS.

The tests were functional and contextualized, and except for the English directions, completely in the foreign language, with all utterances 'natural and complete'. All spoken material was taped by native speakers. The aural comprehension section was presented through headphones and the student responses to the speaking test were recorded on tape. Tasks included sentence repetition, reading aloud, giving single sentence answers, and describing single pictures and sequences. The reading test was multiple choice, with questions based on authentic texts. Writing consisted of open-ended questions and the writing of short dialogues and paragraphs. Two parts, then, were objective, but two required subjective marking.

The new tests were trialled on 40,000 students in 1961, and about a third of the material discarded in the writing of the final forms that were administered in 1963 to 20,000 students for norming. The *MLA–Cooperative Foreign Language Tests* in French (6: 378),[10] German (6: 392), Italian (6: 402), Russian (6: 416), and Spanish (6: 426) were published in 1963. Each included four separate tests: listening, speaking, reading, and writing. Teachers were expected to score their own speaking and writing tests, but professional scoring (at a fairly high cost) was made available at the MLA–ETS scoring centre. The listening section and the speaking section were provided on tape; the speaking section was to be recorded. An instruction manual was published in 1964, but there were no norms or reliability data published.

John Clark (1965)[11] praised the *MLA Cooperative Foreign Language Tests* (7: 254) as a whole 'for their extensiveness and for the emphasis which they bring to the testing of all four language skills'. His criticisms were detailed, but not intended to detract from the place of the tests 'in present day language and teaching endeavors'. He believed, for instance, that the claims of diagnostic usefulness were overstated. The scoring service for the objective tests would not provide useful diagnostic information, and there was no such service available for the subjective sections. The tests, he believed, would be more useful for general purposes such as comparing schools, assigning students to levels, and establishing the general relative level of a student.

Looking at the various sections in turn, Clark wondered if the eschewing of English might not prevent some students from demonstrating their comprehension ability. The listening section presented sound of high quality, raising questions about its generalizability to analogous real-life situations. More serious was the possible confounding difficulty ('method effect') in the written questions on the aural text. Students who had followed an aural before a written curriculum might well be penalized. Some of the passages also included historical or geographical material that might have been studied independently. The writing test also included a good deal of reading; while it was limited in scope, it measured a number of the 'elements' considered to be writing. The speaking tests were, Clark believed, both the most significant and the least successful of the sections. It could only be administered in a language laboratory. There were serious questions about some parts of it: the sound discrimination would be hard to justify, the picture description might favour 'verbose' candidates, the reading aloud item confused modalities. The published speaking norms were largely based on a 'largely native or very fluent' set of speakers. With all his criticisms of details, Clark believed that they were a valuable advance.

There were other reviews of the *MLA Cooperative Foreign Language Tests* in *The Seventh Mental Measurements Yearbook* (1972). Michio Peter Hagiwara (associate professor of French at the University of Michigan) wrote a long review of the French test (7: 277). Like Clark, he considered the tests 'an admirable attempt to introduce innovation as well as renovation in the field of foreign language testing'. He too criticized the 'hybrid' nature of the listening comprehension, with its confounding of reading and listening. He found the speaking test 'original' and 'ingenious', but with drawbacks. Interviews, though expensive, were better ways of testing speaking. He had a number of specific criticisms of the reading section, including the basis for selecting vocabulary and idioms and the absence of stylistic analysis, a normal element in advanced classes. He was also unhappy with the writing section. He thought the tests were now ready to be revised.

The German tests were reviewed by T. F. Naumann, professor of psychology at Central Washington State College (7: 290). In spite of the complete absence of validity data, he considered them to 'set standards which deserve emulation'. One could trust, he assumed, the 'outstanding technical know-how of ETS and the specialists selected by MLA' for the validity of the content. Josephine Bruno Pane, associate professor of foreign language education at Rutgers, considered the Italian tests to be the first and only test for measuring the four skills, and excellent (7: 302).

The Russian tests were reviewed by Raymond Bair (1965, reprinted as Buros 7: 312). He too made the point about the mixture of reading and listening, mentioning his own experiences when he was required on four occasions at summer institutes supported by the National Defense Education Act to take the similar MLA Proficiency Tests for Teachers: 'I vividly recall having had much more difficulty with reading the phrases jammed with polysyllabic words that I had never seen, than with comprehending what was being said by the voice on the tape.' He found the speaking section to be 'cleverly devised' with a praiseworthy rating method. He was uncomfortable with a number of reading items that could be answered without recourse to the text, and unhappy at the balance of grammar items in the writing section. But his main pleasure at the test was in its inevitable effect on teaching: the emphasis on speaking and listening could not but communicate to teachers and students alike their importance in the curriculum.

Robert Lado reviewed the Spanish tests (7: 322), and considered them 'a major effort and accomplishment of the profession'. He saw major points in their favour: the equal emphasis on the four skills, the banning of translation, the near authenticity of items, the professional development and standardization, and (for the most part) the objectivity. He pointed out their limitations: they were general rather than diagnostic, and could not predict real-life use; in addition, the scoring of the speaking and writing sections were costly.

Generally, the MLA Cooperative tests were well received, and both contemporary reviews and one written nearly a decade later showed that they had been successful in incorporating speaking and listening as well as writing into foreign language testing.

Most significantly, these new developments, resulting from changes in the scope and goal of foreign language teaching in the United States, and led by initiatives from teachers working through their organizations, had started to challenge the power of purely objective tests. The difference between the 1954 version of the College Board test and the Cooperative Foreign Language tests published less than a decade later is striking. In the testing for foreign languages, the grip of the reliability-driven, multiple-choice testing of language proficiency seemed to have been loosened.

The Modern Language Association Foreign Language Proficiency Tests

A parallel development was taking place under similar auspices in a testing battery aimed at more advanced learners. In 1959, the construction of tests that would meet the specifications discussed earlier to capture the skills of existing or potential teachers was made possible by a contract between the US Office of Education, under Title VI of the National Defense Education Act, and the MLA.

Wilmarth H. Starr (1962), in the final report on the government funded contract[12] under which the tests were developed, recounted the history of the project. The qualifications statement provided a background to the work of the project, which began in 1959 under Starr's direction.[13]

After a preliminary review of existing foreign language tests, area committees began to meet, to modify the qualifications statements and to use them to define test objectives and specifications. A 'nationally representative cross-section of foreign language scholars and teachers within the Modern Language Association at university, college, and secondary-school levels' formed the test construction committees. For each of the seven areas (except for professional preparation, where there was single committee with a representative of each language), there were separate committees for each of the five languages (French, Spanish, Italian, German, and Russian). Each committee had a chairman (five of the thirty-one committees were chaired by a woman), and two other members. There were more than seventy-five meetings of test construction committees in 1959–60, at which sixty-two preliminary tests were developed. This massive committee effort took place in 'constant and close collaboration' with the ETS, through their 'representatives in each language and area and their testing experts'.

In the course of the extensive discussions, changes were made in the name and wording of the qualifications. The concept of 'qualifications tests' was dropped, for qualifications were seen to be the concern of states and individual institutions; the title, then, was changed to Foreign Language Proficiency Tests. This was to make clear that neither the MLA nor the Government wished to impose qualifications, but rather show 'proficiency as related to national norms'. There were a number of changes in the wording of the qualifications, too. *Aural understanding* became *listening comprehension; language analysis* became *applied linguistics*, and *civilization* was added to *culture*. Mainly, the rewording was stylistic. The speaking qualifications took this final form:

Speaking
Minimal: Ability to read aloud and to talk on prepared topics (e.g. for classroom situations) without obvious faltering, and to use the common expressions needed for getting around in the foreign country, speaking with a pronunciation understandable to a native.
Good: Ability to talk with a native without making glaring mistakes, and with a command of vocabulary and syntax sufficient to express one's thoughts in conversation at normal speed with reasonably good pronunciation.

Superior: Ability to speak fluently, approximating native speech in vocabulary, intonation, and pronunciation. Ability to exchange ideas and to be at ease in social situations.

With the help of the test construction committees, two versions of each of the thirty-one tests were prepared in 1959–60, including a good range of item types. In particular, it was desired not to 'pre-judge sensitive problems in connection with speaking and writing' (Starr 1962: 32). Thirty thousand individual preliminary tests were administered to a population studying at thirty-seven summer institutes funded by the National Defense Education Act, five academic-year institutes, and at the Carnegie Inter-University programmes and the Middlebury Italian summer school. Some 26,000 of these tests were scored. This involved printing, coding, and shipping three tons of material, and training the people who were to score the oral and written parts of the examination. These original tests required a total of six hours and fifty minutes. On the basis of item analysis, the test construction committees in connection with ETS staff developed shorter versions for the 1961 administration, in which each battery now required only three hours and fifty-five minutes.

A revised version was administered to students in National Defense Education Act-supported Institutes in the summer of 1961, and analysed. Each of the tests achieved a desired level of internal consistency: over 0.80 for each individual test (most were close to 0.90) and over 0.90 for the battery as a whole. The high internal consistency scores were as noteworthy as Thibault (1953) had predicted: 'Responsible officers of Educational Testing Service have stated that MLA test batteries are among the most valid and reliable test batteries with which the agency has ever been associated' (Starr 1962: 33).

The two tests of special concern were writing and speaking, for both had to be scored by human scorers rather than machines. In writing, the scorer reliability checks had achieved a phenomenal 0.996 (about as good as machine scoring). There was also evidence that the speaking score, rated by only one judge, was reliable. There was a 0.93 correlation in a sample study for French between scores on Forms A and B, and a correlation of 0.82 between pre- and post-tests. This was also backed up by a sample multiple correlation study. 'All indications, therefore, are that we are dealing with a reliable test in this new area of oral production measurement,' Starr (ibid.) proudly reported.

In sample studies, high correlations (ranging from 0.80 to 0.90) were found between the various linguistic sections of the batteries, but it was still felt to be advisable to maintain the separate sections, both because of the standard error, and because the measurement of individual skills was important to the profession.

The *MLA Foreign Language Proficiency Tests for Teachers and Advanced Students: French* (Buros 6: 379) were reviewed in *The Sixth*

Mental Measurements Yearbook (1965), a year after their publication, by Paul Pimsleur and James Ricks. Pimsleur, director of the Listening Center at Ohio State University, considered this to be 'a major event for the foreign language teaching profession ... the first time that this subject—perhaps any subject field—has provided a reliable standard for evaluating prospective teachers on a nationwide scale'. He pointed out that the test had been prepared by committees and so represented the profession as a whole; the French they contained was 'correct, authentic and representative'; the items were well chosen and constructed. His criticisms were minor. He noted overmuch vocabulary testing in the comprehension section, some problems in the length of one passage in the listening comprehension, some problems with the pictures in the speaking test, and raised questions about bias in the professional preparation test, and about balance in the civilization and culture test. The test marked an 'important milestone in the efforts of the US Office of Education to assist the foreign language teaching profession in upgrading the teaching of foreign languages throughout the country and at all levels'. James Ricks, assistant director of the test division of the Psychological Corporation, was more restrained in his review but also concluded that the tests could well serve as a model for other areas too.

The *MLA Foreign Language Proficiency Tests for Teachers and Advanced Students: Spanish* (Buros 6: 427) were much more harshly treated in a review by Walter Kaulfers: a 'promising attempt' but not yet up to par. The norms were too limited, he thought. There had been no attempt to provide evidence of how a native speaker would perform. The listening comprehension test was not focused, and the instructions were more complex than the items. He recognized the speaking test as a 'milestone': 'one of the first tests of speaking ability in Spanish to be produced for widespread professional use since the days of the Army Student Training Program'.[14] The scoring, however, was too difficult to be done by amateurs. Some of the reading comprehension questions could be answered without reading the passage. There were no dialogues or conversational texts in the reading comprehension. The writing test was misnamed: Part A was what used to be called an 'active vocabulary' test, and Part B tested proofreading and not composition. He also had criticisms of the contents of the other sections.

The *MLA Foreign Language Proficiency Tests for Teachers and Advanced Students: German* (Buros 6: 393) was reviewed by both Dunkel and Schueler. Harold Dunkel, professor of education at the University of Chicago, complained that he was not permitted to cite items 'for obvious reasons of test security'. Usually, with an ETS test this was not a problem because of the high standards of the work, but it made his statements about the test 'appear somewhat vague'. He thought the language sections of the test were 'good' although he was uncomfortable with the reading test. As someone who was not a 'True Believer' in the 'current received opinion' of methodology, he was afraid the professional preparation section tended to be a test of 'orthodoxy'.

In the second review, Herbert Schueler, now director of teacher education at Hunter College, was much more enthusiastic about what he considered 'the culmination of a monumental effort'. He made reference in his review to the foreign language speaking tests which had been pioneered by the United States Armed Forces Institute during and immediately after World War II, but not made available for civilian use. He was impressed by the high reliabilities achieved with the speaking test, which showed the result of 'rigorous training of, and imposition of controls on, expert raters'. The training sessions that ETS organized had achieved reliabilities as high as 0.89. In the writing test, the failure to achieve better than 0.61 inter-rater reliability on experimental free-writing items was, he believed, good justification for abandoning them.

The Italian form was not reviewed until 1970, in a review published in *The Seventh Mental Measurements Yearbook* (1971).[15] Josephine Bruno Pane, associate professor of foreign language education at Rutgers, pointed out the difficulty of writing a review almost ten years after the tests had been produced. The field had moved: in particular the professional preparation, applied linguistics, and culture and civilization sections had become dated and needed to be revised. She was far from comfortable with the other sections too; new studies, like the evaluation by Tollinger and Paquette (1966), were showing up weaknesses.

For all their wider scope, then, the MLA Foreign Language Proficiency Tests had a more limited shelf-life than all the effort that had gone into them might seem to have warranted, but they gave good evidence of high sophistication in language testing. Their requirement of human scorers made them less popular with industrial psychometrists, which is in part probably why their administration was kept so separate from TOEFL when that programme too came to Princeton. Their refusal to allow absolute authority to reliability and their insistence on a degree of subjectivity made them also less attractive as models for those who were thinking of large-scale cheap testing.

The MLA Foreign Language Proficiency Tests were intended for teachers, focusing on the needs of testing at the higher end of the range. But there remained questions about basic skills. With the enormous increase in graduate studies in the post-war period, the graduate student foreign language reading problem was exacerbated. To seek a solution, representatives of eighteen graduate schools, working under a contract between the United States Office of Education and Cornell University, were invited to develop specifications for a test that would serve the purpose. The ETS developed the tests, called the *Graduate School Foreign Language Testing Program* (Buros 6: 356). Separate tests were offered in French, German, and Russian, each containing an option in one part between biological sciences, humanities, physical sciences, and social sciences.

After field testing at thirty-seven institutions, the tests began to be offered four times a year in 1963, and met quite mixed reviews. The French and German versions were reviewed in *The Sixth Mental Measurements Yearbook* (1965). Clarence Turner, professor of Romance languages at Rutgers, recognized the difficult task undertaken by the *Graduate School Foreign Language Test: French* (Buros 6: 377) in its attempt to measure the skills of the many science students who had obtained specialized reading knowledge of French on their own or in courses focused on this goal alone. He thought section I of the test, a test of twenty-five discrete items of French structure, to be irrelevant for these students, 'bewildering and demoralizing as well'. His comments on the reading comprehension section were equally severe: the selection of passages was ingenious, but the questions were not aimed at eliciting detailed comprehension but rather involved 'following the tentacles of the author's thought'. Many correct answers were apparent without reading the text: he himself could have scored in the 63rd percentile without looking at the text. He did not recommend the use of the test.

Jack M. Stein, professor of German at Harvard University, reviewed the *Graduate School Foreign Language Test: German* (6: 391) and found it to be 'an enormous improvement' over the existing chaos. In an informal survey, he found a number of his colleagues agreed with his concern about the lack of specialization in the social science comprehension test; even divided into four areas, the selection remained too general and therefore 'dilettantish'. He was also upset to find that many of the distractors in the physical sciences sections were scientific nonsense and therefore could be rejected without reading and understanding the text. In spite of these weaknesses, he was satisfied that the test was a 'major breakthrough' compared to the 'grossly, sometimes grotesquely inadequate present practices of the graduate departments'. He looked forward to continual improvement in the tests and rejoiced at 'the happy prospect that nation-wide respectability and uniformity can at last be achieved in what has been up to now the shoddiest testing area in our entire educational system'.

More evidence of the sophistication of testing in the 1960s can be seen in the status of the tests intended for assessing the qualifications of college majors for graduate work. Nelson Brooks, who by then was associate professor of French at Yale University, considered that the authors of the *Graduate Record Examinations Advanced Tests: French* (Buros 6: 376) had met the challenge of 'the preparation of a multiple-choice test to estimate a student's fitness for advanced work in cultural and literary studies in the field . . . with resourcefulness and aplomb'. With one minor exception, they had produced a test which 'could well stand as an eloquent rebuttal to those who look upon this kind of test as intellectual heresy'. It tested, he believed, just those qualities that a candidate for graduate study would require.

The test that aroused this enthusiasm consisted of 200 five-choice items, grouped in nine sections, each with its own set of directions in English (but there was no other English in the test). The first three sections consisted of longer passages followed by several questions. The next five tested knowledge of general cultural and historical background, literary vocabulary, famous literary titles and characters, and literary history. The last required interpretation of unidentified quotations. There was a wide range of matters tested, from morphology to literary schools. All, he thought, were appropriate and representative of what would be met in graduate study of French. His one complaint was about reference to the terms 'questions and answers' in instructions for stem-and-completion items. Brooks concluded that this was 'testing at its best'.

This is not the place to deal with the case presented by those who considered such multiple-choice testing of humane knowledge to be intellectual heresy, though one might mention that the arguments are now starting to be made with some effect some thirty years later. But it is perhaps reasonable to note that what Brooks was reviewing was not so much a test of language skills as of the material taught and studied in a foreign literature department.

It is clear from the various tests described in this chapter that, by the mid-1960s, modern foreign language testing had reached a high level of sophistication. The iron grip of the new-type test had been broken, and subjective testing was once again respectable. A good start had been made on usable large-scale tests of aural comprehension in foreign languages; the testing of spoken production was possible in a limited but more or less satisfactory way, and the assessment of writing continued to conflict with the results of the deification of reliability.

The struggle, if one might use the term, between the psychometrists who backed objective testing and their opponents who favoured more creative and freer examining, tended to be focused for the main part on the issue of tests of composition ability. As Nelson Brooks noted in his review of the Graduate Record Examination in French, it was 'intellectual heresy' to some to use multiple-choice items to measure creative or humane literary ability. The problems of essay marking were the centre of much of the criticism of traditional examinations, as was discussed in Chapter 4, and continued to be a central issue in College Board testing during this period. A number of studies, including a major one, did not end the matter. Nearly two decades later, for example, Breland (1983) listed and summarized published studies of direct assessment of writing, and concluded that 'writing skill is inherently difficult to assess accurately' and that any 'assessment is labor intensive, expensive, and cumbersome' (ibid.: 20). A second major study of techniques was to be reported in Breland, Camp, Jones, Morris, and Rook (1987). With writing as with speaking, reliability proved to be a jealous god, making it hard to pay attention to other demands.

Objectivity challenged

All this history so far may serve as introduction, if you will, to the second part of the book, where the focus is narrowed from the historical progress of modern language testing to concentrate the light on a specific case of test development.

At this point of time, a summary state of the art of modern language testing—such as the one provided by Lado (1961)—would have showed the strength and professionalism of the field. It would also have revealed the success of objectivity in America and its contrasting failure in England. Voices were occasionally heard in Britain calling for reliability, but there were equally strong voices being heard in America—as in Carroll (1961)—calling for a recognition that language abilities needed to be measured integratively as well as discretely. A case was beginning to be made for testing that called for judgements rather than the counting of objective marking, and that placed a higher worth on validity than on reliability.

This being the case, the puzzle that Part Two of this book will need to explain is why it was that TOEFL, developed in the early 1960s, should turn out to be narrowly objective, reliability-driven, and resistant to the incorporation of not just later calls for communicative testing, but also the earlier understanding, traced in preceeding chapters, of the possibilities of post-modern testing. To understand this, our history will need to turn from ideas and theories to persons and institutions.

Notes

1 Foggy Bottom is the area of Washington where the Department of State is located.

2 The Foreign Service Institute was established in 1946. Dr Henry Lee Smith, Jr., was dean of the school of languages from 1946 until 1955, during which time it expanded its range of languages taught to thirty-five. He was succeeded as dean by Howard E. Sollenberger, who served until 1966, and was in turn replaced by James R. Frith.

3 There had been an earlier brief report on the test in the first issue of the *Linguistic Reporter* by Rice (1959), but it is intriguing that what Richard Lambert has recently characterized as one of the most effective (and cost-effective) interventions of a US government agency in foreign language testing went virtually unstudied for so long.

4 The fact that Carroll was consulted by his former student Claudia Wilds and others involved in developing the FSI scale, is documented by Sollenberger (1978).

5 Claudia Wilds was appointed his assistant. She later became director of the testing programme.

6 Some of this is reported in Lowe (1988).

7 Jones (1975: 9) cited James Frith as estimating that each speaking and reading test cost $35 to administer.

8 He was at the time associate director of research at the College Board and moved to ETS as research vice-president in June 1954.

9 Presumably by Handschin (1919).

10 Test references are to Buros (1975), where the tests are listed but not reviewed.

11 Reprinted in *The Seventh Mental Measurements Yearbook* (1972).

12 Report on Contract N. SAE 8349, submitted to the Division of College and University Assistance, Bureau of Educational Assistance Programs, United States Office of Education on 15 June 1962. The contract was funded under Title VI of the National Defense Education Act.

13 Starr was then head of the department of foreign languages and classics at the University of Maine, and subsequently head of the all-university department of Romance and Slavic languages and literatures at New York University.

14 His memory both of the name of the Army Specialized Training Program and of its testing history appeared to have lapsed.

15 By then, the name had been changed, so that what was earlier the *MLA Foreign Language Proficiency Tests for Teachers and Students: Italian* was now *MLA Cooperative Foreign Language Proficiency Tests: Italian* (Buros 7: 301), a name-change signalling also a change in administration procedure from internal to external.

PART TWO

TOEFL and the rise of the transatlantic English testing industry

11 English tests for foreigners: 1945–1960

English language testing at Michigan

By 1960, modern language testing in the United States had developed a high level of sophistication, and was starting to draw back from the excesses of objectivization and the unrestrained pursuit of technical reliability. This attempt at more balanced methods also marked tests in English for foreigners.

The *primus inter pares* among these tests in 1960 was the set of tests produced by the University of Michigan. In the post-war period, Ann Arbor in Michigan had joined Washington, DC, Cambridge, England, and Edinburgh, Scotland as a major centre for testing English as a foreign language, as the names of Robert Lado, David Harris, John Upshur, and Leslie Palmer who each at one time taught or studied there bear witness.

Robert Lado's pioneering work with English language tests in the years from 1946 to 1950, when he was writing the dissertation and constructing the tests that established his reputation and that of the institution, has already been described in Chapter 9. As early as 1951, a University of Michigan committee, with representation of the International Center, the English Department, and the English Language Institute, had called for establishing a prospective foreign student's level of English proficiency before the student left for the United States (Palmer 1961).

The first Michigan overseas testing programme was started in 1959, to test ten candidates a year for the School of Public Health, the cost to be paid by the World Health Organization (ibid.). The tradition of test development continued at Michigan even after Robert Lado left in 1960 to become dean of the School of Languages and Linguistics at Georgetown University. By 1961, the service had expanded, making use of 231 examiners in 101 countries and serving 105 US and Canadian universities. A student who wanted to be tested would write to the English Language Institute which would then authorize its local examiner to give the test. One problem for the service was finding local examiners. Besides graduates of the Michigan English Language Institute teacher training programme, US Government officials who were overseas, missionaries, and Fulbright scholars were also recruited to help. There was no direct check on the integrity of examiners, Palmer reported, but no reason to suspect their honesty. The English Language Institute scored the test and then sent a report and its 'recommendation' to the requesting college or university. In most cases, the candidate paid the examiner a fee of $10, $5 of which was sent to Michigan; a requesting school paid $3. In some cases, programme sponsors paid the full cost.

The Michigan Test of English Language Proficiency was, according to *The Sixth Mental Measurements Yearbook* (Buros 6: 360), written by John Upshur, Leslie Palmer, 'John' Harris (surely, David P. Harris), and Geraldine May in 1961.[1] It consisted of three parts. The first was an aural–oral rating by the examiner, based on three five-point scales (aural comprehension, pronunciation, and fluency). This rating was used as collaborative evidence only, Palmer said, for it had been found that raters varied in consistency. Second was a written composition, taking thirty minutes and set on general topics. As no satisfactory scoring grid had been developed, two of a group of four regular readers scored each composition. If there was not close agreement, a third or fourth reader was called on. The fact that there were only four regular readers, all members of the Institute staff, made for consistency. Third was the English Language Test for Foreign Students, a revised form of the Lado test. It contained 100 objective four-choice items, 40 on grammar, 40 on vocabulary, and 20 for reading comprehension. The grammar items included 11 on 'function words', such as choosing between *anyway* and *otherwise* in the following context: 'We have been waiting for you for over an hour.' 'The traffic was heavy; I would have been here 50 minutes sooner.' The vocabulary items were either selecting one of four alternatives to fill in a blank or choosing a synonym or substitute for an underlined word. Thirty of the forty words were in the 4,000–6,000 most common word range in the Thorndike-Lorge general word count. Some of the others were more specialized. The reading comprehension contained four paragraphs of about 200 words, and the items required close reading and careful interpretation.

The objective section of the Michigan test was reviewed in *The Sixth Mental Measurements Yearbook* (1965) by John B. Carroll. He was not clear after reading the manual how it was to be used in relation to the other parts, and had only validity data on the battery as a whole. He felt the items were well selected and constructed, noting that some of them seemed also to involve a 'kind of reasoning' and 'intellectual verbal ability', a contamination that was 'excusable only on the supposition that foreign students would all be of high intelligence if tested in their native language'. He believed some slower students might suffer by having the reading comprehension at the end. Carroll praised the fact that the reading comprehension questions could only be answered by reading the texts. The layout and presentation were generally satisfactory. Carroll regretted the absence of fuller statistical and normative data, and felt the standard error of measurement (around 3.4) was 'a bit too large to inspire confidence in placement based on the test'. Consequently, he was somewhat disturbed that the interpretations offered by the manual were over-precise, noting that the score bands were not much more than one standard error of measurement. He saw no excuse for not providing much more solid predictive validity data. A battery like this, he believed, needed to clarify how it measured English language proficiency and how it measured any other elements that would predict academic success. The test, in spite of these questions about its theoretical underpinnings, was, he believed, 'generally well constructed', and could be used by an experienced user to select and place non-English speaking foreign students. Such a decision, however, must also take into account speaking and understanding ability. 'It would be dangerous to use this test as a sole predictor.'

In principle, as Palmer (1961) pointed out, this had not been not intended, but one can readily imagine the possibility of short cuts taken by those who chose to look only at the objective section of the battery. The proficiency rating was based on the average of the written composition and the English Language Test. Cutting scores were based on a follow-up study of 599 Michigan students. There had been no attempt to generalize beyond Michigan. There were a number of technical problems with the test, Palmer (ibid.) reported; nearly 1 per cent of the mail was lost, and there were 'stand-ins' who took the test in place of the registered candidate. To keep test compromise to a minimum, new test forms were prepared every six months, and in larger test centres like Hong Kong, composition topics were changed frequently. The test was widely used and cited as authoritative, in spite of some concerns, and served as the model for many locally developed tests.[2]

The American University Language Center tests

A second important battery of tests was associated with the American Language Center in Washington. The earliest version of these appears to have been the *Diagnostic Test for Students of English as a Second Language* (Buros 5: 255) published in 1953 by Educational Services and written by A. L. Davis at the American Language Center of American University. The Davis test was far from satisfactory. It contained 150 multiple-choice items where the candidate was required to choose the best of three words or phrases, for example, 'They meet (at) (to) (on) eight o'clock.' The emphasis was on idioms. Items were reported to have been selected from textbooks or submitted by American Language Center teachers. There was no formal pre-testing. Reliability was claimed to be very high, and norms had been established on the basis of experience with many students at the Center. In a review in *The Fifth Mental Measurements Yearbook* (1959), Nelson Brooks said he would have invalidated about a third of the items, which contained impossible forms like 'severals' and 'gooder' or impossible collocations like 'can to write'. There was no place in a test, he believed, for spurious items. To employ them raised issues both of 'fair play' and of wrong learning. He believed a more systematically prepared test would do the job much better. A second review was written by Herschel Manuel, who characterized the test as 'the type of measuring instrument which is developed to meet a need in a particular situation and then made available to other users without sufficient descriptive material on which the new user can base an independent judgment of its value'. He noted the absence of a comparative linguistic basis such as that provided by his one-time student, Robert Lado. He concluded by saying that while the test might well have served its original purpose satisfactorily, it was not clear what it measured nor how idiom knowledge related to other aspects of language ability.

There was improvement when David Harris, in Florida after his time at Michigan and after a spell at ETS, was invited to come to Washington to work with A. L. Davis. By the time he arrived, however, Davis had left, so that Harris took charge of the test development work that followed. The Center later prepared tests for two American Government agencies, the International Cooperation Administration (which became the Agency for International Development (AID) in about 1961) and the Department of State Bureau of Cultural Affairs, to be used for overseas screening of applicants for their various programmes (Harris 1961a). The tests were intended specifically for use with government-sponsored students, and not for the general run of students applying for student visas. The State Department did, however, make an early version of the usage test available for 'service' testing for US universities.

The most widely used American University Language Center test[3] was a combination of the English Usage Test and the Aural/Oral Rating Sheet,[4] based on an oral interview, similar in many ways to the FSI interview described earlier. There were three forms of the English Usage test available in 1961. It consisted of 150 three-choice items, although later forms would contain 100 items. The test took seventy-five minutes; it was scored with correction for guessing (the final score was the number of items a candidate answered correctly minus half the number of items that were answered wrong). One new test form was added each year. In accordance with standard psychometric practice, items were pre-tested, with the content based on typical student errors in classes. The items in Form D, for example, tested nouns, adjectives, and pronouns (20 per cent), sentence structure and word order (18 per cent), verb tenses and modals (44 per cent), and idiomatic usage (18 per cent). There had been some predictive validity studies. For the Aural/Oral Rating Sheet, two interviewers conversed with the candidate separately and rated his or her performance on a six-point scale for comprehension, pronunciation, grammar, vocabulary, and general speed of speech. In one trial at American University Language Center, an inter-rater reliability of 0.76 had been reported. One form of a Vocabulary and Reading Test (25 general vocabulary, 10 two-word verbs, and 25 reading comprehension items) was also available.[5]

Still in preparation in 1961 was a Listening Comprehension Test,[6] to be presented on tape or read aloud, and consisting of forty short questions and answers followed by a multiple-choice interpretation. Harris claimed that the listening test looked promising, and would make up for difficulties of reliability with the interview. In commenting on the battery as it was in 1961, Harris noted that there were diversified needs it did not meet; in particular, it lacked a writing sample.

The two testing programmes so far described are evidence of the mature state of the art in practical testing in 1961. Each used as its core a multiple-choice objective test of selected language items, following thus the discrete-point approach which, Carroll (1961) argued, was good but needed to be supplemented. Each also included a significant integrative section, for both required an oral interview, and Michigan incorporated a written composition. Technologically, then, they shared much with the modern language tests being developed at the same time, but were locally produced rather than the work of national committees or institutions.

Lackland Air Force Base

A third 'local' testing programme running in 1951, and described at the 1961 conference that will be the topic of the next chapter, was the one used by the US Air Force, under the direction of Sidney Sako. Sako had received his doctorate from the University of Texas, where he, like Lado before him, had studied test construction with Professor Herschel Manuel.[7]

English proficiency tests were used at Lackland Air Force Base, which served as the Department of Defense's language teaching institution,[8] to determine the level of students on entrance to courses and on completion of them. Comprehension tests were also used overseas for selection purposes. In the last six years, the School had developed sixty different forms and levels of tests (Sako 1961b).

There were two main kinds of tests used at the Center, Sako reported. The Fundamental English proficiency tests, which included vocabulary, idioms, complex sentences, word order, and grammatical usage, were used for entrance examinations and for progress testing; and there were three Technical English proficiency tests in use in 1961, one for each of technical flying, technical air traffic control, and technical ground control-intercept. All items used were multiple choice and objective. Ideally, tests were pre-tested with at least a hundred subjects. A full validity study was carried out when possible.

The main problems that Sako noted were the compromising of tests (cribbing); distortion by students who wanted to stay in language school; the problem of scheduling experimental tests; and the testing of oral proficiency. This last was one of the issues on which research was underway;

others were the development of a diagnostic language test, classification tests for lower groups, the effect of technological background, and the importance of contrastive analysis.

Sako's report confirmed the high standard of professionalism evidenced in the early 1960s by American English language test constructors, and the close relationship between practical test writing and research in these three institutions. Such high standards were not always achieved, as may be seen from another test from this period, one probably typical of the kind being developed at the time by many teachers of English as a foreign language with little training in psychometrics, and untypical only in that its publication exposed it to review in Buros. *An English Reading Test for Students of English as a Foreign Language* (5: 258) was written by Harold V. King and Russell N. Campbell and published in 1956 by Washington Publications. This test, it appears from the review in *The Fifth Mental Measurements Yearbook* (1959), had been prepared for use in the Costa Rican American Cultural Center. King, a structural linguist from Cornell University, and Campbell, trained as a high school Spanish teacher, spent two years together in the Binational Center, King as director and Campbell as director of studies (Russell Campbell, personal communication, 9 February 1944). The test had been developed to meet local needs and consisted of fifty multiple-choice items, the first eighteen essentially vocabulary and the last thirty-two paragraph meaning, with the texts in common, everyday English. Neither of the reviewers, Ralph Bedell and John A. Cox, Jr., thought the test, coming as it did without statistical data on reliability or validity, could be used by others usefully. Bedell pointed out that the fact that there was a single form made it likely to be insecure. Cox thought it to be too short for screening, and usable only in a controlled research situation. Campbell has told me (personal communication) that the test seems to still be in use. Occasionally he receives a royalty payment, and more often, is recognized by someone at an English teachers' conference as the author of a test they have used. The development of the King–Campbell test is interesting in the light it casts on language testing at the end of the 1950s. Neither of the authors was at the time trained as a language tester. King's background as a linguist and Campbell's as a high school Spanish teacher, however, gave them the rudimentary skills to put together a more than reasonable working test. Campbell later went to Michigan, where he studied with Fries and Lado, and presumably was introduced by the latter's book on language testing to the principles behind his earlier amateur practices.

In the three professional centres, things were different. Reading Sako's report alongside those by Harris and Palmer shows that they all fully accepted psychometric principles. All would no doubt have agreed with a 1952 Test Service Bulletin that Sako sent me: 'It is a statistical and logical fact that no test can be valid unless it is reliable.' The weight of decision fell on objective tests, where reliability could be most easily satisfied, and the measurement of the more global skills of speaking and writing was seen as a problem not yet solved.

Only the Lackland group, with a testing programme well integrated into their teaching, seemed fully satisfied with what they had. For Harris and Palmer, their institutional tests were as good as they could make them, but with serious limitations that cried out for further work. In particular, they felt they lacked the institutional backing to deal with administrative and technical problems and to carry out the pre-testing and detailed analysis they knew was needed. They were to be given an opportunity for this, as we will see in later chapters.

British testing in the post-war period

A description of British Commonwealth English testing by MacKenzie (1961)[9] at the 1961 Washington Conference[10] that will be the central topic of Chapter 11, reveals a quite different picture from the US local tests that have been described so far. Only one of the tests that he described sounds like the American tests, and that was the Australian Commonwealth Office of Education Objective English Proficiency Test, which consisted of a battery of seven multiple-choice or objective tests. While copies of the test are not available in Australia (I was told that they were 'sealed in the archives' for another thirty years), I have been able to see the copy of the test and the accompanying records that Leslie Palmer has kept from the 1961 conference. It is indeed very similar to the Lado test.

MacKenzie saw major problems with using what he characterized as 'Lado tests' for the students he and his colleagues worked with in former British colonies. First, the tests contained many Americanisms,[11] and second, 'to those who have not grown accustomed to ticks and brackets, the tests present a mechanical hazard which almost eclipses their ability to hear or read the test sentences'. Finally, MacKenzie was concerned at the likely diversion of attention from composition to objective test exercises, and the consequent undesirable effects on instructional practice.

The major British examinations that MacKenzie (ibid.) described, then, represented the traditional examination approach rather than the psychometric. The University of London Certificate of Proficiency in English for Foreign Students (CPE), he said, 'has perhaps the highest standards of any such test in the Commonwealth. To obtain it, a foreigner must be able to speak and write "more like an Englishman than not." ' It was intended for prospective teachers of English, but dealt only with linguistic skills. As it was controlled by linguists including T. F. Mitchell (School of African and Oriental Studies), it also stressed knowledge of theoretical and practical phonetics.

The examination for the London certificate consisted of two parts: Part I was a two-hour essay; a set of open-ended questions on the grammar of literary and colloquial English; and a half-hour orthographic dictation. Part II was the test of spoken English, but it too was mainly done in writing: a one-hour composition in colloquial English and some questions calling for the use of colloquial expressions in context; a two-hour phonetics paper; and finally, an oral examination that called on the candidate to read aloud and converse on three standard works by English authors. To receive the certificate, the candidate had to pass the oral examination as well as the written sections.

Translation tests, MacKenzie reported, were a problem. London did not include translation in its proficiency tests, but Cambridge offered to handle twenty languages. British universities required that foreign applicants pass the General Certificate Examination in English intended for native speakers at the Ordinary level,[12] or take one of the special certificate examinations for foreigners. MacKenzie discussed controversies at British universities concerning the poor quality of English of its students, foreign and otherwise. He referred in particular to the ongoing development of a Use of English test for native speakers, intended to replace the hitherto compulsory Latin paper for entrance to Oxford and Cambridge, and to 'reveal whether the candidate has the kind of mind which would profit by a university education'. The examination, proving difficult to devise, would have a pass-fail grading.

MacKenzie also gave details of tests in other Commonwealth countries. An American testing expert was reported to be helping the Central Institute of English at Hyderabad to improve multiple-choice comprehension and grammar tests being devised to replace traditional essay examinations. In Africa, various experiments with objective tests were under way, and MacKenzie expressed the need for a test that was 'thorough in scope, and yet more easily and reliably marked for large numbers of candidates'.

The picture that emerged from MacKenzie's account was of a well-entrenched set of traditional examinations, facing pressure from the field for practical and theoretical reasons: the need for something suitable for less élite students, the concern for reliable measures, together with the problem of large numbers of students. In West Africa, there were to be major changes within five years, but the home country remained less open to innovation. Some years later, Grieve (1964) wrote a highly sophisticated report proposing a number of major changes in the English examination in West Africa that included two kinds of composition (one compulsory), a test of letter-writing, more reliable marking, multiple-choice objective testing of comprehension and grammar, and a compulsory oral test. Grieve's short bibliography includes the 1953 Georgetown Round Table report, Carroll's (1954) mimeographed notes, Lado (1961), the report of the 1961 Center for Applied Linguistics meeting, and two articles by Wilmarth Starr. The innovations he proposed were to be adopted for the 1966 examinations. His rcport is evidence that there were many British applied linguists who shared American concerns for psychometric developments. But many British examination boards remained virtually impervious to the new influences. Such was the case with the Cambridge English examinations.

The Cambridge examinations in English after 1945

In earlier chapters, the development of English language testing at Cambridge until the end of World War II has been sketched, and the story is now taken up at the point where it left off in Chapter 6. With the ending of the war, Nalder Williams retired as secretary of the Board. There ensued a period of somewhat unpleasant Cambridge politics. The appointment was first offered to his deputies, John O. Roach and William Brereton jointly. At one stage during these negotiations, it was suggested to Roach that he might want to take a separate post as secretary for the examinations in English as a second language, but an offer from the Civil Service Commissioners and the promises of later positions were too appealing, and Roach followed his wife's advice to go where he was wanted (Roach, 1986). 'Of course they treated you abominably', was the comment of Roach's new colleague at the Civil Service Board, Charles P. Snow. Readers of Snow's novels on life in Cambridge will be able to imagine some of the machinations that took place.[13] Brereton succeeded to the secretaryship, and the English examinations were left in less capable hands. In a letter[14] to Roach written in 1976, the then-ninety-one-year-old Sydney Grose, commented on the 'furious differences' over the selection of secretary, and the fact that years later, Stanley Bennett, who had led the opposition to Roach, conceded his error. 'You were quite right: Roach was the man we ought to have taken', he is said to have told Grose.

   The 1945 examinations, then, were the last for which Roach was directly responsible. The English Language with Literature paper took three hours. The required first question consisted of a reading passage dealing with foreign students at an English university. Candidates had to summarize it and explain the meaning of underlined words and phrases. They then could choose any four out of thirteen questions, which offered a wide range of options: a letter or composition, a paraphrase of a passage of blank verse from Shakespeare, a description of a man on the basis of a description of his house, the correction of some ungrammatical sentences, the recommendation of two books of English literature, an essay on love stories in English, an essay on Shakespeare's view of tragedy or comedy, a consideration of Wordsworth's view of the aim of poetry, an essay on what is characteristically English about English literature, or about English principles, or about English cookery, or about Englishmen's propensity to take their pleasures sadly.

It is clear from the kind of questions set that the objective question had no place in the thinking of the Cambridge examiners. The English Literature paper had questions on the prescribed texts, which included such modern writers as Aldous Huxley and E. M. Forster. The Survey of Industry and Commerce paper (UCLES Certificate of Proficiency in English examination paper, Thursday 14 June 1945) required students to answer six out of twelve questions, such as

 2 Why does capital occupy a position of such great importance in modern industry and commerce? How is capital obtained by a public joint-stock company?
 11 Distinguish between Customs Duties and Excise Duties, and justify the need for both.

The English Life and Institutions paper (UCLES Certificate of Proficiency in English examination, Thursday 14 June 1945) required responses to five or six out of fifteen questions, such as

 1 What do you consider to be the *real* powers of the English Crown as distinct from its *legal* powers?
 6 Explain why 'mandated territories' were created after the last war (1914–1918) and give an account, with illustrations, of **two** types of such territories.
 14 What are the elements in the British character which, in your opinion, have made the British so successful as colonial pioneers?

Examinations like these were invitations to the candidates to display their linguistic prowess in a variety of formally proscribed situations. The examiner was then expected to apply educated and moderated judgement in order to arrive at a fair and equitable decision on the standard that had been achieved. While we have no detailed account of the concern taken within the system to assure that this moderation worked in written examinations, we can see from his work on the oral examination the kind of care that Roach considered must be taken to make these judgements as fair as humanly possible.

For 1945, for example, there were two alternative reading passages for the oral examination and a dictation passage. Oral examiners received copies of Roach's (1945) study, revised mark sheets and instructions, and a heading for their reports. They were invited to describe (1) the general conditions of the examination (Was it better to give the reading first? Was it possible to prevent communication between candidates? What was the average time? Would more time be an advantage?); (2) the reading test (Did two separate reading tests help? What did the examiner listen for in each? How would the examiner define the degree of proficiency expected at the different levels? Were any of the early candidates retested?); (3) the conversation (What degree of fluency and range of vocabulary was expected at each level? Were questions based on the reading passage? Were all candidates asked the same questions? What was the balance between questions requiring short answers and those encouraging free conversation? Did specific questions test specific vocabulary, the use of tenses, the knowledge of numerals, days of the week, and English names of countries? What do you suggest as a syllabus to define the range of the conversation test?); (4) the standards for the test as a whole (Would examiners prefer that standards be suggested or fixed? Should the standards be the sum of the various parts of the test? Should a candidate pass after failing one section of the test?); and (5) the dictation (Manner and speed of reading? What is it designed to test? What should be the principles of marking?). Examiners were also invited to comment on Roach's report, to report on any experimental testing, and testing of joint examining, to make general suggestions for improvement, and to suggest 'semi-oral' tests. It is evident from this that Roach was planning to continue his ground-breaking research, and that the Cambridge test suffered from his resignation.

The minutes of meetings of the Joint Committee on English Examinations, established by the University of Cambridge Local Examinations Syndicate (UCLES) and the British Council in 1941,[15] provide some sense of the attitudes of the examiners. Most of the discussions were routine approval of examiners and testing centres, but others were more interesting. On 21 November 1945, there was a report of a standardization meeting of examiners in Egypt; a year later, there was a report of difficulty in finding someone to set a translation paper for Syriac. In March 1947, there was discussion of the commercial bias for some items. It was decided to continue research into the standardization of oral tests, and to begin research into methods of testing knowledge of English. The possible use of gramophone records was discussed in the July meeting of that year. In 1950, it was agreed to use the General Service Word List as a guide for the Lower Certificate. In June 1951 a proposal was made to include a Use of English paper for all candidates.

In October, there was further discussion in which it was made clear that grammatical terminology was not to be tested. Experiments were to be made in the 'objective' methods of testing reading. The word 'objective', it should be noted, remained in inverted commas in the committee's minutes for some years.

In April 1952, the committee was informed that the Use of English paper had been tried out in Portugal. A request was noted for phonetics to be tested again. The 1953 meeting considered modifications to the Certificate language paper, and opined that candidates should not be failed because of weakness shown in the translation examination in their native language.

The 1955 examination had a compulsory three-hour Use of English paper in the afternoon. Question 1 was a reading passage followed by a number of comprehension questions. Other questions (candidates were to answer all but one) involved rewriting sentences and paragraphs, showing the effect of punctuation changes, correcting errors in a passage (and saying why they were wrong), describing objects, and showing knowledge of prefixes. Before this, in the morning, candidates could choose among a number of papers: English Language (a passage for summarizing and a formal essay—the topics included: 'The ordinary man' and 'The customer is always right'); English Literature (a wide choice of questions); Survey of Industry and Commerce ('Describe a suitable method of insuring a valuable cargo of radio and television sets to be sent from London to New York'); English Life and Institutions ('What are the principal outdoor recreations of the English schoolgirl? How do they compare with those in your own country?'); and English Science Texts (summarizing a passage, paraphrasing another, and writing an essay on a topic such as 'Give an account of poisons produced by animals'). For the Oral Examination, there were six possible reading passages. With this number of options available, the chance of achieving anything like minimal psychometric equivalence, let alone internal or inter-rater consistency, was obviously nil. With regular moderation and constant meetings of examiners, however, some degree of fairness would be possible.

Not everyone was satisfied with the Cambridge dominance over English language testing. By 1956, John Roach, by now at the Ministry of Education and involved with education in Europe,[16] prepared two documents for an Inter-Departmental Committee on the Teaching of English Abroad claiming that there were signs that the Cambridge mechanism was not filling all of the needs for English language testing. In the first memorandum, Roach (1956a) set out the history of examinations in English as a foreign language, pointing out that the main brunt of development had fallen on Cambridge. For a while, the British Council had subsidized their programme (but never by more than £1,400 a year), but since 1955, the programme had been self-sufficient. It continued to grow, with an increase of between 12 per cent and 21 per cent for each of the last five years, the total in 1954 being over 15,000 candidates.

While former colonies were slowly taking responsibility for their own school leaving examinations, reducing the overseas demand for the Cambridge Overseas School Examinations, the examination in English was not 'felt as a tutelage' but a test in a skill and 'who better to test it than an English examining body backed by a world famous name?' With this continued growth, it might well be prudent, Roach felt, to consider adding a second examining body to assist UCLES. He argued for the newly established Joint Examining Board of the Universities of Bristol, Exeter, and Southampton; they would be in a good area also to attract foreign students.

Roach recognized the attractiveness of controlling examinations: 'Examinations are an unusual element in cultural work abroad, in that they pay their way, once established, and are also a source of revenue and influence through the sale of text-books.' UCLES had no 'profit motive', but saw the value of maintaining fees at a level that would cover development costs and related fields. He even envisioned local examinations secretaries abroad as politically useful substitutes for British Council officers where there was 'political prejudice' against the Council.

In a second memorandum written four months later, Roach (1956b) cited in support of his arguments the fact that at the Joint Committee meeting in May, the British Council staff in at least one European country had reported that they could cope with no additional centres. The Secretary of UCLES had raised the suggestion that in the foreseeable future it might be appropriate to decide in some countries that the 'first phase of encouraging the study of English is over', and that attention might be turned to raising standards, which would mean withdrawing the Lower Certificate. Roach's comment on this was as follows:

> It is true that about 1929 I formed the modest ambition of making English the world language. I was not alone, and some of my most satisfying memories are the plans and dreams I shared with e.g. I.A. Richards and C.E. Carrington. But from the outset my basic concept was the reaffirmation and extension of British influence, in reaction against the limp and creedless spirit of the late twenties, a spirit which has recently become a subject of historical appraisal. Let it be said frankly that English may now become the world's second language without the help of Cambridge examinations, and that the encouragement of the study of English is no longer synonymous with the spread of British influence, if ever it was. English is an instrument and as such could just as well favour the spread of American influence, or even Russian and anti-British influence, if, e.g. Russia floods a foreign country with cheap text-books (as I understand is happening, or may happen, in Indian and Pakistan). The cardinal consideration now is, how far the examinations themselves can be used to turn people's thoughts, not merely to English, but to England; how far, that is, they can best serve as an *instrument of cultural and even commercial influence.* (emphasis in original)
> (ibid.)

There is an interesting echo of this in I. A. Richards' comments at the 1961 Anglo-American Conference (British Council 1961):

> An important consideration here is that English, through its assimilations, has become not only the representative of contemporary English-

speaking thought and feeling but a vehicle of the entire developing human tradition: the best (and worst) that has been thought and felt by man in all places and in all recorded times. It is equally the key to the prodigious mysteries the swift oncoming years will bring upon us.
(cited by Phillipson 1992: 167)

I am grateful to Robert Phillipson for drawing my attention to this conference and to Richards' role in it. I suspect, though, that Phillipson exaggerates somewhat in considering this as such egregious 'imperialism' as he does. Note, for instance, that Richards acknowledged that the power of English is to be attributed to its having borrowed so freely—one senses here none of the chauvinism associated with more puristic claims for the greatness of a language like French—and argued that it records the good and the bad. Even if the young Richards and Roach had imperialistic plans, they appear not to have ever had major success in persuading the establishment to support their implementation.

Roach (1956b) was arguing for a new examining body because he felt that UCLES itself had tended not to take the English examinations seriously, and would be unlikely to 'appreciate the need for a drive for cultural expansion'. Nor did UCLES have high priority itself in Cambridge, where the college-centred system considered it to be marginal. It lacked financial incentive; it paid its way, and was a source of occasional capital for the university.

Roach concluded with a restatement of the potential value of English and of the examinations as a method of maintaining cultural influence 'without the need for public funds'. While Roach saw the value of adding the 'encroaching power' of examination to the service of what Phillipson (1992) labels as linguistic imperialism, the effects of what he proposed only came later, in much changed circumstances, and in spite of rather than because of official British efforts.[17]

The response to Roach's initiative was minimal. The major issue at the Joint Committee's meeting in 1956 was whether to continue to include a book of modern verse in the Certificate of Proficiency examination. To allow more time for discussions like this and relieve the Joint Committee of excessive routine business, at the May 1957 meeting, it was decided to set up an Executive Committee, consisting of four Syndics, two representatives each of the British Council and the schools, one representative of the London Educational Authority, one university teacher of English as a foreign language, and one or two examiners to handle the establishment of examination centres the appointment of examiners.

At its first meeting in November 1957, the new committee had its role explained. Some 20,000 candidates had applied for the two examinations in December. The committee learnt that more guidance was needed for the oral examiners, who should try not to be influenced by the intelligence of the candidates, or ask questions requiring factual knowledge or literary judgement. Roach was not invited to the Executive Committee, where the basic study of oral examinations he had written a decade earlier now seemed to have been forgotten, but continued to attend the Joint Committee.

At the May 1958 meeting of the Executive Committee, Professor J. A. Noonan reported on modifications being tried in the first part of the English Language paper, with comprehension questions being used in place of the précis. The Joint Committee in June 1958 learnt of an investigation of the problems of oral examining. When the Executive Committee met in November, it decided that Shakespeare was no longer to be compulsory in the literature paper. In May 1959, it made a further change to the literature paper, dropping Part II (a second set of optional essays). At that meeting, it was decided to prepare a draft phonetics paper and to raise examination fees.

A year later, in its June 1959 meeting, the Joint Committee had an opportunity to consider new developments in testing techniques, and I cite in full the item from the minutes:

> The possibility of using 'objective' tests was briefly discussed, and it was agreed that this should be borne in mind in future. The possibility might well be a limited one, however, since examining bodies using such tests in English language use a test in composition of the type set by the Syndicate, and some of the Syndicate's questions (e.g. on the meaning of words and phrases) resemble 'objective' questions to some extent.

The comment is an interesting one, showing that the committee members had very little appreciation of the problems that objective testing (with 'objective' still in inverted commas) was intended to deal with. They clearly lacked the sophistication that had been developed across the Atlantic in members of the College Entrance Examination Board by their professional staff since the 1930s, and were deaf to any advice offered by British applied linguists.

The 'objective' question issue came back to the Joint Committee at its June 1960 meeting, in which specimens of the examination of the English Language Institute of the University of Michigan, and the syllabus of the programme of the American Language Center of the University of Pennsylvania were received and briefly discussed. The Committee remained quite unimpressed. This event appears to have followed a visit reported to have been made to UCLES in 1960 by Robert Lado, who met there, Shephard (1989) reported, the people in charge of the English examinations: T. S. Wyatt, a modern language don who had been assistant secretary since the 1950s, and his two assistants, Marie Overton and Janet Birchnall-Wild. Shephard believed that UCLES staff (and perhaps the committee members) expressed some surprise at the American English in the tests. In any case, they did not change their methods of testing. However, Wyatt did make a visit in 1960 to ETS in Princeton, and Overton and Birchnall-Wild were sent the following year to Edinburgh to meet some of the applied linguists there. One result was that John Sinclair was appointed to the Executive Committee in 1963, and another applied linguist, Peter Strevens,[18] was appointed some years later. Strevens casts some light on this attitude of UCLES to psychometric principles:

> I had acquired a reputation for saying publicly that the UCLES exams, FCE and CPE, were already old-fashioned and should be modernized . . . After two years with no visible signs of change in the exams being accepted, I rebelled, at a stormy meeting where the Chairman, with the full approval of the committee, said to me that the reason why the Cambridge exams should not be changed was that '. . . they force the teacher to teach according to the best possible methods'.
> (Strevens 1989: 5)

In May 1961, the Executive Committee learnt of the failure of the new punched card readers to produce lists in time. In November, it decided to drop the literature period requirement; as of 1965, there would be twelve texts: a Shakespeare play and six other works of English literature written before 1900, and five after. The committee was also informed that examiners did not penalize the use of 'normal American spelling and usage', but that this concession would not be listed in the regulations. In 1962, the committee rejected a proposal from the British Council to increase the proportion of post-1900 literature texts.

The committees continued to fight a resolute battle against what I would designate as scientific testing and against associated notions from applied linguistics. Finally, in June 1962 the Joint Committee reluctantly agreed to inquire about the demand for a 'more purely linguistic type of exam'. At its meeting a year later, the words 'more purely linguistic' in the minutes of the 1962 meeting were replaced by 'more flexible'. However, a letter seems to have already been sent out using the unwanted term. In October 1961, the Executive Committee was informed that forty-nine centres supported a purely linguistic examination, twenty-six had some hesitations, and fourteen opposed. As a result, a new syllabus was proposed, with a compulsory English language paper and a choice of any two out of literature, use of English, and translation. A subcommittee was set up to consider 'synthetic and analytic items'. It was further decided to consult John Trim, an applied linguist at the University of Cambridge, about oral examinations. In May 1964, the report of discussions with Trim established that a more systematized form of oral testing would require fairly extensive research.

At the same meeting, a subcommittee reported on a new form of the examination to be introduced in 1965. Major changes were proposed. In the English language paper, composition would be reduced from 60 per cent to 50 per cent, and the formal précis would be replaced by comprehension questions and an informal summary. The Use of English paper would include 'a series of short analytic tests of basic linguistic skills' (60 per cent) and longer questions including varieties of English (40 per cent). It also called for:

> Further research to be done into tests of 'objective' type, as a matter of urgency, with a view 1) to finding out the linguistic skills which could be most satisfactorily tested objectively and 2) to building up batteries of tests which could be used in the Use of English paper.

In July 1964, the Joint Committee approved the revised syllabus, with literature now an option. The following year, the committee was informed that UCLES had set up a research committee. John Roach, now retired from the Civil Service, had started work on a revised oral examination that included prepared topics, such as were being used for O level French.

The barbarians were finally let inside the gates in 1967, when a revised Lower Certificate examination syllabus for 1970 was approved, which included multiple-choice items in an optional language test. A staff member with psychometric training was finally added to the UCLES staff in 1970, when E. F. Chapen was appointed research officer.

Chapen immediately started to make his presence felt, just as Carl Brigham had when he joined the College Entrance Examinations Board over forty years earlier. The following year, he criticized the absence of 'a substantial compulsory element of objective testing as a yardstick for the assessment of candidates' and 'incompatibility, in terms of measures of attainment, of the present range of optional tests'. The absence of inverted commas around the word 'objective' supports the notion that psychometrics had at last made its way into UCLES, but as it turned out, it was to have no easy way once it was through the doors.[19]

In 1960, then, British testing of English as a foreign language, in spite of the psychometric sophistication of British applied linguists, did not offer a model for those faced with the problem of creating effective and efficient tests of English for prospective foreign students. The continued concern about curriculum rather than proficiency, the confusion of trait and method, and the failure to develop any theoretical basis for moderation, meant that the newer tests developed at Michigan and American University provided much better models than longer-established Cambridge examinations.

Notes

1 The manual was prepared by the Division of Testing and Certification of the English Language Institute in 1962, and distributed by Follet's Book Store.

2 The *Michigan English Language Assessment Battery* has continued to exist, and is available in revised form.

3 The *English Usage Test for Non-native Speakers of English* (Buros 5: 259) was written by A. L. Davis and Kenneth Croft, first published in 1955 (Form A), revised in 1957 (Form B) by Washington Publications, and available for distribution only to the International Cooperation Agency or the International Educational Exchange Service of the US Department of State. There were a number of later forms: Form C appeared in 1958, with Harry Freeman added to Davis and Croft as author; Form D appeared in 1960, the work of David P. Harris and Winifred D. Jones; Form E was issued in 1961, written by Harris; and Form E appeared in 1962, the work of Harris and Leslie A. Palmer (Buros 6: 358).

4 The *Oral Rating Form for Rating Language Proficiency in Speaking and Understanding English*, also called the *AULC Interview Rating Form* (6: 363) was prepared by David Harris in 1959 and revised in 1962.

5 *A Vocabulary and Reading Test for Students of English as a Second Language* (Buros 6: 363) had appeared already in 1960 and another form was written in 1962 by Harris and Palmer for the Agency for International Development and the Department of State.

6 The *Listening Test for Students of English as a Second Language* (Buros 6: 359) was later published in two forms by the American Language Institute (Form A in 1961 and Form B in 1962). Written by Harris and Palmer, it was restricted to the Agency for International Development and Bureau of Educational and Cultural Affairs of the US Department of State (Buros 6: 239).

7 Other teachers of his were Professor Pierce-Jones who taught courses in psycholinguistics and Professor Benjamin Fruchter who taught advanced statistics, factor analysis, psychological scaling theory methods, and educational psychological measurement (Sako 1991). Herschel Manuel, as noted earlier, was author of the Inter-American Tests, and one of the three people to whom Robert Lado dedicated his 1961 book, *Language Testing*.

8 The Air Force and Lackland focused on teaching English to foreign service personnel, while Monterey (under Army control) specialized in teaching foreign languages to US personnel.

9 It should be noted that MacKenzie did not attend the conference; British interest was represented by D. P. Martin of the British Embassy. According to the agenda of the conference, this paper was submitted by MacKenzie and G. E. Perren. The paper certainly seems to have been co-authored by George Perren, founding director of the British Council's English Teaching Information Centre and later of the Centre for Information on Language Teaching and Research; in any case, it seems clear that the paper builds on Perren's extensive experience in East Africa.

10 From its beginnings, the Center for Applied Linguistics had recognized its common interests with the British Council and its potential partnership with the other major organization sponsoring or exploiting the spread of English. In May 1959, it convened a conference on the topic of teaching English abroad (Center for Applied Linguistics 1959), to which the British Council sent five representatives. A second meeting was organized by the British Council two years later (British Council 1961). In organizing the 1961 testing meeting, then, it was natural that the organizers should invite the British Council to send someone to describe the state of British Commonwealth English language testing.

11 I have been told by Bill Shephard that it was the Americanisms rather than the objective items that so shocked the Cambridge testers during Lado's 1959 visit to UCLES. The nature of the problem may be illustrated by the fact that at the 1989 meeting of the Advisory Committee on the Cambridge–TOEFL Comparability Study, British testers were surprised to learn that the Americans present did not know what a doctor's *surgery* mentioned in the test item was, because they called it a doctor's *office*.

12 After three years of secondary education.

13 Roach has recorded them in a number of unpublished documents (Roach 1983, 1984, 1985, 1986).

14 A photocopy of part of the holograph letter is included in Roach (1986).

15 The committee had members from UCLES and its staff, the British Council, the University of London (especially the Institute of Education), and the Foreign Office. Roach continued to be invited to meetings even after he left UCLES. The following notes are based on the minutes of the committees named. I am grateful to John Reddaway, secretary of the Syndicate, and Peter Hargreaves, director of the English Examination, for access to these documents from the archives of UCLES.

16 In 1955, he published a report on French public education in French, a translation of which appeared in German the following year, and prepared another for the Foreign Office and the Ministry on *Some Political Aspects of German Education.*

17 For a more thorough consideration of this issue, see Fishman, Rubal-Lopez, and Conrad (forthcoming), including my article in that volume.

18 He was invited to serve on the UCLES English as a Foreign Language Executive Committee, after having served on the staff of the School of Applied Linguistics at Edinburgh, and having been appointed to the new chair of contemporary English language at Leeds.

19 See, for example, the report by Bachman, Davidson, Ryan, and Choi (1989) on the Cambridge–TOEFL comparability study. This will be discussed in Chapter 19.

12 The idea of TOEFL

Plans and participants

In 1961, the prevailing belief in American academic and governmental circles in the inadequacy of existing English language tests for foreigners supplied the impetus for the creation of the Test of English as a Foreign Language. There was, I now believe, only limited justification in this belief. While it is true that the administrative structure of the existing tests was inadequate, as valid tests of language proficiency they showed much broader sophistication than the test that came in their place. In TOEFL, I will argue, the modern language test—purely objective, psychometrically pure, machine-scored and machine-like, cost-effective and profitable, secure and efficient—reached its pinnacle, successfully armoured, for two decades at least, against the threats of more subjective, fuzzy, integrative, expensive, and human testing approaches that were already starting to be understood in 1960. Efficiency and technical reliability won out over validity. Essentially, the chapters that follow can be read as a story of how practical and institutional needs came to dominate and distract attention from theory-driven concerns.

TOEFL, like many other organizationally-inspired American programmes, started with a meeting. This conference, sponsored by the Center for Applied Linguistics in co-operation with the Institute of International Education and the National Association of Foreign Student Advisers, and held in Washington on 11–12 May 1961, adopted the goal of establishing an 'omnibus battery testing a wide range of English proficiency' that could meet the needs of all US colleges and universities who were considering the admission of foreign students (Center for Applied Linguistics 1961c).

Foreign student advisers and admission officers had for some time been worried about the lack of a suitable English language test. In November 1960, Paul M. Chalmers (1960a), foreign student adviser at Massachusetts Institute of Technology, wrote a five-page letter to Edward Noyes, then acting president of the College Entrance Examination Board, in which he urged the Board to 'take some action in the field of selection of foreign students by the universities of this country'. There were, he noted, already 48,000 such students, 25,000 of them undergraduates. The weight of screening fell on the colleges and universities, and it was 'in the interests of our foreign policy that this selection be made as wisely as possible'. The 'English for foreigners test' was, he knew, an area in which ETS had 'done a little work'. A month later, Richard Pearson (1960), executive vice-president of the College Board, replied to Chalmers that a special committee on foreign student selection was to be formed. In the same letter, he mentioned that the Board had just received a letter from Arthur Adams, of the American Council on Education, passing on a recommendation from the Council's Commission on Education and International Affairs, that the Board should develop a test of English proficiency for foreign applicants.

Government officials had also noticed the problem. At the US State Department, James Alatis was appointed, in 1959, to a position established to deal with the problems of the English proficiency of sponsored and unsponsored foreign students coming to study in the United States (Alatis, personal communication. See also the Bibliography reference to Alatis 1961). Alatis recalls discussions with Freeman, his predecessor in the State Department, who had been persuaded to move to the International Cooperation Agency, and with Melvin Fox of the Ford Foundation, who was surprised to learn that no suitable test was available. Alatis and Fox both talked to Charles Ferguson, just arrived in Washington to be first director of the newly established Ford Foundation-supported Center for Applied Linguistics, who was looking for relevant projects. At the March 1961 meeting of the Advisory Committee of the Center for Applied Linguistics, the plan for the May conference on English proficiency testing was mentioned, and there was discussion with Howard Sollenberger of the Language School of the Foreign Service Institute about a proposal to the Office of Education for a standardized proficiency testing project. James Alatis, John B. Carroll, and Melvin Fox were all members of the advisory committee (Center for Applied Linguistics 1961a).

The task of organizing a conference on English proficiency was, according to David Harris (1989), handed to Sirarpi Ohannessian. Harris, who was to be first chairman of the National Council on the Testing of English as a Foreign Language, and first director of the TOEFL programme, identifies her as the 'Prime Mover'.

Born and raised in the Armenian Quarter of the Old City of Jerusalem, Ohannessian had studied at Harvard with Charles Ferguson, and joined him on the staff in August 1959 as the second employee of the new Center. In 1961, she was head of English as a foreign language at the Center. TOEFL was only one of her 'creations', her other initiatives including TESOL (Teachers of English to Speakers of Other Languages) and a number of programmes in bilingual and American Indian education.

The invitations to the conference (including an offer to reimburse travel and per diem expenses) were sent out in February by Ohannessian (1961). In the invitation, the organizing committee[1] described the aim of the conference as 'the exchange of information on present testing needs and practices and the drafting of proposals for setting up appropriate machinery to prepare and administer annual English examinations which will set up standards of competency acceptable to universities and institutions in the United

States'. All the key groups involved in foreign student affairs or in language testing were represented at the meeting.[2]

Charles Ferguson, director of the Center for Applied Linguistics, opened the first morning session on 11 May 1961, after which John Carroll gave his keynote speech.[3] Background papers written for the conference were discussed during the rest of the day. The second day dealt with criteria for test construction and the mechanics of test administration and implementation. After a dinner addressed by Albert Sims and Joe Neal, a set of conference decisions was accepted and an interim committee was appointed to implement them.

Language testing scholars remember the 1961 Washington testing conference chiefly for the paper given there by John Carroll (1961) which has been reprinted and cited regularly. At least one of the participants, Sydney Sako, already recognized this paper as 'most important'. Its twenty-fifth anniversary was celebrated by an international symposium. The symposium, entitled 'LT+25' was sponsored in May 1986 by the Israel Academic Committee for Research on Language Testing, in association with the AILA Commission on Language Testing, the Interuniversitäre Sprachtestgruppe, and the journal *Language Testing*.[4] Carroll himself now tends to downplay it somewhat:

> When I wrote that paper, I had no idea, of course, that it might have any great or lasting effect. As I recall, it was prepared and presented at the request of Charles Ferguson, then director of the Center for Applied Linguistics in Washington, and I thought of it as a fairly pedestrian attempt to set forth and summarize some more or less self-evident truths about language testing. I thought of its publication as being perhaps a good idea at least as a matter of record. So I was greatly surprised that my views came to be looked upon as approximating a kind of first-draft gospel in language testing.
> (Carroll 1986: 123)

In 1961, Carroll noted, large-scale testing was in the air. In April 1961, he had attended another conference on testing, this one on the problems of 'government language testing', that was attended by people from the Foreign Service Insitute (FSI). The April meeting, according to Carroll's account, was concerned with the development of objective tests in twenty to thirty languages. Howard Sollenberger and Claudia Wilds, who were then in charge of the testing programme at the FSI and responsible there for the development of the scale and the oral interview, were at the April but not at the May meeting. In this way, the direct testing that came to be associated with the FSI was kept distinct from the objective testing of the Educational Testing Service, just as the testing of English as a foreign language, as Starr recalled, was later to be kept separate from foreign language testing. Carroll's paper, written after he had read the papers circulated to participants, set the keynote, and by summarizing the state of the art, cleared the way for practical decisions.

Reading the full account of the conference, one realizes both the strength of the institutional demand for such action, and the extent to which it overlapped and built on existing testing programmes. In her report on the conference, the College Board representative, Katharine Salter (1961a, 1961b) paid no attention to the more theoretical interests, but responded instead to what she considered its political action programme:

> Contrary to our original view of the conference, which we gathered from bits of correspondence, it quickly became apparent that this group intended to put in motion all of the wheels necessary for the development of a new test of English language proficiency, including an aptitude test of language skills, under the joint sponsorship of groups represented at the meeting . . . There was no thought of adapting an existing test program, or of asking an existing group, such as the College Board, to set up such a program.

There is no record that I have so far been able to find of Charles Ferguson's opening remarks at the conference, but, as John Carroll (1989) suggests, 'doubtless he pointed out the need for a more systematic, comprehensive, and nationwide testing program as opposed to the numerous "local" programs then in operation.'[5]

The background was spelt out in detail in two papers. The first, by Joel Slocum (1961) summarized the problems faced by the admissions officers of US colleges and universities when dealing with applications from foreign students, echoing the 1930 approach by registrars to the College Board described in Chapter 7.[6] Among the information needed for intelligent admission decisions, he said, was some objective way of assessing the candidate's proficiency in English. Existing methods were generally subjective, and admissions officers had no way of deciding what standards lay behind a judgement that someone was proficient or not. Slocum pointed out difficulties in interpreting the two 'local' test programmes that were widely used, the English Language Test of the University of Michigan Overseas Testing Programme, and the American University Language Center two-part English test. Firstly, it was not widely known how to interpret the scores on these tests. Secondly, there were problems with the objectivity of the tests, to do with the uniformity of the conditions under which they were administered, and the whole question of test security. He believed that 'one is not necessarily a cynic if he assumes that an unsupervised student might cheat, in view of the eagerness of foreign students to come to this country and their anxiety lest an insufficient command of English prevent them from doing so' (ibid.: 100).

Slocum called, then, for tests with greater standardization and objectivity, and pointed out the urgency of developing such a programme, noting the harm done both to foreign students and to American institutions when under-prepared students arrived. At the same time, he recognized that standardized objective tests would still need local interpretation: each university would need to develop its own understanding of the meaning of test results for its demands, and the test itself would need not to give absolute results but information permitting a US institution to determine whether an applicant knows 'enough English to accomplish a given objective at a given institution' (ibid.: 102). There is here a striking contrast with the philosophy of British examinations, which are assumed usually to have a requirement of determining some absolute pass-fail point.

The point of view of the US Government was presented at the conference by James Alatis (1961), in a paper written while he was still at the State Department. Alatis said that the issue of determining the English proficiency of foreign students before they left their home country had been of long-term concern to the US Government. The Government's responsibility for the overseas English testing of unsponsored students fell under two main heads. The first of these was to be sure that students who applied for visas had sufficient knowledge of English or would be given it; the second was to help administer tests. Alatis summarized the difficulties overseas posts found in carrying out these tasks, and described various efforts under way to tighten up the procedures and to find an independent certification of English proficiency. The general thrust of what he said was to move the responsibility to the admitting institution. He focused not on government-sponsored students, already served by the AULC tests, but unsponsored or privately sponsored students, suggesting that test development should follow the procedures used for developing modern language tests under National Defense Education Act contracts, and that the Center for Applied Linguistics should co-ordinate the project, with the advice of other agencies and organizations.

The papers by Slocum and Alatis showed how much university administrators and government bureaucrats felt the need for a new testing battery. With increasing numbers of foreign students applying for admission to American colleges and universities, the absence of some standardized and reliable way of assessing candidates' English proficiency was leading to personal hardship, institutional waste, and bureaucratic frustration. Department of State officers were aware of the problem but limited in their power to find a solution to it. A more centralist governmental policy might have proposed mandatory government testing; a less responsible élitist view might have said, let the students and the universities work it out for themselves. Rather, as Alatis demonstrated, the various government agencies involved, working through a range of public and semi-private organizations, set about to encourage a co-operative approach to the problem.

While there is no hard evidence on who first suggested that the Center for Applied Linguistics be involved, it is likely that the idea came up in discussions between Alatis, Fox (who was responsible for the Ford Foundation funding of the Center), and Ferguson (who was its first director). These and other unrecorded preliminary conversations with people at the Institute of International Education (also Ford-funded) and the National Association of Foreign Student Advisors probably led the College Board representative Katharine Salter (1961a), resenting the invasion of the Board's traditional territory by upstarts, to remark on the speed and ease with which the conference moved to an action agenda.

The 1961 conference was a response to a practical administrative problem. Its solution, as in much good applied linguistics, started not with the linguistics but with the application. And as in all businesslike applications, the first step was to analyse what was available at the time. Thus, the conference spent its first afternoon hearing about existing testing programmes. The state of the art in US English language testing in 1961 was portrayed in the description of three existing local programmes,[7] summaries of which have already been given in Chapter 10. Salter, in a report to her colleagues, noted how the participants quickly ruled out the use of these existing tests:

> In fact, at this meeting, the participants helped kill and subsequently bury the overseas testing program of English proficiency currently administered by the University of Michigan Language Center.[8] This test, as you will remember, was developed by Robert Lado, now of Georgetown University. According to many people, this was a good thing. However, the current Director of the Program, Leslie Palmer, was not aware of this proposal, and I am sure, premeditated action, until shortly before the conference.
> (ibid.)

Salter's confused syntax is a symptom of her strong reaction to what was going on. She was sufficiently moved to telephone one of her colleagues during the meeting. In addition, she mailed a copy of her report, written immediately after her return to the office, to Richard Pearson, executive vice-president of the College Board, even though he was in France at the time visiting the College Board president, who was on leave there (Salter 1961b).

Her view that there was a 'premeditated' plan to 'kill' the local tests is echoed in the comment by David Harris that he was surprised at the lack of objection from those responsible for the local tests to the new plan. It is interesting that Harris did not see the new test as a threat to his own government-funded American Language Institute test. Harris and Palmer, recognizing the practical difficulties of their own tests, appeared to have welcomed a better-funded attempt to build an improved test.

The descriptions of current practice were followed by the theoretical paper by John Carroll. Looking back twenty-five years and re-reading his

1961 paper, Carroll (1986) found some memories stirred and issues revived that he had not thought about for a long time, 'but I found nothing in it that I wished I had not said. My reaction was: yes, these "considerations" I set forth were fundamental, and they still are' (ibid.: 124).

Carroll's paper dealt quite quickly with the objections that had been raised by MacKenzie against objective tests, noting that 'most testers can recite all the arguments pro and con the use of objective tests . . .' (Carroll 1961: 31). Language testing was a professional field, and a whole book on it was about to be published,[9] so that there was no need to go over elementary matters. He reminded the audience, already well indoctrinated by the papers it had presumably read in preparation for the meeting, that 'The purpose of testing is always to render information to aid in making intelligent decisions about possible courses of action' (ibid.). The tests being contemplated were intended to help make decisions about university admission, and therefore 'American universities should try to get together to specify what kinds and levels of English language proficiencies they desire in foreign students . . .' (ibid.: 32). He said that 'There is need for surveys of the kind of linguistic situations faced by these students and the success or failure of students of various levels of English proficiency in meeting these situations . . . What are typical social situations in which foreign students must engage?' (ibid.: 32–3). Tests of this kind must be validated like aptitude tests: 'External validation in this case would be solely against the criterion of having sufficient English to operate in given situations' (ibid.: 33).

Carroll set out the grid of language aspects (phonology or orthography, morphology, syntax, lexicon) by skill (auditory comprehension, oral production, reading, writing) that he believed to be involved in language proficiency. While each cell was logically independent, in practice they were not. There were eleven aspects that might be tested: knowledge of structures (sample of structure-points); knowledge of general usage lexicon; knowledge of specialized lexicon; auditory discrimination (of phonemes, allophones, and suprasegmentals); oral production; reading (word pronunciation); writing (spelling); rate and accuracy of listening comprehension; rate and quality of speaking; rate and accuracy of reading comprehension; and rate and accuracy of written composition. Robert Lado and others had focused on testing specific items, which made for reliable and valid testing. This would suit the first six categories, but one might miss 'facility'; therefore, he made his now classic plea for the addition of integrative items:

> For this reason I recommend tests in which there is less attention paid to specific structure-points or lexicon than to the total communicative effect of an utterance . . . Indeed, this 'integrative' approach has several advantages over the 'discrete structure-point' approach. It entails a

broader and more diffuse sampling over the total field of linguistic items and thus depends less upon the specifics of a particular course of training. It thus may lend itself somewhat more effectively to the problem of an external examination in which the examiner does not ordinarily know, in any detail, what was covered in any particular course of training. Furthermore, the difficulty of a task is subjectively more obvious than in the case of a 'discrete structure-point' item . . . Finally, the 'integrative' approach makes less necessary the kind of comparison of language systems upon which much current language test[ing] is premised.
(ibid.: 37–8)

This may well have been the first call for testing *communicative* effect. An ideal English language proficiency test, Carroll suggested, would distinguish levels of performance on those dimensions which are more relevant to the kind of situations in which the candidates will be expected to find themselves: its validity would be established on the basis of this predictive power more than on its appearing to be a good sample of the English language. Thus, while he placed himself firmly with the psychometrists, his call for integrative testing had set them a challenge that would prove very difficult to meet, and that was virtually ignored in the test that was put in place.

Carroll (1986) reiterated that his argument twenty-five years earlier for integrative tests had not been intended as a criticism or attack on discrete-point testing. He felt that the discrete-point approach, associated particularly with Robert Lado (1961), was 'valuable, commendable, and well-grounded theoretically' (1986: 124), but that it needed to be supplemented with tests measuring skills of speaking or writing or understanding connected speech or writing in more or less real-life situations:

Language understanding entails weaving together all the discrete points in a linguistic stimulus to gather its total meaning. Often this understanding does not depend so much upon knowledge of particular words or points of grammar, as upon an ability to make inferences from the context as a whole. The discrete-point approach, if the 'points' are adequately sampled, is often a good way to measure the language competence upon which effective language performance is based, but it needs to be supplemented by measures of integrative performance.
(ibid.: 124)

Carroll concluded his 1961 conference keynote paper with three added points: the need to control 'extraneous variables or influences' such as auditory comprehension tests that required reading difficult textual material to find the answer; problems of sampling bias; and the fact that different objectives might well require different techniques. Finally, he mentioned the problem of score interpretation and suggested that reports be not of percentage or percentiles but of difficulty levels or expectancy tables.

We have no reports of immediate reactions to Carroll's paper. It was followed at the conference by a day discussing the papers that had been circulated before the meeting.[10] While it had important influence on the subsequent development of language testing theory, its major innovation in proposing to test what Bachman (1990) calls communicative language ability ('functioning in the "target language" in appropriate social situations', as Carroll put it) has not been fully appreciated by those who date this trend from 1980. Nor did the paper have the major influence on the decisions arrived at by the conference that one might have anticipated.

Discussions and decisions

There is no verbatim record of the discussions that took place at the conference,[11] but the report by Sako (1961a; see also Peters 1961) on his return from the conference included a list of the questions discussed, presumably on the second day. Sako divided them into two parts, criteria for test construction and criteria for test administration: the frequency of new forms and the public availability of the old ones; the advisability of test-taking orientation for candidates, in the form of a specimen test; how and where overseas administration should take place; and whether the tests should be scored locally or centrally.[12]

Carroll (1989) recalled discussion of one point in particular, the writing sample. 'My notes suggest that this was a big issue at the conference, and that I seemed to have persuaded people not to contemplate trying to score that part.'[13] In spite of the call for integrative testing in the keynote address, the conference was not ready to go into the development of reliable composition-scoring methods. Carroll wrote that

> I simply don't remember details of the discussion of linguistic skills; much of it was in response to ideas I had presented, and I believe most of those ideas were accepted in principle. Nor do I recall much about the decision to put the main emphasis on objective testing; objective testing seemed more practical and feasible than testing of oral production, for example. At least some of the 'local' programs put considerable reliance on objective testing. Slocum, my notes indicate, was one of the proponents of a writing sample, but people like Godshalk and myself pointed out the great difficulties (both technical and logistic) entailed in any professional scoring of such samples. Discussions of these and related issues must have occupied most of the second day of the conference.
> (ibid.)

Carroll's account was confirmed by Harris (1989), who wrote:

> I don't recall whether there was divided opinion on the omission of a direct sample of writing . . . As a compromise, it will be noted, we agreed that a writing sample could be sent to universities for their own analysis. (No doubt the Educational Testing Service representative suggested this, for CEEB was, I think, doing the same thing then.)

Harris reported that the ETS representative at the conference, Fred Godshalk, was a 'very persuasive figure'.

Godshalk (1961a), in his own report of the conference, said that 'the matter of an essay, unscored, to be sent with the reports, was strongly supported by some conferees and was accepted'. He added that 'the major proponent was won over later, and so it is possible that this "writing sample" problem is still a matter at issue, to be decided upon the basis of user demand'.

Godshalk was at this period just starting work on the major project that would lead to the reintroduction of holistically marked essays in the College Board English tests. His colleagues on his retirement recalled him as the person most responsible for reintroducing the scoring of essays. One must conclude that while he personally would have been in favour of including writing, he felt it would complicate matters to have the new test of English as a foreign language, which he already saw as a potential part of his own bailiwick at ETS, infected by association with what must have been an unpopular cause. Godshalk reported to his colleagues at Princeton that the conference had satisfied itself with limited goals so as to get the programme in operation as soon as possible, leaving what he called 'fringes and frills' for future research.

Harris also confirmed Carroll's comment on the problem of oral production, when he recalled 'no objection to the omission of a direct test of speaking ability, for the logistical problems of directly testing the speech of huge numbers of candidates around the world was generally recognized . . . the conference called for future experimentation' (Harris 1989). Thus, it seems that for the testing experts like Carroll, Godshalk, Harris, and Palmer, logistics, rather than linguistics or psychometrics, was the driving force.

The published decisions of the conference (Center for Applied Linguistics 1961c: 3–9) were based on discussions on the second day, and start with a statement of the need for a generally accepted programme of proficiency testing, 'a comprehensive program using carefully constructed tests of the English proficiency of foreign students, suitable and acceptable to all educational institutions in the United States and to various other organizations, chiefly governmental' to be developed by a permanent test organization. No objections were made to the new test, not even from those with a 'vested interest' (as Harris put it) in the old ones.[14]

The decision on specifications for the test was speedy and amicable, Katharine Salter (1961a) reported to her colleagues at the College Board. The test, it was decided, should have two parts. The first should be an English proficiency test, described as 'an omnibus battery testing a wide range of proficiency and yielding meaningful (reliable) subscores in addition to total score'. It should take two and a half hours and be aimed, at first, at the college level. The second part should be a language aptitude test, needed 'In view of the importance of predictions of subsequent English attainment . . .'

The idea of including an aptitude test seems to have come through the work of Harris at the American University Language Center; he referred to it in his paper and so did Alatis. A paper by Marquardt (1961) on the topic was also among those circulated to conference participants. Carroll's keynote paper referred to validating the proficiency test on the basis of its predictive power, just as one would validate an aptitude test, but he did not propose including aptitude in the battery. On this issue, he comments (1989) that 'Though this was planned, it was never carried out; it seems that conferees hoped that I could work something out, but I never did, thinking the task too difficult or impractical, or not having the time.'

Carroll proposed that the English Proficiency Test should have four subtests:

1 control of English structure
2 auditory comprehension
3 vocabulary and reading comprehension and
4 writing ability.[15]

Oral production was not to be tested in the meantime, but research should be initiated on how to do this. Nor was writing to be scored: 'Writing ability is to be tested by objective techniques, not by the scoring of writing samples. However, an unscored composition will be furnished to test users for whatever use they may wish to make of it.' (Carroll 1989)

Thirty minutes would be allowed, according to Carroll's notes, for the composition. Harris (1989) recalled that

> Though the conference specified the sections of the tests (that is, the general skills to be tested) it did not go into the matter of specific techniques to get at the skills. These decisions were made at a meeting held in the TOEFL [presumably, Center for Applied Linguistics] office following the conference.

A number of decisions were made about the administration and the scoring of tests. Testing was generally to be carried out in the student's country of origin. There were to be three test administrations a year, with new forms for each administration for the first two years, after which reuse of the test material would be possible. All scoring was to be done in the United

States. Candidates for the test should be recommended by US universities or agencies. The testing programme should provide additional services: interpretive manuals, specimen tests, norms and central validation, seminars on meaning of tests and on local norms on campuses and at meetings, correlation of the new test with existing tests, and liaison with government agencies. Groups for pre-testing should include native speakers.[16] The programme might be able to make use of government posts for overseas test administration.

Organizational and funding questions, according to Carroll's notes, were left to the last evening. The conference called for co-operation from US Government agencies and proposed international co-operation, first with Canada and then the British Commonwealth. It proposed that the testing programme be independent, controlled by a National Advisory Council drawn from university organizations, professional associations, government agencies, and testing organizations. There should be a project director, a testing committee including linguists and professional testers as well as representatives of users, test construction committees, and an organization for the construction, administration, and operation of the test. While on the surface all was calm, there was considerable concern about who would control the programme.

On the issue of 'effective' control, Godshalk (1961a) noted in the account he circulated to his colleagues at Princeton, that there had been 'undercurrents of partisan feeling'. Katharine Salter had explained how the College Board was organized and how it used a professional testing organization (ETS) to conduct the tests. A number of possible permanent centres were proposed. According to Godshalk, Ohannessian favoured an inter-university activity housed in some place such as the Center for Applied Linguistics. However, Godshalk himself was satisfied that 'there is no question [but] that the conference group intends Educational Testing Service to be the testing organization'. In his report to his colleagues and supervisors at ETS, he stated that he felt his position was strong, for he was on the interim committee.

> There is a nice question in this of the effectiveness of personal–professional versus official relationship, which I mention because it was discussed at our planning session here. My unofficial status perhaps disarmed opposition or relieved suspicion, and promoted the 'corporate image' of Educational Testing Service as a service agency, to our great advantage. (ibid.)

Salter (1961a), as noted above, was very disturbed with plans for the new organization, sufficiently disturbed to call a colleague about it on Friday and send a copy of her report to her supervisor who was on a trip to France (1961b). She had told the conference, she said, about the College

Board's interests, as evidenced by the *ad hoc* committee that it had just established on foreign student admission. She also indicated the Board's 'past involvement in English language proficiency testing'. She personally thought the College Board would need to decide whether to swallow the new venture ('bring it within its organizational structure and work with the National Advisory Council and suborganization, the testing committee, in the same manner as we do with our own committees'), seek to become one of the sponsors of the test, or develop its own test.

Various participants suggested that the programme might be funded by the National Defense Education Act, by users, and by foundations. Harris recollects that Mel Fox from the Ford Foundation was encouraging from the start. Salter (1961a) too reported to her colleagues that the significance of his attendance 'was not lost on any of the participants'.

No doubt this optimism was a little exaggerated. Fox did not find it very easy in the event to convince the senior officers of Ford of the viability of the project. From my reading of the documents, I suspect that part of the problem was with the failure to develop the needed relations with the College Board. In a response to Salter's letter and report after the meeting, College Board vice-president Pearson (1961) said he 'was not inclined to be too disturbed'. Frank Bowles, the president—at the time on assignment with UNESCO in France, with whom he was meeting in France, had some ideas on the 'whether' of English proficiency testing, which made the issue less important. This, it seems, was related to an interest at the College Board in preparing other language versions of the Scholastic Aptitude tests. 'Ongoing financing' would also be a real question, and Bowles, correctly as it turned out, doubted that 'the Fund', presumably the Ford Foundation, would handle that. He concluded that 'we're in a strong position and I don't think we need worry about being out-maneuvered'.

The participants in the Washington conference finished their work by agreeing to set up an interim organization. The representatives of the Institute of International Education and the Center for Applied Linguistics offered to provide the interim secretariat; an interim committee was chosen consisting of Ohannessian, Godshalk, Swope, Slocum, and Harris (chairman),[17] and the three sponsors, the Center for Applied Linguistics, the Institute of International Education, and the National Association of Foreign Student Advisers, agreed that they would pay for reports and interim operations.

The conference casts interesting light on the nature of applied linguistics and the implementation of its ideas. First, the whole exercise started not with a desire to apply some new notion in linguistic theory, but rather as what Henry Widdowson would call a principled effort to solve a language-related problem. As the papers by Slocum and Alatis make clear, and the statement of conference decisions reaffirms, the conference was called to find a practical solution to a socially relevant problem, the assessment of the English language proficiency of the increasing number of foreign students seeking to study in American universities.

The people called together to discuss this issue were American scholars and administrators with experience with language tests from two points of view: as test makers and as test users. A number of them had been trained as linguists, and among them were those who brought their knowledge of linguistic theory to bear on the topic. But the knowledge of linguistic theory was firmly counterbalanced by knowledge of psychometric theory, and both sets of theories were strongly constrained by practical experience and demands. This was not a meeting where a single linguistic theory would or could be proposed as the panacea for a problem. In this, the conference's work can be clearly distinguished from a number of less successful interventions by linguists who have proposed that some aspect of theory will form the basis for a new and successful method of teaching, for example, reading or foreign languages. By their careful balance of invited participants and by the selection of invited papers, Ohannessian and Harris had organized a group who would blend knowledge of two fields of theory with considerable experience of practical testing and its uses.

In these circumstances, it is interesting to trace the source of proposals and the nature of the final decisions made at the conference. The conference was presented with a set of theoretical notions (mainly in Carroll's keynote paper, but also in other presentations and certainly in the discussions), a number of possible models (especially the Michigan and the American University Language Center batteries), and a set of practical administrative and institutional constraints, among which funding was the most serious. Assuming a world without the financial and practical limitations, the kind of battery that the language testers at the meeting would presumably have favoured would have consisted of a large objective section to test reading and grammar, improved (that is to say, more psychometrically reliable) versions of the speaking test used in the American University Language Center battery and the composition-writing test of the Michigan battery, and a language aptitude test that would help relate the synchronic measurement of the test to the diachronic prediction it was intended to make.

Such an ideal test, for which we are still waiting, would have doubtless been much more capable than the test battery that was actually developed of bridging the gap between traditional and modern tests, by combining the demands of psychometric reliability with those for naturalistic and integrative performance. In the circumstances, it seems probable that the greater intellectual value attached to objective testing principles, not unrelated to the then still fairly firm alliance between structural linguistic theory and behaviourist psychology in foreign language learning theory, meant that the conference opted for immediate use of the objective items, with the speaking test and the scored writing left for further development. Thus,

Carroll's important call for integrative testing, with its relation to real-life situations, was not specifically echoed in the decisions, and was satisfied, in actual test development, by the use of mini-dialogues in the listening comprehension and of short connected passages in the reading comprehension. The absence of any spokesperson at the conference for the oral testing that, by 1961, was proceeding efficiently at the FSI, and the decreasing status for prognostic tests that had once held equal place with proficiency tests, made it easier for the practical arguments of a machine-scorable test to win out.

The conference thus recognized a tension, but was constrained to suggest a resolution of it that was heavily weighted towards the psychometric principles that drove the industrial practices at ETS. Any doubts about the wisdom of omitting tests of speaking or writing were quickly pushed aside for 'later research', the common filing cabinet for the desirable but unfeasible academic idea. The conference came up with a very valuable set of prescriptions that should have permitted designing the best possible testing programme, given the state of language testing knowledge and the general intellectual atmosphere of American language teaching theory and practice at the time. The research effort that was stressed in the decisions provided a way to deal with the areas where the participants wisely spotted weakness in that knowledge. As things turned out, the lack of resources, and the institution strait-jacket that came with the financial bail-out, meant that the research took much longer than participants had anticipated, with the result that the test that was implemented was much narrower in its scope than might have been hoped.

Notes

1 The committee in charge of organizing the conference consisted of David P. Harris as chairman; Raleigh Morgan, Jr. and Sirarpi Ohannessian (Center for Applied Linguistics); J. Morgan Swope (Institute of International Education); and Grant Taylor (New York University, representing the National Association of Foreign Student Advisors). In 1961, Harris was director of the American University Language Center in Washington, having been recruited from a position in Florida to work on the Davis test. He had previously taught at the University of Michigan, during which time he worked for a spell at ETS in Princeton. Fred Godshalk (1961a), in an internal ETS report on the conference, was pleased to note that Harris was 'an Educational Testing Service alumnus'. The inclusion of Swope and Taylor reflects the fact of co-operation with two other Ford Foundation-backed organizations, the Institute of International Education and the National Association of Foreign Student Advisors (later to be renamed National Association for Foreign Student

Affairs in recognition of the role of admissions officers and English language teachers in the organization).
2 Alphabetically, they were:

Janes E. Alatis (Department of Health Education and Welfare). Alatis had just joined the Office of Education but until shortly before the conference he had been English language specialist at the Special Activities Branch of the Bureau of Educational and Cultural Affairs of the US State Department. His doctorate was in English, but a Fulbright fellowship to Greece had been important in his new area of concern. Subsequently, Alatis became associate dean of the School of Languages and Linguistics at Georgetown University, and succeeded Robert Lado on his retirement in 1973.

John B. Carroll (Harvard University). Carroll's activities in work at the junction of linguistics and psychology—being chairman of the group that met at Cornell and first defined the field of psycholinguistics (Carroll 1951)—and in language testing and in developing language attitude tests, have been discussed in earlier chapters. After 1961, he was to spend some years in a senior research position at ETS, and then moved to the University of North Carolina.

Frederick N. Cromwell (Department of State Bureau of Educational and Cultural Affairs).

Thomas L. Crowell (Columbia University). According to Salter (1961a), Crowell represented 'some of the testing interests of NAFSA'.

Charles Ferguson (Center for Applied Linguistics). Ferguson was the first director of the Center and had previously taught at Harvard.

Melvin J. Fox (Ford Foundation). Fox was associate director of the International Training and Research programme.

Harry Freeman (International Cooperation Administration). Freeman preceded Alatis as English language specialist at the State Department, but moved to the International Cooperation Agency, which had large numbers of sponsored foreign students.

Fred I. Godshalk (ETS). Godshalk joined the Service in 1954 as head of the communications section in test development, and retired, twenty years later (past the usual 65 retirement age) as senior examiner in the test development area of higher education and career programmes. Born in Bangor, Pennsylvania, he had received a masters degree and doctorate from the University of Illinois, and had taught for fifteen years as English department chairman at Staunton Military Academy. During the war, he served as a reserve captain in the Army's morale unit, rising to the rank of colonel. Before coming to ETS, he spent the post-war years at the University of Illinois and as a school principal. He became chairman of the ETS test development humanities department in 1956, after which he worked more as an editor of tests than as a test-builder (*Examiner* 1974). He worked with Trudy Conlan from 1961 until 1979 to invent the idea of holistic scoring for the Admissions Testing Program English Composition Test (*Examiner* 1979). In the detailed summary of the conference proceedings that she wrote for the College Board staff, Salter (1961a) noted after Godshalk's name that he was 'primarily asked to represent himself'. In his own internal memorandum reporting to his colleagues at ETS and the College Board on this, Godshalk (1961c) noted the advantage of this 'independence'. Though his affiliation with ETS was known to all, he was elected to the resolutions committee and the interim committee.

Edward T. Hall (Washington Institute of Psychiatry).

Robert Lado (Georgetown University). Lado was dean of the School of Languages and Linguistics at Georgetown University from 1960 until his retirement in 1973; he had moved there from the University of Michigan, where he had developed the first version of the Michigan test, as described earlier. His book on language testing (Lado 1961) had just appeared.

D. P. Martin (British Embassy).

Leslie A. Palmer (University of Michigan). Palmer worked in the English Language Institute; he later moved to Georgetown to be with David Harris and became associate director of the TOEFL programme when it started and first programme director at ETS. Subsequently, he became director of the Maryland Language Institute.

Sydney Sako (US Air Force). Sako was director of the language testing programme at the Language School of Lackland Air Force Base.

Katharine A. Salter (College Entrance Examinations Board). Her title was assistant director of associational activities.

Inez H. Sepmeyer (University of California Los Angeles). Sepmeyer was senior administrative assistant in the Office of Admissions. Chalmers (1960b) had suggested her name as the ideal representative for the college admissions officers on the proposed College Board committee on foreign student selection; she had just published 'some very helpful comparisons' of credits allowed for foreign study.

Joel B. Slocum (Columbia University).

Wilmarth H. Starr (Modern Languages Association). Starr was director of the Foreign Language Program Research Center, where he was involved in the development of the MLA foreign language tests, as recounted earlier. Starr (1992) later recalled that

the interdisciplinary relationship between teachers of and specialists in foreign languages and those in English as a Foreign Language was casual and not well organized if at all. It is true that I served for a time in meetings and councils that attempted to straddle the two disciplines, but this was one of personal interest and stemmed from a modest and happenstantial 'reputation' as director of the FL Testing project. However, such relationship was rather short lived . . .

In addition, Joe W. Neal (University of Texas), who was president of the National Association of Foreign Student Affairs served on the College Board special committee on foreign student admissions, and Albert G. Sims (executive vice-president of the International Institute of Education) attended the conference dinner on 12 May.

3 For this reconstruction of the meeting, I have relied on notes made at the time by John Carroll (1989) and Sydney Sako (1961a), (Peters 1961) and a copy of the original agenda (Center for Applied Linguistics 1961b) which Leslie Palmer has kept. Another report of the meeting, from the point of view of ETS to whom it was distributed, is provided by Godshalk (1961a). A somewhat different account, much of it an expression of College Board concerns, was written by Salter (1961a and 1961b). A more imaginative account is given in Neal (1984). According to the agenda, discussion of criteria for test construction was to start at 4.15 on 11 May; Carroll, however, notes that this discussion started the next morning.

4 Papers from the symposium, which honoured Carroll's paper and the publication in the same year by Robert Lado of his book on language testing, were published in *Language Testing* (Volume 3/2, December 1986).

5 Leslie Palmer's handwritten notes made at the conference start with the following words, which may well have come from Ferguson's opening: 'Problem of multitude of tests and lack of correlation. Shooting for one test suitable acceptable to all colleges.'

6 Sepmeyer and Clifford Prator, supervisor of the UCLA English as a second language programme, had read and 'heartily' endorsed the paper by Joel Slocum; she believed that it represented the opinion of most admissions officers and teachers of English as a second language (Sepmeyer 1961). Salter (1961a), however, thought it was to be regretted that the conference places for representatives of admissions officers were filled by NAFSA people, biasing it presumably towards foreign student concerns.

7 The term 'local' is used in two distinct contexts and meanings in this study of English tests. In the present US context, it refers to tests developed and controlled 'locally', i.e. by individual US institutions (in particular, Michigan and American University, later also Georgetown and others). The other use is in the title of the University of Cambridge Local Examinations Syndicate (UCLES), where it is used to mark the fact that this was the first Syndicate to administer examinations 'locally', i.e. at schools and places outside Cambridge. It might be useful to note at this point another crucial transatlantic variation in definition: for TOEFL and ETS a testing centre is a physical space hired for the purpose of administering a test; for UCLES, it has traditionally been a school which has applied and been approved to follow a defined syllabus, after

which its students will be examined 'locally' on their achievements. The introduction of the Local Examinations in 1858 by Oxford and Cambridge has been characterized as an attempt to change the curriculum in secondary schools and at the same time to change society by being able to 'bring forward able boys and girls from a lower social level' (Roach 1971: 9).

8 Actually, the English Language Institute. Her prediction was wrong, too, for the Michigan battery is still alive and well.

9 His reference was to Lado (1961). Robert Lado's book *Language Testing* appeared first in 1961, published in Britain by Longman. A second impression followed the next year. The American impression, the same at the British 'without abridgment or change' except for a couple of paragraphs added to the Preface, appeared in 1964 published by McGraw-Hill.

10 Sako's official report (Peters 1961) made after the return from the conference also refers to a talk by Starr on the MLA language testing programme; this is not included in the printed proceedings (Center for Applied Linguistics 1961c), nor in the listing at the end of that document of additional material made available to the participants (p. 103); nor is it included in Carroll's own notes on the items discussed (Carroll 1989).

11 Neither Harris nor Ohannessian knows of any, nor has the Center for Applied Linguistics kept its files from those years. The destruction of these archives is a serious handicap to studying the history of applied linguistics. Some of the less ephemeral items (reports and documents such as Carroll 1954) were fortunately transferred to the Georgetown University Library with other books from the Center's library.

12 On Leslie Palmer's copy of these questions, a few cryptic notes are written. According to these notes, there should not be separate versions for linguistic areas, but there should be separate forms for different proficiency levels. Vocabulary and reading comprehension should be included, and there 'must be some kind of measure' of writing. Test materials should be field-tested in the United States, and an attempt should be made to test language aptitude.

13 See Chapter 9 for Carroll's opinions, ten years earlier, on the testing of writing ability. Godshalk (1961a) also took credit for the omission of a writing test.

14 In a talk given over twenty years later, Joseph Neal (1984) recalled that there was 'long and eloquent debate' on the whole question of having a new test developed, but neither Al Sims (who attended the evening session with Neal) nor David Harris (who presumably conducted it) remembers any serious disagreement being expressed with the fundamental goal. Neal's talk does contain a number of other mistaken recollections—the time of year and location of the conference, the amount

of time he spent there—so one might reasonably suspect that he was confusing the occasion in which he heard the opposition to the test expressed. It is perhaps also relevant that he is one of those who have publicly criticized TOEFL.

15 According to Carroll's notes, these four parts were to take (1) 95 minutes, (2) 30 minutes, (3) 95 minutes, and (4) 30 minutes. Sako, however, was under the impression that the four parts would take two hours, with an extra 30 minutes for writing: he had perhaps conflated the objective writing section and the proposed unscored writing sample.

16 Carroll believed that this was his suggestion.

17 According to the Center for Applied Linguistics (1966) report, Hattie Jarmon of the American Association of Collegiate Registrars and Admissions Officers was also a member of the interim committee.

13   TOEFL: gestation

The ETS interest and the end of the English Examination for Foreign Students

After the success of the May 1961 meeting, there was a burst of interest and activity at Princeton, where senior staff, buoyed by Fred Godshalk's enthusiastic reports, were expecting a major role for the Educational Testing Service. A summary history of TOEFL prepared by ETS (1988) cites a November 1961 meeting of the interim committee at which, it contends, ETS had been invited to 'submit a proposal to develop a test in English to replace the five-hour "English examination for foreign students" administered by the College Board at centers overseas in the 1940s and later made available for purchase by colleges for their own use'. I have found no record of such a meeting. By 1988, when the TOEFL programme at ETS was preparing to celebrate the twenty-fifth anniversary of the second largest testing project in the agency, it is not surprising to find a little myth-making about the early days.

The anticipation of the actual decision in the 1988 document may well have been derived from a misreading of a memorandum that Fred Godshalk (1961c) wrote on 14 November 1961 to some of his colleagues and supervisors (Chauncey, Dyer, Ebel, Solomon, Turnbull, and Wantman), inviting them to a meeting to be held in the next two days to discuss the share of ETS and the College Entrance Examination Board in the proposed new programme.

Godshalk had been paying close attention to developments. In September, he wrote to William Turnbull, executive vice-president, requesting an appointment to discuss the involvement of ETS and possibly the College Board in the new test (Godshalk 1961b). He and Turnbull seem not to have met at this stage. In November, he reported to Turnbull and Solomon that the interim committee had decided the previous weekend[1] to schedule the meeting of the National Advisory Council for 12–14 January 1962. Turnbull and Solomon suggested an internal ETS discussion, which Godshalk convened with an explanatory memorandum.

In the memorandum, Godshalk (1961c) said that the interim committee would ask interested organizations to nominate official representatives to the council meeting. When this had been done, the committee would select nominees for a permanent executive committee, finance committee, and testing committee (or at least its nucleus) to be recommended to the council. Godshalk went on to say that the interim committee 'will recommend that ETS be approached as the service organization for test construction and administration, with the intent to negotiate a contract'. Godshalk had been asked by other members of the committee, on the basis of his access to information, to come up with a tentative estimate of the cost of developing tests, including pre-testing, to be used for two years, and the cost of administering (including scoring and reporting) a series of three administrations. He predicted cautiously that the tests would ultimately replace existing tests, and by the third year, should be between 15,000 and 25,000 candidates a year, and even more than that if the State Department required it to be taken by applicants for certain non-student visas.

I have not found any independent confirmation of Godshalk's confidence that ETS would be selected. It is quite clear that no formal decision or offer had been made. This is shown by the fact that in the internal ETS report by Godshalk (1962a) written just after the January 1962 council meeting, he again expressed confidence that ETS would be selected as the testing/administration organization for the new programme. If the committee had already, in November 1961, asked ETS to develop the test, why was this still open in January 1962? Nor is there any mention of a decision in any of the three reports of a November 1961 interim committee meeting. In the draft minutes of the January meeting, both Harris and Godshalk make reference to 'test service' and 'testing service' and its function, but not to ETS as the organization.

The January meeting in fact specifically decided to leave the decision on a testing service until the next meeting, in May 1962, reflecting in part David Harris's reluctance, after his experience working there, to have ETS involved, but there was ultimately no feasible alternative (Harris 1989). The formal invitation to ETS was finally issued at the May 1962 meeting of the National Council.

I have not seen a report of the internal ETS meeting in November 1961 but, from the people invited, it seems to have finally put paid to an abortive earlier initiative by Dean Seibel to have ETS revise the English Examination for Foreign Students, developed by the College Board in 1947, which it had taken over. When, in February 1961, Godshalk had told Turnbull of his invitation to the May conference, William Turnbull (1961a) asked him to find out first what he could about the state of this test.

Seibel's proposal (Evaluation and Advisory Service 1961) had been developed by him for Morey Wantman (1961a), who sent it to Turnbull on 17 March 1961, perhaps in response to a request from the College Board.[2] The proposal noted the need for a test of written and spoken English for the selection, placement, and counselling of foreign students. The existing English Examination for Foreign Students suffered, they believed, from a number of disadvantages. It was sold to colleges in sets of ten tests only, without any provision for overseas testing. Administration took five hours. It provided more information than was needed on students of lower ability, and included parts, such as science vocabulary and non-verbal reasoning, the relevance of which was doubtful. The essay produced scoring problems. Interpretive data were limited. There were norms for only 507 students, and only two studies had been done, one on reliability with seventy students at Queens College and one on validity with fifty-seven students.

Seibel proposed a three-hour test with four parts: reading comprehension and vocabulary, grammar and usage, 'pronounciation', and listening comprehension, with separate scores for each. The tests were to be scored a section at a time, and students permitted to go on only if they passed the previous section. They further proposed two levels, depending on whether English had been the medium of instruction or just a second language. The test would 'easily' be administered abroad by US cultural centres, perhaps, and would need to be tried out experimentally at first.

Turnbull (1961b) liked the proposal and thought that Henry Chauncey, the president of ETS, who had been involved in the earlier College Board English test, might be invited to a meeting to discuss it. He thought scoring the examination in progress would be impractical, and would involve candidates in a full day of being tested. He also thought one level would be enough, but this could be decided empirically.

On 4 May 1961, a fortnight before the Washington conference, a group met at ETS to discuss the English Examination for Foreign Students. Further development of the Seibel proposal seems to have lapsed after this meeting, which determined the ETS position for the May conference (Godshalk 1961c). According to a report of that meeting (Educational Testing Service 1961; Wantman 1961b), it was agreed that there certainly existed a need for an achievement test in English to be used in the selection of foreign students. There was also a need for an aptitude-like test. ETS, however, would prefer a group of organizations like the International Institute of Education, or the US Office of Education, or the State Department to form an advisory board to seek funds for the test, which ETS would run. If such a board were not formed, ETS would 'probably proceed to work'. Foundation support should be sought because of the complexity of the task. Norms would have to be established for various groups, and a good deal of research would be needed.

At this internal meeting in November 1961, then, ETS rejected the proposal to revise the College Board test it owned in favour of supporting and exploiting the initiative of the Washington meeting. In a note to Bob Solomon in 1966, Turnbull (1966) wrote the last word on the English Examination for Foreign Students. 'It was a dandy test,' he believed, but 'superfluous' now that TOEFL was in place. From then on, it was decided, 'any requests for the EEFS should be referred to TOEFL'.

Both William Turnbull and Fred Godshalk saw from the beginning the value to ETS of the establishment of a 'front organization', if one may use the term. Such a group would develop the appropriate funding and acceptance for a testing programme that ETS could operate, just as it was running programmes for the College Board and the Graduate Record Examination Board. Turnbull (1961c) set his priorities for the organizational structure to be aimed at. The first choice on his list was that the grant should come to ETS which would set up a 'responsible committee'. A less desirable choice was that the grant should go to another agency, perhaps the College Board. While this strategy of sheltering behind controllable organizations infuriated some like Nairn (1980), it gave ETS the maximum protection in its role as a testing agency and a research institution.

In November 1961, then, ETS decided to work towards effective control of the initiative for a new test of English for foreign students. To the extent that this strategy ultimately succeeded, the date is a reasonable one for ETS to choose to celebrate an anniversary, but to other members of the interim committee and the National Council, the question of a testing agency was at that date still open.

Implementing the plan

The May 1961 conference had adopted a set of recommendations and appointed an interim committee to implement them. Taking into account the normal summer hiatus in US academic activity, the committee seems to have tackled its work with good speed, and by the beginning of the next school year in September, it had sent out invitations to a follow-up meeting to take place in Washington on 12–13 January 1962.

In New York, the College Board was now, like ETS, starting to take a close interest in the initiative. Its new *ad hoc* committee on foreign student admission was already at work. After a meeting between Richard Pearson and Katharine Salter on 16 June 1961, the Board staff set out their plan to take over the test:

> The advisory group [the National Advisory Council] that has been set up to consider the development of such tests will apply for a grant to develop the tests and produce the first form. After this, the Board would be willing to take on the administration of the test in our overseas centers, and to re-issue new forms of the test, thus, to bring it under the umbrella of the Board. An examining committee would be set up to watch the control and administration of this particular test. Regarding the aptitude section of this test, it is felt that counter-part testing would be a far better way of arriving at the hoped-for answer, i.e., the ability of the student to learn in an American institution, and that the level of English Language Proficiency of the student is a secondary question, only to be asked and answered after the ability of the student is known. (College Entrance Examination Board 1961)

Counter-part tests had as their objective 'the same kind of measurement, in both aptitude and in achievement, as is now available for American students who take the tests of the CEEB' and might need to be given in the student's language, and 'in the context of his own culture' (Chalmers 1960a). Thus, the College Board too was watching developments closely, not intending to be out-manoeuvred, as Bowles had put it, in this new initiative by a group of Ford-supported organizations, and ready to assert control over what it considered its own territory.

Members of the interim committee, for the most part unaware of the independent plans on the part of ETS and of the College Board to bring the new test under their respective 'umbrellas', continued to plan for independence. The second conference in January 1962 (National Advisory Council 1962a) 'represented the first step' in implementing the decisions of the May 1961 conference. Invitations were sent out[3] to all who had taken part in the May 1961 conference, and also to representatives of other organizations suggested by participants.[4]

The vice-president of the College Board, Edward Noyes (1961a), gave some warning signals in his letter accepting the invitation: 'We surely do not wish to be uncooperative', he cautioned. Katharine Salter would represent the Board and 'assist in the formation of the advisory council', but for the more technical matters, Fred Godshalk was better qualified. 'Since he had worked with our College Board examining committees in English, since I know he has an excellent technical background, and since he is willing to act for the Board as well as for Educational Testing Service', Noyes nominated him as College Board representative for work on actual test construction and administration.[5]

Many of those who had been at the first conference came,[6] but some, by this new academic year, had new affiliations.[7] Although a number of foundations were invited to the meeting, only Melvin Fox from the Ford Foundation was present, a clear indication of funding problems to come. Considering that participants in the January 1962 meeting were expected to have their organizations or institutions pay their way, the strong representation[8] is a sign of the seriousness with which the purpose of the meeting was taken.

On the first day of the meeting,[9] after a welcome by Charles Ferguson, David Harris, chairman of the interim committee, explained that the conference had two main purposes. It would review the report of the May 1961 conference and then set up a National Advisory Council which would carry out the test development programme it had adopted. In a review of this programme, Fred Godshalk stressed the idea of an 'omnibus' two-and-a-half-hour test.

Godshalk's presentation ruled out the more integrative kinds of tests that Carroll (1961) had favoured. He also said that the language aptitude test, which involved extra cost, was 'desirable but not necessary'.[10] A letter from

Noyes (1961b) reveals that Godshalk had talked to people at the College Board, and may have learnt of their notion of using counterpart tests rather than including aptitude in the battery. Godshalk further said that the development of an oral production test did not seem possible at the moment, because of the lack of equipment of high enough fidelity.

In a further attack on direct testing, Godshalk drew attention to the difficulty and expense of tests of written production. Sending essays by airmail would be much more expensive than sending answer sheets. In continuing the campaign against direct tests of written ability, the level of argument moved in this more bureaucratic context from theoretical to financial considerations.

Godshalk himself was at this time in the midst of the debates at ETS over essays versus objective measures of writing ability. Although at Princeton he was involved with the projects that restored essays (for a while) to acceptability for first language testing, in the second language context he proved an effective opponent of their use. The planned tests were to be administered overseas and in some US centres, but scored only in the United States. Many foreign students would have problems with objective tests. To start off, it would be necessary to obtain foundation support for development, but Godshalk believed that government agencies should in time find the programme useful.

In the discussion, Starr talked about the difficulty of administering tests abroad. Robert Lado proposed the kind of indirect oral measures that he himself had used, to which David Harris replied that he had not seen any satisfactory oral production test. Harris (1989) noted that he assumed at that time that there would be high priority for such a test once the project was under way, but as it was necessary to get something started fast, he did not want to become involved in the extra complication.

After the morning coffee break, the discussion continued to range widely. Topics included the possibility of pre-testing in the summer or in the armed forces, agency funding for Fulbright students within a year or so, the need for about $10,000 extra for the aptitude study, the need for more than just English proficiency tests for foreign students, and anecdotal accounts of individual foreign students at American universities who had failed because they did not know English. John Winterbottom said that the Association of American Law Schools had no funds to support the proposed organization.

When Leon Bosch of the Association of American Collegiate Schools of Business asked why existing tests could not be used or revised, David Harris replied that the new test would in fact be based on existing ones.[11] The Michigan tests, he said, had been fully revised and would provide a good starting-point. However, it was pointed out that no existing test was either comprehensive or focused enough to serve the required purpose. University students, Harris said, were only a small proportion of those tested by the American Language Institute test. Existing facilities for administration could not be easily expanded. Existing test forms were insecure because they were used too many times and they had not been satisfactorily validated. When Bosch went on to ask why a new organization was needed, Harris answered that no existing organization was able to offer or control a world-wide testing programme, obtain the agreement of all potential users, and validate the new test. The exception, which he did not mention, was the College Board, but it had nothing like the system that the University of Cambridge had developed.

Discussion continued about the scope and administration of the new test, showing conflicting views. When it was argued that the new test must be more focused on university-relevant English proficiency, the Army representative said this would be a disadvantage from their point of view. Another speaker thought the test should be broad enough for all types of people, including those aiming to work in factories. Harry Freedman thought wider use might be achieved by using sub-tests. This might make it possible for the test to be used for short-time visitors on Agency for International Development programmes. Godshalk discussed the feasibility of sub-tests, which he said would involve administering different versions in different rooms, but might be achieved by a test with detachable pages. Harris pointed out that this raised the problem of security when giving tests overseas. How could the universities be guaranteed that the secrecy of the test forms had not been compromised? If there were too many different populations and tests, tests would have to be given very often. Rather, he expressed the hope that there was agreement that there would be a single test, but with subscores available.

A participant from the universities asked for research on open-ended responses and essays, mentioning that a student of his was working on this topic. Harris's response was negative. He cited Starr to the effect that one could not obtain objective results with essay responses, but only subjective judgements of things like style. 'Our experience is', the notes of the meeting quote him, 'we don't want to put time and money into this'. He asked Godshalk to comment on the experience at ETS. Godshalk agreed, and pointed out further the expense involved in essays. If an essay is written, it must be read, which takes more time and expense. Unfortunately, there was no objective way to score essays, nor could test users agree on criteria. But it was still planned to include a written sample for test users to use as they saw fit.

Harris ended the morning session by asking if agreement existed on having a limited number of test administrations every year. After the Army and Air Force representatives pointed out their difficulties with this, he presented two related proposals:

1 Three administrations of the test a year for universities and other
groups.
2 Arrange to make tests available to other agencies for administering
their own tests and being responsible for their security and making
their results available to us.
(National Advisory Council 1962a: 5)

Finally, a set of proposals was voted on and passed.[12] The meeting then
broke for lunch, during which time the extra details in the proposals were
presumably worked out by some of the committee.

Harris started the afternoon session by recapitulating the three main
points on which he had found consensus: an identical form of the test for
everyone, a regular administration three times a year, and special users (as
approved by the Advisory Council) who would be permitted their own test
administrations. The conference next turned to organizational issues.
Harris outlined the plan set out in the May conference.[13] There would be
a National Advisory Council at the top, to be established formally at this
meeting, and to be responsible for financing and operating the programme;
an executive committee to carry out policy; and a part- or full-time project
director.[14] The project director would be a 'professional man' assisted by
a clerk-typist, and would be aided by test construction committees, made
up of 'test construction men'. The committees would find item writers for
the various parts of the test. A central test committee with about nine members would set specifications for the items and make technical decisions.
Thus, the council would make policy decisions and the test construction
committee technical ones. The National Advisory Council members would
not be paid, but their meeting expenses would be reimbursed. The testing
committee would be paid on a per diem basis for meetings, and receive a
fee for reviewing items. Harris (personal communication) later explained
that he felt it was important that test writers should be chosen from the
leading professionals in the field of English as a foreign language.

Because the council would be financed by private funds and not governmental money, it would not need to seek competitive bids for test services.
A test service (still unnamed) would carry out the technical work, but the
test writing would be done by experts in the field of English as a foreign
language. Godshalk added that these items would then be submitted to the
test construction committee for review. The tests would be administered
in the students' countries of origin, and sent to the United States for scoring
by the testing service.

Discussion of details of overseas administration of the test continued
after the afternoon coffee break. An expanded test would stretch consulate
and US Information Agency resources. Various methods of shipping test
forms and answer sheets were discussed, as was the issue of co-ordinating
administration dates around the world and avoiding local national holi-

days. One participant asked about using US shipping, but was told (presumably by Harris or Godshalk) that it was better to use KLM Airlines to return answer sheets by airmail express.

At 4.30 p.m., a formal meeting of the National Advisory Council, made up of all organizational representatives present, took place, at which David Harris was elected temporary[15] chairman.[16] The draft notes for the day's session concluded with a statement that 'the Interim Committee Chairman, Dr Godshalk, will prepare [a] schedule of costs for setting up this test'.

The Saturday morning session began with what Winterbottom (1962) characterized as the 'crucial topic of funding'.[17] Godshalk, for the interim committee, presented an estimated cost of $368,000 for two years, assuming six test administrations, each with a new form, with 200 centres and an average of 5,000 candidates for each administration:

Cost estimates for two years for TOEFL, 1962

1	Test construction	$145,000
2	Test administration	134,000
3	Scoring and reporting	24,000
4	Director's office	65,000
	Total	$368,500

The test would cost about $10–12 per candidate, which was comparable to the cost of existing tests such as the Scholastic Aptitude Test, the Graduate Record Examination, and the Law School Aptitude Test and had also been the price for the 1930 and 1946 College Board tests.

In the discussion of finances the Ford representative, Melvin Fox, commented that his Foundation was becoming increasingly interested in the general field of language,[18] and while this interest had not yet 'developed its full momentum', a proposal to fund the testing programme 'would probably find a sympathetic ear'. At the same time, the Foundation would probably expect governmental agencies and others interested to make a contribution, so that he suggested forming a consortium of foundations and of agencies that would commit themselves to buying tests and services. Before an approach was made to any foundation, a survey of potential users should be carried out to find out how interested they were and what support they would give. Ford could not consider a proposal before 30 September 1962,[19] and the informal approach should not be begun before June 1962. Foundations might be prepared to pay for the costs of developing and launching the programme—test production and the director's office, for instance—but programme costs such as administration, scoring, and reporting would need to be recouped from users. Another suggestion Fox made was to develop a five-year rather than a two-year budget, both to allow the programme to become firmly established and to show this eventual self-reliance to a foundation asked to help in the initial period.

The conference accepted the point that after 'the developmental stage', the programme would be 'largely or wholly self-supporting'. It agreed to seek the support of several foundations. It agreed that approaches should be made only after a five-year budget had been drawn up and a survey carried out of prospective test users, namely the university, the government, and the military.

After a break for lunch, the conference met for an hour as the National Advisory Council, and arrived at a number of decisions about the next steps to be taken. The council should meet again in the spring (30 April to 1 May was proposed), at which time it would determine a site for the permanent centre of the testing programme, set up key committees, approve a five-year budget, select a 'test construction organization', and agree on how the proposal was to be presented to the foundations. In preparation for this meeting, people who had attended this January meeting were to ask their organizations to appoint them as permanent members and to make a commitment to the programme and to its support.

The interim committee was to continue in office (albeit with what Winterbottom characterized as the 'more grandiose title' of *Interim Executive Committee*) and with three additional members. The Council further voted to ask the three sponsoring organizations (the Center for Applied Linguistics, the Institute of International Education, and the National Association of Foreign Student Advisors) for more funds for ongoing operations. The committee was instructed and authorized to prepare a report of the conference,[20] add other appropriate organizations to the council, review the costs and prepare a five-year budget, carry out a survey of prospective users, prepare a job description for the project director, and prepare the agenda for the spring meeting.[21]

With the second conference the pattern of action became clear; the general specifications had been agreed on; and the role of ETS was assured. In the internal ETS report he wrote on the 12–13 January meeting, Godshalk (1962a) summarized the main points of the meeting exactly as they have been outlined here. On one matter of concern, he added that he assumed the decision would eventually be made not to include a 'secure' writing sample in the battery. He believed that the interim executive committee would move soon to select a testing committee and propose a project director. Even more important, he felt confident that the role of ETS as the testing service for the programme was now quite secure, and believed that work should start on drafting an ETS contract:

Action to select a testing committee and propose a director of the Testing Program will be taken by the Executive Committee, I feel sure. It might also be advisable for ETS to be ready with the bare bones of a contract proposal. The Executive Committee will choose ETS as the professional testing organization for test construction, administration, and routine procedures; the chance that the National Advisory Council will not approve this choice is extremely remote ...

Godshalk also drew attention to the statement by Melvin Fox that Ford would not pick up the full bill.

In one year of work, a good deal had been accomplished and the general design of an English testing programme had been developed. While both ETS and the College Board had strong hopes of gaining major control of the new programme, most of the others involved seemed to think it could work independently. But in any case, the blueprint was useless without money. Now a good proposal was needed to raise funds to implement the design.

Notes

1 It is not clear if the interim committee actually met or if it made the decision by telephone.
2 It is probable that Wantman's interest in this test revision was raised by Katharine Salter's inquiries about the test in February; her copy of a letter from Bretnall (1961) has Wantman's name written in a margin, and also the words 'Proposal—Mr. Turnbull').
3 The invitation, typed on Center of Applied Linguistics paper, to Edward Noyes was dated 20 November 1961, and signed by David P. Harris (1961b) as chairman of the interim committee.
4 Newly represented at this second meeting were the National Council of Teachers of English (Harold B. Allen), the American Association of Collegiate Schools of Business (Leon Bosch), the Department of Defense (David Quant), the United States Navy (John Falco), the Department of the Army (Rowland Foulstone), the United States Air Force (William Looney), the African Scholarship Program of American Universities (Stewart Fraser), the American Council of Education (C. H. Walter Howe), the African American Institute (Henryk Uznanski), the Association of American Medical Colleges (Joseph Whiting), and the American Association of Law Schools (John A. Winterbottom). Representing the Division of International Education of the US Office of Education, Thomas Cotner joined Frederick Cromwell. The United States Information Agency was represented by Ainslie B. Minor. John Thurston represented the Institute of International Education.
5 Noyes seems to have completely forgotten this confidence in Godshalk when he presented Fox's request for College Board reactions to the funding proposal a year later. See Chapter 15.
6 Present with unchanged status were James Alatis (US Office of Education), Charles Ferguson and Sirarpi Ohannessian (Center for Applied Linguistics), Melvin Fox (Ford Foundation), Harry Freedman

(except that the International Cooperation Agency had now become the Agency for International Development), Fred Godshalk (Educational Testing Service), Robert Lado (Georgetown University), Sydney Sako (Language School, US Air Force, Lackland), Katharine Salter (College Entrance Examination Board), Inez H. Sepmeyer (University of California, Los Angeles), Joel B. Slocum (Columbia University), Wilmarth Starr (Modern Language Association), J. Morgan Swope (International Institute of Education), and Grant Taylor (New York University). John B. Carroll was neither invited nor present.

7 David Harris, who had moved from American University to Georgetown, taking with him the American Language Institute, now represented the National Association of Foreign Student Advisers. Leslie Palmer had joined Harris at the American Language Institute of Georgetown University, with the result that John Upshur represented the English Language Institute of the University of Michigan. Raleigh Morgan was now at Howard University.

8 Of those who had participated in the May conference, the only people missing were Thomas L. Crowell (Columbia University), Edward T. Hall (Washington Institute of Psychiatry), and D. P. Martin (British Embassy).

9 I have found three separate reports of this conference.

10 In the formal report of the conference, this is interpreted somewhat more positively: 'The language aptitude test shall not be included in the initial tests, but a separate proposal shall be prepared for experimental work in developing such an aptitude test for which supporting funds independent of the major proposal should be sought' (National Advisory Council 1962d: 2).

11 According to a report written by John Winterbottom (1962).

12 Details appear in the official report:
    Test forms and answer sheets shall be made available to certain special kinds of users (chiefly governmental and military) approved by the Council, for use at their discretion after the regular administrations of a test on a specified date, each of these special users to handle its own administrations and scoring, and to furnish the Project Director with the data so obtained for use as additional normative data. (National Advisory Council 1962d: 2)

13 Winterbottom's report refers to this as the November meeting.

14 The draft minutes cite Harris as saying the organization would be 'based on N[ew] Y[ork] C[ity]'. However, the official version of the decisions say that location of the permanent centre was to be decided at the next meeting, in May.

15 The notes and Winterbottom do not list the appointment as temporary, but the official report does.

16 Winterbottom has this election taking place at the end of the Saturday morning meeting, but as he points out that he had to leave before lunch, I follow rather the notes and the official report.

17 Winterbottom's is the only detailed account of this part of the meeting.

18 For a survey of the many Ford programmes in the language field, developed with Fox's help over the next decade or more, see Ford Foundation (1975).

19 Sutton (1992) guesses that that date was related to Ford's fiscal year which began on 1 October. Howard and Fox had presumably committed their 1962 budget and planned to include TOEFL in 1963. Fox's suggested timetable was followed, and the proposal was mailed on 5 October.

20 Two were in fact prepared, one by Winterbottom, and one probably by Harris. Winterbottom worked without the detailed notes that were kept of the first day's discussions.

21 Winterbottom, who left before lunch to catch a train, has a slightly different summary: 'I was instructed', he reports, 'to call a meeting of the Council during May and, in the meantime, to begin the survey of potential users and to draft a prospectus for presentation to foundations'.

14   The birth of TOEFL

The National Council starts work

If committee meetings and institutional politics bore you, you would be wise to skip the next two chapters,[1] and turn to Chapter 16, where the testing committee meetings are reported. However, for those who wish to understand (as I did) the way that institutional, political, commercial, and personal factors regularly and freely dominate scientific and theoretical considerations in the field of language testing (just as they do in language teaching and many other applied fields), Chapters 14 and 15 will provide raw data to develop hypotheses of how things really work.

The most intriguing story-line to follow is the way that the testing establishment (the College Entrance Examination Board, the Carnegie Foundation that backed it, and the Educational Testing Service that they had together created) kept careful tabs on a potentially independent programme being built up by a new coalition of Ford Foundation-backed organizations (the Center for Applied Linguistics, the National Association of Foreign Affairs, and the Institute of International Education). There are also many sub-plots to watch. The College Board and ETS already had divergent interests. The foreign student enterprise was somewhat cautious of the newly established Center for Applied Linguistics. Within each organization, there were personal and factional interests (such as, at ETS, the English testers—Godshalk among them—and the foreign language testers, each competing rather than co-operating).

David Harris, on whom fell the major brunt of welding these multiple interests together, was a young language tester, in his first years in Washington, not yet aware of the complex institutional political scene that he had stepped into. He certainly did not know many of the details that have turned up in internal memoranda recorded by some of the people he was working with. His first and main concern was to get the test started, but there was still a lot of fund-raising and even more institutional political manoeuvring to be done before test writing could start.

After the successful second meeting of the newly established council, the newly named interim executive committee[2] moved rapidly to carry out its tasks. Its first, all-day, meeting took place in Washington in David Harris's office on 9 February 1962 (Harris 1962a) and its second on 13–14 April. By May, Harris (1962b) was able to report to the council that the committee had used $350 promised by each of the three sponsoring organizations to appoint a secretary on an hourly basis.[3] Seven new organizations had accepted invitations to be represented. Seven others declined but asked to be kept informed. The three sponsoring organizations were authorized (subject to the approval of the council) to send two representatives each to the May meeting, and the Department of Defense was invited to send three observers. Most significantly, the committee had carried out a survey of the colleges and universities who would be likely to use the results of the test.

The failure to be sure of the potential market had played a major role in the early demise of the two other major US English testing initiatives, in 1930 and in 1946. Both Fox from the Ford Foundation and Godshalk from ETS had good reasons to insist on a user survey. A questionnaire was prepared by the committee at its February meeting. It was to be sent out accompanied by a covering letter, signed by David P. Harris as chairman of the National Advisory Council, that explained the background to the initiative and included a one-page summary of the decisions of the May 1961 and January 1962 conferences, and a list of member organizations of the council.[4] It asked institutions if they agreed that there was 'a definite need for the new and improved programme for testing the English proficiency of foreign students' and whether they would be make use of it.

Given the lack of funds, Fred Godshalk asked William Turnbull on 27 February 1962 for ETS to pay the costs up to $500 of printing the survey. Turnbull's senior colleague, Robert Solomon (1962) was reluctant to do this, arguing that the Advisory Council should look for 'foundation support of a modest sort' to carry on its feasibility study. He thought that 'given the evidence of genuine interest and activity to date by a most prestigious array of educational activities', a foundation should be happy to give three or four thousand dollars for this. Turnbull agreed to Godshalk's request, and the materials were photocopied at ETS. The survey was mailed between 28 March and 18 April by Allene Guss to the presidents of the 965[5] US universities and colleges which, according to the 1960 edition of Open Doors, had at least five foreign students. The mailing cost of $51.50 was paid by the committee.

By May 1962, 575 replies had been received and almost all (97.8 per cent) agreed that there was a need for the new programme. Most agreed that the English preparation of foreign students had been a problem, and half said they would use the testing programme. Further analysis showed that results held true for big schools as well as small ones; that almost all of the forty-four schools with more than two hundred foreign students would probably be interested; and that sixty-five of the sixty-eight institutions currently using the Michigan English Language Institute Testing Service, who replied, would probably be interested. Most of those answering no were small schools with so few foreign students that they could screen all their applicants themselves. Seven big schools said no; five were music or art colleges that felt their students did not need high proficiency in

English; one was satisfied with the Michigan service, and one felt that the test 'would keep too many good foreign students out of the country'.

The main worry was the cost of the test. Schools were most reluctant to pay for the service, and some wondered whether foreign students would be able to afford to take the test, or whether English results might be used to exclude deserving students (Harris 1962d). The survey results reassured the committee and the council that their efforts to get the test started were worthwhile and likely to meet with a market.

Affiliations and plans

At the second meeting of the interim executive committee on 13–14 April 1962, critical decisions were taken on institutional arrangements, the question that had been uppermost in many minds. The committee decided to recommend to the council that the Center for Applied Linguistics should be the permanent centre for the new programme, and that ETS should be the test construction and administration organization.

It might be argued that the deck was stacked. Each of these organizations had a voting representative on the committee—though there was no serious concern over conflict of interest in these matters. Fred Godshalk abstained on the vote to select ETS, which was unanimous. In a letter to John Morse, director of a congressional study of Federal Educational Programmes, College Board vice-president Pearson commented on the politics:

> The three groups which sponsored the original conference in the Testing of English Language Proficiency of Foreign Students are the Center for Applied Linguistics which is an appendage of the Modern Language Association (receiving a large hunk of its money from the Ford Foundation), the Institute of International Education (receiving money from the Ford Foundation and the State Department), and the National Association of Foreign Student Advisers (a child of the Institute of International Education and a membership organization which does receive grants of money from time to time from such foundations as Ford and Danforth). If this looks like an 'interlocking directorate', it is.
> (Pearson 1962)

But the choices made were logical ones. ETS was already far and away the leading testing agency, with a strongly developed machinery for test construction, administration, scoring, analysis, and result reporting. Its close relations with the College Board gave it access to overseas centres. And the Center for Applied Linguistics was a sound choice for a headquarters site, offering not just a physical base in Washington, close to the major centres of English language testing at American University and Georgetown University and to the governmental and international agencies involved with foreign student matters, but also a source of connection to the developing fields of applied linguistics and English as a foreign language.

The general views that had jelled inside the committee can be seen from the statement[6] of proposed job responsibilities of the programme director and associate (Interim Committee 1962b) and from the five-year budget proposal (Interim Committee 1962a) prepared for the May 1962 council meeting. There would be two professional staff members[7] who would run the central office where tests would be constructed. The full description makes clear that the programme would be independent, with its own office and staff, arriving at its own policy and implementation decisions, but collaborating with a test construction and administration organization, now recommended to be ETS. The responsibilities of the professional staff would be to establish a central office, with office staff, and keep appropriate records; plan conferences, preliminary testing, the final forms of the tests, and overseas administration; make progress reports and maintain liaison with funding agencies, the test construction and administration organization, and the various committees; negotiate contracts and develop grants, control budget and payments; recruit test committees, make policy decisions about testing specifications, proof-read tests and decide in cases of controversy, look at item analyses, collect and disseminate information on norms and validity, and supervise the language aptitude and other studies; and handle publicity and public relations.

The budget proposal[8] (restricted in distribution at that time to 'members of the Council and their principals who have a legitimate special interest in the testing programme') was an extension to five years of the earlier two-year budget presented to the council in January 1962. The estimate for the first two years of the programme was fairly close to the earlier estimate ($383,440 instead of $368,500), although within the budget a good deal seems to have been moved to the heading of programme direction, doubled from $65,000 in the first budget to nearly $122,000 in the second, from test construction and administration. One might surmise that this change reflected the increased responsibility of the programme staff beyond what Godshalk had at first envisaged. It also follows logically from the decision to have a professional associate to the director.

The budget was based on eleven assumptions, many of which have been seen in embryo form in discussions and decisions reported so far, but some of which show evidence of new conclusions reached in the intervening period:

1 The tests were to follow the recommendations of the May 1961 conference.
2 They were to have about 250 questions, and take two-and-a-half hours.

3 Two forms were to be prepared in the first year and three each year after that; all forms were to be new, but material could be reused 'judiciously' three to four years after the first use.
4 The first two forms were to be experimental, to test administration procedures and revise the testing pattern.
5 The first two forms were to follow rigid specifications, but to be pre-tested only in classes conducted by members of the test construction committee.
6 All subsequent tests were to be fully pre-tested, and to be as nearly parallel as possible.
7 The fee charged was to be $8.00 per candidate plus $2.00 per score report.
8 Forms of the test were to be sold to government agencies for their own secure administration at a lower cost.
9 Some sale of forms was possible under similar conditions to other US institutions.
10 Language aptitude test development was to be included in a separate proposal.
11 The programme was to aim to be self-supporting 'except for further research and possible different lines of development' by the end of the five-year period.

The five-year cost of the programme was estimated at $1,148,440,[9] based on the assumption of a total of 95,500 candidates over the five-year period, which made a cost per test of just over $12. To cover the expenditure, it was estimated that ultimately individual and institutional fees would suffice; while the first two years were expected to run at a deficit of $120,000–140,000 each, in the third and fourth the deficit would drop to $30,000–50,000, and in the fifth to $5,000. The estimate of 22,500 candidates a year for the third to fifth years turned out to be conservative. By the fifth year, the figure was close to 50,000. To provide a hedge against variation in institutional and government support, the maximum sum that was to be requested from foundations was $558,440 for the five years. The budget was carefully broken down into cost areas and particular items.

It is interesting to look in some detail at the first-year budget for the underlying assumptions about programme operation that it made. Test construction was estimated at $21,500. This provided for meetings of the test construction committee ($6,000) and the committee on testing and research ($2,000), the services of two ETS consultants at these meetings, the actual meeting costs ($1,500), and honoraria for 15 test writers ($1,500). Once written, the items would be reviewed and revised by ETS and prepared for committee review ($3,725). ETS would then prepare final copy for two tests ($4,160); extra costs for the listening tests were estimated at $1,615. The printing cost for the test forms was estimated at $15,600. Test administration, which involved arranging for up to 200 centres, was estimated at $44,000; $10,660 of this was for the bulletin of information; $16,000 to establish 200 centres, use 150 of them for each administration, and pay honoraria to supervisors; $16,550 to ship and receive test books, via KLM; and, finally, $490 for a supervisors' manual and $360 to file the candidates' tickets of admission. The cost of scoring and recording of results was estimated at $4,656; sending reports to colleges and to the programme director was estimated at $3,344. The final budget heading was the office of the director of the programme. A staff of four was envisaged: a director (salary of $17,500), associate director ($11,000), administrative assistant, and clerk typist; salary costs came to $43,450. Office space and supplies were estimated at $5,160; phones, duplication, transportation, and travel 'to professional meetings and Princeton' at $4,340; there was a further $4,340 for office furniture and equipment and other non-recurring costs; and $5,800 for informational and promotional activities (including entertainment of special guests).

The budgets for following years followed much the same pattern. After the second year, there was an added $16,490 for pre-testing of materials for the forms; test construction then went down slightly, printing and test administration became higher, as did the estimate for scoring and reporting. The director's office was also reduced, on the assumption that promotional activities would gradually decrease and some of the activities of the office would become chargeable to otherwise-supported research programmes.

The plan for test construction and preparation followed closely the ETS working arrangement, with professional test developers working as intermediaries between subject-matter specialist test writers and committees and the test administration, standards being controlled by psychometric principles implemented by statistical analysis and reporting. The subject-matter specialist in this arrangement may propose an item, but the make-up of the final form of the test is essentially determined by its statistical properties; as assumption 6 in the budget proposal written by Godshalk spelt it out:

6 That all forms after the first two be prepared from pretested materials to meet predetermined content and statistical criteria and therefore to be as nearly parallel in content and difficulty as may be achieved by standard psychometric procedure.
(Appendix 6, page 1 Report of the May 1962 meeting)

This decision to follow the ETS model, was, I am convinced, a significant step in the development of the test, marking its firm capture by the psychometrists and the machinery they used, with the applied linguists effectively restricted to the drafting of individual items. The interim executive committee had created a model which determined not just the organizational shape but also the testing principles that were to dominate.

The second council meeting, May 1962

The second meeting of the council took place four months after the first, and almost exactly a year after the first planning meeting, on 10 and 11 May 1962. By now, the weight of participation had moved to professional administrators,[10] who quickly accepted the recommendations prepared by the interim executive committee.[11] The council agreed unanimously that all its decisions should be by a two-thirds vote of official representatives present at a meeting of the council. The council was to meet at least once a year, ensuring that any changes would now require a solid consensus of the varied groups represented and that no one faction (government, associations, universities) could dominate. Harris also brought to the council two decisions by the committee concerning the make-up of the council: that there should be two representatives for each of the three original sponsoring organizations, and that the Army, Navy, and Air Force should have non-voting status.

Harris reported the results of the questionnaire and its evidence of widespread university support for the new programme. In her notes on the meeting, Salter (1962) commented that this study provided 'a strong vote of confidence in the program' and believed that it would 'serve as good ammunition' in seeking funds from either foundations or government. There was discussion of the name for the council, and on the recommendation of a subcommittee,[12] the name chosen for the programme was Testing of English as a Foreign Language (TOEFL), and for the council the National Council on the Testing of English as a Foreign Language. A year later, the name was modified to Test of English as a Foreign Language.[13]

The two major affiliations proposed by the committee were accepted. ETS was to be invited 'to propose a contractual relationship with the testing program whereby ETS would serve as the program's test construction/administration organization'. This was the triumphant culmination of Fred Godshalk's efforts, from his very first involvement at the beginning of 1961, to set up this arrangement. Salter (ibid.) wrote to Pearson 'It will not be surprising for you to learn that the Educational Testing Agency was selected as the testing agency . . .' Godshalk (1962b) had more details on this:

A recommendation by the interim executive committee that the services of ETS be sought as the test construction and administration agency was approved without dissent (one abstention, mine) and almost without comment. The call of the chairman for comment upon the motion for approval produced, after a pause, well-phrased endorsements of ETS by Dean Talbott, representing the AALS, and by Kay Salter, representing the CEEB.

The Permanent Executive Committee was empowered to act on the ETS proposal when it came in. But the programme itself was not to go to Princeton or even to New York. Rather, it was to stay permanently in Washington, and to be housed there, if both the Center and its parent body, the Modern Language Association, agreed, at the Center for Applied Linguistics.

The council also approved the job descriptions and, after a long discussion, the proposed budget. In future each member organization was to have one official representative. In addition, the chairman was authorized to designate non-voting 'consultant representatives' who could serve on committees other than the executive.[14] David Harris was elected permanent chairman, an Executive Committee was established that guaranteed control to the nuclear group, and other committees were approved.[15] A subcommittee (Starr, Ferguson, and Talbott, chair) proposed that the executive committee consist of the chairman, three members of the council elected for one year, and three appointed by the chairman for one year. The proposal was accepted, and the three members elected were Ferguson, Godshalk, and Talbott; subsequently, Harris appointed David Quant, Sims, and Boynton as the three additional members of the committee. The confidence this structure expressed in the chairman is noteworthy, as is the complete lack of concern over potential conflict of interest in appointing Godshalk to a committee that was charged to negotiate a contract with his employers. A finance committee was later appointed by Harris, chaired by Boynton and including Godshalk, Slocum, Ferguson, Dangerfield, and Sims.

The College Board representative, Katharine Salter was sensitive to the political structure.

> This group (the Interim Committee) has been in existence since May 1961. It has carried on the negotiations and planning for the programme on behalf of the council between its three meetings. Thus it has been a key group which was enlarged slightly between the second and third meeting of the council. The enlarged group will probably wield a controlling interest. Even though it has technically been dissolved, its members are now on the key committees.
> (Salter 1962)

In May 1962, a year to the day after the first conference, the institutional lines of the new organization had been set. The new testing programme was to be independent, its independence guaranteed by clear division of authority. The council, acting through a powerful chairman and committees, with a professional and executive staff of director and associate and a physical home in the Center for Applied Linguistics in Washington, would have a contractual arrangement with ETS in Princeton. In theory, this independence should have meant that testing philosophy would be determined by the council and its staff, which would enable a merging of candidate and institutional needs with language testing and psychometric principles, although as we have seen the mix was already fairly well predetermined. But real independence depended on financial backing. No foundation representative was present at the May 1962 meeting, which had estimated a five-year deficit of at least $500,000 to produce a self-supporting but minimal test, with much more needed to carry out the important research proposed in the May 1961 meeting to develop the kind of test that the experts believed was needed.

Negotiating

The institutional arrangements had to be negotiated and a start made on the search for funding. One organizational connection was straightforward, thanks to the dual role of Fred Godshalk. The relation with ETS was ratified when ETS and the Modern Language Association signed a formal letter of agreement on 1 July 1962 (Educational Testing Service and Modern Language Association 1962).

Other relations took a while longer. Discussions with the Center for Applied Linguistics took place in June and July. Damon Boynton (1962a), who was dean of the graduate school at Cornell University, wrote to David Harris on 7 June 1962 agreeing to serve on the executive committee and at the same time reporting on a meeting of the finance committee. At this meeting, attended also by Fred Godshalk, Albert Sims, and Joel Slocum, a proposal had been considered from Charles Ferguson, director of the Center for Applied Linguistics, for how the programme should be integrated into the Center. The negotiators (none of them a linguist) felt that Ferguson was asking for too much control. They wanted the programme to remain independent, with the Center for Applied Linguistics providing space or services for it on a cost basis. It is tempting to speculate on how different things might have been for TOEFL and for the Center if a more permanent relationship had been established!

The financial arrangement took some time to settle. In a later letter, dated 27 July 1962, Boynton reported on a meeting he had had with George Winchester Stone (executive secretary of the Modern Language Association, which was fiscally responsible for the Center for Applied Linguistics), who had agreed to discuss with Ferguson modifications to the proposal which would give the programme more independence (Boynton 1962b). Stone would also raise the question of the 15 per cent overhead, which Boynton thought was too high. No final decision had been made in September, when Sims (1962b) wrote a letter to Harris about it. In September, Boynton (1962c) wrote to Harris again about the issue of the relationship between TOEFL and the Center for Applied Linguistics. He also suggested adding to the proposal a sentence on the complementary development of an 'evaluation' test; one assumes he was referring to the proposed attitude test.

In the meantime, between May and 5 October the chief activity of the committee members was writing the grant proposal to the Ford Foundation.[16] Fred Godshalk (1962c) reported on 21 September 1962 to his supervisor at ETS, William Turnbull, on the progress of the proposal writing and on its contents. The TOEFL budget was estimated at $558,440 for three years. Melvin Fox was ready to act on the proposal, which would go only to the Ford Foundation. Writing to Edward Noyes a few months later, Godshalk (1963c) was not happy with this: 'The proposal has gone to Ford only, through Fox. This was perhaps an error of judgement.'

In his letter to Turnbull, Godshalk (1962c) wrote, 'The proposal has suffered from randomitis, growing in odd ways to [resemble the saying that] the camel is a horse assembled by a committee.' Making things more difficult, David Harris, chairman of the executive committee, was ill and had been 'pretty much out of gear' for several weeks; he had just gone to his parents' home for at least a month of convalescence. While Harris was away on convalescent leave, his post had to be forwarded to him in South Carolina. On 10 October, Harris (1962c) wrote to Fox answering some questions about the draft proposal and advising him that Godshalk would be acting chairman for the rest of the month. He reassured Fox that the fees were reasonable, although there were some institutions who naively thought they should be free. Fox (1962a) replied that he would study the proposal 'within several weeks'. He mentioned also that he had spoken with Jane Alden (in the State Department) who had reaffirmed the Government's interest and thought it might be possible to obtain 'stronger assurances' about government use of the tests.

In spite of the difficulties, Godshalk (1962c) assured Turnbull that the job of writing the proposal should be finished by mail and phone by the end of the following week. Godshalk included a detailed budget for test construction, printing, administration, scoring, and reporting, and it was hoped to have trial administrations early, with foreign trials in May or June 1962. The test was to follow the May 1961 plans; there were to be 250 questions and it would take two and a half hours. Two forms were to be prepared in the first year; three each year after that; new forms would be used for each administration. Items could be used again after three or four years. The first two forms would be experimental and informally pre-tested. After that, there would be formal pre-testing 'as nearly parallel in content and difficulty as may be achieved by standard psychometric procedure'. The fee for taking the test would be set at $8, with an additional fee of $2 for extra reports. Use by government agencies (including the armed services) and other institutions was envisaged. Aptitude test research was to be conducted parallel to the other work but was not included in the budget. The programme should be self-supporting after five years except for the cost of additional research and development. The writing, or perhaps, more accurately, the cobbling together[17] of the proposal was completed by early October and sent off to Fox at the Ford Foundation. On 13 December 1962, David Harris (1962e) reported to members of the TOEFL executive committee that it had been mailed to the Ford Foundation on 5 October. In his letter of transmission addressed to Melvin Fox, Harris (1962c) stressed the need for a guarantee of funds for five years, explaining that more exact figures would be known each year as the programme developed.

Tally-ho

Action now moved to the Ford Foundation and Melvin Fox. On 17 October, Fox acknowledged receipt of the proposal, and a month later, on 19 November, he told Albert Sims that the foundation should make a decision by February 1963. At this meeting, Fox asked about the prospects for Government help. Following up on this, Albert Sims went to Washington, and together with David Harris met with Don Cook, director of the Bureau of Educational and Cultural Affairs at the State Department. Cook said it would be difficult but not impossible for the Department of State to help; he suggested approaching the Agency for International Development.

Fox himself later checked out possibilities. On 5 December, Alfred Boerner (1962), Acting Assistant Secretary of State responsible for Educational and Cultural Affairs, wrote to him: 'I have meant to write to you ever since the meeting at Brookings to comment on your brief remarks on English language programs abroad and the role which the Government and the Foundations can play in this major effort . . .' Boerner was pleased by the prospect of Ford grants to Cornell University and other institutions to expand the 'resource base' for training Americans in linguistics and English language teaching. The Department of State was working towards 'formulating a broad policy statement which will set forth the objectives of our English language activities in terms of the national interest' but it would take some months of work with the several agencies involved to accomplish this. In the meantime, they were waiting to hear reports from posts abroad on the testing question, which he considered a much needed effort. There were no positive results from either of these approaches, so that the development of the test, though originally stimulated by the Government, was in fact to be left to the private sector.

Having had time for a first reading of the proposal, and once Harris was back from his convalescence, Fox now started checking details. He sounded out his colleagues at Ford, responding to or anticipating questions that would be asked as the various levels of foundation executives considered the proposal. The kind of constructive compromise work that middle-level staff like Melvin Fox carried out so well, forming the bridge between those controlling the funds—foundation and government officials with limited knowledge of the field and complex political and philanthropic agendas of their own—and those asking for them—mission- or theory-oriented professionals and scholars with hazy notions of feasibility—was an essential feature of the success of initiatives like TOEFL, and deserves much wider recognition. In practice, research and development brokers like Fox are treated by both sides as not altogether trustworthy, and certainly as a nuisance. Looking back over the full record, though, it is clear that TOEFL would never have been funded without Fox's careful negotiation and compromises.

How he worked can be reconstructed from the records. On 10 December, Fox (1962b) asked Harris for 'the dimensions of your most current budget estimate' and asked to meet him in Washington on 19 December. He raised three questions. Could the programme be started with a grant of $225,000? This setting of Ford Foundation funding at less than half the amount requested was critical in that it allowed the programme to be started but effectively ruled out its chances of independence. Would the Government use the new test in place of the American Language Institute tests they were at present using? And how much government use was there of these tests? While there is no documentary evidence that anyone raised the questions specifically, it would be surprising if someone had not recalled the fate of the earlier College Board attempts to start an examination like this. It is my guess, as I will discuss a little later, that College Board officers were probably in touch with senior Ford Foundation officers, independently of the work that Fox was doing at a lower level, and unknown to him. The doubts they raised would explain both the funding limitation and the request for reassurance of government support.

Harris (1963a) replied to Fox's questions in a letter on 16 January, having in the meantime talked with Fred Godshalk and other members of the executive committee. First, he told Fox the reaction of ETS. Godshalk, he said, had discussed the matter with ETS officials who expressed the belief that ETS would probably be willing to negotiate a contract on the basis of the Ford grant but that they would be 'unwilling to commit themselves for more than one or two years without guarantees of additional funds'. Harris made an 'educated guess' that a grant of $225,000 would not quite cover two years of operation. They would therefore need to find more money, and he was trying to set up an executive committee meeting to discuss this. He asked for a further meeting with Fox on the possibility of additional Ford funding at a later date.

On the question of government use, he told Fox about two meetings where the Department of State and the Agency for International Development had said they would use the tests. On 7 December, Donald B. Cook (director of educational and cultural programmes of the Bureau of Educational and Cultural Affairs of the Department of State) had told Harris and Sims that the Bureau would use the new tests and, subsequently, Harry Freeman (English language specialist of the International Training Division of the Agency for International Development) had said that the Agency for International Development would also use them. While there were no records of the number of tests that these agencies needed, this could be inferred from the fact that in 1962 the American Language Institute had sent out 38,762 answer sheets for the basic structure test for use by government posts abroad. The potential market was good.

Pressure of business kept Fox (1963a) from accepting the invitation to meet the executive committee in Washington on 25 January, but he expressed himself willing to meet anyone in New York. Noyes and Godshalk went to see him. Strange as it may seem to the observer sensitive to conflicts of interest, it was indeed the case that staff members from the College Board and ETS were conducting these key negotiations on behalf of an independent organization that they later jointly swallowed.

Fox had prepared some detailed questions about the budget that were passed to Fred Godshalk, who submitted his answers two weeks later, on Friday 8 February 1963. Fox's first question concerned the size of the testing committees; he had counted thirty-two members. Godshalk replied that the test writing committees consisted of fifteen people, and the testing and research committee (which directed the work of the others) of six, a total of twenty-one, needed to prepare at least 750 questions. Fox asked about the honoraria, set higher than the $100-a-day Ford Foundation maximum. Godshalk replied that the testing and research committees were being paid at the rate of $71.50 per day, and members of the test writing committees would receive $66.67 per day for meetings, and an additional $100 to write fifty items and review one hundred. In subsequent years, experienced writers would receive $3.00 per acceptable item. 'The first year's writing', he noted, 'is a learning operation, basically. Prospective members of the test construction committees will be offered a "token" honorarium, therefore, for item writing in Year A, on [the] assumption that later professional work at a realistic fee will be a possible outcome.' Fox asked a third question about the number of overseas centres for test administration. Were as many as two hundred needed to start with? Godshalk answered that for the first year a number of 'stand-by' centres had been proposed, in order to allow for widely scattered test administration. If only a hundred centres had to be used, there would be a saving of $3,450; if only seventy-five, there would be a saving of $5,175.

Fox asked other questions about staff and budget. He further asked if overheads for the Center for Applied Linguistics had been included in the budget. Godshalk reported that they were not. Following the 25 January executive committee meeting, Malcolm Talbott was to meet George Winchester Stone to negotiate the MLA/Center for Applied Linguistics agreement. The finance committee had earlier rejected the proposal that Ferguson had made for the Center for Applied Linguistics arrangement. As Godshalk understood things, there were two basic difficulties. First, the Center for Applied Linguistics had assumed too much authority over the TOEFL operation; and second, it was asking for too much money for this. Talbott had broad power to negotiate both arrangements and the payment, within the limits of 5–7½ per cent of the cost of the programme director's office, estimated to run between $3,000 to $5,000 a year, in addition to direct costs for office rental and administrative or professional services. Another question concerned fringe benefits for programme staff. These had been set at 10 per cent. Godshalk explained that the figure would include employer payments to social security, retirement, and health insurance. The budget included 'cash fringe benefits', which, he explained was an ETS term for a sum paid by the employer that would otherwise have to be paid by the employee, that was 'a salary increment (beyond stated salary) not included in annual salary for income tax purposes'. He noted that 'legal provision for eventual taxation of employer contributions to retirement' would apply. Godshalk also reorganized the budget as Fox had requested into seven categories: salaries, fringe benefits, conference and travel, rental of space and equipment, printing and publication, office expenses, and indirect costs.

In this exchange, Melvin Fox played an auditing role, checking that the proposed budget was realistic. Fox also raised with the National Council questions about the formal responsibility of the various groups, and asked for formal letters and resolutions. At his request, a formal resolution was prepared for the executive council of the Modern Language Association which spelt out the willingness of the Association to be involved, its role as fiscal agent, the fact that ownership and policy for the tests was vested in the National Council, the housing of the programme at the Center for Applied Linguistics, which would provide facilities and services while not interfering with its independence, the right of the Modern Language Association, the Center for Applied Linguistics, and the National Council to terminate the arrangements, and the role of ETS as sub-contractor. Malcolm Talbott (1963), a member of the executive committee of the National Council and a professor and assistant dean of law at Rutgers, had worked out details of the resolution with George W. Stone (MLA executive secretary) and his successor, John Hurt Fisher, together with Charles Ferguson (director of the Center for Applied Linguistics) and Willmarth Starr (director of the MLA foreign language programmes) at a meeting on 6 February, the same day that Fox was meeting Noyes at the College Board. The resolution would come to the MLA Board in March. Fox (1963b) was very pleased with the agreement, which he credited to the good work of Talbott, and especially with the decision of the MLA 'general staff' (presumably Stone and Fisher) on overheads, in that they seem to have projected Ferguson's earlier position. 'In thus responding to your persuasive logic, they have shown more statesmanship and good sense than at the time of our conference I honestly thought possible.'

When it met, the Modern Language Association executive board approved the resolution, and on 14 March 1963, a formal letter was written by George Winchester Stone (1963), executive secretary of the MLA of America to Henry Heald, president of the Ford Foundation, reporting their decision and affirming that while the Association had no funds to support the proposal, it was willing to act as fiscal agent 'via its Center for Applied Linguistics' for the National Council. David Harris (1963c) wrote to Fox on 19 March saying that the members of the National Council for TOEFL executive committee were in basic agreement with the major terms of the resolution, although some sharper definition of some points might be needed later. Should the Center for Applied Linguistics and the MLA ever withdraw from participation, the National Council would retain full ownership of 'all products of the testing program'. He was ready to recommend that a representative of the MLA serve on the executive committee. While the programme director would be responsible for expenditures, he would recommend a constitutional amendment to establish a finance committee to oversee expenditures and seek additional funding.

Fox asked now for a similar statement on the role of ETS, and an assurance that the National Council would continue its search for financial support. Because he was also anxious about the attitude of the College Board, at their 6 February meeting he spoke to Noyes, who promised to take the case to his Trustees. How Noyes did this shows again the College Board's worry about the TOEFL programme initiative, and its intention to gain control if it could.

Notes

1 And certainly the footnotes.
2 Harris, Godshalk, Swope, Ohannessian, and Slocum were the continuing members; two additional members were added: Hattie Jarmon (of the American Association of Registrars and Admissions Officers) and Frederick Cromwell (from the Department of State).
3 This was Allene Guss, then on the staff of the Institute of Languages and Linguistics at Georgetown University, who, as Allene Guss Grognet, subsequently became a senior staff member of the Center for Applied Linguistics.
4 A copy in the archives of the College Board has a title with the heading 'Department of State: Bureau of Educational and Cultural Affairs'. It ascribes the writing of the questionnaire to James E. Alatis ('formerly with the Department of State'). The data were compiled, it says, by Eugene Shiro (of the American Language Institute, Georgetown University) and the report was by David P. Harris.

5 It was sent to 1,600 institutions, according to the version in the College Board archives, with responses from 993.

6 This had been drawn up by the committee with the assistance of Wilmarth Starr, who had directed the MLA foreign language testing programme.

7 Rather than the single director identified in earlier documents. The description, as expressly pointed out in the committee report signed by David Harris, did not attempt to describe how the two officers would divide up the work. There is no evidence that Harris had already been asked to consider taking the job. But it might have been based on his experience at American University, where he had been hired to assist A. L. Davis but left to carry out the job alone.

8 It had been drawn up for the committee, Harris pointed out, by Fred Godshalk, and reviewed and approved by the committee (Interim Committee 1962a).

9 At the subsequent May meeting of the Council, the total five-year budget was $1,182,950 (Pearson 1962).

10 Present at the two-day meeting, which also was held at Meridian House, were twenty-eight representatives and observers from member organizations. Sixteen had been at the January 1962 meeting: Cromwell from the State Department, Falcao from the Navy, Ferguson and Ohannessian from the Center for Applied Linguistics, Foulstone from the Army, Freeman from the Agency for International Development, Godshalk from ETS, Harris representing the National Association of Foreign Student Advisors, Howe from the American Council on Education, Minor from the United States Information Agency, Palmer from Georgetown, Sako from the Air Force, Salter from the College Board, Slocum also from the National Association of Foreign Student Advisors, Starr from MLA, Swope from the International Institute of Education, and Upshur from Michigan. Robert Allen replaced Harold Allen as representative of the National Council of Teachers of English; Albert Sims represented the Institute of International Education; William Shamblin represented the US Office of Education, and Malcolm Talbott the Association of American Law Schools. A number of major organizations were represented for the first time: the Association of Graduate Schools (Damon Boynton, later to succeed David Harris as chairman of the Council), the Council of Graduate Schools (A. J. Prahl), the Association of State Universities and Land-Grant Colleges (Royden Dangerfield), the Association of American Colleges (G. L. Wormald), the American Economic Association (Merrill Gay), and the American Association of Collegiate Registrars and Admissions Officers (Hattie Jarmon). With the presence of this latter group, the Council could be said to have arrived, to have been joined and recognized by the most important US organizations concerned with foreign student admission.

11 The report of the meeting (National Advisory Council 1962a) is in summary form and organized by topic, without detailed accounts of the
discussion. Many of the decisions of the Council were later included in
the Constitution (National Council 1962b), a copy of which is printed
as Appendix 7 of the Report, although there is no formal statement of
when it was adopted.

12 Slocum, Godshalk, and Foulstone, chair.

13 The abbreviated history prepared by ETS in 1988 mistakenly claims
that this designation was determined at the May 1962 meeting. Salter
(1962) in her report to Pearson also shared this mistaken view, but was
possibly instrumental in the change a year later. See below.

14 Harris then used this provision to appoint the second member for the
sponsors, the Center for Applied Linguistics, the Institute for International Education, and the National Association of Foreign Student
Advisors, in this capacity. The same arrangement was later used to
make Godshalk a consultant when ETS sent a second representative.

15 What was originally (in the May 1961 meeting) proposed as a testing
committee was specified to be a test development and research committee; it would consist of the programme director, a testing specialist, and
the chairmen of the test construction committees. Two *ad hoc* committees were also proposed and subsequently appointed by the chairman:
a services committee (Jarmon, Upshur, Foulstone, and Swope, chair)
and a selection committee to propose director and associate (Freeman,
Palmer, and Starr, chair).

16 A letter from Albert Sims (1962a) to David Harris in August 1962
reports that Joel Slocum wrote the draft. I have not seen a first draft,
but a second draft (National Advisory Council 1962b) is dated 3
August 1962, and headed: 'PROPOSAL: THAT A NEW AND IMPROVED PRO-
GRAM FOR TESTING THE ENGLISH PROFICIENCY OF FOREIGN STUDENTS
OVERSEAS BE DEVELOPED UNDER THE DIRECTION OF THE NATIONAL
COUNCIL ON THE TESTING OF ENGLISH AS A FOREIGN LANGUAGE (NC/
TOEFL)'. It opened with the stark statement of the problem: 'The inad-
equate English proficiency of many foreign students in the United States
causes a waste of time, money, and institutional and human resources.'
The final version (National Council 1962c) was more restrained and
academic in tone:

The past decade has witnessed a dramatic growth in the number of
students and trainees coming to the United States from parts of the
world where English is not the native language. Quite clearly, the
determination of their English competence is a matter of prime
importance; yet it remains the consensus of the academic community
that current screening procedures fail to measure the English proficiency of these students with the diagnostic accuracy necessary to
make sound judgments concerning the feasibility, duration, and

proper nature of their study programs in this country. As a result, they are all too frequently misassigned to institutions and study programs, undue burdens are put upon instructional staffs, educational programs must be extended, adding unanticipated financial burdens to students and their sponsors, and failure or major disappointment is quite likely to be the unhappy outcome of study or training in the United States.

The proposal identified four major shortcomings of existing testing programmes: inadequately trained examiners, insufficient number of test forms, limited test coverage, and limited pre-testing and statistical analysis. It supported these claims by reference to the results of the survey of universities. The plan had been drawn up by 'representatives of universities, governmental agencies, and experts in the teaching and testing of English as a foreign language' who had held a number of conferences and agreed on a testing programme as has been described. The tests would be prepared by experts. ETS would be invited 'to propose a contractual arrangement for the construction, administration, and scoring of the tests, and for reporting test scores to users' and would advise the programme director on statistical analyses. The 'general supervision' of the programme would be by the National Council, on which test users were well represented. The headquarters of the programme would be located on 'an adjunct basis' in the offices of the Center for Applied Linguistics, provided the arrangement was approved by the MLA. The goal was to have a first experimental administration of the test by late spring of 1963.

17 It included numbers of appendices, with reports of meetings, lists of participating institutions, and reports of the survey, as well as the budget.

15 Action in the boardrooms

The College Board defends its turf

One of the intriguing administrative sub-plots in the early years of the Test of English as a Foreign Language affected the College Entrance Examination Board which, with some justification, saw itself potentially threatened by a new group attempting to move in on its territory. When Melvin Fox approached Noyes for help, the College Board had a chance to make sure its interests were safeguarded.

The claim of the College Board for primacy in the English as a foreign language testing business had been staked by its leadership in the two earlier short-lived tests described in Chapters 4 and 8. Its responsibility to meet the gap left by the demise of these tests was reasserted in 1960, in a five-page letter from Paul Chalmers, foreign student adviser at Massachusetts Institute of Technology, to Edward Noyes, acting president of the College Board, urging the Board to 'take some action in the field of selection of foreign students by the universities of this country'. There were, Chalmers remarked, already 48,000 such students, 25,000 of them undergraduates. The weight of screening fell on the colleges and universities, and it was 'in the interests of our foreign policy that this selection be made as wisely as possible'. The College Board's main professional interest would be in the tests used, and one such area of importance was the 'English for foreigners test', an area in which he believed ETS had 'done a little work'. The College Board accepted Chalmer's suggestion, and in December, Richard Pearson (1960), executive vice-president of the College Board, wrote to Chalmers informing him that the special committee on foreign student selection was shortly to be formed. In the same letter, he mentioned that the College Board had just received a letter from Arthur Adams, of the American Council on Education, passing on a recommendation from the council's commission on education and international affairs, that the Board should provide a test in English proficiency for foreign applicants.

As Chapter 11 described, the initiative that led to the development of TOEFL came from elsewhere, and while the College Board was not included in the sponsoring group, it was invited to the May 1961 Washington meeting.

At first, it seems the Board did not take the new initiative too seriously, with the result that Katharine Salter, a programme officer, was chosen as their representative rather than a vice-president. Salter quickly realized the significance of the development. Her report on the May 1961 meeting, the

College Board's apparent initial complacency, and its increasing wariness[1], resulting in the nomination by acting president, Edward Noyes of his old colleague[2] Fred Godshalk as the College Board representative for work on test construction and administration, are described in Chapters 12 and 13.

It was Godshalk who in February 1963 involved Noyes in the key meeting with Fox. Godshalk (1963b) sent Noyes a good deal of material in preparation for the meeting. He provided support for Bowles' prediction when he noted the problem that had arisen with the proposal:

> ... the Executive Committee made a decision to try Ford *solus* because Fox's interest *at the time* led us to believe that Ford might well support the program in its entirety. We were wrong, of course. If any immediate support is forthcoming, it will be limited to $225,000 of the more than half-million requested.

He warned Noyes that Fox was coming to the meeting on 6 February to ask that College Board interest should be expressed 'in financial support', and promised to arrive at 10.30 for their 11.00 a.m. meeting with Fox so that they could co-ordinate their case.

Noyes (1963a) prepared himself some brief notes from the material that Godshalk sent him.[3] At the meeting, Noyes (1963b) made notes of Fox's questions and suggestions and of his reply, explaining the extent and nature of the College Board's overseas activities and commitments, and the fact that it was not a foundation and must draw the line somewhere. Fox, he noted, had 'an exaggerated idea' of the College Board's financial commitment to the programme for selection of African students. He believed the Board should make a financial contribution to TOEFL. He was taking a $250,000 proposal to the Ford trustees' meeting, where he knew he would be asked about the College Board's attitude. A token contribution from the Board would show support. Noyes sensed, though, that Fox believed the Ford funding would not depend on this. The Board had twice in earlier years offered an examination in English for foreign students, and 'our members and Trustees might balk at contributing to an operation not at all under our control in an area in which we had had experience and still, supposedly, had some competence'.

Noyes recorded that he warned Fox that because of previous experience, the trustees would 'shy away from the prospect of steadily increasing support for TOEFL' even if they would come up with a token contribution. He said he would discuss the matter with senior officers. If they agreed, he would propose a token grant of not over $10,000 for each of two years. He thought someone might propose some way in which the College Board 'could share in policy making or administration'. He also advised Fox of the number of test centres that the Board had overseas, which would reduce the problem of security and even perhaps of the number of forms used.

After the 6 February meeting between Fox, Godshalk, and Noyes, Noyes spoke to his colleagues and wrote to Fox, as he stressed, at the suggestion of the College Board president, Mr Bowles (Noyes 1963c). He said that he wished there 'to be no misunderstanding about the Board's genuine interest in the proposed test', noting the fact that the Board had had 'tests roughly similar in intent, if not in kind' at two earlier periods. The Board could not offer financial assistance, but might be willing to make its overseas test centres and supervisors available.[4] This would need action of the Board and depend on 'their judgment as to the commitments which the Board already has, and the relative importance of the new project'. He asked therefore to see the full details of the test and the budget, so that they could be studied in preparation for the College Board meeting in March. Fox (1963c) wrote back at once, saying that he looked forward to the reaction of the College Board trustees, and that Godshalk had now sent a set of materials to Noyes.

At the College Board trustees meeting, Noyes (1963d)[5] fulfilled the promise to present the plan, but did so in a much less favourable light than he had given Fox to believe. He was coming to the trustees, he said, at the request of Melvin Fox, 'Associate Director, International Training and Research, Ford Foundation'. The use of the full title showed his low status. Mr Fox, he said, had asked that the Board make a grant to the National Council on the Testing of English as a Foreign Language. Noyes explained the history of the council, starting with its May 1961 meeting, the establishment of a council, a home, and the election of a permanent chairman. David Harris was identified by Noyes as being 'of NAFSA', an organization of which Salter (1961a) had expressed the Board's distrust, rather than 'of Georgetown University'. One can imagine the suprasegmentals at this point. He listed the number of organizations besides the College Board involved in it. 'I shall read a few of the member organizations, to give you some idea of the company in which we find ourselves . . .' was how Noyes presented this.

To appreciate the effect, one might recall the setting: the trustees of the College Board, with its distinguished history and collegial self-certainty, sitting comfortably in a boardroom in Princeton, listening to a long list of acronymic Washington-based organizations. These people, Ford and the 'interlocking directorate' it had created (Pearson 1962), wanted the Board to 'subscribe' and show interest 'in some substantial way'.

He said that Ford would be making a final decision a week later on a grant request. I quote Noyes's next sentence:

Mr. Fox told me that at first he believed that Ford's answer would depend considerably on whether the College Board thought well enough of this enterprise to subscribe to it; but that he believed on February 6 that the answer would be favorable, in any case, though the amount of the grant will not be quite enough to meet the two-year budget. His plea was that, as a member of the Council, the College Board should show its interest in some substantial way, and he asked me to bring the matter to your attention.

Note the word 'substantial'. In the notes he made after his meeting with Fox on 6 February, Noyes (1963a) referred to the request as of 'token contribution', and spoke in his response of 'a token grant (probably not over $10,000 for each of the two years)'. Noyes was clearly stacking the deck further.

He went on to describe the test, which would be 'wholly objective in type, although there will be an unscored writing sample to be sent to the colleges desiring it'. This too is a strange error, considering how sensitive the issue was at the College Board. I cite from the *Review of College Board Research 1952–60*:

> Undaunted by the lack of success with the General Composition Tests, some member colleges argue loud and strong for an essay measure of writing ability. The Board states its opposition to such a test at the present time and prefers to embark upon further research and developmental work. But member colleges cannot be silenced.
> (Pasanella 1961: 22)

The issue was still very much alive in 1963, so one can only assume that Noyes must have had some reason to misinterpret not just the proposal but also his own notes written on 6 February: 'An additional Writing Sample was suggested but thrown out by vote' (Noyes 1963a).

'Hopefully', he went on, the test would be ready in 1964. 'Hopefully, again', it would become self-supporting. The council also 'hopes' to start research on speaking and aptitude tests, but these were not included in the present budget. At this point, Noyes expressed the further hope that his presentation so far had fulfilled his promise to Fox.

If I have not purposely misread his text, I am fairly certain that he had successfully set up the trustees for the kill that followed, when he finally moved on to his own comments and suggested course of action. He saw no reason to doubt the need for the test. But there were problems:

> On the other hand, no one on the Board staff as yet knows enough about the test to say whether or not it looks like a good one. We do not know who will construct it, and only its very general specifications. The experience we have had with the PSAT and SAT in Africa shows that cultural bias has to be overcome somehow,[6] and I do not as yet understand how a single test can do this for students from Asia, Africa, and the Continent. I do not like to buy a pig in a poke.

Thus, in spite of Salter's involvement as College Board representative from the beginning, his own recognition of the ETS interest, and his former colleague, Fred Godshalk's close participation,[7] Noyes, certainly after talking to other officers of the Board, was taking a strongly negative tack.

He suggested approving the plans in principle, but delaying action until something was known about the instrument itself. He had another suggestion: if the test looked satisfactory, and Ford made a grant sufficient to get the programme under way, then the College Board might arrange with ETS to use the Board's overseas centres. If this were done, the fee for the overseas operation might be at the Board's 7.5 per cent rate rather than the 15 per cent included in the proposed budget. I suspect the trustees would have enjoyed the idea of making their contribution at the expense of part of the fee they paid ETS. He concluded by noting the coincidence that the number of centres proposed for the new test was 150, 'almost precisely' the number of centres the College Board operated.

The trustees voted to 'receive the request with interest and view it with sympathy', but left any decision to their next meeting in September, by which time they hoped to have more details from the staff about the test, its content, administration, and financing (College Entrance Examination Board 1963).

In spite of his disappointment at the lack of real support from the College Board (and surely not realizing how much Noyes had personally contributed to it, and, if my suspicions are correct, to the other difficulties he had with senior officers at Ford), Fox subsequently made sure that Noyes was more centrally involved in the affairs of the new programme. Noyes was invited to the meeting of the executive committee on 3 May 1963, and subsequently elected to it.

After the College Board meeting Noyes (1963e) wrote to Harris to cover himself. He told Harris that Katharine Salter had married and left the staff of the College Board and that he would now represent the Board on the council. 'As a former teacher of English and one long connected with the College Board's own examinations in English,' he looked forward to working with the council. Indeed, he had just had an opportunity to tell the trustees about the work of the council 'as far as I could assemble from the data left by the former Miss Salter or provided by Fred Godshalk'. He would be happy to meet with Harris in due course 'to be brought up to date on the work of the Council'. Harris might have guessed from this evidence that Katharine Salter had not kept her colleagues at the College Board fully informed on the developments. Not being a member of the executive committee, she would not have been personally privy to all the developments. Considering the major experience that the Board had had with the two previous tests, it is easy to understand how it might feel slighted to be asked to support a fully developed proposal.

However, in the light of the evidence, it is obvious that Noyes was being more than a little disingenuous. Clearly, from the first, the College Board had been well aware of all the details of the programme. Salter and Godshalk had kept other Board staff informed of all developments; Noyes himself had proposed Godshalk as their representative on technical matters; and Noyes had seen all the documents that Godshalk had. It is very hard not to see this action by Noyes as a further step in the Board's plan, enunciated in the letter by Pearson (1961) to Salter after his meeting with Frank Bowles in France, to make sure that the Board was not out-manoeuvred.

Beginning with the rapid reaction of Katharine Salter (1961a, 1961b) to the 1961 conference with its threatened invasion of the Board's territory by a Ford-dominated 'interlocking directorate', as Richard Pearson (1962) characterized it, the College Board had been on its guard. Like ETS, it was not unhappy to have someone else take responsibility for the third attempt to develop an examination in English for foreign students. However, they would not have wanted it to stay independent, and were waiting in the wings, ready to go on.

Ford decides

Noyes had kept his promise to bring Fox's request to the College Board, but had presented the case in a way that guaranteed failure. The Board's endorsement was lukewarm at best, and Fox (1963d), not realizing that Noyes had betrayed him, and unaware of the Board's other manoeuvring, was clearly dismayed by the lack of enthusiasm of such an important constituent. Some of the technical questions that were being raised at this stage, he said, seemed to be quite fundamental and he had been given to believe that the College Board would be fully supportive. He urged Harris to follow up on this before the September meeting.

In the meantime, active discussions were taking place within the Ford Foundation. Melvin Fox and John B. Howard (director of the international training research division) had by now prepared and sent in material for the Ford trustees meeting. In the March docket item (Ford Foundation 1963a) as it was called, the action recommended to the Ford Foundation trustees meeting was to approve 'a terminal[8] grant of $250,000 to enable the Center for Applied Linguistics to develop a new series of English language proficiency tests for foreign students'. The recommendation joined together two separate proposals: that from the Modern Language Association for the National Council for TOEFL, and one from Boston University (working together with Boston College, Harvard, MIT, and Brandeis University) for $174,000 to develop a joint summer orientation seminar for newly arrived foreign students. The docket pointed out that 'Even the Boston–Cambridge group of universities have problems with the inadequate preparation of foreign students they admit.' The two proposals were said to meet two of the criteria laid down by staff of the division for issues concerning foreign students: that the initiative come from the universities and colleges, and that the efforts be co-operative.

The recommendation summarized the proposal, emphasizing the need for the programme and the planning that had so far taken place. It pointed out that the council would work under the Center for Applied Linguistics, which Ford already supported. The director would be responsible for planning and developing the programme. The test forms, as designed by the council, would be developed, administered, and scored by the ETS, serving 'solely in the role of a contractor' and having waived its normal 15 per cent fee.

The grant was 'predicated on the assumption that the program would become substantially self-supporting by the beginning of the third year and totally so by the end of the fifth year'. (This of course is not what Harris had said, and must be considered a somewhat disingenuous tactic by the staff to assure passage in the face of higher-level doubts.) It recommended that the $250,000 be paid in a lump sum, so that the grant plus interest should cover the deficit for the first two years. It concluded that

> The College Entrance Examination Board, the Association of American Law Schools, IIE, and several other organizations of the twenty-one which are closely related to the Council and the academic users of the service have indicated a readiness to seek any necessary underwriting during the last three years.

At the beginning of the month of the trustees meeting, on 4 March 1963, John Howard and Melvin Fox met with Ford Foundation president Henry T. Heald and vice-president Clarence T. Faust to discuss the docket items. There is no record of that meeting, but two memoranda later that week provide information on the issues that were raised.

In the first, Howard and Fox (1963) explained that they might have given a misleading reply concerning the 'uniform character of the test' when they said there would be a series of tests designed to accommodate the special problems of different areas and languages; instead, the test would be uniform but long enough to permit screening out of special linguistic effects. When I first read this, I assumed the reference to have been to Lado's proposals to base language tests on contrastive analysis, but it seems improbable that the president and vice-president of Ford would think up such a point. It seems much more probable that they got the idea from someone at the College Board, where this was to be the key substantive point in Noyes' criticism of the proposed test in his presentation to the trustees' meeting later that month. I see this as further support for my hypothesis of the existence of earlier contacts at this level.[9]

The second memorandum dealt with the complex administrative arrangement. After their meeting with Heald and Faust, Howard (1963) said that he and Fox had met again with a number of key people: John Fisher (secretary elect of the Modern Language Association), Charles Ferguson, David Harris,[10] Malcolm Talbott, and Albert Sims. With them, the question of some alternative structure was raised. Reconsideration of this issue too would seem to point to Heald's being well aware of College Board concerns. Various plans were proposed: placing the operation entirely within the ETS, associating it with a university, setting up an independent body, or placing it completely under the Center for Applied Linguistics with the council as an advisory committee. 'Solid and unanimous reasons were voiced against each of these alternatives.' Only with an active and independent National Council could one be assured of the active support of the council members and their organizations. Separate identity was needed for effective promotion. The ETS would serve best in a technical role, and could not manage the enterprise or handle the 'user' problems. Attaching it to a university would stir up competition which had so far been subdued. It would cost more and involve delay to set up a completely independent organization. The proposed structure was to be preferred for it assured maximum support of the users, put control in capable hands, and made use of the Center for Applied Linguistics and ETS in suitable roles.

In spite of doubts expressed by the senior officers, including the President, Henry Heald, it was agreed to recommend the grant to the trustees. The Ford Foundation decision came, as Fox had hoped, at the meeting of the Board in March. By October, Fox had known that Ford would come up with only half of the $500,000 that had been requested.

Thirty years later, Fox could no longer recall how the amount was set. There was some doubt, he believed, about what the test would cost in the long run. The amount might also have been determined by factors internal to Ford, he surmised (personal communication), but there is evidence of concerns at higher levels of the Ford staff, quite possibly under the influence of contacts from senior College Board staff. Some light is cast on this matter by a handwritten note from Fox to Elinor Barber in the Ford archives. Barber (1972), who had succeeded Fox as the Foundation staff person working with the grant, wrote a final summary for the files at the closing out of a later, second grant in 1972. She felt that the end-of-grant report prepared by the College Board and ETS was an excellent one, telling 'everything one can possibly expect a grantee to tell'. All perceived problems had been remedied. She felt, however, that it would be necessary to go to a qualified outsider to get a really critical view. She hoped in particular that research would continue, though it might produce deficits. She sent a copy of this memo and the report to Fox. Fox (1972) thanked her, and continued:

The report on the TOEFL program was particularly gratifying to me, as [it] was with some initial personal uncertainty, and in the face of sneering skepticism on the part of certain officers* that we got the first grant through. It is one of the more dramatic ITR [International Training and Research division of the Ford Foundation, of which he was associate director] program success stories.
* particularly Heald

It is my guess that Heald's 'sneering skepticism' was influenced by conversations with the senior staff of the College Board. There is good evidence of a contact at the highest level between the College Board and the Ford Foundation just as the final decision on funding was being made in March 1963. I think there are good grounds for suspecting a similar contact a few months earlier that might have been passed back to Fox in the form of a limitation on possible funding.

In any case, the non-renewable grant of $250,000 to the Modern Language Association of America for 'development of English language proficiency tests for foreign students' was approved by the College Board at its meeting on 28–29 March 1963.[11] The news reached Harris immediately. On 4 April, when Harris (1963d) sent out invitations to a meeting of the National Council to take place in May, he was able to include the good news that 'sufficient foundation funds have been promised to enable us to put our own testing program into operation'. Harris was, however, disappointed, as he later recalled:

As for the original funding, it will be noted that Mel Fox representing the Ford Foundation, then supporting the Center, was an active participant at the [1961] conference. It is my recollection that Ford was encouraging from the start. For the purposes of approaching Ford, a proposed five-year budget was worked out, the chief figure here being Fred Godshalk. He estimated that it would take $500,000 over a 5-year period to make the program self-sufficient. Instead, Ford provided just half that amount. I took that as a bad sign, for there was no possibility that TOEFL could become self-sufficient in $2\frac{1}{2}$ years. Such proved to be the case.
(Harris 1989)

None the less, it had already been decided to go ahead, with the hope that extra funds could somehow be found.[12]

The council acts, May 1963

The executive committee met on 3 May 1963, and the council on the next day (National Council on TOEFL 1963b).[13] At the executive committee meeting, Edward Noyes was present, having been invited, in response to

Fox's request, by Harris (1963e) in an apologetic letter. Now that the programme was under way, the College Board wanted a senior person keeping a close eye on it. Noyes was subsequently appointed to the executive committee. At this meeting, the ETS also beefed up its representation on the council, sending Robert Solomon, a vice-president, to bolster Godshalk. According to the chairman's report, Noyes expressed interest in the NC/ TOEFL and areas of possible co-operation were discussed.[14] Other topics discussed by the executive committee included membership of the council (the Asia Foundation and the Education and World Affairs organization were invited to join); the need for publicity; the problem of funding; and the membership of a nominating committee (Joel Slocum, Allene Guss, and Frederick Cromwell were selected).

The council[15] meeting next day decided to go ahead with plans even though it had been granted only part of the funds that it had requested, and to start work on the testing programme immediately, aiming to have the first test administration by February 1964. Godshalk was to work on new proposals and the budget. Publicity should be put out as soon as possible, and a new short name for the test should be found. A single test fee, $10, which would include sending a report to two or three schools, was agreed on; there would be a charge for additional reports:

> The Council also agreed on the principle of a single testing fee (which will probably be $10) to be charged the candidate or his financial sponsor. This reversed an earlier decision that called for both the candidate and his prospective educational institution to contribute toward the cost of testing and score reporting.

The decision to drop the proposed $2 cost of score reports kept the programme in the red for many years; the cost of preparing reports by hand for the many institutions to which foreign students applied meant that the administrative costs overburdened the programme. Ironically, having rejected direct tests of speaking and writing because of the expense involved, it was a fiscally unwise step that caused the major expense to the programme over the first years of its operation. A finance committee was established, and there was an inconclusive discussion of how to finance research on a language aptitude test. The finance committee was to approach foundations and government agencies to secure more funds for this and other purposes.

David Harris, reluctant though he was to abandon his new position as director of the American Language Institute at Georgetown University, 'was persuaded, as the first choice of all concerned, to accept the position of TOEFL Program Director', provided Georgetown would grant him leave. He was to appoint other staff. There were other changes in the committees, on which both the College Board and ETS had key positions.[16]

Enough money having been promised, it was time now to get the new test under way.

Notes

1 From 1962 until 1964, three studies were conducted by ETS for the College Board, looking at the usefulness of the existing College Board tests for candidates of non-English language background. The third of these, by Howell (1964), showed the 'language handicap' they suffered.

2 They had worked together on the writing ability problem.

3 For someone like Noyes, who had long been involved in the controversy over essay testing, one would have expected more accuracy.

4 This was ultimately done and resulted in a considerable savings to the programme.

5 The text prepared for this presentation has been preserved in the College Board Archives.

6 Noyes will have learnt about this no doubt in the research started at the College Board when Joshua Fishman was director of research there (Fishman 1957) and continued under Pasanella (1961).

7 See Chapter 13, where Noyes remarked on Godshalk's expert technical knowledge.

8 This term discouraged any thought of continuing support.

9 Francis X. Sutton, a former vice-president of the Ford Foundation, in a letter to me dated 13 September 1992, finds it 'quite plausible' that Heald was resistant to the original proposal and its organizational design. 'Heald, as an educator well acquainted with the College Board and ETS, would have had views of his own on how this project should be organized and friends who would call him about it'. But this, he stresses, is 'only speculation' and he doubts that there is a 'paper trail' to be found (Sutton 1992).

10 The $38 that his trip to New York for the meeting cost was paid for by the Ford Foundation as the National Council had only limited funds available for interim operations (Harris 1963b).

11 The grant approval was signed by the vice-president of the Foundation on 3 April, by the president and the secretary on the 5th, and by the treasurer on the 8th (Ford Foundation 1963b). The grant letter from the secretary of the foundation to the MLA was dated 8 April (McDaniel 1963).

12 The treasurer of the MLA, Alan Hubbell (1963), wrote to the foundation on 9 April asking for payment so that interest could start to accrue at once; the payment was approved internally and made on 22 April (MacLeod 1963).

13 Some of the decisions can be reconstructed from a later summary report (Center for Applied Linguistics 1966) and from a description prepared

and sent out with invitations to the June 1963 testing committee meetings (Harris 1963f).

14 From notes by Noyes (1963g) himself, he told the story of Fox's request to the College Board and of the trustees' decision (but presumably not of his suggestions) and said he was to report to the trustees on the project in September. He also told them about the planned Puerto Rican Scholastic Aptitude Test that would include a forty-five-minute section testing English comprehension and usage; it was agreed this would not interfere with the council's plans.

15 There were twenty-nine organizations represented at the May 1963 meeting of the council.

16 Damon Boynton was elected second chairman of the National Council on TOEFL. The 1966 summary singled out Malcolm Talbott as the member of the executive committee 'that was instrumental in obtaining the services of Dr. Harris as Director of the TOEFL Program'. The report also identified Boynton as serving on the finance committee that developed the 1964 budget proposal, which was an attempt to fill the financial gap and led to the Danforth grant. Charles Ferguson, Fred Godshalk, and Al Sims were elected as members of the executive committee. After the meeting, Edward Noyes (College Board) and Quant (Defense Department) were added, and at the October 1963 executive committee meeting Joel Slocum was appointed.

16   TOEFL in action

The TOEFL programme starts work

More than two years of preparations and intensive negotiations bore fruit when the office of the TOEFL programme opened for business on 1 July 1963. The staff of four was made up of David Harris and Leslie Palmer[1] as director and associate director, with Lois McArdle[2] as their administrative assistant, and Elizabeth Shanahan as secretary. They occupied three and a half rooms rented from the Center for Applied Linguistics[3] at 1755 Massachusetts Avenue NW, Washington DC, in a building owned by the Brookings Institution.[4] Harris considered the location, with its embassies and elegant office buildings, to be 'spacious and showy' but he was pleased to report that the rent would be well under the amount budgeted.

The embarrassing problem of deciding on a name for the new test was resolved when Boynton, chairman of the National Council, told Leslie Palmer to use the name 'Test of English as a Foreign Language' (TOEFL) on all correspondence and publicity material. There had been several other suggestions. 'Diagnostic English Proficiency Test' was Boynton's preference, while Harris and Palmer favoured 'Comprehensive English Language Test (for non-native speakers of English)'. 'No doubt the acronym CELT bubbled forth from the molten magma of our Director's ancestry', Boynton (1963a) quipped, as he invited members of the committee to comment. Noyes did not send in a written response, although he pencilled 'Proficiency Test: English as a FL' on his copy of the memorandum. But he spoke to Boynton and others must have too, so that Boynton (1963b) reported 'continuing disagreement'. He therefore settled on the name 'Test of English as a Foreign Language', which had the advantage of being 'noncontroversial' and maintaining the use of the letters 'TOEFL', an acronym that preceded its full form. Noyes (1963f) thought this a wise choice: 'It seems to me impossible, as I told you here, to have a very brief title that would be honestly indicative of the purpose of the test, and it seems to me that you have come as close to truth and honesty in a single phrase as can be expected.'

Now that the necessary preliminary organization and funding were in place, the work of preparing a test could start. The first step was a meeting of the test committees in June 1963, two years after the founding conference and a bare two months after funding had been approved. By 6 June, all but one member of the test writing committees had been selected. Because he believed that wide involvement of leading professionals would be vital to the new testing programme, Harris had modelled the structure of the committees on those that Starr had set up for the Foreign Language Proficiency Tests (see Chapter 9). The tradition of committees of teachers as test writers has been a strong one in the language testing field. There was also to be a test planning committee, made up of David Harris, Leslie Palmer, Fred Godshalk ('specialist in test construction'), and the chairmen of the five test construction committees.[5] The people involved were all active in teaching or testing English as a foreign language—their names include many of the leading professionals in the field—and each subcommittee came from a single university or locality to make their close collaboration feasible.

The committees met in Washington from 27 to 29 June 1963, the planning committee meeting the first two days at the American Language Institute and the construction committees on 29 June at the Jefferson Hotel, where committee members were staying. During the general sessions, committee members were to receive instruction in item-writing techniques, and would then have July and August to complete their assignments and send in test items.

The agenda planned a general orientation at 1.00 p.m. on 28 June for chairs only. The test planning committee would discuss auditory comprehension that afternoon, vocabulary in the evening, reading and structure next morning; structure and writing in the afternoon and possibly in the evening. Saturday morning, when the rest of the committee members would arrive, would start with an orientation, followed by assignment of duties. In the afternoon, from 2.00 until 3.30, there would be 'discussion of principles of item writing'. The time from 3.45 to 5.00 p.m. was then allocated to meetings of the individual committees.

The 'general outline' of the test sent in advance to committee members started by citing from the report of the May 1961 conference the specifications for the test. It was to cover 'a wide range of English proficiency', provide 'meaningful (reliable) subscores', require a 'maximum of two and one-half hours', and be suitable for the 'sub-college level as well'. The subtests that had been designated by the 1961 conference were control of English structure, auditory comprehension, vocabulary and reading comprehension (note that these were divided in the agenda), and writing ability. There was not to be direct testing of oral production, but research should start on techniques. Nor was there to be direct testing of writing: 'writing ability is to be tested by objective techniques, not by the scoring of writing samples'.

The agenda proposed that the examination should be divided as follows:

		Items	Minutes
1	Auditory	50	35
2	Writing	50	25
3	Structure	70	30
4a	Vocabulary	40	20
b	Reading	30	40
Total		240	150

It included detailed suggestions for each section, which were to be refined in the course of the three days of discussions.

Leslie Palmer chaired the meetings, as David Harris was away on annual leave. During the first two days, the planning committee set the outlines for each section of the test, spelling out for each sub-test the number of sections, items, item types, testing time, problems to be tested, and sources for testing material.

The final form of the first test

The decision of the testing committee, left open for further modification after pre-testing, was that the battery as a whole should contain 270 items, each offering four choices, and take 180 minutes. As the purpose of the test was to determine 'English proficiency of non-native speakers of the language for academic placement in US colleges and universities', participants agreed that the test should have a high ceiling. The special problem of overseas testing of candidates from different language backgrounds was a second consideration. The test should 'present language problems in as realistic a context as possible within the limitations of test design'. Other points on which there was consensus were that all the sub-tests were to test 'English *qua* English' and not special problems from specific language backgrounds, that the item stems and answer choices should have vocabulary controlled to reduce the reading factor to a minimum, and that items should be 'written in the simplest, most straightforward manner' but at the same time present 'as realistic a context as possible'.

Two points are of particular interest. The decision not to test special problems can be explained by the fact that one of the committee members, John Upshur (1962), had just published his attack on Lado's proposal to test only those errors that were predicted by contrastive analysis. There is no evidence that Noyes made any attempt to pass on the suggestion he had made to the College Board trustees about the need for different versions for each language and area, though he had been sent the agenda for the meeting, and did ask to see the pre-tests before the trustees met in September.

The second issue concerns the view of the goal of the test. While the description did not use the word 'communicative'—the term did not make it into language testing circles until Cooper (1968) used it, and did not become popular for another decade (see Spolsky 1989b) it is clear from the concern for the spoken language and for realistic context that the original intentions of the planners were in the direction of communicative and integrative testing. However, practical exigencies, time pressure, and the constraints of industrialized psychometrics effectively narrowed the range of the test battery. It will be interesting to see whether the most recent pro-

posal of the TOEFL committee of examiners to revise the battery to measure 'communicative language use in an academic context' (Taylor 1993)
will be any more successful in breaking away from the industrial and psychometric limitations that so completely stifled similar ambitions thirty
years ago.

The test planning committee ended its preliminary work on Friday afternoon at 4.40 p.m. Next morning, the full committees first heard the
detailed outline, suggesting a few modifications. Test writers were told how
to submit items and how to get paid for them. Leslie Palmer gave a talk
on some of the principles of item writing. The timetable for item writing
was presented. 'Throughout the three day session, the importance of meeting the deadlines set by the time schedule was emphasized again and again.'
At 3.30 p.m., the subcommittees began their separate meetings.

In the plan for the auditory comprehension section in the preliminary
agenda, David Harris and Leslie Palmer had pointed out that it was not
safe to assume that good tape recorders would be available at all testing
centres, with the result that the test might sometimes have to be given live.
This would rule out dialogues or conversations. They did, however, suggest
dialogues among the item types. Three item types were finally accepted:
twenty statements and questions, where the candidate chose the appropriate written response or paraphrase from four possibilities; fifteen dialogues,
'short interchanges between two or more speakers, with a question based
on it asked on the tape or in the test book', and one five-minute lecture,
followed by fifteen questions or statements. The original proposal had
included news broadcasts and telephone conversations in this section. Candidates were to take notes; one voice would read the directions and give
the lecture; a second voice should answer the questions. The lecture should
be an introduction to a course, or one speaker introducing another, or a
college campus or library orientation. A suggested type of item in which
candidates had to decide on the probable location of an utterance was
rejected.

Harris and Palmer had posed a number of questions about the vocabulary section. The committees chose to emphasize reading vocabulary, but
not to attempt to include words from specific fields of study. Most vocabulary should be chosen from the 10–20 words per million level of the
Thorndike-Lorge or other lists, but the 5–25 levels could be used. Bor-
rowing and cognates need not be avoided; two-word verbs should be
included; equal numbers of verbs, nouns, adjectives, and adverbs should
be tested. Two item types were finally selected, the sentence completion
and the phrase synonym. This second type was to be pre-tested, as there
were doubts about its usefulness with foreign students.

Harris and Palmer pointed out the advantages in space and speed of
simple synonyms, but thought it was 'better to use items in which test
words appear in context'. This appears to be one of the areas where TOEFL

showed sensitivity to curricular effect, with a concern to avoid an item type that might seem to suggest the value of memorizing lists of words.

Harris and Palmer originally proposed that there be thirty reading comprehension questions based on five or six brief passages, which should be 'typical of college-level reading' and of a wide variety, requiring outside knowledge. Questions should be simple and not tricky and the stems should be as full as possible. The committee decided on five passages, each followed by four- or five-choice items. Forty minutes were to be allowed. The questions should be on three different levels: specific facts in the passage, interpretation of facts and sentences, and understanding the passage (inference and tone). Passages should be 100–250 words long, selected from three areas (social sciences, fiction, and natural sciences), with no attempt to control vocabulary.

In the agenda, Harris and Palmer described the problem of selecting grammar points for a 'high-level English test', noting the absence of any inventory or frequency count. Five areas were singled out for attention: noun, adjective, and pronoun forms; verb forms and tenses; word order; prepositions; and elliptical expressions. Vocabulary was not to be tested here. The level of style to be tested was left open, but dialectal variation was to be avoided. There should be items that demonstrated interpretation of the grammar. Three-choice items seemed desirable. Two item types were proposed: selecting an item to complete a sentence, or choosing an interpretation (or a logical response). The testing committee was satisfied that only one item type, the completion, was needed. Fred Godshalk, Clarence Derrick, and Jack Upshur argued convincingly that four-choice items were 'statistically desirable', and it was decided that this was to be adhered to even if in pre-testing a choice 'pulled no more than one or two responses in a sample of 370'. It was further decided to focus on the 'grammar of spoken English'. Finally, the area to be covered was narrowed to word order, function words, and inflections.

Having already conceded that writing was be tested not by an essay but indirectly, Harris and Palmer stressed that this section should test neither grammar nor vocabulary, but rather 'grasp of English style', so that even native speakers might not achieve a perfect score. Spelling was probably not of sufficient importance, punctuation and capitalization probably varied too much in different varieties of English to be testable, and organization of material might be hard to cover properly. Two areas they suggested testing were 'overloaded' or overlong or 'awkward' sentences on the one hand, and inappropriate style (florid or excessively colloquial language) on the other. Item types that they proposed included: combining sentences, completing a paragraph with a stylistically appropriate section, selecting a correct form, and sorting out scrambled sentences. The committee finally selected two item types. Thirty-five items were to be sentences with a mistake or a 'wrong element' and twenty-five were to be completion of paragraphs. Punctuation, paragraph organization, and spelling were not to be tested, except for the spelling of some grammatically relevant items such as *there* and *their*. Items were to be pre-tested on native as well as foreign speakers.

The main accomplishment of the test committees, it can be seen, was to narrow the range of possible items, no doubt increasing the efficiency of item writing and also the internal consistency of the test, but building into it an even narrower focus on the aspects of English proficiency that it could sample. It was during the testing meetings that any chance was lost of TOEFL moving beyond the limitations of what could be tested in multiple-choice format, easily, efficiently, economically, and objectively. Harris and Palmer's first concern was to get the test under way as quickly as possible. They were willing to postpone any improvement in the testing method for the next few years of operation. As things turned out, the industrialization of the test after it moved to Princeton slowed down any modifications, so that the test has continued virtually unchanged, with supplementary direct tests of speaking and writing finally added (see Chapter 18).

The timetable was indeed tight, and test writers were asked to send items to the programme office no later than 3 September. After review by Harris and Palmer, they would go to ETS for production of the pre-tests on 19 September. Ten days later, they were to be shipped out for pre-testing to take place between 4 and 11 October. The following week, item statistics were to be prepared, and from 21 October until 15 November, the programme staff would review the items and assemble the first draft. This would be sent to ETS by 18 November for their review and editing; the first form of the test should then go to the printer on 11 December 1963.

David Harris was able to report to the April 1964 council meeting (National Council on TOEFL 1964b) that this demanding timetable had been adhered to, although, as will be noted later, only because Harris and Palmer worked very hard to revise poor items that were sent to them. Writing assignments had been completed on time, and the pre-test had been administered as planned to foreign students in fifty-five American universities.

The first form, MEF-1 of TOEFL, a 270-item, three-hour test, was sent to ETS to be printed and sent abroad. Godshalk (1963d) advised Noyes that they were planning on 100 of the 150 centres being used, with 1,000 candidates at each of two test dates; the centre cost for the year would be about $5,750. The College Board trustees at their September 1963 meeting agreed to make their centres available for the first three administrations of TOEFL. It was given in thirty-four countries at fifty-five testing centres to 920 candidates, of whom 548 paid fees and 372 formed a special group to be compared to examinees already in the United States. The comparison showed correlations ranging from 0.76 to 0.87. In order to deal with problems that had arisen, the test writing committees were reorganized in

January 1964, and assignments for the next three forms (MEF-2, NEF-1, and NEF-2) were given out, with the aim of being ready to administer new forms of the test in November 1964 and winter and spring 1965. The programme committee had collected two thousand items that were being reviewed and would be pre-tested late spring or summer.

The programme in operation in 1964

Writing and producing a test was not enough. Universities and colleges now had to be persuaded to require their foreign applicants to take it. During 1964, information about the programme appeared in fifteen organizational publications, the programme officers and test committee members made formal presentations to thirty organizations, three mailings were sent to 2,600 college presidents and admissions officers,[6] and more than four hundred written inquiries were answered (National Council on TOEFL 1964b). As a result, more than eighty colleges and universities agreed or planned to include TOEFL as a requirement for foreign applicants, and the Department of State had started to use it experimentally with grant applicants.

There were still uncertainties about the fiscal arrangements, and the Modern Language Association was nervous that it might be liable to pay more than it received. On 23 October, John Hurt Fisher (1963), executive secretary of the Modern Language Association wrote to Dean Damon Boynton, chair of the National Council on the Testing of English as a Foreign Language, with copies to David Harris, Fred Godshalk, and Charles Ferguson. In his letter, he tried to limit the association's liability for ETS expenditures, which were (as usual) on a cost plus fee basis. Ford had refused the association's request for 15 per cent overheads in the grant. Was it reasonable, then, for the association to be responsible for payments to ETS under the terms of the agreement?

This was one item on the agenda for the meeting of the executive committee of the National Council on the Testing of English as a Foreign Language, which took place in Washington, at the TOEFL programme office, on 25 October 1963 (National Council on TOEFL 1963d).[7] The programme director, David Harris, reported on test preparation, pre-testing, promotion, and publicity. The ETS representative, Fred Godshalk, said that institutions would receive the total scores and subscores expressed both in terms of the College Board scale (a mean of 500 for total scores and of 50 for subscores) and of percentile ranks. They would also receive reports of normative testing at US colleges and universities. As soon as they were available, correlations of TOEFL with other tests would be published.[8] To establish norms, the committee agreed that foreign students on US campuses could be tested free of charge if they were part of a group of at least ten students taking the test at the campus. It was also decided to make Form A of the test available as a specimen, following 'established ETS procedures for distribution of secure tests'. Non-US institutions were to be permitted use TOEFL services in the same way as domestic institutions. The test was to be described as 'available to "schools, colleges and universities" ' to encourage secondary school use. TOEFL was not to be sold to educational institutions, at least until after the issue was reconsidered after the second administration, but would be available for sale to US Government agencies 'at a negotiated price'. Work on the stalled English aptitude test was postponed again, at least until there was evidence that TOEFL would continue, but the programme staff was authorized to seek funding for a preliminary study of development in language aptitude testing and to be ready to work on a 'product' later on.

Leslie Palmer, associate director of the programme, presented a financial report. The sum of $2,500 would shortly be paid to item writers, bringing the total expenditure for the programme office from 1 May 1963 until 30 September to $13,742.44. The committee agreed, when the question was raised by Palmer, that 'guest expenses' such as lunch for the members of the committee, could appropriately be 'absorbed' by TOEFL in its promotion budget.

A letter was read from the College Board offering to underwrite the expenses of the TOEFL examination centres for the first three administrations to the amount of $17,250. The election of Noyes to the executive, and Sims' move from the Institute of International Education to the College Board as a vice-president, meant that the rift that had worried Fox just before the grant award was clearly healed.

The fiscal arrangement with ETS, as set out in the proposed contract between the Modern Language Association (acting for the National Council on TOEFL) and ETS was next considered. There is no indication that Fred Godshalk left the meeting at this stage, but neither is any participation in it by him included in the summary minutes. Boynton summarized the financial history of the programme and gave committee members copies of the proposed contract[9] and of John Hurt Fisher's 23 October letter questioning items in the contract.

Four decisions were made. First, Albert Sims was to speak to Dr Talbott to find out the Ford Foundation's attitude to the 15 per cent fee that ETS was asking. If he thought that Ford would object, the issue was to be reopened with Ford. If not, the fee was to be paid. Second, a decision was made on Association liability, which would be limited to the amount of the Ford grant plus interest and income from test fees and sales.[10] Third, Sims was to find out the effect of the schedule of payments in reducing the amount of interest earned by the grant. Fourth, section VIII of the contract was to be revised by ETS to make clear that the final payment would be based on variable costs.

Finally, the committee turned to the worrying problem of future funding. Harris (personal communication) found members of the committee to be somewhat reluctant to make the necessary effort in fund-raising. A 'concentrated approach to the foundations' was left until spring 1964, after the first test administration.

The disagreement with ETS was finally resolved. William Turnbull sent the revised version of the contract with ETS to John Fisher and Damon Boynton on 6 December 1963, together with a three-page letter clarifying certain aspects of it. He asked that the letter be signed and returned to signify agreement (Turnbull 1963). The contract had been amended, he noted, to limit the liability of the National Council and the Modern Language Association to the $250,000 subvention from Ford. He pointed out that ETS had already committed itself to 'considerable risk' and expense in support of a 'professionally most worthwhile' project. The Ford grant was only 'seed money', being two-year support for a programme that would not be self-supporting for at least five years. Thus, the full financial risk had fallen on ETS. The original contract, Turnbull went on, had been written on the assumption that the programme would continue even after the Ford grant was exhausted, with the support provided by financial returns from the testing and further foundation grants, to the pursuit of which he assumed the National Council was committed. Without this, the programme would 'fall of its own weight'. He set out then four 'points of interpretation' that he considered necessary.

The first point was that any additional funds collected would be used to supplement the Ford grant and test fees in order to meet ETS costs. Secondly, he assumed that it was understood that test preparation and administration would continue beyond the two years of the contract, with the cost to be charged to 'then available and future income'. Thirdly, he assumed that the fee for ETS was not to be limited to the $110,000 included in the Ford budget, but its full fee should come from any available funds. Fourthly, he expected that the National Council would 'resolve the problems of contractual relationships with ETS' so that preparation for testing after June 1965 could continue.

In a memorandum dealing with the arrangement, Turnbull expressed the opinion that 'TOEFL seems to me to be one of the most significant and promising developments on the educational horizon' and wrote that ETS was committed to it. Turnbull had learnt the lesson from the early College Board experiences with English tests for foreign students. This third test was not to be allowed to fade away when initial enthusiasm waned, but was to be institutionalized, something only a major testing institution could guarantee.

When the TOEFL executive committee met next on 25 March 1964, it agreed that Albert Sims and the programme officers should develop a proposal to be submitted to the Carnegie Foundation and later to others. A further meeting took place on 17 and 18 April 1964. A list of officers for election at the National Council meeting was approved.[11] Noting that ETS had now appointed Robert Solomon as its representative to the council, the executive committee decided to appoint Fred Godshalk as a consultant to the National Council as well as to the executive committee.

Finally, the executive committee agreed to tell the National Council that it thought the time had come to 'disassociate' the council from the Modern Language Association of America. Discussions were already under way about a similar break for the Center for Applied Linguistics, which had begun operations in 1959 under the fiscal authority of the Association. The Center was to be incorporated as an independent body in late 1964. The executive committee was ready to consider 'feasible alternatives' to the existing arrangement. Perhaps TOEFL too could become independent?

A bid for freedom

With preparations for the first test administration in February 1964 under control, the attention of the programme officers, David Harris and Leslie Palmer, began to turn to freedom, especially from the entanglement with the MLA. Harris and Palmer convinced Boynton that the best course to follow was the legal incorporation of TOEFL, both because it would eliminate the personal liability of officers and because it would provide the 'maximum opportunity for initiative and control' by the officers, particularly in determining relations with the MLA, the Center for Applied Linguistics, and the ETS. It would give them control of their own budget and let TOEFL keep and use money from the planned sale of tests. After he had talked to them, Boynton (1963c), the chairman of the National Council, wrote to members of the executive committee in December, asking for their reactions to the idea of incorporating TOEFL as an independent body. The incorporation idea was to be on the agenda for the executive committee in March.

In the meantime, on 17 February 1964, the first administration of TOEFL took place at fifty-five centres in thirty-four countries to 592 examinees, a large proportion of them applicants for Department of State grants.[12] Most of the others were unsponsored students who had learnt of TOEFL from American colleges and universities, eighty of which were already recommending the test to their applicants.

A total of 512 candidates was included in the scaling (other papers had not arrived in time).[13] There was at the same time a special administration of the test for purposes of comparison at three institutions: Columbia University, New York University, and the University of Michigan. Some 215 students, ranked on a five- or six-point proficiency scale, also took the test. The total scores correlated 0.78 with the proficiency ratings at one university, 0.87 at a second, and 0.76 at the third. In reporting this to the executive committee at its meeting on 25 March 1964, Fred Godshalk noted that the comparison testing had yielded 'an extremely high validity figure' (National Council on TOEFL 1964a).[14] The meeting started with routine business. The American Friends of the Middle East were invited to join the council. Leslie Palmer reported that expenditures were running below the budgeted amounts, but this was because only four forms would be completed in the grant period. Mr Anderson agreed that the Modern Language Association would provide a monthly financial statement in future. Albert Sims reported that the Carnegie Foundation had agreed to accept a proposal for funding. Five administration dates for 1965 were proposed. A committee of Boynton, Slocum, and Noyes was set up to nominate officers at the National Council meeting. A contract for the additional 9 May administration was approved. The committee turned to the incorporation proposal. Boynton suggested asking Malcolm Talbott, dean of the law school at Rutgers University and a member of the executive committee, to help find out how to incorporate with the New York State Board of Regents under New York law.

The doubtful future of the programme was in Fred Godshalk's mind, too, when he wrote to colleagues at ETS[15] about a possible conflict of dates between TOEFL and the College Board examinations. He opened in a tone suitable for a letter written on 1 April:

> The infant TOEFL may die of fiscal malnutrition or creeping paralysis before his second birthday. Meanwhile, one prescription is that he gain vigor by dancing to a two-piano tune as theme, with variations in the GRE[16] brass, counterpoint in the singing cello of LSAT, and a leitmotif posing, in piccolo and percussion, the problem of the ATGSB. In short, everybody wants to get in the TOEFL swing—or maybe it is vice-versa. (Godshalk 1964)

Translated into simpler terms, his proposal was to have TOEFL administered on the same day as, or the day before or after, other College Board and ETS examinations, an arrangement that should encourage more candidates to take it. In spite of the levity with which the proposal was presented, and noting the implied threat to sections that were unrepresented at the meeting, one suspects that the issue was very serious, and in fact it was not resolved before the April council meeting.

Albert Sims was also making preparations for the council meeting. On 1 April (in the afternoon) the retiring chairman, Damon Boynton, who would be overseas the next year, visited Sims at his New York office at the Institute of International Education, at the corner of Second Avenue and 42nd Street, conveniently close to the Ford Foundation, to discuss TOEFL. The next day, Sims (1964a) wrote to Noyes, now firmly entrenched as chairman of the nominating committee, at the College Board, reporting that the two of them had agreed that the new chairman should be ideally 'someone from the academic side (as distinct from someone in the testing or language field) who can give the programme as much prestige and vigorous direction as possible'. Some names were canvassed: a graduate dean from Harvard University (their preference), a dean of international activities at Michigan State University, the president of a liberal arts college like Carleton or Earlham. He also gave Noyes some suggestions on nominations for the executive committee. He saw no reason to keep a Defense Department representative, so Quant should be replaced. In the case of Godshalk, although his membership of the committee was 'an extraordinary arrangement' for him to both run the programme for ETS and sit on the committee of the organization that controlled the contract, Sims 'personally would not be inclined to question it'. This offhand attitude to potential conflicts of interest continued to characterize proceedings.

When the National Council met on 18 April 1964, the first test administration had already taken place, and Harris and Palmer's proposal that the Council should become independent had already been canvassed. Following its normal procedure, the executive committee met[17] the night before the council meeting to prepare recommendations about committee membership[18] and other routine matters. A recommendation to permit US institutions to administer TOEFL to their foreign students at a special fee (up to twenty-five students for $50), using old forms, was to go to the council. It was agreed that there could only be three test dates for 1965; one should be tried concurrently with a College Board date. It was agreed that the programme staff were overworked with test preparation and needed extra help for promotional duties. An expansion should be provided for in the new funding proposals.

The committee convened again early next morning, with Talbott, Boynton, and Charles Ferguson now present. The first new topic was incorporation. The minutes of this fateful discussion read as follows:

> It was agreed that a statement would be made to the Council indicating that the Executive Committee believes it preferable eventually to disassociate the National Council from the MLA. The Council therefore must consider incorporation and certain alternatives, chief among which is merging with an existing non-profit organization with similar or related objectives. The Council will be asked to approve this course of action. Mr. Sims suggested that the Council invite reaction from CAL, IIE, CEEB and ETS regarding the acceptability of a possible merger.

Some further background on this decision is provided in a memorandum that Noyes (1964a) sent to his colleagues at the College Board reporting on the council meeting. Things were going smoothly, although there was a heavy burden in item writing on Harris and Palmer. The data on the first administration suggested that the test was a 'good one'. But there were financial difficulties ahead. The Ford grant was not enough, and a proposal to Carnegie was in preparation. No candidates had appeared from the Department of Defense, and the Department's interest seemed slight (the representative they sent had been in his job for only six days before the meeting and knew nothing about past arrangements). The 'marriage' with the Modern Language Association had not been a happy one: the Center for Applied Linguistics was also thinking of 'separate incorporation and a divorce from MLA'.

While independent incorporation was still at the top of the list, the alternative plan, raised by Sims and Noyes, of merging with an existing organization now seemed to be in stronger favour, marking a defeat for Harris and Palmer, but their personal needs were not ignored. The final item that the executive committee approved, before it adjourned at 10.05 a.m., was a policy on fringe benefits (including optional Teachers Insurance and Annuity Association and College Retirement Equities Fund contributions, the retirement plans used by major American universities) for TOEFL personnel.

The full National Council meeting, with twenty-five representatives present and chaired by Damon Boynton, began half an hour later, at 10.30 a.m. (National Council on TOEFL 1964b). After describing test development in some detail, Harris reported that the programme would be left with about $20,000 at the end of the grant in June 1965, not enough to continue. A printed report signed by George L. Anderson, associate executive secretary and treasurer of the Modern Language Association, revealed that the balance in hand on 31 March 1964 was $168,533.02; Harris projected a balance of $21,303 by June 1965, which was the end of the grant period. ETS would receive $110,000 out of the grant, and an additional unspecified amount out of fees to cover other expenses. The Modern Language Association and the Center for Applied Linguistics were to receive $4,700 and $3,500 respectively in indirect costs. The direct costs of $117,497 for the programme office and test committees included 25 per cent of the salary of an accountant in the Association office.

The chairman of the finance committee, Albert Sims, described steps to find money for the future. Only Ford had responded to the proposals sent out in 1962. Now that the test was in operation, a revised proposal was about to be submitted to the Carnegie Foundation (which had agreed to receive it) and others. The proposal was eventually submitted to the Carnegie, Danforth, Fels, Johnson, Kellogg, and Rockefeller foundations. Because of the critical need for active government involvement, Sims had been disappointed at the lack of participation by the Department of Defense (their representative to the council meeting, Richard Beym, was designated as 'acting'). Fred Godshalk endorsed the concern that Sims had expressed; without government involvement, he thought it unlikely that the programme could ever be self-supporting. The council next discussed institutional testing and dates for tests. The committee on test dates for 1965, chaired by Hattie Jarmon, had recommended five administrations, but the executive committee felt it was too early to try this number. After discussion by the council, three dates were approved.

After Malcolm Talbott raised the question of the future status of the programme, a resolution was unanimously accepted to 'affirm the need expressed by the Executive Committee to eventually sever the relationship of TOEFL with its fiscal agent, the Modern Language Association of America'. Three alternatives were to be considered: merger with 'a registered, established tax-exempt organization' (now first in order), independent incorporation, or independent incorporation followed by merger. The organizations that the programme could merge with included the College Board, ETS, an independent Center for Applied Linguistics, and the Institute for International Education. After accepting the nominations for chairman and executive committee proposed by the executive committee, the council adjourned at 4.30 p.m.

As it became increasingly evident that the existing arrangement could not continue for long, both the College Board and the ETS saw themselves as natural heirs. On his return to New York, the College Board vice-president Noyes (1964a) shared his impressions of the meeting with his senior colleagues, giving them his frank assessment of the situation in the TOEFL programme office. Of interest also is his note on the division of roles at the ETS between Solomon and Godshalk. Solomon, a vice-president, did not 'intend to get entangled in these administrative operations at all'.

Palmer and Harris had been heavily burdened, Noyes commented, by less than ideal item writers. Some had sent in no items at all, and only a third of the items that came in could be used without complete revision; another third had to be 'discarded as hopeless'. Noyes appreciated the programme directors' hard work on test construction, their problem with the 'needless' interruptions from the Modern Language Association, and their speeches about TOEFL at thirty meetings. 'All this granted', he still thought there was urgency in finding 'an aggressive executive secretary' who could run the office better, keep after people in government, keep in touch with the chairman and executive committee, and provide support to Albert Sims in developing and writing proposals. (Harris for his part was disappointed at the lack of fund-raising support he felt he was receiving.) There had, Noyes noted as an example, been no up-to-date list of delegates available when he started his work on the nominating committee. All this led to his conclusions that the Board should be ready to take over TOEFL, even if it involved a deficit 'on the order of $125,000 a year at first'; 'at least one vigorous person' should be added to the staff; and the Board should consider having its own office in Washington DC. His complaints were not about the quality of the programme officers' work as language testers—it was taken for granted that they could write good items themselves—but about the administrative operations. From the vice-presidential suites that were becoming increasingly involved in TOEFL, these were the issues that seemed more important.

The College Board executive vice-president Richard Pearson (1964) replied to Noyes, agreeing to bring the issue to the December trustees' meeting as part of a consideration of the Board's involvement in international education. The TOEFL activity, he said, was necessary and should be kept alive; if it should fail, it would have to be resurrected. Considering the Board's commitments, however, he believed an effective but independent TOEFL would be an asset. The Board should be ready to help.

There were discussions at Princeton as well as in New York, when Solomon (1964) reported on the TOEFL council meeting to his colleagues. He clearly liked the idea of a merger, noting that Noyes, Sims, and Solomon himself had all expressed their organization's receptivity to it. At the council meeting, he had stressed the need for a policy-making body like the TOEFL council, working with ETS in an arrangement like the one that had been set up for the Law School Admission Test (LSAT). He confided that both Boynton and Talbott had 'informally' told him that the project might have done better 'if ETS had had more responsibility from the beginning'. Responses at ETS were not uniformly favourable: Dyer (1964) thought that 'we should think long and hard before locking arms with a deficit producer like TOEFL'.

As these discussions portended, the TOEFL programme was to have just over another year of independent operation, until in August 1965 it was taken over by the College Board and ETS in a unique structural arrangement.

Notes

1 By 3 June, when Harris (1963f) sent out invitations to the testing committee meetings, Leslie Palmer had been appointed associate programme director.

2 In his progress report on 6 June, Harris (1963g) reported that she was 29, had graduated Phi Beta Kappa from the University of Kansas, had taught English conversation in Japan; and had previously worked for the CIA, NBC, and Electronic Teaching Laboratories. Her starting salary would be $6,500, with a $400 increment for the second year.

3 Until then, the programme had been operating out of Harris's office at the American Language Institute, 3605 O Street in Georgetown.

4 I spent the academic year 1992–3 writing this book in a building not far from Brookings, eating lunch in the Brookings cafeteria.

5 The five test construction committees and their members (the chairman is listed first) were: I. Auditory comprehension: David P. Harris, Winifred

E. Jones (also Georgetown University), Fred J. Bosco; II. Writing: Clarence Derrick and Jayne Harder (both of the University of Florida); III. Structure: Betty J. Robinett and Janet Ross (both from Ball State College); IV. Vocabulary: Ralph P. Barrett (Michigan State University) and Randolph Thrasher (University of Michigan); V. Reading comprehension: John Upshur, Alan Howes, and Lidie M. Howes (all from the University of Michigan).

6 One example of the published information was a small Ford Foundation report, reprinted from *Overseas* (Fox and Harris 1964) and distributed by the Foundation.

7 Damon Boynton chaired the meeting; also present were Charles Ferguson (director of the Center for Applied Linguistics), Fred Godshalk (ETS), David Harris and Leslie Palmer, Joel Slocum, Dr Noyes and, in the afternoon, Albert Sims (both from the College Board); Peter Loret (programme director of the MLA Foreign Language Proficiency Testing at ETS), was a guest of the committee in the afternoon session, and David Quant (Department of Defense) was absent. The meeting began at 10.05 a.m. and was adjourned at 4 p.m.

8 The first published report of such a study appears to be Dizney (1965). But other such comparisons were made. Robert L. Cooper (1964) carried out a study at Columbia University at the request of the National Council on TOEFL and reported that TOEFL seemed to rank students in much the same order as the test used there.

9 The contract was enclosed with a letter from Godshalk (1963a) to Boynton.

10 A footnote states that 'this decision was somewhat altered subsequent to the meeting', but does not say what the alteration was. A holograph note on Noyes' copy of the contract reads: 'Amplify to protect MLA against costs in excess of Ford and other income.'

11 Royden Dangerfield (associate provost of the University of Illinois, representing the Association of State Universities and Land-Grant Colleges) as chairman of the National Council, and Virgil Crippin (American Friends of the Middle East), Frederick Cromwell (Bureau of Educational and Cultural Affairs (CU), Department of State), and Joel Slocum (representing the National Association for Foreign Student Affairs) as elected members of the executive committee.

12 This section is based on a memorandum issued soon after (National Council on TOEFL 1964c) and on a corrected version of an April press release (Program for the Testing of English as a Foreign Language 1964).

13 It is to be noted that one of the criticisms offered by Reibel and Wantman of the College Board English Examination for Foreign Students (EEFS) was that it had been normed on only 507 candidates. None the less, this 512-candidate norm has remained the basis for TOEFL ever

since, having been maintained even after the five-part test was changed to a three-part test in 1976 (TOEFL Programs and Services 1990: 11).

14 All members of the committee except Quant (from Defense) were there, and George Anderson, of the MLA, was an invited guest.

15 Bretnall's copy was forwarded to the College Board.

16 GRE was the Graduate Record Examination, conducted by ETS but its policy set by a board with representatives of graduate school organizations. LSAT was the Law School Admission Test. ATGSB was the Admission Test for Graduate Study in Business.

17 Informally from 7 p.m. until 10.40 p.m., but final decisions on matters discussed then were only made at the full meeting early in the morning, at breakfast. Sims (1964a) had advised Noyes that this arrangement was because Boynton 'had a firm commitment in New York' the afternoon and evening of 17 April. Charles Ferguson did not attend the evening session either.

18 The nominating committee presented its short list. For chairman, they nominated Royden Dangerfield, representative to the Council for the Association of State Universities and Land-Grant Colleges; he was associate provost and dean of administration at the University of Illinois. Sims' earlier suggestions were not followed; they chose an administrator from a Big Ten university rather than a graduate dean or a president, but they did manage to avoid choosing a language or testing person. Godshalk and Slocum were renominated, together with Fred Cromwell from the Department of State to replace the again absent Quant from Defense. Godshalk, however, pointed out that as Robert Solomon would now be the ETS representative, he would could not serve, so the name of Virgil Crippin from the American Friends of the Middle East was proposed. It was agreed that Godshalk should be 'consultant representative' to both the executive committee and the National Council.

17 Dividing up the pot

The second and last year

During the second year of the Ford grant and of the Educational Testing Service–Modern Language Association contract, the various responsibilities continued to be shared between the council, the programme office, and ETS. The council laid down policy which the TOEFL programme office implemented by co-ordination with ETS, supervision of test development, and publicity and promotion. ETS responsibilities were to co-ordinate and consult with the programme office in Washington, to produce and distribute informational materials, to produce, print, and administer the pre-tests and final forms, to score and report results, and provide statistical information. ETS reported that its membership of the National Council 'and close association with its developmental activities' took it beyond the normal role of contractor. Its staff helped with developing a seven-year budget to be used to secure extra funds, in promotion activities with membership groups, and 'the handling of a very heavy correspondence questioning or criticizing the administration of a new program—dates, costs, uses, centers, reporting procedures, and the like'.

It was a year of major growth, with the number of candidates in the May 1965 testing session equalling the number tested up until then (National Council on TOEFL 1965).[1] But the financial problem remained a threat to this third American attempt at a test for foreign students.

All the same, it was not until August 1964 that a request to foundations for the funds needed to start meeting a projected six-year deficit of $434,585 was finally sent out, as Sims (1964b), still at that time with the Institute of International Education, wrote to Mel Fox at the Ford Foundation. The first proposal went to the Carnegie Corporation, asking for $250,000 to support the National Council's work for the next six years (Dangerfield 1964). Similar requests were made to the Danforth Foundation (for $100,000), the Rockefeller Brothers Fund ($50,000), the Kellogg Foundation (for $100,000), the Johnson Foundation (for $50,000), and the Fels Foundation (for $100,000). In spite of Sims' earlier optimism, the immediate response from Carnegie was discouraging, as Mosher (1964), the executive associate responsible for the area, reported that their charter did not permit them to operate overseas (although, as was noted in Chapter 8, there was a way to handle this if they had wanted to) and that it did not fit their current interests.

In the meantime, regular testing continued. During the 1964–5 year, there were three international administrations. Further attempts were made to encourage government use of the tests, but none of the initiatives bore fruit. A proposal was developed for a short form of the test, to be called the Basic Test of English, and to be used by the Agency for International Development in screening non-academic participants. The proposal was also sent to the Defense Language Institute.

The continued attempts to interest the Defense Language Institute in the tests are intriguing, for reading Sako's (1961) account of the complexity and developmental stage of their own highly specialized and focused testing programme, one wonders who in the Department of Defense could have thought that they might be interested in a global battery. Sako has confirmed this:

> Since the initial English Proficiency Examination was developed by Dr. John A. Cox Jr. of the Air Force Personnel and Training Research Center at Lackland Air Force Base, we have largely based our tests on his model for the development of subsequent English Proficiency Examinations of the 6200 series. The initial test was validated on foreign military students attending the United States Air Force pilot training under the Mutual Defense Assistance Program back in 1953–54. Because these tests were doing the job satisfactorily, we didn't consider the TOEFL, mainly because this test was geared for selecting foreign students for academic education in American universities. Then, too, the military tests were normed by use of foreign military personnel for United States military training purposes.
> (Sako 1991b)

Sako knew of no formal discussions on the possibility of Defense use of the TOEFL. But as late as 1965, Albert Sims was hopeful; his conversations, it seems, were with a Colonel Gomes, whose posting elsewhere seems to have finally set the issue to rest.

During 1964, studies were carried out by ETS and by a number of universities, and adequate internal consistency and good correlations with other tests were reported. By the end of that year the efforts of the language testers and their supporters had produced an efficient and psychometrically satisfactory test, but any thought of making it an even better test was blocked by the clouded fiscal outlook. A good deal more money would be needed to get the operation onto a sound basis, let alone to develop the needed attitude test or start working on a more integrative and communicative instrument. By November 1964, only the Danforth Foundation had responded to the request for further funds with any significant amount (Cuninggim 1964), and the $50,000 that they offered was not enough keep the programme going. In November, Noyes (1964b) acknowledged the announcement of the Danforth grant to members of the executive committee, but passed on his own news. Shortly after 1 January 1965, he himself would retire, and be replaced at the College Board as vice-president by Albert Sims. Noyes would miss his activity on the Board, which he had enjoyed. The task of salvaging the foundering test was to be left in other hands.

Salvage operations

Sims duly arrived at the College Board, and very soon set to work on the TOEFL issue. Within a month of crossing from the East to the West Side of Manhattan,[2] he was hard at it. In the middle of February, he met with Malcolm Talbott, the legal expert on the executive committee, to discuss the question of how to handle the money expected from Danforth (Sims 1965a). The original agreement with the Modern Language Association had only dealt with the original $250,000 Ford grant, and this new money would offer a chance to break free. Talbott suggested incorporation of TOEFL, after which Ford might be prepared to give additional support. This issue, 'as well as some ETS- and/or Board-type of sponsorship' would come up for discussion at the executive committee meeting on 22 February.

The Center for Applied Linguistics was to break free from the Modern Language Association and incorporate independently on 26 February. However, the fragility of the link with the Center had been revealed during the period that Martin Joos was 'Visiting Director' in the absence of Charles Ferguson. Harris (1964) wrote to Ferguson that, but for a 'spirited defense' by Ferguson and others, Joos was 'seriously considering putting TOEFL out on the street'. After Harris had explained the situation, Joos offered a continued relationship.

It was at this stage that Sims formed the coalition that would put an end to the notions of independent incorporation. In discussions with Solomon and Turnbull at ETS, he negotiated an agreement on how the two major members of the testing establishment would take over and divide up the newborn programme.

In Chapter 12, a description was given of the steps that the College Board took to make sure it held a strategic edge in any developments with TOEFL. The opportunity to take advantage of this position of strength came in the chaotic days in early 1965 when the newborn test, threatened with fiscal starvation, and hoping for independence, was most susceptible to a take-over bid. As much as the College Board may have liked to become the sole proprietor, it could see no way of doing this without involving its own special creation, ETS. The English test thus became another pawn in the ongoing match between the College Board and its offspring. The leading players in the drama that followed were Albert Sims, formerly with the Institute of International Education and now vice-president at the College

Board, and William Turnbull, executive vice-president (and later, president) of ETS.

A day or so after hearing about Talbott's support for independence, Sims (1965a)[3] spoke on the phone with Robert Solomon, vice-president at ETS, who told him of a conversation that he had had with College Board president Richard Pearson at the last ETS board meeting. Solomon reported that Pearson had broached the question of whether ETS and the College Board might not, in some appropriate form, take over joint responsibility for the TOEFL programme. Sims and Solomon agreed that the present programme arrangements had been 'inadequate from a management point of view'. The Washington office and the CAL–MLA overheads arrangement were unnecessarily expensive. One might note that they were not disturbed by the much larger 'fee' that ETS received from the programme. Since David Harris would presumably be giving up the programme directorship when he returned to his position at Georgetown University at the end of the academic year,[4] a take-over of management would be 'timely'. Sims and Solomon agreed to meet in New York and explore this further.

With assurance of Solomon's support for the College Board initiative, Sims now sounded out Melvin Fox at the Ford Foundation. He told him about the Danforth grant and the hopes for another from the Johnson Foundation. Even with these, the shortfall predicted over a seven-year period was about $350,000. Fox said that additional Ford money was unlikely unless there could be 'a substantial showing of additional support and the assurance of a sound long-term management arrangement'. If for instance 'an organization like the Board' would take responsibility and find $100,000, the Foundation might well be able to find the other $250,000. He warned Sims that no grant could be considered until later in the year.[5]

Before the TOEFL executive committee meeting on 22 February 1965 at Princeton, Sims had a chance to talk to William Turnbull (as well as Joel Slocum and Royden Dangerfield) confirming, one assumes, his earlier talks with Solomon. The latest figures, prepared for the meeting, suggested that TOEFL might just squeeze through the next fiscal year but then would be in trouble (Sims 1965c).

The new ownership arrangement was proffered at the TOEFL executive committee meeting at Princeton on 22 February 1965.[6] With Turnbull's endorsement, Sims put forward the idea of the new arrangement: 'The College Board, together with ETS, would, if agreed by the executive committee, carefully study during the next four to six weeks the status of the program and the conditions under which either organization or both might assume responsibility for the program.'

There was extensive discussion, Sims reported. George Anderson thought TOEFL might be integrated with the Modern Language Association's language testing programme, but could promise no additional finances. Joel Slocum finally proposed an arrangement with the College Board; Malcolm

Talbott amended the proposal to include the ETS, and the motion was passed. Some points were made about the new arrangements. Someone in the programme should be responsible for promoting the test. The chief programme officer need not be a test production expert, but one should be included. Harris was committed to return to Georgetown, but offers should be made to the other three staff members. It was agreed that the new arrangement should be worked out as quickly as possible. Talbott, Dangerfield, and Slocum were designated as a subcommittee for liaison with the 'study' which Turnbull and Sims promised to start on the following week, as soon as their organizations had a chance to react to the plan they themselves had developed. The rest of the executive committee meeting dealt with routine business.

Now that the idea of an independent TOEFL was dead, serious negotiations began between the College Board and ETS on how to divide up control. Three days after the meeting in Princeton, Sims (1965d) met with Richard Pearson to establish an agreed College Board position for the bargaining with Turnbull at ETS. One argument for a shared investment was that the Board dealt with undergraduate studies, while half of the foreign candidates for TOEFL were graduate students. Sims' first priority was an agreement whereby the Board would have 'full program responsibility', keeping a place for the National Council and the executive committee. If ETS were to take 'full responsibility', the Board would probably not want to put up any money. A third arrangement might be to share financial and programme responsibility, in a mode still to be worked out.

Within two weeks, presumably after consultations with other officers, Pearson (1965b) sent a clear and encouraging response to Sims. The College Board's general position, he told him, is that 'we will be prepared to do anything necessary to keep this test in use and to continue its development'. He would like a formal letter from the test's present sponsors asking the Board to take an interest. The transfer operation should be handled in two stages: in the first stage, it seemed simplest for the Board to take over full responsibility. For the second stage, 'joint sponsorship' seemed worth exploring as part of a larger renegotiation of the relations between the Board and ETS. Sponsorship by ETS alone should not be considered 'realistic'. He would be reluctant to have the National Council or the executive committee continue as other than an examining committee. He demonstrated the strength of his support when he said that if an immediate commitment to a take-over were needed, he would be willing to make it administratively in advance of the trustees' meeting in September.

The view from Princeton was very similar.[7] Turnbull believed that although the programme had been run over the past two years at a deficit about equal to the $250,000 Ford grant, and was unlikely to break even before 1969–70, it was a worthwhile project. Ford would come up with more money if a responsible organization took over. One of the causes of concern was that the director's office was 'separated spiritually and physically' from ETS. He favoured a 'partnership agreement' with the Board.

Sims (1965e, 1965f) met with Turnbull and Solomon at ETS in Princeton on 19 March 1964. They agreed that the TOEFL programme must be continued, and that there were three alternative ways to do this. They also saw the need for extensive promotional activities, including an effort to win over the Fulbright personnel who thought a test like this was too expensive, and preferred local manufactured tests.

Turnbull and Solomon were successful in convincing Sims to support a partnership plan. The negotiators proposed that the Board take responsibility 'in cooperation with ETS', with a sharing of financial responsibility up to a limit of $100,000. The TOEFL council could in the meantime serve as an advisory committee. ETS would be responsible for test development, production, and administration. The College Board would handle the council, promotional activities, and finding external support. Leslie Palmer should be offered the programme directorship, provided that he were ready to move to Princeton, where he should be given an assistant knowledgeable about internal ETS matters. Jobs should be found for the other two programme staff members. The commitment of the Board would be for four or five years. Sims agreed to put these ideas to Fox and then to Harris and Palmer (Sims 1965f). In his letter to Turnbull summarizing their agreement, Sims also raised the possibility of modifying the test to make it 'more economic and efficient'; such a test should not have to take three hours.

Seemingly unaware that the College Board, ETS, and Ford had already tied things up, Royden Dangerfield made another direct appeal to the Ford Foundation at the beginning of March for the kind of help that would permit independent incorporation. Fox (1965a) made quite clear that this was impossible. He pointed out that the original grant had been terminal, and only if there had been substantial support from other foundations might Ford consider coming up with a proportion that would help the programme to break even.

Later that week, on 23 March, Sims (1965g) met with Mel Fox and reported on his agreement with Turnbull. Fox recounted his surprise at the request for funds from Dangerfield. There was no chance of it being accepted without a change in responsibility for the programme. Sims said he had not been aware of Dangerfield's initiative. He assured Fox that discussions were going along well with Princeton, and suggested an early meeting. Fox preferred to 'get a sounding' within the foundation first, and was persuaded to do this before a lunch meeting the two would have on 15 April.[8] Fox did not seem dismayed when Sims mentioned a $200,000 request.

Following up on his promise to Turnbull, Sims went to Washington on 25 March to meet with Leslie Palmer. He told him the shape of plans, and asked for his reaction and interest in continuing with the programme. In the first of two records that he made of this meeting, Sims (1965h) said that Palmer seemed happy at the idea of Board direction, but would need to learn more about the internal arrangements proposed at Princeton. Palmer would wait for an invitation from Solomon. In the second confidential record, Sims (1965i) disclosed that Palmer had misgivings about working with Solomon. Godshalk, who had been overburdened with work on TOEFL, would no longer be with the programme after 1 July. There was an impression in the programme office that Solomon was unsympathetic to the programme, or eager for a change in it. The memorandum also mentioned that Palmer was concerned about an orderly transition; Sims did not think that closing the Washington office and moving his wife and two children to Princeton by early autumn would cause undue hardship. Pearson (1965b) responded to Sims immediately: 'we would object strongly if the programme direction for TOEFL at ETS was not placed under Henry Dyer's supervision'. Sims should make this clear in his negotiations.

On 8 April, William Turnbull and Albert Sims were guests of Mel Fox for lunch at the Ford Foundation. Before they met with Fox, Sims (1965j) reported that he and Turnbull went over the financial projections, which now showed a continuing and increasing deficit. They passed this on to Fox, who thought the Ford Foundation might well be able to find about $150,000. They agreed to look at the estimates again. A few days later, when Malcolm Talbott called Sims to ask about progress, Sims (1965k) hoped something would be known in time for the 15 May National Council meeting.

After speaking to Fox on the phone on 14 April, Sims asked his assistant (PK 1965) to call Turnbull to say that the Ford Foundation would like to see a revised budget; Turnbull replied that it should be ready within the week. He also reported that Palmer was in Princeton on a visit that day. On 11 May, just before the executive and council meetings, there was still no definite word from Fox, so Sims called him. Sims (1965m) was urged to wait a day or so. He assured Fox there would be no opposition from the National Council to the proposed take-over. Nor was there.[9]

The National Council concedes

The meeting of the National Council in May 1965 (National Council on TOEFL 1965) opened optimistically with a report of the excellent progress of the testing programme. Over one hundred universities, including nineteen of the fifty with the largest foreign student enrolment, already required or recommended foreign students to take the test. Marita Houlihan of the Bureau of Educational and Cultural Affairs (CU) of the State Department reported they would use the test for candidates for awards from non-English speaking countries, with some 3,000 expected in the next two administrations. Leslie Palmer reported that, with the end of the Ford support, there was a balance in hand of $43,000. Albert Sims, chairman of the finance committee, reported that proposals had been sent to a number of foundations. A grant of $50,000 had been promised by the Danforth Foundation, and a small grant was expected from the Johnson Foundation. The Danforth grant would be paid in May and October, and ETS would be custodian of the funds, thus anticipating the break from the Modern Language Association.

The financial crisis and steps to overcome it were then disclosed. Royden Dangerfield reported that in February the executive committee had appointed a subcommittee chaired by Malcolm Talbott (with Dangerfield and Joel Slocum) to consider future organizational structure and affiliation. The subcommittee had held discussions with representatives of the College Board and ETS. In these discussions, Talbott reported, there had been four major issues: fiscal responsibility; location of the programme office; personnel; and responsibility for test policy. A proposal had now been received from the College Board in association with ETS. The proposal, dated 11 May 1965, was appended to the report of the National Council meeting. It is headed 'A general proposal by the College Entrance Examination Board, in association with the Educational Testing Service, with respect to the program for the Testing of English as a Foreign Language (TOEFL)' and opened by saying that it was a response to the request of the executive committee of TOEFL, meeting in Princeton on 22 February 1965, to indicate the terms under which the College Board and ETS individually or together might assume responsibility for TOEFL. The request, it will be recalled, was suggested by Sims for the Board and Turnbull for ETS. But the proprieties must be observed.

Five items were included:

1 The College Entrance Examination Board 'in cooperation with the Educational Testing Service' offered to assume responsibility for TOEFL from 1 July 1965, or as soon as possible after that.
2 The programme office should be moved to Princeton.
3 The College Board would take 'over-all responsibility for the program, in consultation with the Educational Testing Service', including funding, relations with co-operating agencies, and promotion through its regional offices and publications.
4 The two organizations would continue the programme for one year, expecting foundation support for the next five or six years.
5 The College Board and the ETS 'would use their discretion' to effect economies and improve the programme.[10]

The subcommittee supported the proposal, which had been discussed with Ford. Albert Sims and Robert Solomon, representing the College Board and ETS, said that they planned to keep the National Council 'in an advisory position'. Continued Ford support was anticipated. There was no recorded opposition to the take-over, although some council members stressed the importance of maintaining the identity of the programme. The council authorized the executive committee and chairman[11] to negotiate these arrangements with the College Board and ETS, and to negotiate the continuation of the council as an advisory body. David Harris announced his resignation as programme director and paid tribute to his staff, the testing committees, and the council. The chairman commended Dr Harris for his contribution. While his name does not appear in the official ETS histories, there is no doubt that the existence and form of TOEFL owed more to his hard work than to anyone else. The meeting adjourned at 12.30 p.m., having voted to give up on its transitory (and perhaps illusory) independence.

TOEFL at Princeton

In summer 1965,[12] TOEFL came under new management. The programme office was moved to Princeton and combined, under single direction, with other ETS responsibilities for the test. Leslie Palmer became programme director and Florence Curran was assigned to be assistant programme director.[13] The National Council was dissolved 'with the retention of an effective advisory group'. Fiscal responsibility for contributed funds would move to the College Board–ETS when the contract between ETS and Modern Language Association (for the National Council) expired on 30 June 1965. The test was flourishing. The number of candidates for 1965–6 was expected to be three times that of 1964–5; over 175 institutions were now asking prospective students to take it.

The details of the new arrangement between the College Board and ETS took a while to work out, and were finally settled at a meeting of Sims and Mullins (for the College Board) with Sterling, Brodsky, Solomon, and Bretnall (for ETS) (Bretnall 1965b). The agreement, to be separate from the basic contract already in place for the Scholastic Aptitude Test between the two institutions, would run retroactively from 1 July 1965 (even though formal responsibility for the programme would not be taken at that date) for four years. ETS would not add a 7.5 per cent fee to the costs of the programme, and the College Board would charge only publications, conferences, and travel to the programme. ETS would keep a single account. Contracts with other parties would be negotiated by the College Board, drawn up by ETS, and reviewed and signed by the Board.

Well before the change-over, the new owners were already at work looking for more money. In April 1965, Sims (1965l) wrote to Fox reporting that he and William Turnbull had reviewed the financial position of the programme, and now felt that it should be self-sustaining in five years.

They projected a five-year deficit of $400,000 and, accordingly, asked for a supplementary $250,000 grant from Ford. On 6 May, Fox (1965b) recommended to the officers of the Foundation that they consider a renewal grant of $200,000, to cover half of the expected deficit. On 14 June, Sims (1965n) heard from Fox that Ford would be ready to provide funds on a matching basis.

There were some months of discussions, before, in November, Sims (1965p) sent in a formal request for a grant of $175,000. The proposal recounted the history of the test and of the take-over. It said that early in 1965 the National Council, facing the loss of its director in June 1965, and seeming 'in any case, to need the backing of a well-established organization to offer the program prospects of continuity so necessary to its acceptance by US Colleges and universities', and because the time and capital needed were now more than the original five years and $500,000, had asked the College Board and ETS to offer terms under which one or the other would take over the programme. The College Board, in association with ETS, proposed acceptable terms and took over the programme in July 1965.

The College Board and ETS undertook to underwrite 'from their own funds, on an equal sharing basis' up to $100,000, and to look for any more money needed. The budget projection expected a deficit of $427,000 before the break-even point during 1970–1. Once this happened, it was the intent of College Board to reduce fees, since the amount of $10 constituted a 'burden' for foreign students.

The request came before the Ford Foundation board on 9–10 December 1965, and a grant of $175,000 was approved (College Entrance Examination Board 1966). It had the following condition:

> It is understood that the College Entrance Examination Board, in collaboration with the Educational Testing Service, will assume responsibility for carrying the test program to the point of self-support, currently estimated to be 1970–71, without further grants from the Ford Foundation, and that any income over and above costs after that point will be used to reduce the fee charged to foreign students taking the test.
> (Ford Foundation 1965)

Now that the programme was under the effective institutional control of the old establishment, there were funds for its continuation.

As Harris looked back on the story some twenty-five years later, it seemed to him that the restricted first Ford grant, half the amount that had been needed, was the heart of the problem:

> I took that as a bad sign, for there was no possibility that TOEFL could become self-sufficient in $2\frac{1}{2}$ years. Such proved to be the case. From the very start, the small TOEFL staff, under my direction, was assigned the

duty of looking for additional funds. While one other foundation gave a small (but much appreciated grant), we didn't have luck obtaining the necessary $250,000 called for under the 'Godshalk budget', and it was necessary then that Educational Testing Service agreed to assume responsibility for the TOEFL program.
(Harris 1989)

I think there was another point that, with the benefit of hindsight, one can make. Once the test had been designed and the first form prepared, the task was not just one of test development, in which Harris and Palmer were experts whose competence has been memorialized in the fact that the item types they piloted are still used thirty years later. What was needed was a kind of industrial management, with strong attention to good sales and promotion and efficient production. In this chapter, it will have been noted how little attention was paid to the quality of the test, although there are references to the hard work of item writing and the satisfying reliability and validity data that were produced. The interest moved to the power question: who would control the test? It came down to a struggle among three competing elements. The first was the *ad hoc* alliance of language testers and foreign student advisers with Ford support that had formed the National Council. The second was a solidly established testing policy group, the College Board. The third was a fast-growing independent test-producing agency, the ETS.

From the beginning, the testing agency had managed to keep a firm grasp on matters through the successful infiltration of Fred Godshalk into the central planning and management group. The College Board had kept its distance until it was clear that the programme was going to work, and then made its bid for control of what was going to be a profitable and important business. But the College Board was not able to out-manoeuvre Turnbull and Solomon at ETS, who found a way to satisfy the Board without giving them any effective power.

Once TOEFL had moved to Princeton, the full industrial power of ETS, for good and for bad, came to bear on it. Some of these developments, which might be characterized as the high point of modern objective language testing, will be described in the next chapter.

Notes

1 The activities are described in the report of the May 1965 National Council meeting and in an ETS (1965) annual report on the project.
2 The offices of the International Institute of Education are close to the Ford Foundation, and those of the College Board are on Columbus Avenue.

3 Much of the account in this chapter is made possible by the detailed memoranda that Sims wrote to the College Board files, usually with copies to his senior colleagues at the Board.

4 Although there were hints of some dissatisfaction with Harris as programme director, all the evidence suggests that he was ready to leave and eager to return to Georgetown.

5 The Ford fiscal year began in October.

6 In a holograph note (in the personal papers of James E. Alatis), Joos noted on 21 February that he had met Malcolm Talbott at his home the night before the meeting and learnt of their plans: to merge TOEFL with ETS or (preferably) with the College Board, to move 'the Washington shop' to 'that home office, terminating DPH[arris] and keeping Palmer'.

7 An unsigned and undated two-page document in the Turnbull papers looks very much like a presentation by Turnbull (1965) to his colleagues describing the situation.

8 The luncheon meeting was pushed ahead to 8 April, but Fox did not have word by then.

9 See Chapter 14.

10 The ETS (1965) annual report referred to the changed status with slightly different wording. The College Board in co-operation with ETS assumed 'financial, policy making and operational responsibility'.

11 Royden Dangerfield was re-elected as chairman; elected members of the executive committee were George Anderson (MLA), Allan Farnsworth (Association of American Law Schools), and General Lloyd H. Gomes (Department of Defense); appointed by the chairman as members of the executive committee were Virgil Crippin (American Friends of the Middle East), Albert Sims (College Board), and Joel Slocum (NAFSA). All of these were listed on the Executive Committee Resolution dissolving the National Council and transferring its assets (Dangerfield 1965).

12 The dating of the change is a little complex. It was 4 August 1965 according to a memorandum from Leslie Palmer (1965), which was also the date the agreement between the College Board and ETS was signed. It was July 1965 according to the College Board (Pearson 1965c). It was 1 July according to the director of College Board programmes at Princeton (Bretnall 1965a). It was 30 September 1965 according to a letter Charles Ferguson (1966) wrote to George Anderson, associate secretary-treasurer of the Modern Language Association. Ferguson was instructed in a letter from Dangerfield (1965) dated 22 July to hand over the assets in accordance with a formal resolution dissolving the National Council dated 16 July 1965. Ferguson's (1966) letter was written ten months later in order to try to clear up some complications with the accounting for the Ford Foundation grant. With

so many agencies and people involved, it was not until December 1966 that all the appropriate explanations had been made and it was possible to close the Ford Foundation records on the grant.

13 She had been head of the testing services group at ETS.

18 The English testing industry

Growth of the TOEFL industry in Princeton

The language testers who were involved with TOEFL in its formative period—David Harris, Leslie Palmer, and Fred Godshalk, in particular—had assumed that, once testing was in progress, they should be able to deal with a number of intriguing but postponed issues, such as attitude tests and more direct testing of writing and speaking. Had this been the case, TOEFL might well have broken out of the strict adherence to the principles of the psychometric-structuralist model of language testing, and taken advantage of the post-modern, communicative-integrative approaches that were already appreciated and being implemented in 1960. For reasons that had nothing to do with the state of language testing theory, these hopes were to be disappointed or at least put into cold storage for nearly two decades. Instead of carrying out the delayed research and incorporating the new ideas, the TOEFL programme, once it was swallowed by ETS, developed an industrial infrastructure that was effective not just in making the test efficient and profitable, but also in resisting changes in it for as long as possible. There certainly was research, as time went on, but its directions were determined not by growth in understanding of language testing, but by a concern to defend the test against consumer complaints. TOEFL had become a product, like a car, and its proprietors were driven by considerations of marketing and profitability.

Over the next few years, as TOEFL became more established and the number of candidates grew, so too did the administrative structure. When the TOEFL programme office (with Leslie Palmer as its director) moved to Princeton in 1965, the members of the former National Council for TOEFL became a purely advisory body. The fiscal, policy, and operational responsibilities passed (in a unique arrangement) to the College Board and ETS jointly. Palmer remained at Princeton for only one year, finding the job much less interesting than he had hoped. When he returned to academic work at Georgetown University, the programme continued under the administrative control of the assistant director, Florence Curran, who had been brought in to make sure the new programme fitted into the organizational structure. From then on, the effective authority over the test was to be managerial rather than academic.

Any responsibility for academic guidance passed, in line with the practice with other testing programmes at ETS, to a committee of examiners formed in 1967. While committees of examiners at ETS were usually subject matter rather than testing experts, the TOEFL committees over the years have included a number of language testers. I was a member from 1967 to 1970 and chair in 1970; I was succeeded as chair by John Oller. These commit-tees are described as 'independent' but their members are selected by the programme managers, the agenda of their meetings is set by staff, and their meetings are paid for by ETS. In spite of these limitations, the committees of examiners have over the years been the main source of new theoretical input to the test, and a continued voice calling for innovation. Their lack of access to central management and the absence of decision-making power kept their potential influence for change to a minimum.

For some time, the committee had a second chance of trying to influence testing policy through the College Board, but this changed in 1975, when there was a major reorganization of programme management. In that year, Albert Sims (to his considerable later chagrin) was finally persuaded that the College Board should drop financial responsibility for TOEFL, which, together with operational responsibility, now became uniquely the domain of ETS.[1] The substantive argument was that TOEFL was largely being used by graduate students, and the College Board had left graduate admission to the Graduate Record Examination Board. The initial agreement had pro-vided for close co-operation and shared responsibility, including shared finances. Following its terms, Sims (1965o) had suggested to Bretnall that the members of the now-defunct National Council be appointed to the promised advisory committee, and this was done. But effective daily control of the new testing programme and of its finances remained in Princeton, and the programme continued to show a loss, until a year or so after the College Board gave up its financial interest.

When the agreement between the College Board and ETS to operate TOEFL 'jointly' expired on 30 June 1975, a new agreement was established between them and the Graduate Record Examination Board (GREB). After a decade of 'joint responsibility', ETS became the 'sole executive agency' for TOEFL, with financial responsibility, including deficit risks, and copyright ownership of tests and materials. The fees were to be fixed after consulta-tion with the TOEFL policy council. As compensation, ETS was to receive direct and indirect costs, which by 1976 or 1977 started to produce signi-ficant profits. The fee was about 12 per cent of testing activities and special projects and services expenses, and was estimated in 1987–8 to be between $1,620,000 and $1,657,000. The number of candidates per year reached 50,000 in 1968–9; 100,000 in 1974–5; 300,000 in 1979–80; and 500,000 in 1988. Income seems to have exceeded expenditure in 1975–6, the first year the financial responsibility passed fully to ETS. In 1977, TOEFL had a budgeted revenue of $1,927,000 and a profit of $206,000 (Nairn 1980: 488).

The new 'understanding' did, however, continue joint sponsorship for the programme and its policies. There were now to be three sponsors: ETS, the College Board, and GREB. The latter two Boards each elected three members of a TOEFL executive committee; these six members selected nine members at large and served with them on the fifteen-member policy council. The TOEFL policy council, which is considered the 'governing body' for TOEFL, constitutes one of the 'client groups' which ETS claims are independent of ETS:

> Each of the policy groups is representative of and elected by the educational constituency it serves. The decision to use ETS services rests, in each instance, with the educational institutions and their representatives. Moreover, ultimate review of these programs rests with the educational community that uses them.
> (cited by Nairn 1980: 302–3, from the 1975 report, 'ETS: Students, Institutions and Programs', p. 7)

The notion of the independence of these bodies is repeatedly stressed by ETS, with the word regularly occurring in documents mentioning them. For instance, to quote from Taylor (1993): 'The TOEFL program, through its Policy Council (an independent 15-member council . . .' And in the next paragraph, 'The TOEFL Committee of Examiners (an independent seven-member committee . . .)'.

There are reasons, as Nairn (1980) pointed out, to consider this claim of independence somewhat disingenuous, to say the least. With the exception of the College Board, the client groups are puppet bodies established by ETS itself, and have no independent existence, no legal incorporation, no ownership of the tests or test materials, and no right to choose any other testing agency to conduct the tests, which always legally belong to ETS. The policy boards meet twice a year, conduct business prepared for them by ETS staff and monitor the budget for which ETS has responsibility. Their expenses in coming to meetings are paid by the ETS programme with which they are affiliated. While it is true that they can influence the corporation, it is hard to consider them other than creatures of ETS.

With the 1975 agreement, ETS finally took effective control of the TOEFL programme. While the logo on publications of the TOEFL Program Office modestly downplays the ETS role ('TOEFL Programs are administered by ETS for the College Board and the Graduate Record Examinations Board'), the copyright statement on the publications is quite clear: 'No part of this book may be reproduced, in any form or by any means, without permission in writing from ETS, Princeton, NJ, USA.' The TOEFL policy council functions as a respectable but captive sounding-board for TOEFL staff to try out ideas on test users: the 1990–1 members included three present or former graduate school deans, six present or former admissions officers, a couple of other deans, and three English professors (two with extensive English as a second language experience). Thus, the industrialized testing agency finally succeeded in gaining full control, and it was in this atmosphere that TOEFL was to grow and develop into a major testing programme, producing a good proportion of the non-profit body's not inconsiderable income.

There are other committees. The committee of examiners is responsible to the policy board; it had six members in 1990–1, seven in 1993, rotated regularly; one was chair of the core reader group described below. An *ad hoc* research committee was established in 1975, and given increased authority to approve research in 1985. There was also a services committee.

The somewhat negative tone of what I have written so far needs to be tempered by considering the advantages to the consumers in this arrangement. As a market-driven producer, ETS has made sure that its test has always shown the highest possible standards of efficiency and reliability. Results appear on time; test security is as good as modern technology permits; psychometric reliability is constantly monitored. The *TOEFL Test and Score Manual*, revised and republished every two years, is a model of useful psychometric data and information about the test that makes possible intelligent use of the test scores.

The *Manual* provides a somewhat oversimplified history of the test, leaving out, for instance, any mention of the original relation with the Center for Applied Linguistics. It describes fully the three-part test, formed in 1976 by combining the original five parts with the Test of Written English. The most valuable section is the full explanation of how scores are reported and the discussion of how they are and can be used. The reader is warned that 'rigid "cut-off" scores' should not be used, 'because test scores are not perfect measures of ability' (TOEFL Programs and Services 1990: 15). For those who wish further details, the *Manual* explains reliabilities and the standard error of measurement. For the test as a whole, it is pointed out, approximately two-thirds of the candidates have 'true scores' within 14.8 points of their reported scores, and 95 per cent have 'true scores' within 29.6 per cent of their reported score (ibid.: 25).

To assist in interpretation, the *Manual* provides data on the ranges of scores earned by speakers of different languages (Maltese, with 607, is the highest, and Trukese, with 443, the lowest, but these are certainly effects of small samples) and countries of origin (the highest mean, 605, from the Netherlands is probably well-earned) (ibid.: 23–4). There is also a survey of institutional use of the scores, carried out in 1989. Here, the range of practices shows either confusion or a wise unwillingness to make rigid use of the scores. For instance, 124 of 324 respondents (the survey was sent to 2,200 institutions, of whom 761 replied) allow students to begin academic work without restriction if they score between 500 and 547, while 192 make the same decision between 550 and 600. At the other end, 111 refer students to full-time English as a foreign language programmes when their scores are between 450 and 497, while 107 do so if their scores are between 500 and 547 (ibid.: 19).

In less responsible hands, the search for profit might well have led to skimping on these matters. Research has also been supported, but within a narrow range determined by the industrial testing mode. Perhaps a good part of the blame might be attributed to the status of the TOEFL programme within ETS, where testing rather than language testing has much higher standing.

Research and development at TOEFL

From his first association with the College Board in the early 1930s,[2] Carl Brigham had insisted on the need for research, and, later on, in 1937, it was his opposition that blocked a move to establish a separate testing agency. Brigham expressed his opposition to this idea in these terms:

> One of my complaints about the proposed organization is that although the word *research* will be mentioned many times in its charter, the very creation of powerful machinery to do more widely those things that are now being done badly will stifle research, discourage new developments, and establish existing methods and even existing tests, as the correct ones.
> (From a letter dated 3 January 1937 to Conant in Nargil 1992)

His appreciation of the effect of the 'powerful machinery' in perpetuating a test form was unfortunately prophetic.

As a non-profit corporation, ETS intended from the beginning to carry out research and development in support of its testing functions. Because its financial records are not open,[3] there is no easy way to determine what proportion of funds goes to these functions. In fiscal year 1975–6, two years after the College Board gave up financial responsibility for TOEFL, the programme enjoyed its first significant surplus, and during 1977 a financial policy on reserves was established. The first was a 'general contingency reserve', to meet unpredictable needs to wind down TOEFL testing operations without an adverse effect on other ETS programmes should the flow of foreign students ever dry up. It was to be 20 per cent of the total expenses of the preceding fiscal year, and available for such contingencies as 'abrupt shift(s) of public policy, including the severing of diplomatic relations, armed conflicts, civil war or "bloc" treaties' that could result in sudden drops in registration, or economic developments that might have similar effects, or the unnoticed first two years of 'erosion of confidence in the American educational system'. A second reserve fund, set at 10 per cent of the previous year's expenses, was to be established for 'development'.

Development was specified as follows:

> The kinds of investigation, exchange and preliminary study which, while not necessarily directly related to current programs, are designed to

stimulate proposals for improvement of current endeavors and/or extension of research and program services into new areas appropriate to the
TOEFL program. Included in this would be the development of special
equating forms, speaking tests, measures of language proficiency at different levels, specialized area tests, conduct of surveys, new scoring procedures, experimentation with advanced technological equipment, new
forms of test presentation, etc.
(Educational Testing Service 1977)

For a definition of product-, market-, and profit-oriented industrial research
and development, one need go no further. The main goal of research at
ETS was necessarily the maintenance of the product and of the marketing
edge.

While there were a number of earlier studies carried out, the series of
TOEFL Research Reports began in 1977, with a study of the performance
of native speakers of English on TOEFL (Clark 1977). From 1979, about
two research reports appeared each year addressing items of interest to the
programme and to test users. The first study (and some others on related
topics) was concerned with the question raised in the late 1970s about the
use of TOEFL with Mexican American, Puerto Rican, and other minority
group members who, while actually native speakers of English, might be
assumed to have some of the language problems of foreign students. Some
reports were concerned with preliminary studies of new tests like the writing and speaking tests described below. Others were responses to challenges
to TOEFL, such as those of cloze tests or of communicative testing (Duran,
Canale, Penfield, Stansfield, and Liskin-Gasparro 1985) or of special purpose testing.

It would, however, be naive to assume that changes in TOEFL were
driven by lessons learnt in research. Just as the original version of TOEFL
managed to disregard research evidence of the value of integrative testing
and of the possibilities of valid tests of speaking and writing, so changes
in TOEFL were unlikely to follow from research evidence but rather from
technical innovations or strong consumer demand. This can be seen from
the eventual development of a test of spoken English.

The Test of Spoken English (TSE)

When the specifications for TOEFL were being developed in the early
1960s, there seemed to be no pressure to give high priority to the testing
of foreign students' speaking ability. While speaking had been important
for the University of Cambridge Certificate of Proficiency in English, which
was originally intended to certify non-native English language teachers, the
focus of the American test (like the two earlier College Board English tests
for foreigners) was on people who were coming to study at university. For

them, listening and reading comprehension were important, and writing ability needed to be measured, but the testing of speaking ability, it was assumed, was something to be left for later experimental work. This belief may well explain why none of the people then involved with the development of the Foreign Service Institute Oral Interview were invited to the 1961 planning conference that led to the development of TOEFL.

As a result of developments in engineering and science education unanticipated pressures, quite unrelated to language testing theory, later built up for a test of spoken English. The rapid growth in the 1960s of the computer industry meant that few native-born American computing and engineering students saw much reason to stay on for graduate degrees when they could start working with a bachelor's degree at a salary higher than that of many of their professors. American universities were consequently hard pressed to find the graduate students they needed to help staff their beginning mathematics and computing classes. They welcomed with open arms the applications for graduate study of increasing numbers of foreign students, who quickly received graduate and teaching assistantships and fellowships.

However highly these foreign graduate assistants might have been qualified in their disciplines, a large number of them turned out to be seriously handicapped as teachers by their lack of ability to speak English. Students' complaints that they could not understand their teachers multiplied, and found their way to TOEFL. In 1975, the TOEFL staff recommended to the policy council that a survey should be made of graduate admission officers to see if there was in fact a demand for a speaking test for foreign graduate assistants, and when the survey was conducted, a significant enough level of interest was found to start experimentation (ETS 1991: 42). Thus, the development of a speaking test came not from some theoretical concern for communicative testing, but as a result of direct pressure from test users.

Experimental study of direct testing of speaking had started at ETS as early as 1969, in collaboration with the Peace Corps (Clark 1978b). To start with, staff of the ETS language department were trained at the Foreign Service Institute in the oral interview and its methods, and subsequently tested a large number of Peace Corps volunteers in the United States and overseas. Starting in 1971, the focus changed to the training of 560 interview testers in 55 different countries, who later administered 18,000 interviews. A second project started in 1974, when ETS provided testing in English-speaking ability under contract for secondary schools in the province of New Brunswick, Canada (Albert 1978). In 1977, New Brunswick (a third of the population of which was French speaking) was to become officially bilingual, and the Department of Education decided to add evaluation of the oral components of the language programmes. English and French as a second language teachers were trained by ETS staff to conduct interviews and to score the tapes collected in the interviews.

The TOEFL research committee and the policy council approved in 1976 a study of technical issues involved in interview testing. It was assumed from the start that face-to-face testing would be precluded by the cost and complexity of administration at the hundreds of world-wide TOEFL testing sites, and that therefore the format would be a tape-recorded test supplemented by a printed test booklet.[4]

The first part of Clark's study was an investigation of the psychometric properties of the oral interview: inter- and intra-rater reliability, as it was effected by initial training of interviewers, realistic interviewing, varying interview length, and on-site scoring compared with delayed scoring of tapes. Four native speakers of English with various levels of undergraduate and graduate training and teaching experience were given two days' training in interviewing and scoring, following the model used in the New Brunswick project. Three weeks later, the interviewers carried out three days of interviewing, the candidates tested being eighty-six foreign students in the American Language Program at Columbia University. All candidates were given a long (usually twenty-minutes) and short (aimed to be five minutes) interview by different interviewers. Interviews were conducted one-on-one, and each interviewer made a written note of a rating immediately afterwards. Two weeks later, each of the interviewers rated the tapes of all the interviews. Other data (age, self-report, level, and multiple-choice placement test) were available for each subject.

These studies showed that raters could be trained and suggested that the interview could be about twelve minutes (Clark and Swinton 1979). First, raters were found to perform about as well in the operational rating as they had in the training sessions. Second, their later ratings of tapes correlated on the average 0.867 with their on-the-spot ratings of the longer interviews (0.817 in the case of the shorter interviews). The tape scores tended to be slightly higher than those given face-to-face. Inter-rater reliability was also checked, and found to average 0.735 (with the longer interview) and 0.758 (with the shorter). The mean ratings given by the five raters ranged from 2.47 to 2.79, with a good deal of overlap. The interview scores correlated significantly with self-rating and placement scores, and had about as much predictive power as the latter. There was a high correlation (0.939) between the longer and the shorter interviews, but the latter might be viewed as too short. Clark concluded that a ten- to twelve-minute interview might well turn out to be appropriate.

The growing interest in direct testing led to the organization of an important conference on the topic in 1978. Protase Woodford,[5] together with John Clark, who was leading the studies of direct oral testing at ETS, were the organizers of the conference, which was conducted by ETS in collaboration with the US Interagency Language Round Table[6] and the Georgetown University Round Table on Languages and Linguistics,[7] and funded by the US Office of Education.[8] The conference, whose proceedings were published by ETS (Clark 1978a), brought together testers inside and outside the government with experience and interest in the oral interview.[9]

The conference marked two important historical developments in language testing. It was the first detailed public scholarly consideration of the already twenty-year-old FSI Oral Interview.[10] It also helped to make the connection which had long been lacking between foreign language testing and testing English as a foreign language, two fields that had long kept their distance. Woodford (personal communication 1990) told me that when the TOEFL programme first came to Princeton, it had no contact with the foreign language testing programme already there, though the two programmes had offices in the same corridor. The original development for TOEFL at ETS had been done by Fred Godshalk, who was concerned with English and not foreign language testing programmes. How serious this gap was can be realized by considering the much greater sophistication of the foreign language tests developed in the 1960s, their incorporation of integrative and communicative testing, and their readiness to move beyond the constraints of psychometric reliability that hamstrung TOEFL.

In further studies conducted at Princeton, Clark and Swinton (1979) produced and tried experimental forms of an English-speaking test, the final form consisting of six sections: 'autobiographical warm-up, reading a paragraph aloud, sentence completion tasks, describing a picture sequence, answering multiple questions about a single picture, and interview type questions'. The total test time allowed was fifteen minutes. Four separate scores are reported: overall comprehensibility, and three diagnostic area scores for pronunciation, grammar, and fluency (ETS 1991: 42).

Trial uses of the new test began in 1979–80, with the testing fee set at $30.[11] Work began on more test forms, and by 1981–2, the test was being offered regularly five times a year. A form for institutional use was also made available.[12] By 1983–4, there were over 800 registrations at the six testing sessions, as increasing numbers of institutions required the test.

The main development concerns appear to be maximum reliability, achieved by strict rater training and selection, and cost. More rater training sessions were held, as demand increased, and efforts continued to be made to reduce cost. A study by Bejar (1985), which was 'undertaken to provide information about the feasibility of reducing scoring costs by using one rater instead of the two that are now used for the TSE' concluded that the existence of different standards among raters made this impossible. In 1987–8, there were over 9,000 applicants.

Thus, twenty years after the plans for a test of spoken English were shelved 'for later research', demand from test users led to the development of a workable test. At the same time, the strength of the need to defend the existing test was revealed in the publication of a report on a research project on the ability of the existing testing battery to measure communicative language ability. Duran *et al.* (1985) reported on a collaborative study that included among its authors two researchers from outside ETS, Michael Canale and Joyce Penfield. The report carefully tones down any faultfinding ('The analysis of TOEFL that is summarized here at times might be interpreted as having a critical tone that may be misleading . . .' ibid.: 61), and praises the value of TOEFL for its purposes. It does, however, gently suggest ways of improving the battery. However this may be, the main pressure for modifications came not from the language testers, but from state legislators whose children could not understand their foreign graduate assistants. Similar non-theoretical pressures, this time from college and university administrators and EFL professionals, led to the development of a direct writing test.

Reliability of essays

The psychometric problems surrounding the use of compositions in examinations were most fully explored in a series of studies concerning the testing of native rather than foreign speakers of English. From 1916, the year it was started, until 1940, the Comprehensive Examination in English of the College Board had included an hour-long essay and two hours of questions on set books[13] and on unseens.[14] After Brigham's study described in Chapter 4, efforts continued to increase the reliability of composition marking. These efforts met with some success: Edward Noyes, in the introduction to Godshalk, Swineford, and Coffman (1966: iv), could report that its reliability had been brought to 0.88 by 1939, partly because the essays were re-read whenever they did not agree with the more reliable grades of the other sections of the examination.

In 1941, the College Board's Comprehensive Examinations were replaced by a series of one-hour achievement tests. In the first phase of the change, the English test became a one-hour essay only, but reliability was unsatisfactory. In his final report as associate secretary of the College Board, Stalnaker commented on the problem in these terms:

> In a field like English composition, the objective test is a feeble instrument. One can but urge that more effort and attention be given to the many problems of improving the preparation and evaluation of the discursive type of test which now seems so essential in a field like English. The Board must continue to work in this difficult and discouraging area. (College Entrance Examination Board 1945: 27)

Various attempts to achieve reliability, such as replacing the single hour-long essay by three twenty-minute or four fifteen-minute essays, to be marked analytically, failed in their purpose. Coward (1950) found no evidence of any difference between analytical markers and holistic markers. With the continued weakness of the reliability of marking written essays, the College Board examiners then turned 'reluctantly', Noyes noted, to objective tests. Part of the motivation was obviously financial. In 1946, Fuess (1950) had reported, the English composition test had cost $50,000 to set and score, which was double the total research budget of the College Board. There was considerable opposition to the proposed change, with arguments being made about face validity (how could these objective items be called a test of composition?) and pedagogical effect (how could composition be taught if it was not being examined?). A general composition test, with a two-hour structured essay and analytical grading, was tried in 1954, but the reliability was low. While there was a case put forward for continuing to test writing, as a creative skill (Eley 1955), the composition test was once again abandoned in favour of cheaper and more psychometrically reliable methods of assessing related skills.

Pressure from schools and universities for the inclusion of writing in the College Board examinations continued, and the 'compromise' that was instituted to soften the demand was the writing sample, a one-hour essay that was written under examination conditions but was not graded. The resulting essays were then sent to the schools to which the candidate applied. How and indeed whether they were used there was uncertain and seemingly of no interest.

Meanwhile, the English achievement test included objective items and a new semi-objective 'interlinear exercise', in which candidates were asked to make corrections of errors in a passage of prose. These new types of items were studied by Huddleston (1954), who found, as Diederich had, that the verbal sections of the Scholastic Achievement Test correlated so highly (about 0.76) with teachers' grades and ratings for English that there seemed little point in adding other measures.

While the correction task was criticized as regards face validity (it tested editing and not writing) and pedagogical impact (it exposed candidates to errors), its concurrent validity was again shown by Swineford and Olsen (1953) and Swineford (1955). Anderson (1960) presented the whole enigma clearly. The inadequacy of the essay as a perfectly reliable examination method had been indisputable ever since Edgeworth's papers in 1888 and 1890, but rather than giving up on it, investigators had tinkered with it, trying (without avail) to remedy 'its more glaring defects'. But there remained a fundamental problem: 'The hope of ever finding a valid measure can be dismissed immediately for the simple reason that different examiners disagree about the criteria of excellence or merit to be adopted' (Anderson 1960: 95)

The most one could hope for was internal consistency among examiners—'the average verdict of a number of examiners'—but simply choosing a group of examiners who agreed did not mean that their agreement would be correct. In this argument, Anderson was obviously ignoring Thorndike's suggestion, discussed in Chapter 4, that the truth resided *only* in the differing opinions of the examiners; he missed the basic point that this disagreement on criteria is not only inevitable but also appropriate.

To see if the new Sequential Tests of Educational Progress essay test developed by the Cooperative Test Division would help, Anderson administered the test to fifty-five students, each of whom wrote eight essays on four occasions. The anonymous essays were marked by three experienced judges using the scale and approach developed for the Sequential Tests of Educational Progress. There remained major fluctuations among markers and among essays, the reliability achieved being only 0.451. There seemed, then, to be little reason to try further.

However, in 1960, the English examiners asked the College Board to test the validity of the items that they were using. The state of concern in 1961 was judiciously reviewed in a paper by an ETS researcher, John French (1962). The issue of essays, he noted, was a 'perennial bone of contention between English teachers and psychometricians', leading to the 'crazy ups and downs' in the College Board's policies and practices that has been charted here. Until 1945, the essay had been part of the examination. Once the psychometricians showed that a test of verbal ability was a better predictor of English grades, it was dropped, an action that was met with 'shouts of horror'. It was reinstated 'ingeniously garnished', research again showed its unreliability and it was again abandoned, only to be restored in response to public demand as an unscored 'Writing Sample', virtually unreadable carbon copies of which were sent out with the score reports.

French concluded:

So, if we psychometricians can encourage testing and further clarification of those aspects of writing that objective tests cannot measure, encourage the use of readers who favor grading those particular qualities that are desirable to grade, and see to it that the students are aware of what they are being graded on, we can enlighten rather than merely disparage the polemic art of essay testing.
(ibid.: 12)

These were the three main questions set for the major study that ETS next undertook. The first was the validity of the interlinear exercise and its contribution to the test. The second was whether the various kinds of items varied in validity according to the ability of the candidates. The third was the possible contribution of a twenty-minute essay.

The results of this study were finally reported in Godshalk *et al.* (1966). As Noyes summarized the work, they showed that all but one of the objective item types were effective predictors, and that two objective item types and an interlinear exercise were also very reliable. Score two for the psychometrists! But the English teachers had their day too. The twenty-minute essay, read 'impressionistically and independently' by three readers, made more contribution than the interlinear essay to the validity of the test.

In planning their study, the first problem faced by Godshalk *et al.* was to find a satisfactory criterion measure. Until then, the various studies had used teachers' grades or grades in freshman composition courses, but these were not necessarily or purely measures of writing ability. The logical criterion must be a piece of writing. The problem was how to overcome the lack of reliability. Two major sources of error were known. The first was variance in performance on different topics: this could be handled by having students write on a number of topics. The second concerned reader variation. The approach of training in analytical methods had proved unsatisfactory, and Coward (1950) had shown the potential value of what she called 'wholistic' over 'atomistic' grading of essays. A study of the characteristics of readers had shown the existence of correlations between them, so that using enough readings (say, ten), it would be possible to reach a high level of reliability (about 0.90) (Anderson 1960; Diederich, French, and Carlton 1961). Thus, it was decided to use as the criterion measure five essays each written on different topics and each to be read holistically by five different readers.

The researchers administered a test consisting of five essay topics and eight different types of objective tests to a sample of secondary school students in their junior and senior years. The free-writing consisted of two essays and three extended paragraphs. The tests were administered to over 1,300 students in twenty-four different schools, some public and some private, in various parts of the United States.

The interlinear tests were scored by a team of twenty-five trained scorers, who also graded the essays in a single five-day session. They gave holistic ratings of 3 (superior), 2 (average), and 1 (inferior), and were encouraged to give high and low scores. Each passage was scored by five different judges; thus, each student had twenty-five ratings, usually by different judges. The analysis of the reading scores provided a number of interesting facts. First, the desired reliability was obtained. The reliability of the reading was 0.921 and for the total essay score (assuming different topics and scorers) was 0.841. Some topics turned out to have received higher scores than others, showing the problem of tests with a single essay. The large variance across topics reinforced the notion that options should not be provided. The variance across readers could best be dealt with by assuring multiple readings, with readings spread across the reading period to minimize the effect of time. The scores of individual essays were no more reliable than in earlier studies, as the reliability was a result of summing the five essays.

The eight objective items were next correlated with the total essay scores; the highest correlations were the usage and sentence correction (about 0.706); the lowest was the paragraph organization (0.458). Various com-

binations of three-item type tests, each making up a one-hour test, produced validity (correlations of 0.71 and higher). Combinations including
the interlinear exercise also produced valid tests. These various combination tests were generally found to be more highly correlated with the criterion measure than were Scholastic Aptitude Test total and verbal scores
for those groups of students for whom they were available.

Godshalk *et al.* (1966: 21) were satisfied that 'the one-hour English Composition Test does an amazingly effective job of ordering students in the
same way as a trained group of readers would after reading a sizable sample
of their actual writing'. It was shown that adding an essay in place of the
interlinear exercise increased validity. The study up to this point suggested
the desirability of including in a one-hour test a twenty-minute essay and
two kinds of objective tests. A number of problems needed to be resolved.
Could the same results be achieved with the hundreds of readers who
would be needed for a full administration? Could satisfactory reliability be
achieved with three readings for each essay (which would take no more
time than one marking of an interlinear exercise, and so cost no more)?
Would a four-point scale be an improvement (by adding to reliability) without reducing speed of reading?

For the study of these issues, two twenty-minute papers from 533
cases were selected and scored, some five times on a three-point scale,
some four times on a three-point scale, and some four times on a
four-point scale. The resulting scores were analysed in various ways, but
basically these readings and the four-point scale were found to be more
reliable. The tests with fewer readings remained valid predictors. Tests
including essays read even once were better predictors than those with
only objective items.

The report highlighted its three most significant findings, which, it noted,
were consistent with a study reported by Vernon (1957) in Britain:

1   The reliability of essay scores is primarily a function of the number of
    different essays and the number of different readings included. (39)
2   When objective questions specifically designed to measure writing
    skills are evaluated against a reliable criterion of writing ability, they
    prove to be highly valid. (40)
3   The most efficient predictor of a reliable direct measure of writing
    ability is one which includes essay questions or interlinear exercises in
    combination with objective questions. (41)

It was true, Godshalk *et al.* (1966) conceded, that interlinear exercises
and essays were expensive in time and money, but to include them was
important for the pedagogical feedback.

These studies of essay marking for native speakers of English had a
major influence on the development of the Test of Written English for
foreigners.

The Test of Written English (TWE)

In the design of TOEFL in the 1960s, the issue of a writing sample, such as was then included in both the Michigan and the American Language Institute tests that served otherwise as models, was a matter of controversy. Initial opposition from testers such as Carroll and Harris, concerned about scoring difficulties, led to a modified proposal to follow the College Board practice then current of sending test users an unscored writing sample along with the test results, but the ETS representative, Fred Godshalk, was successful in persuading everyone of the practical problems and low utility of this option. The writing sample was therefore omitted from the 1962 test specifications.

For a number of years, the standard answer to questions about TOEFL and writing ability was that the structure, vocabulary, and written expression sections provided an appropriate indirect measure. One early internal study by Pitcher and Ra (1967) reported a satisfactory correlation between items in the structure and written expression sections of TOEFL and essay scores, but it did not conclude, as did the slightly earlier and much more thorough study by Godshalk *et al.* (1966), that the best strategy was to combine an essay question with indirect measures. The fact that Godshalk was no longer responsible for the TOEFL programme once it moved to ETS, and the continued unanticipated expense of score reporting, appeared to have blocked any thought of plans to add a writing test.[15]

None the less, members of the TOEFL policy council and the committee of examiners continued to apply pressure for direct testing. ETS commissioned a major research study by Pike (1979) but his comparison of test items did not show any internally generated need for including a writing section.

Over the next few years, TOEFL policy council members took a somewhat different tack, one that was more suited to the industrial context they were working in. Rather than funding additional psychometric studies, they called for market-directed studies. The first of these, by Hale and Hinofotis (1981), reported interviews with twenty-five leading ESL professionals, many of whom expressed support for a direct writing test which, they believed, would provide better 'face validity'.[16] A similar conclusion was published the following year by Angelis (1982), who had found that the teachers of graduate students in engineering and business (where most foreign students went) were concerned both at the low written ability of their students and the failure of TOEFL to make this clearer. Two further surveys were carried out. In 1983, Kane (1983) sent questionnaires to administrators and ESL teachers at 600 US institutions, and found that the change in TOEFL that was most often suggested was a direct measure of writing ability. The following year, in a study of 194 community colleges with significant numbers of foreign students, there was a similar preference for direct testing of writing (Stansfield 1986: 225).

Convinced by market surveys as they had not been by psychometric research, the TOEFL programme funded a study by Bridgeman and Carlson (1983) of what kinds of writing foreign students were likely to be asked to do while they were at university. Bridgeman surveyed teachers in 190 departments at thirty-four large universities in the United States and Canada, learning from this survey that engineering and natural science students were most often required to write short laboratory reports, while undergraduates in other fields and graduate students in business were more liable to be expected to write longer research reports. In computer science and some engineering fields, skill in descriptive writing would be adequate, but in business, students were expected to be able to argue a position. As a result of the study, Bridgeman and Carlson recommended that the test should include tests of two distinct kinds of writing skill, the one descriptive (including the ability desired in some science fields of interpreting a chart or graph) and the other argumentative (comparing or contrasting two things, or taking a position).

A group at ETS (Carlson, Bridgeman, Camp, and Waanders 1985) experimented with a prototype writing test. A sample 638 candidates each wrote four thirty-minute compositions, two argumentative and two describing a chart or graph. These samples were scored by twenty-three English composition instructors and, independently, by twenty-three ESL instructors. There were two kinds of scoring, the first holistic and the second, in a separate session, calling for separate scores for sentence level and discourse level skills. In addition, some essays were scored by engineering and social science graduate instructors. TOEFL scores were available for all candidates. Analysis of the results showed that TOEFL scores and essay scores were related, but (as earlier research had shown) did not measure exactly the same thing, providing some statistical support for the market-generated position. The data further indicated that there was little difference between the holistic scores and the more analytic scores. They revealed also little variance either between the two topic types, providing hope of a one-topic test that would be shorter and cheaper. There was also a very high correlation between the various types of markers, convincing the researchers that 'individuals in all groups could be trained readily to score using common criteria' (Stansfield 1986: 227). It is this emphasis on the achievement of high reliability even in essay marking, as a result of stringent training techniques, that was criticized by Nevo (1986): 'ETS put much effort into establishing the reliability of the scoring procedures and less effort into establishing the validity of the new test.'

Stansfield (1984) reported the results of his studies to the TOEFL policy council and submitted a proposal to develop a direct writing test. Showing the importance of market response rather than testing theory as the basis for test design, the first stage of this development involved a new survey, this time of admissions officers (the primary users of TOEFL results) at over 800 institutions that received many TOEFL scores. Strong support for the proposed writing test was reported among the three-quarters who responded; community colleges were also interested (Adams-Fallon and Stansfield 1985). The respondents were also asked about the design, administration, and score reporting system for the new test. Large majorities agreed that it should be compulsory, its topic general rather than discipline-specific, and its score reported separately and not incorporated with the structure and written expression score. A majority preferred a numerical score to a letter grade, but a third favoured a description of the candidate's writing skills.

While the justification and design of the writing test were in large measure based on responses from test users, the development of suitable topics and of scoring techniques was handled (as the original writing of the first version of TOEFL had been) by a committee of experienced and practicing teachers. In 1985, a group of such experts, called core readers, were selected by TOEFL staff. Before their first meeting in Princeton in August, they were each asked to prepare ten possible essay topics. At the meeting, the seventy topics were discussed, and eleven selected that seemed both appropriate to the TOEFL population and also 'in compliance with the racial, cultural, and other sensitivity guidelines used by ETS test development specialists' (Stansfield 1986: 227).

The topics were included in the 1985 pre-testing programme,[17] and 200[18] thirty-minute essays were collected on each of the eleven. The core readers read these essays at a meeting in Berkeley, California,[19] in November 1985. Stansfield (ibid.) reported that six topics were approved for use in real testing as they were, three were discarded, and two sent to be further revised and tested. The core readers met twice early in 1986 and were to continue regular meetings.

Work next started on developing a scoring guide, which was to be anchored to the essays included in the earlier study by Carlson *et al.* (1985), in order to assure greater agreement with the rest of TOEFL. Kyle Perkins was asked by TOEFL staff to examine the characteristics of the 200 essays in the Carlson study on which there had been the highest agreement among raters, and to develop a 150–250-word description of the lexical, syntactic, and communicative strengths and weaknesses of the papers in each level. These descriptions were modified after discussion with the core readers, to consist of single statements for each level followed by short characterizations of selected discourse features typical of the level. This shorter guide, Stansfield (1986: 228) suggested, would be more suitable for the TOEFL scorers in the Bay Area who were expected to rate thirty-five essays an hour.

The choice of the Bay Area (Berkeley) office of ETS for essay scoring was based, Stansfield (ibid.) reported, on its extensive experience with essay reading, meaning that it had available a large body of experienced readers with known reliability. This issue of reliability was chosen as the most important criterion for choosing a reader, and only those readers who, after training, demonstrated a high enough level of agreement, were used. Initially, equal numbers of experienced English composition teachers and ESL teachers were used as scorers, the goal being to assure that scores were both 'anchored' in standards for native speakers and cognizant of special problems of foreign students. During the November pre-test reading, the descriptions were tried and revised twice, and the guide was subsequently validated independently with other groups of readers. Only minor revisions were made in the version that was set in March 1986. Scorers underwent training, which involved five hours of use of the scoring guide, followed by the reading of thirty papers whose official scores were already known (ibid.). Only readers whose scores correlated highly with the official scores would be used, Stansfield stressed. During the first year described by Stansfield (ibid.), considerable effort was also expended on developing specifications for writing topics involving descriptions of charts and graphs, which were found to be much more difficult to write than topics of the 'compare, contrast, and take a position' type. A number of technical problems concerned with test administration also had to be dealt with. The answer sheet had to be redesigned so that the two parts could be scored at Princeton and Berkeley, and systems established for computer combination of the two scores. One unsolved problem was a technique for equating forms of the new test.

The name 'Test of Written English' (TWE) was selected in 1986. The first formal administration of the test took place in July 1986; it was also included in the November 1986 and May 1987 administrations. Altogether, 106,500 TOEFL candidates wrote essays in 1986–7. Two training sessions were held, at which 150 composition teachers were trained as scorers (ETS 1991).

The use of the Test of Written English continued to grow. In 1987–8, a fifth of institutions surveyed planned to require it. In the 1988–9 programme year, 40 per cent of TOEFL candidates wrote essays. The core reader group was given formal status, with its chairperson appointed to the committee of examiners. New readers continued to be trained and the programme became official rather than experimental in 1990–1, a year also marked by the reading of the one millionth TWE essay (ETS 1991). Currently (for the 1993–4 TOEFL testing calendar), TOEFL is offered once every month of the year, and TWE is given with it on five of these months.[20]

In the case of the writing test, too, it took two decades to fulfil the promise to add a writing section to TOEFL. Again, the development was market-driven rather than the result of test research. The method of training and selecting readers to agree, reported in Stansfield (1986), is in direct contradiction to the principle enunciated by Thorndike (in Monroe 1939) that scores on matters such as composition, where there is reason to assume differences in the opinions of good judges, should be based on the mean of disagreeing judges rather than being the result of forcing compliance with an official version.[21] Thus, the practical needs of commercially viable mass testing, justified by the concern to maintain reliability, continue to dampen efforts to improve validity.

Other TOEFL initiatives

From its beginnings, the TOEFL programme followed the basic psychometric principle of other College Board types of examinations in that it was intended to be a norm-based test of proficiency. The method of scoring introduced to the College Board examinations by Carl Brigham in 1937 established the use of a scale from 200 to 800, with a median of 500 and a standard deviation of 50. At the crucial meeting of Fred Godshalk with Melvin Fox concerning Ford Foundation funding in February 1963, Godshalk had explained this concept to the Ford Foundation representative. From its earliest publicity, and in all test manuals and explanations, ETS had emphasized that the interpretation of the score at that time involved all test users in developing their own validation studies, to see the relevance in their own institutions of any specific score for students from specific countries and in the various disciplines. There was no notion (as in the competitive examinations that had developed in Britain in the eighteenth and nineteenth centuries) of a desire to rank the top students, although, of course, norm-referenced scores were reported as percentiles. Nor was there any concern to provide a criterion-referenced passing point: the interpretations, it was continually stressed in the *TOEFL Test and Score Manual*, were not pass-fail, but indicated the probable need of further instruction in English as a foreign language before a candidate could be expected to handle full-time work at an English-speaking university.

One might wonder if this was not somewhat disingenuous. The continued stressing of this point reveals ETS awareness that TOEFL scores are widely used as criterion-referenced pass-fail indicators. It is also clear that the original US Government interest in testing foreign applicants in order to exclude those who were seeking a loophole in immigration regulations would be satisfied if TOEFL were to be a method of certification of minimal proficiency. But for the first twenty years of TOEFL, there was no public recognition of this possibility, which was in opposition to fundamental psychometric principles adopted by the College Board and continued by ETS.

In 1986, however, there was a major reversal of policy with the development of the English Proficiency Certification Program, or, to use its more marketable title, EUROCERT.[22] The idea of EUROCERT originated in 1986 in conversations between staff members at ETS and at the Centraal Instituut voor Toetsontwikkeling (CITO), the Institute for Educational

Measurement in the Netherlands. It was felt that with the increasing interest in language in Europe,[23] there could well be a market for a method of certifying English language proficiency. CITO and ETS agreed in November 1986 to develop a joint 'venture' that would make use of the three available ETS tests, TOEFL, TSE, and TWE.

The first step in this was a 'benchmark' study of 250 candidates who took the tests in centres in Norway, France, Greece, and Turkey. From the study of these results, two levels for EUROCERT certification were determined, 'certified' and 'certified with honours'. The term 'honours', like the notion of 'certificate', is clearly more British than American, providing strong support for an interpretation that suggested the new programme was intended to compete with the long-established Certificate of Proficiency in English awarded by the University of Cambridge Local Examinations Syndicate. Candidates not reaching the required certification standard were to receive an English Proficiency Profile, a letter showing areas where their scores were weak and suggesting how to improve them. The rating of the Test of Speaking English was to be carried out in Europe at CITO, so during 1987 and in January 1988 ETS staff members helped select and train a pool of CITO staff as TSE raters.

The first advertised administration of EUROCERT was conducted in March 1988 at twenty-five test centres in eleven European countries. Of the sixty-four candidates who registered, twenty-three were awarded certificates, one with honours. There was a second administration in May 1988, at thirty-five centres; of the ninety-eight candidates, twenty-one received certificates (not with honours). During the 1988–9 testing year, the EUROCERT tests were offered four times, with the number of candidates reaching five hundred and seventy-eight certificates awarded. Major advertising campaigns were conducted the following year, with a resulting 25 per cent increase in candidates, the majority being in France. In 1990–1, however, the programme appeared to have passed saturation point, so that a decision was made to phase it out after the 1991–2 testing year.

The EUROCERT programme would appear to illustrate more clearly than other programmes the industrial and marketing basis for large institutional tests like TOEFL, and the relatively easy way in which testing principles are temporarily forgotten when there is the chance of a commercially viable enterprise making use of an available test. Clearly, any developmental costs for EUROCERT were purely administrative: there was no need to investigate new methods or develop new testing approaches; one suspects that a good deal of the cost was promotional.

TOEFL 2000

There has continued to be internal as well as external pressure for changes in TOEFL. The most recent initiative appears to have started in the committee of examiners, which in 1987 made a number of proposals that were considered impractical.[24] Four years later, staff presented to the committee a list of possible changes. A year later, the policy council received permission from ETS to start TOEFL 2000, a project 'to develop a new language proficiency test or test battery'. The emphasis for the test will continue to be on evaluating students applying for admission to North American universities, and it is to be 'a measure of communicative language proficiency that focuses on academic language and the language of university life'. The work of developing the new test was assigned in 1993 to a development team. While the team is working to modify a 'conceptual framework' developed by language testers, Taylor (1993) stresses that any changes must also take into account 'TOEFL score users and their needs'. 'Construct validity' must be tempered by 'consequential validity'.

The effect of the industrialization of TOEFL was to establish the priority of efficient production and successful sale over theoretical issues of construct validity. This was accompanied by an unquestioning devotion to psychometric reliability, the pursuit of a kind of certainty that the pioneers of testing such as Edgeworth, Thorndike, and Brigham realized was unattainable. The goal of maintaining equivalence means that the scaling of the current forms of the test is still linked to the scores of the first 512 papers that arrived in 1964.[25] The goal of the highest possible internal consistency for the indirect objective core of the test involved narrowing its focus and ignoring the integrative communicative side of language ability. In the reluctantly introduced direct measures of speaking and writing ability, high inter-rater agreement was achieved by the ruthless suppression and exclusion of individual differences in judgement.

TOEFL 2000 is therefore an important initiative, recognizing ETS's responsibility to improve the test, and bearing witness to the continued discomfort of the language testing profession with the fossilization that has been a logical corollary of industrial and commercial success. How successful this latest effort remains for a future historian to assess.

Notes

1 The Graduate Record Examination Board was one of the earliest of ETS 'client groups'. Its members are elected by members of the Association of American Universities and the Council of Graduate Schools, and meet for two days twice a year. The Board is unincorporated and is served by ETS staff. (Nairn 1980: 305).

2 See Chapter 4.

3 The financial arrangements of the various testing programmes were complex. For TOEFL in 1987 there were five categories of expenditures. ETS did not collect a fee for council and committee meeting expenses, or for

developmental activity expenses. The TOEFL policy council established a ceiling on research; any additional research expenditures were absorbed by ETS (presumably from its fees). All special projects and services were reimbursed to ETS, and in addition a 12 per cent fee was paid. The largest part of the policy council expenses was testing activities, about 89 per cent. For each expense category (such as printing test books, mailing, supervision, scoring services, score reports, test development, equating, and students' publications) ETS prepared an estimate based on testing volume. Thus, for 1987–8 testing year, the volume was estimated at between 475,000 and 495,000 tests. If ETS kept to the estimated expenses, it received a 12 per cent fee; if expenses ran over, the fee was lowered, and if expenses were under the ceiling, it kept half the savings. For the year cited above ETS would receive more than $15,000,000 over and above all its expenses in administering and operating TOEFL. While ETS was a non-profit corporation, senior staff appear to have been quite well paid; Nairn (1980: 343) reported that in 1976–7, the top officers were paid more than double the salaries of equivalent university administrators.

4 The results of this study are also reported in Clark (1979).

5 At the time associate director of the international office at ETS.

6 This group was formed originally by language teachers at the various US Government agencies, including the Foreign Service Institute of the Department of State, the Language School of the Central Intelligence Agency, and the National Security Agency. In 1978, James Frith, dean of the school of language studies at the FSI, was chair of the management committee of the Round Table. The testing committee of the Round Table was chaired by Dorothy Waugh.

7 The conference met at Georgetown University on 14–15 March 1978, as a pre-session for the main Round Table, which was chaired by James E. Alatis, dean of the school of languages and linguistics at Georgetown University. It joined a tradition of meetings on language testing associated with the Georgetown Round Table that started with the fourth annual meeting in 1953 (Hill 1953) and included the meeting organized by Randall Jones and Bernard Spolsky in 1975 (Jones and Spolsky 1975).

8 The conference and much of Clark's research at ETS was supported from a grant under Title VI, Section 602, of the National Defense Education Act. This programme, started originally in response to the USSR's launch, in 1957, of Sputnik, the first artificial Earth satellite, provided funding for major development in foreign language instruction in the United States and for the parallel development of area studies.

9 For discussion of the development of the FSI Oral Interview, see Chapter 9.

10 There had been a two-page article describing the interview in the first issue of the *Linguistic Reporter* (Rice 1959), but the first major

published discussion was a paper given at Georgetown University in 1975 (Wilds 1975). The 1978 meeting then brought all this activity, previously confined to internal professional discussion, into open scholarly debate.

11 Just under 200 candidates were tested in October 1979, and nearly 500 in March 1980.

12 Called SPEAK, it included a manual and tape for training local scorers.

13 Books that the candidates were assumed to have read in class.

14 Passages from books or poems assumed not to have been read by the candidates.

15 In writing this section, I was helped by the short history of TWE by Stansfield (1986). Stansfield was at the time of writing still employed by ETS.

16 Cited by Stansfield (1986).

17 In the TOEFL pre-testing programme, new items would be included in selected examination papers, but the scores for the items were not reported in the normal way.

18 According to Stansfield (1986: 228). The abbreviated history of TOEFL (ETS 1991: 51) says 400.

19 The Bay Area office of ETS received a contract to be responsible for scoring TWE essays (ETS 1991).

20 August, September, and October (the results of which are available by University application deadlines in December, February, and May). The efficiency of the operation may be noted by the fact that score reports are mailed one month after the examination date, whether TWE is included or not.

21 See Chapter 4.

22 The account in this section is based on details provided in ETS (1991: 54–6).

23 The first major programme of the Council for Cultural Co-operation of the Council of Europe started in 1962, leading ultimately to work on the Threshold Level in the 1970s; a major new project was started in 1982 and completed in 1988 (Girard and Trim 1988). More recently considerable interest has developed in standardizing methods of proficiency assessment (North 1992).

24 I am grateful to Carol Taylor (1993) for supplying these details. I have not yet had an opportunity to consult the internal documents involved.

25 See Chapter 16. The *TOEFL Test and Score Manual* published in 1990 explains that the three-section TOEFL (dating from 1976) was linked to 'a group of foreign students tested in February 1964' (p. 11).

19 The Cambridge–Princeton test race

The Cambridge examinations examined

As structural linguists and deconstructing literary critics have proclaimed, meaning emerges in difference. In order to appreciate what happened to TOEFL after ETS absorbed it, a comparison with developments across the Atlantic in the United Kingdom is useful. Here, too, English testing for foreigners has become highly centralized, under the control of the University of Cambridge Local Examinations Syndicate, but with many others sharing in the academic action.

While Cambridge is the *administrative* centre of these British testing activities, the *academic* connections have been elsewhere—with London and its Institute of Education before World War II, and more recently, in a nicely balanced sharing of activities and reviewing, with applied linguistics programmes at Edinburgh, Reading, and Lancaster. Until it endowed the new Centre for English and Applied Linguistics and the foundation professor, Gillian Brown, added a language tester to the staff of the Centre in 1991, UCLES had generally to rely on its own internal staff or go to other universities for language testing expertise.

In the history of English language testing so far presented in this book, the central theme has been the reluctance of UCLES to recognize the seriousness of all the research arguing for the need to reduce errors of measurement. The Cambridge examiners continued a humanistic concern for subjective judgement that was combined with a smug certainty in the infallibility of their unexplained collective opinions. Their views were traditional and élitist: they were examining the extent to which foreigners who wanted to teach English or be recognized as knowing it had assimilated the ability to perform like ideal British candidates, and to share in their common literary culture. They therefore resisted the challenge of proponents of explicit theories such as psychometrics and linguistics to open up the process to external scientific validation.

Roach's prophecy about the growth of English language testing has been borne out at the institution where he spent his formative years. From the tiny programme with which UCLES entered the field before World War I, a major cluster of complementary tests has emerged. The Lower Certificate (later, First Certificate) was added in 1939. A higher level Diploma of English Studies, begun in 1941 for the élite candidate, was balanced at the lower end by a Preliminary English Test in 1980. In 1984, the Cambridge Examination in English for Language Teachers took over the original task of the Certificate of Proficiency in English. In 1988, UCLES took over the Royal Society of Arts' Schemes in English as a Foreign Language and responsibility for the accompanying communicative tests. It subsequently became responsible for the English Language Testing Service (later renamed the International English Language Testing Service or IELTS)[1] and its battery intended for foreign students, the development of which will be traced later in this chapter.

With all this increase in testing activity, UCLES remained for a long time firmly in the grips of traditional language examining, with a continuing distaste for psychometrics. However, under the pressure of its growing programmes, and with the increasing employment of professional testers on its staff, there has been an increase in psychometric sophistication, especially in the light of the criticisms of Cambridge testing practices that emerged in the recent comparison of the Certificate of Proficiency of English with TOEFL.

The encounter reported between UCLES and the ETS, proprietors of the two currently most widely used and most profitable English tests for foreign students, had long been threatening. For about sixty years, the earlier versions of the English tests on either side of the Atlantic had been used in relative isolation, with only occasional indirect contacts. In 1987, however, pricked on by the attempt of Princeton to invade Cambridge turf with EURO-CERT,[2] UCLES invited a leading American language tester to make a detailed side-by-side study of the two tests. The report by Bachman, Davidson, Ryan, and Choi (1989) found many good features in the Cambridge examination, and much evidence of overlap in the areas that the two test batteries measured, but also revealed many lapses in test reliability of the kind noted earlier by Edgeworth (1888) or criticized by Hartog and Rhodes (1935).

By 1987, a year before the comparative study began, the First Certificate in English (FCE) and the Certificate of Proficiency in English (CPE) were only two out of nine examinations in English as a foreign language offered by UCLES, but they formed the blue-ribbon core, as it were, of the cluster. One of the points made by commentators on the Bachman study was that it would have been more to the point to compare TOEFL with IELTS. Such a comparison, it was suggested, would show the psychometric sophistication of British testers in a much more favourable light, for this test battery is much closer to TOEFL in form and philosophy.

The Certificate of Proficiency in English, dating from 1913, and the First Certificate in English, added by Roach in 1939, had grown by the late 1980s to examine about a quarter of a million students a year in sixty countries. The examination syllabus in effect in 1987 (University of Cambridge Local Examinations Syndicate 1987) was the result of a major revision in 1975, with modifications in 1984. It had four underlying principles: the communicative approach, the importance of listening and speaking, the authenticity of reading and listening texts, and the 'need to avoid culture bias'. In accepting these, UCLES had shown sensitivity to the major trends in language teaching in general and English language teaching in particular. From this point of view, the content of the syllabus and of the examinations were completely up-to-date. The technology of testing, in contrast, was to prove much less satisfactory.

The FCE and CPE examinations consisted of five separate papers or tests. The reading comprehension paper had forty multiple-choice items, twenty-five of which tested discrete-point items and fifteen of which were based on reading passages. The composition paper offered five topics, with the candidate required to write on two of them. A use of English paper included items such as filling gaps and writing paragraphs. The listening comprehension paper consisted of taped passages with a variety of written and visual prompts. The fifth paper was an interview, given individually or in groups, for which a number of topics were proposed.

Only the reading comprehension paper was machine-scored; all the others were marked by hand, following pre-determined marking schemes which set out criteria for scoring. Composition and use of English were marked subjectively, listening comprehension was marked by clerical staff according to a key, and the interviews rated locally on a analytic scale (with separate ratings for fluency, grammatical accuracy, pronunciation of sentences, pronunciation of sounds, interactive communication, and vocabulary). The marks for each paper were scaled and summed, and reported finally with a single letter grade, with A, B, and C as passing grades, D as a narrow failure, and E as a failure.

UCLES justified this approach historically and as a result of its experience:

> The current system has been developed in the light of the Syndicate's experience of over a century as a public examining board, of over 70 years of examining specifically in English as a Foreign Language, and most important of all, in the light of the introduction of an integrated and comprehensive language testing syllabus in 1975. This was preceded by an intensive research programme in which the desirable relative weighting of subjective and objective elements, in the testing of the written and spoken language, was established, together with ways of incorporating valid and administratively viable forms of test. The subsequent very large increases in entries, despite the differences in teaching programmes, have indicated a high degree of public confidence in the fairness and consistency of the examinations.
> (University of Cambridge Local Examinations Syndicate 1987: 3)

There followed, the *Handbook* explained, a complex process of balancing and scaling the various papers, so that 'appropriate adjustment' is made to the composition mark on the basis of the reading comprehension mark, the use of English mark is adjusted to allow for 'examiner variation', the listening comprehension mark is adjusted to allow for the various forms used, and the results of the first four papers are used to adjust the 'tradition-ally problematic mark of the interview'.

While the Cambridge procedure is not fully described, it is very similar to the method of 'limen-referencing', a term introduced by Christie and Forrest (1981) and defined by French, Slater, Vassiloglou, and Willmott (1987: 18) as the application of standards that 'have never been formalised and written down as precise criteria. In the British system, the standards exist, by and large, in the minds of the examining profession, not on paper'. They depend, as Roach (1945) made clear, on the establishment of a consensus.

One of the first questions tackled by Bachman and his colleagues con-cerned the statistical characteristics of the two test batteries he was compar-ing, as might be expected from scholars trained in what Bachman (forgetting Edgeworth, Hartog and Thomson, and many other British psychometrists) calls the 'American measurement tradition'. There were three potential sources of measurement error. For the objective, discrete-point tests in the reading comprehension paper and for parts of the use of English and listening comprehension papers, the appropriate question was internal consistency. In listening comprehension, classical internal consist-ency estimates—coefficient was the measure calculated—were very low, so that over half the variance in scores resulted from measurement error. Even for the objective reading comprehension paper the internal consistency was around 0.73 (Bachman *et al.* 1989: 61–2).

A second source of measurement error was the subjective marking of items by different examiners. As a result of the administrative procedures followed it proved impossible to establish the intra- and inter-rater consist-ency of the subjective papers. Some compositions were re-marked, but the second marker knew the first mark, with the result that reliability could not be estimated (ibid.: 62–3). The interesting point to note here is not the lack of reliability, but the complete lack of concern for it evidenced by the Cambridge method of administration.

A third source of measurement error was introduced by the multiple topics offered in the composition and the multiple forms used in the lis-tening comprehension paper and in the interview. A preliminary study of variance by topic showed a high degree of consistency (ibid.: 66). However, a study of the variance introduced by using different forms of the listening comprehension test suggested that their use introduced a considerable degree of measurement error (ibid.: 67). Variations in examiners and methods (individual versus group) masked the variance introduced by having alternative forms for the interview (ibid.: 68).

Bachman and his colleagues summarized their reaction to this particular area as follows:

The finding with the most serious implications for the Cambridge EFL examinations is that they have serious problems with respect to several

aspects of reliability: internal consistency of questions, equivalence of forms and consistency of ratings. The internal consistency reliabilities of scores from FCE Papers 1 [reading comprehension] and 4 [listening comprehension] are below generally accepted levels for standardized tests, as are those for the parts of Paper 3 [use of English]; the score differences across Paper 4 forms are unacceptably large, and the intra- and inter-rater reliabilities of ratings for Papers 2 [composition] and 5 [interview] are essentially unknown.
(ibid.: 121)

While they appreciated the strengths in the complex integrative and communicative examining involved, Bachman and his colleagues believed that 'the complexities of test design, test administration and marking procedures provided numerous sources of uncontrolled variation in test scores, and thus constituted serious hindrances to demonstrating that Cambridge examination scores are reliable indicators of the abilities they are intended to measure' (ibid.: 122).

In all this, their comparison was with the psychometrically-driven testing of ETS. In commenting on the final report, Alan Maley (1989) drew attention to differences in the purposes of the tests, with the CPE and FCE serving only a minority of those seeking university admission. He also provided a charming metaphor when he characterized the ETS tests as representing a factory system, as opposed to the UCLES cottage industry. The latter produced, he suggested in a somewhat mixed image, a 'herbaceous border, characterized by the charm of the unexpected, gradual approximation, and rule of thumb or eye'. 'Cottage industrial' methods, however, are not likely to be very successful in producing a quarter of a million fair test scores a year. Since the report was completed,[3] UCLES has put into effect many of the recommendations needed to increase the reliability of the CPE.

The lesson to be derived is the relative invulnerability of institutions to change and like other institutions, testing agencies have a high resistance to theoretical innovation. Just as ETS managed to hold off the claims of integrative communicative testing for some decades and then find psychometrically acceptable ways of incorporating tests of writing and speaking, so UCLES managed for a long time to resist the claims of objective testing, even when its staff members were well acquainted with it and were actively involved in developing innovative modern and post-modern batteries of tests.

The other British tradition

The CPE and the FCE were, as already noted, only two of the nine batteries controlled by UCLES in 1987, albeit their most widespread and most lucrative.

The British Council, established by the British government as the main institution for spreading British language and culture, had formed a Joint Committee with UCLES as early as 1944. From Roach's accounts,[4] there was tension between UCLES and British Council representatives, many of whom were associated with the University of London Institute of Education and the Cambridge Syndics. The British Council members had an understandable concern for practical English language teaching and testing, while the Syndics had a much more traditional view of English as the vehicle for culture and literature. While the British Council members were successful in chipping away at the literary bias of the Cambridge examination, it was clear to them by the early 1960s that the CPE could not meet the needs for a test of English for growing numbers of students seeking admission to British universities.

In 1964 the British Council gave the task of developing such a test battery to Alan Davies, at the time studying towards an MA in English at Birmingham after a spell as a teacher of English as a second language in Kenya (Davies 1990: vi). The goal of the British Council, Davies reported, was to find a 'more objective' method of selecting candidates for scholarships and fellowships. Put in other terms, the goal was to apply the measurement tradition, British in origin but so highly developed in America as to be commonly regarded as American, to this testing task.

Until this could be done, the British Council had been relying, Alderson and Clapham (1992: 149) reported, on the British Council Subjective Assessments, which guided British Council officers overseas in rating candidates on a five-point scale for listening, speaking, reading, and writing ability, just as, before TOEFL was developed, many American universities had relied on informal reports of consular and United States Information Service officials overseas. There were no testing materials provided, but some suggestions on how to do this testing.[5]

The first version of the British Council English Proficiency Test Battery, known also as the Davies test after its developer, was available in 1965. It was similar in some ways to the Michigan and American Language Institute tests, in consisting of a combination of discrete-point items testing grammar, sound discrimination, and identification of prosodic features, together with more integrative items including versions of cloze items. It showed, as did the collection of theoretical papers subsequently published in Davies (1968), that English language testers were well aware of developments in American language testing.

Over the next twelve years, three new versions of the Battery were developed.[6] This test, Davies (1990: 47) asserted, had a single cut-off point, raised over the years, based on the argument that minimal English proficiency was necessary for overseas students, but not sufficient, as a predictor of their academic success.[7] Neither Davies's Battery, nor a similar English Language Battery designed by Elisabeth Ingram for students entering Edinburgh University made any effort towards special versions for students in different subjects, but the validation of the Ingram test (on 1,600 students over seven years at Edinburgh) showed that the different faculties had different needs in English.

These and other local initiatives in British testing of English as a foreign language have, over the last few years, slowly but surely come under the administrative control of the Cambridge Syndics. In Britain as in the United States, centralization of English testing has been needed to cope with the growth of a major influx of foreign students and an unprecedented increase in the status and use of English internationally.

Improving and internationalizing ELTS

The original English Language Testing Service test, Alderson and Clapham (1992) claim, quickly became outdated. The willingness of its owners to revise the test must be considered a point in its favour. Indeed, whereas the Cambridge English Proficiency examinations appear as traditional, pre-scientific examinations that only slowly and self-consciously incorporated objective testing technology, the ELTS test was from the beginning intended to embody current ideas of language testing.

It was first proposed in the late 1970s by the British Council, who asked UCLES for assistance in designing a test of English for Special Purposes suitable for making decisions about foreign students seeking to study in the United Kingdom.[8] The test was to be based on the model developed by John Munby (1978), in the elaboration of what was called the 'notional/ functional syllabus', itself influenced by work of British applied linguists like Wilkins (1976) and Trim (Girard and Trim 1988) in expanding on the model of communicative competence proposed by Hymes (1967).[9]

Though there had been criticism of the notional-functional model quite early, it seemed logical to the test developers that the test should differentiate according to a student's field of study, respecting the widespread acceptance of the notion of teaching English for Special Purposes. The new test was therefore to include modules in such fields as technology, life sciences, and medical sciences.

The test was described as 'a systematic and continuously available means of assessing the English language proficiency of non-native speakers of English wishing to study or train in the medium of English' (Westaway, Alderson, and Clapham 1992: 239).[10] In 1986–7, it was taken by about 14,000 candidates at 150 centres world-wide, and was recognized by all British universities and polytechnics and some in Australia and Canada. In this version, there were two main tests, one academic and the other non-academic. The academic test had two general sub-tests, a forty-item multiple-choice test of reading and a thirty-five item multiple-choice test of listening comprehension. There were also three subject-specific sub-tests, a forty-item multiple-choice study skills sub-test, a forty-minute extended writing test with two items, and a twelve-to-fifteen-minute individual guided interview. Modules were available in specific subjects (life sciences, medicine, physical sciences, social studies), and general subjects. The non-academic test had three sub-tests: thirty multiple-choice listening items, forty-five multiple-choice and sentence-writing items for reading and writing, and a fifteen-minute interview.

Recognizing no doubt the innovative and controversial nature of the test, within a year of its introduction in 1980 the British Council and UCLES commissioned two Edinburgh applied linguists, Clive Criper and Alan Davies, to conduct a validation study, which was completed in 1986 (Criper and Davies 1988). Their study showed that the test predicted academic success about as well as other similar English proficiency tests, correlating around 0.30 with the grades in other subjects of foreign students admitted to study in Britain. The multiple-choice items were quite reliable (ranging from 0.80 to 0.93), but the open-ended sub-tests had reliabilities of only about 0.50. The test correlated well with other English language proficiency tests (about 0.80), but not with supervisors' or tutors' rating (about 0.30). Candidates and supervisors found the test generally fair.

But the attempt to provide for subject specialization was much less successful. In the predictive analyses, it was the general sub-tests that had most of the power. Criper and Davies (1986: 99) were critical of the theory: 'Like register analysis before it, ESP [English for Special Purposes] both in teaching and testing falls down when it moves from the process of variation, variety, specific purposes to discrete entities which appear to be impossible to delineate and keep apart.' They were also unhappy with the practice: 'ELTS was constructed in what was, as we have now seen, a highly unsystematic and also in a thoroughly unempirical manner.'

The evaluation report by Criper and Davies was discussed at a conference of language testing specialists in 1986 (Porter, Hughes, and Weir 1988). At this meeting, it was the general view that the high acceptance of the new test by receiving institutions made it wise to revise it rather than to scrap it, a decision that will be familiar to most manufacturers. With the loss of support for the Munby model, there were grounds for a new approach to content. The test should be streamlined and the reliability improved.

The test owners accepted this approach, and in January 1987, the British Council and UCLES, with the participation later of the International Development Programme of Australian Universities, set up a three-year project, directed by Charles Alderson and Caroline Clapham of the University of Lancaster, to develop a revised test.

Westaway, Alderson, and Clapham (1990), in a paper written in 1987, detail the first stage, in which reactions to ELTS were collected from test administrators and the staff of receiving institutions, British Council staff, and language testers and teachers. In addition, a thousand test report forms were analysed and papers were commissioned from applied linguists. Overseas administrators wanted a simplified procedure. Receiving institutions felt the number of modules could be reduced; admission offices used overall scores while individual departments liked the profiles; and there was no need seen to separate undergraduate and postgraduate students. Teachers were concerned about washback. Language testers agreed that the number of modules could be reduced. The British Council staff thought the test was a great improvement but a bit too long. The language testers agreed that the Munby model was outdated, but did not agree on a replacement.

Alderson and Clapham (1992) reviewed in more detail the theoretical or ideological basis for the changes proposed. By 1986, an influential article by Canale and Swain (1980) had widened the view of communicative competence,[11] and work in the United States adapting the Foreign Service Institute Oral Interview to more general use had made it a major force, although, Alderson notes, none of the British testers who wrote papers for the project referred to it or to work by Bachman developing a model of communicative language ability. While they did not see a new paradigm emerging, they seem to have agreed that the Munby model was no longer a dominant force.

The conclusions of the first six months' work by the project were presented to a conference of consultants in July 1987, and a revision plan was drawn up. The new ELTS would contain three general components (grammar, listening, and speaking) and two modular (academic reading and academic writing), the latter to be offered in arts and social science, physical science and technology, life and medical sciences, and general training versions.[12] The choice of the three subject area modules divided the 1,000 students whose test forms had been studied into three more or less equal groups, as good a way as any of resolving a problem for which there was no obvious theoretical criterion.

Alderson and Clapham (1992) deplored the failure of the attempt to find a theoretical consensus among the applied linguists invited to comment in 1987 on the revision plans. The practical effect of this lack of a single agreed model was to allow greater freedom for the test writers: 'Since the results of our consultations proved to be inconclusive, we were advised to take an eclectic approach to the establishment of specifications for our test writers' (ibid.: 164).

This very complaint, however, makes it apparent that with the development of ELTS, its validation and revision, and its subsequent rebirth as the International English Language Testing Service (IELTS), British applied linguists and language testers had been proffered just the kind of independence and control of English language testing that their American predecessors, such as David Harris and Leslie Palmer, had hoped to obtain twenty years earlier. That a consensus did not emerge is, I would suspect, not evidence of the lack of sophistication of the field, but rather of the underlying error in assuming that language proficiency can be simply measured. The paradox of the success of the English testing industry on either side of the Atlantic is that it has revealed the underlying theoretical weaknesses of the enterprise.

The flourishing English testing industry

The enterprises continue. UCLES played a leading role in forming the Association of Language Testers in Europe, by whom its English tests are fully recognized. The Association is (appropriately) registered as a European Economic Interest Grouping within the European Community.[13] It is working to establish common standards for testing among European testing agencies, and, presumably, to guard against new attempts like the EURO-CERT of ETS to break into the European market.

In the meantime, ETS has established the TOEFL 2000 project to propose ways of improving the effectiveness and the marketability of its own competing set of English tests. The spread of English and its diffusion throughout the modern world has made English language testing international big business.

And big business, it is clear, has its own logic and rules, quite distinct from the logic and rules of an academic field like language testing. Between them, Cambridge and Princeton now test the English proficiency of a million non-native learners of English every year. To treat these commercially profitable and institutionally entrenched testing enterprises in the same way that scholars treat an article published in a journal is naive. TOEFL and its English counterparts are to be explained not by a theory drawing on linguistics and psychology, but by an understanding of the social and economic and institutional forces that control them.

These forces explain why UCLES was reluctant to give up on a formula of minimizing attention to psychometric considerations, and why, with all the goodwill in the world, ETS was unable and unwilling to give up on a working TOEFL test in favour of theoretically induced innovations. The best test for its purposes was a highly reliable and highly efficient one, with the result that, from its beginning under the influence of Princeton, TOEFL developed into the acme of the objective modern language test, with all its strengths and with all its weaknesses.

Notes

1 This is the name of the test, although it is often referred to as the ELTS (or in the latest version, IELTS) test. Foucault would surely have had

something to say about using the name 'service' for a test which asserts power over foreigners seeking admission to universities.

2 See Chapter 18.
3 Its publication has been promised but is still awaited.
4 See Chapter 11.
5 A doctoral dissertation by Moller (1981) discusses the reliability of this assessment method.
6 Alan Moller worked with Davies on the third version, and Charles Alderson on the fourth.
7 Davies (1990: 44) noted that such English proficiency tests correlated only about 0.03 with students' scores at the end of a year of study.
8 For a brief background, see Seaton (1981). Alderson and Hughes (1981) includes papers by Brendan Carroll, Criper, Alderson, and Clapham discussing the development of these specifications.
9 The same model is also set out in a book by B.J. Carroll (1980), and formed the basis for tests other than ELTS.
10 The paper by Westaway (of the British Council) and her colleagues (from the University of Lancaster) was first read at the Applied Linguistics Congress in 1987.
11 For a fuller background, see Spolsky (1989b).
12 This was to provide for a growing number of candidates aiming to follow vocational courses.
13 Its membership in 1993 was the Alliance Française (France), CITO (the Netherlands), the Generalitat de Catalunya, Instituto Cervantes, and Universidad de Salamanca (representing the three major Spanish languages), the Danish Language Testing Consortium, the Goethe Institute (Germany), the Universidade de Lisboa (Portugal), the Universita per Stranieri (Italy), and UCLES.

20 Jubilee: an envoi

Objectivity dominant

Objective modern language tests reached a high point in 1965, just over fifty years after the call of the Modern Language Association committee for objective language tests, when TOEFL moved to Princeton and the institutional protection of ETS. TOEFL marks the maturity of a particular kind of psychometrically driven objective test. It was a very successful maturity, as TOEFL grew into the most profitable single language test ever developed. Mature, certainly, as befits something reflecting fifty years of development, and such an effective and efficient and psychometrically polished test deserves all the financial success and product recognition that it has had.

At the same time, dinosaur-like, TOEFL signals the end of an epoch of language testing. Efficient as it was for its context, strongly armoured enough to withstand puny attacks, and big enough to bully its way into new contexts of use, TOEFL showed the ultimate sterility of the purely reliability-driven approach to the problem of language testing This is revealed in its continued outflanking by the much more integratively designed Test of Written English and Test of Spoken English that ETS finally produced and the related, less ideologically pure, approach represented by the International English Language Testing Service and other tests offered by UCLES. ETS, too, has acknowledged the need for major rethinking of its approach, with the launching of TOEFL 2000, its internal programme to consider the new goals and testing methods that have grown up in what I call post-modern testing.

Looked at in this wider context, purely objective language testing appears to have failed, for, while it measured something reliably, what it measured was not the language proficiency that was assumed. The improvements that objectivity brought seem to have been illusory. One alternative offered within language testing, and still enjoying a fading fashion among modern language teachers, has been the notion of an absolute scale.

The search for the holy scale

The dream of an absolute scale for measuring language proficiency has been around certainly since Thorndike (1910). It was embodied in the American Council on the Teaching of Foreign Languages' (1982, 1986) reincarnation of the Foreign Service Institute scales. While the absoluteness of these scales has been mitigated, following Carroll's (1954) assertion of the need for different scales for the various skills, there has continued to be an assumption that scales will provide scientifically accurate control of subjective measurement.

The FSI scale has been transported to Europe, too, and interpreted there in a number of different forms. North (1992) set out the scales developed in 1967 by Wilkins, in the late 1970s by the English Language Teaching Development Unit, later by IELTS, and in 1989 by the English-Speaking Union. North attempted to calibrate these with scales proposed by Euro-centres and the UK National Curriculum, and implicit in other organization of curricula into levels. He mentioned how these scales might be broken down into skills (the traditional reading, writing, speaking, and listening, or an alternative comprehension, oral interaction, and production).

Attractive as these attempts at scale construction are to those who wish to design language teaching syllabuses, and useful as they no doubt seem to those who want an easy presentation of the results of language testing, it is my argument that this ease is possible only as a result of excessive over-simplification, and that it ultimately misrepresents the nature of language proficiency. Furthermore, it leads to necessarily inaccurate, and therefore ethically questionable, statements about individuals placed on such a scale.

How much does it hurt?

A helpful analogy to language testing is in the field of pain measurement and assessment.[1] The development of techniques for measuring and assessing pain has been one of the most important advances in pain research and therapy (Melzack 1983a). Since 1984, US law has laid down how pain must be evaluated for determining disability benefits, thus raising serious questions about its assessment (Osterweis, Kleinman, and Mechanic 1987). In this field, as in language testing, scientifically established multidimensionality places difficult constraints on the search for a unidimensional scale.

In the study of pain, the complex relationships that exist between sensory and psychological components have been recognized. For the former, known stimuli such as a tourniquet can be applied to a subject in laboratory conditions, and physical responses (sweating, dilation of pupils, excessively rapid heartbeat) can be observed (Sternbach 1983). The psychological components are more likely to be studied using verbal judgements by sufferers, collected in clinical conditions by using some more or less standardized instrument. One of the simplest is the Visual Analogue Scale, a 10 cm. line defined as representing no pain at one end and severe pain at the other

(Huskisson 1983); the obvious analogy in language testing is self-assessment. Another is the McGill Pain Questionnaire (Melzack 1983b), which calls for a subject to specify various aspects of the pain he or she is suffering in a designated body area by selecting among a number of sets of adjectives, such as 'flickering, quivering, pulsing, throbbing, beating, pounding', or 'pinching, pressing, grating, cramping, crushing', or 'nagging, nauseating, agonizing, dreadful, torturing'. A single subject, it seems, can deal with not more than a quarter of the 102 terms, but the technique has shown itself useful in exploration of the phenomenon.

In summarizing their findings on methods of assessing pain, the Committee on Pain, Disability and Chronic Illness Behavior of the Institute of Medicine of the National Academy of Science noted that the very complexity and multidimensionality of the area made it extremely difficult to agree on a measure:

> A number of well-defined instruments are available for assessing pain and related variables. Each is bound to a theoretical position, and each has its strength and weaknesses. None can yield unequivocal evidence of the presence of painful activity within the nervous system apart from the patient's reports and behaviors. Most experienced clinicians tend toward the eclectic: subjective data are used to build up a broad picture of the individual patient. Decisions for diagnosis and treatment are based on interpretations drawn from patterns evident among the combined measures.
> (Osterweis *et al.* 1987: 227–8)

Rather than expecting some simple mechanical device to translate the complex data of individual language proficiency into a single measure, language testers, too, would benefit from intelligent and responsible 'interpretations drawn from patterns evident among the combined measures'.

Re-embodying language proficiency

Part of the confusion, I suspect, has arisen out of attempts to deal with language proficiency out of context. The decontexualization of language—in its most extreme form in the quest for an autonomous linguistics—marked the triumph of Cartesian rationality over the more humanistic scepticism of earlier approaches. The promise of absolute certainty, promoted by modern science and eagerly espoused by bureaucracies, encouraged the mistaken belief in the possibility of absolute reliable measurement of a complex human skill.

One of the major problems with measuring pain is that those who do so seek in some way to separate the phenomenon from the person, treating it as a physical rather than a psychological object. Blood cholesterol levels, or weight, or heartbeat can, with all their complexities and variations from time to time and situation to situation, be measured with some reasonable degree of confidence. Love, or pain, or, I suggest, language proficiency, are so inseparable from the possessor and his or her socio-psychological context that any simple measure is necessarily flawed.

Some understanding of this problem can come from some recent proposals concerning epistemology by Lorraine Code.[2] She argues that the kind of objective knowledge that is normally assumed as basic (as in the form of knowing that something is an X or knowing that X is a Y) is not necessarily the only or the most useful kind of knowledge. I quote her description of what she characterizes as cognitively autonomous knowledge:

> Belief that knowers can and should be self-sufficient, and that objects of knowledge are independent and separate from them, yields a composite picture of knowledge in which autonomy is a privileged value. A dominant feature of this picture is the assumption that knowledge is the *product* of inquiry that stands alone in the sense that details of its production are irrelevant to its structure, content, and/or evaluation. This assumption connects with the view that knowledge worthy of the name is timelessly and placelessly true, and that its objects are independent in the sense both of being disconnected from knowing subjects and of being inert and unaffected by the knowing process.
> (Code 1991)

After analysing other alternatives, she suggests as a basic notion the reciprocal, subjective knowledge involved in knowing a friend. Such knowledge is necessarily reciprocal, contextualized, affectively coloured, dynamic.

It is, I would claim, also a better model for understanding language knowledge and proficiency than is the objective approach, adding a much needed scepticism to the approach to a complex topic.

Oedipal? But what if I don't like my mother either?

In a strange way, language testers (with a few outstanding exceptions like Henmon and Carroll) are not unlike the person who murdered his parents and then made a plea for clemency as an orphan. Our field has been remarkably ahistorical; we have too often satisfied ourselves with patricidal fury on a named or unnamed predecessor before launching ourselves into our own rediscovery of a slightly circular wheel of our own.

This study has been salutary for the writer, at least, in discovering how earlier scholars understood the problems as clearly as later ones. If students of language testing were required to read Edgeworth, Brigham, Henmon, Kaulfers, Roach, Lado, Carroll, and Grieve, as students of physics are taught the historical development of their field, and if replication of others' work regularly preceded new experimentation, I am certain that we would find much more modesty, and many more useful advances. Looking back on my own quarter of a century in the field, I now realize how much time I wasted before I came to appreciate the other traditions.[3]

A central issue underlying this history has been the question of whether language proficiency can be measured on a definable dimension, like the time of a race or the distance of a jump or the number of goals, or whether it must be judged on a subjective set of criteria, like the performance of a diver, gymnast, or skater. But this dichotomy, like all other binary choices in two-valued logic, is almost certainly a false and unnecessary one. It is not too hard to realize that both sides of the argument are correct; that there are language abilities that are measurable, and that there are others that are only judgeable. The analogy of pain assessment shows the need for accepting the underlying complexity of these human phenomena; from the feminist epistemology, it can been seen how an objective view of knowledge is not the only alternative. It is surely not unreasonable to accept a similar open and contextual approach to language proficiency.

Check your answers before you hand in the paper

An invitation to give a plenary address to the Fourth Applied Linguistics Congress in Stuttgart first enticed me to address myself to the historical context in which I had been working for ten years as a self-trained English language tester. My intent then, as today, was not just to try to understand the development of the field over time, but rather to understand the basic issues I was facing as a tester and the multitude of often competing solutions offered.

In the talk I gave at the congress (Spolsky 1977), I put forward the notion of a three-stage history of language testing. The earliest I called the traditional or pre-scientific phase. It was marked by the use of essays, open-ended examinations, or oral examining, with results determined intuitively by an authorized and authoritarian examiner. This was succeeded, I suggested, by a psychometric–structuralist (or scientific) period. The adjectives alluded to the highly productive collaboration of psychometrists and linguists, the former seeking objective and replicable methods to measure as consistently as possible an individual learner's control of the items identified by the latter. This was the basis of the discrete-point testing demonstrated by Robert Lado in his pioneering book. Dissatisfaction with some aspects of this approach, expressed in John Carroll's trail-blazing call for the equal relevance of integrative and communicative language testing, had led, in turn, to what I at first labelled the psycholinguistic–sociolinguistic stage, with its quest for unifying psychological principles (such as my

pursuit of reduced redundancy or John Oller's parallel proposal of expectancy grammar), or the growing interest in functionally and socially contextualized testing of language use. I hastened to point out that there was
overlap between the stages, so that the approaches underlying them had
survived their succession, and existed as uneasy bedfellows. In later papers,
I suggested some other names, proposing for the first period the term *traditional* (for it can be dated back to the Chinese civil service examinations
started two thousand years ago, although it seems to have taken its present
shape more from the eighteenth-century Cambridge Tripos), the second
modern (by which I meant applying psychometric principles invented at
the end of the last century and sharing with those inventors a belief in
progress and science), and the third *post-modern* (a fashionable term, but
apt, none the less, for its suggestions of the dissatisfactions with modernism
that started to emerge in the 1960s).

There is no doubt a good deal of truth in this tripartite division, for it
has been frequently cited and widely accepted. It was based, however,
strictly on the generalized impressions and unsystematic reading of someone who was untrained in language testing and whose reading in the historical background of the field was very limited.

For the past few years I have been trying to expiate, as it were, the *ex
cathedra* pronouncements on the history of the field that I made seventeen
years ago, by a more thorough exploration of the documentary sources.
With this wider perspective, I offer an alternative conjecture, which sees
the development of language testing not as three periods but rather as an
unresolved (and fundamentally unresolvable) tension between competing
sets of forces.

These forces are both practical and ideological. One fundamental
factor—we might call it the test user's practical motivation—arises from
the institutional context of any testing, which sets limits on the time and
money that can be devoted to the test, as well as encumbering the process
with a number of constraints (such as speed and form of reporting, security
and uncompromisability, efficiency and profitability, etc.).

This is most clearly to be seen with the institutional test user—the person
charged with using test results to control the admission or certification or
other aspect of the career of a subject. Reading the history of modern tests,
starting, say, with the 1913 committee of the Modern Language Association, which wanted oral testing to encourage direct-method teaching, but
finished up with written tests because they were easier to administer, one
regularly finds that the solutions to testing problems are compromises governed by practical concerns. This explained the failure of the 1927 Modern
Language Study led by Henmon to develop the oral–aural tests he thought
necessary, or of the National Council on the Testing of English as a Foreign
Language or its successor owners of TOEFL to develop the promised aptitude tests, and the twenty-year delay in providing the promised speaking

and writing tests. Rather than testing everything that one believes needs to be tested, one looks for a short cut, a 'quick dirty' method of approximating the complex testing battery that intelligent analysis demands. The overall effect of this pressure is to encourage people to test what is easy or cheap to test, rather than what is harder or more expensive. Testing is done in a real world, with fiscal and time and equipment constraints, and their effect on the form of tests cannot be ignored.

A second factor, equally contextual, is the need for some general acceptance (on the part of test taker, user, and public) that the test appears to capture suitably a performance of the ability it is claimed to measure and that it provides some easily interpretable result. The test, in the words of the head of a major testing institution, needs to be 'felt fair'. This feeling can be engendered in different ways. The simplest one is to proclaim the authorized expertise of the examiners. It is no accident that tests and testing agencies are happy to clothe themselves with the aura of universities or university towns. Another is the appeal to scientific accuracy and certainty, advertised by the reporting of complex and doubtfully relevant statistical properties of the numbers produced almost by chance by modern testing. The claim of 0.9 reliability seems to suggest a sufficient basis for confidence, although very few people would cross a street if they were told they had a 20 per cent chance of being run over, which is about the probability that a score with 0.9 reliability is wrong.

This factor, which we might label the test user's confidence and ease of use, also explains why it is that complex score reports and profiles (fully justified as they are by the facts) are spurned in favour of simple answers. The unsophisticated test user, like the lawyer badgering the expert witness in court, asks for simple yes-no, pass-fail answers to extremely complicated questions. The carefully explained and regularly repeated statement in the *TOEFL Test and Score Manual* about the need for local validation and interpretation of scores bears witness to the sad truth that most users act as though the score a student receives is a real absolute measure with an immediate non-contextualized interpretation, and as though there is a real difference between a student who scores 597 and one who scores 601.

As was noted in Chapter 18, the *TOEFL Test and Score Manual* is quite clear when it points out that in fact only a 30-point difference between two scores is significant (TOEFL Programs and Services 1990: 25). It does, however, present data suggesting that the use and interpretation of test scores may fall far short of the ideal it postulates. Only 800 of the more than 2,200 institutions receiving TOEFL scores responded to the 1989 survey of users. Only 26 institutions (4 per cent of the respondents, and 1 per cent of the institutions) had carried out their own internal validity studies as recommended, although another 53 said they were planning or conducting such studies (ibid.: 18). Put more negatively, 90 per cent of the institutions use the scores without locally established validity. These real-world desires for easy answers set major ethical challenges to testers who know the complexity of the task of assessing language proficiency.

The third factor, and the one that has been the professional tester's primary focus, is the challenge of the 'unavoidable uncertainty' and 'probable error' that Edgeworth (1888) identified as inevitable accompaniments of all attempts to measure human abilities. Since the first serious work on testing, we have known how inaccurate all measures are and must remain. We know about many of the causes of error: the illness or other distraction of the test taker, the inadequacy or bias of the tester, the accidental variation in selecting the items, the inaccuracy of the marking. In spite of this, we regularly fail to treat the test results with the healthy respect for fuzziness and inaccuracy that they demand and that are evinced by experts.

Remember what Carl Brigham said in 1932. He told the College Board about the issue of the unreliability of measuring devices. Testers, he said, had long been aware of this problem, so that they thought of a grade not as a fixed point but rather as 'one particular grade drawn by chance from a hat which contains all of that candidate's grades obtained from an infinite series of examinations set and read to measure exactly that same trait'. Unlike the colleges, which acted as though a reported grade were an exact and fixed number, testers saw it surrounded by its standard error, 'which would include two-thirds of the grades above and below it'. The purpose of the 'new-type' movement was essentially to reduce this error and so to rate an *individual* more fairly. But one can never expect complete accuracy: as the *TOEFL Test and Score Manual* regularly reminds those users who take the time to read it, 'test scores are not perfect measures of ability' (TOEFL Programs and Services ibid.: 15).

These three factors, feasibility, usability, and reliability, must be considered as constraints on the possibility of developing a valid test, one that measures (if that is possible) or assesses in some other way the specific abilities with which we are concerned. In an ideal world, the provision of an adequate assessment would be the only concern; in practical language testing, compromises must be made. Each of the approaches made different choices.

The *traditional* test emphasized the first two factors, paying minimal attention to reliability: it was enough that the test be 'felt fair'. The *scientific* test concentrated on technological developments (the use of multiple-choice items, the selection only of well-schooled judges whose agreement is known) that minimize statistical unreliability, and at the same time provide businesslike and potentially lucrative tests, with a hazardous disregard for some aspects of validity. Ideologically, there was a basic distinction in the training and perception of the two kind of testers.

There was another fundamental difference between the two approaches. The traditional examiners were pre-eminently trained in the humanities, and had inherited the kind of scepticism and acceptance of pluralism (there is no one correct answer) that marked Renaissance geniuses such as Montaigne and Shakespeare. But many of them were easily drawn, by institutional needs or by personal predilections for élitism, to believe that examination scores obtained in a humanistic pluralistic way still had the *imprimatur* that called for absolute certainty and accuracy. At their best (and worst), they resisted those who would find ways to improve the reliability and replicability of their scores; at their worst, they often acted as though their grades were divinely inspired and infallible.

The psychometrists, in contrast, had a more consistent ideology as well as practical needs on their side. While earlier students of the human mind tended to be pluralistic collectors of new and interesting cases, the stronger trend in psychology turned out to be the attempt to apply the Cartesian search for absolute certainty to the measurement of human abilities. It is intriguing to compare Francis Galton, the cousin of Darwin, who happily collected measurements of anything that would stand still (and of things that wouldn't, such as the efficacy of prayer and the leadership potential of oxen) with his younger contemporary, James Cattell, who felt psychometrics was the basis of a new science: 'Psychology cannot attain the certainty and exactness of the physical sciences, unless it rests on a foundation of experiment and measurement.' Psychometric reliability made one believe one had measured something relevant; while psychometrists (like Brigham or John Carroll) were able to avoid falling into the trap of reification, the lay users of test results are much less sophisticated.

What I have labelled *post-modern* testing may be seen as an approach that accepts the equal importance of all three identified factors. Readers may recall the story of the Rabbi who, being chided by his wife for saying that two contending parties were right, agreed that she too was right to point out the contradiction. The point is that neither traditional Jewish thought nor humanistic ideology assume that binary choices must be made. Post-modern testing also adds a sincere, ethically driven, consideration of the potentially deleterious effects of testing on the test taker, on the instructional process, and on other facets of the social context in which we test.

This may usefully be seen as part of the conflict, so well described by Stephen Toulmin, between the pluralistic scepticism of the humanities and the search for unique certainty of the rationalism of the modern sciences. It is, I suspect, a tension worth maintaining. The rejection of some of the worst features of modernism need not mean rejecting its strengths as well— we might dislike many features of modern life, but it is hard to give up all the advances that have been made. We cannot simply return to the village, or to the pure traditional test, without considering the demands of feasibility and reliability.

The fundamental flaw of objective modern language testing has been to presuppose that language proficiency is measurable and unidimensional, in the sense that the speed of a runner or the weight of a shot-put is measurable on a single defined dimension. Language proficiency is more like pain, the external assessment of which has many analogous properties: it varies from person to person, from context to context, and can only be inferred from self-report and the observation of impaired performance.

It is also a mistake to assume that knowledge of a language is best considered as the possession of something external and autonomously measurable, like money. In this approach, we assume that the language is autonomous and external to the knower, and we ask how much of it is under the learner's control. A more useful model, I believe, is that suggested by Lorraine Code, knowledge of a friend. The knowledge in 'knowing a friend' involves properties—contextualization, dynamism, reciprocity—all of which mitigate against measurement. In the same way, knowledge of a language is dynamic (at different times of day, I know more or less French), is contextualized as to domain (place and topic, certainly), and person (my language ability varies with my interlocutor). To assume that all this complexity can usefully and meaningfully be squeezed into a single number or a single point on a unidimensional scale, is, on the face of it, absurd.

The analysis I have provided is not meant to prevent language testing. Just as the scientist does not wait until he or she has a final understanding of the nature of the universe before he or she risks using navigation aids based on less sophisticated methods, the humanistic sceptic need not sit paralysed because he or she is never certain of the truth of his or her answers. There are practical ways to behave.

In language testing as in all other testing, as Bachman (1990) emphasizes so strongly, the first step must be an honest decision on the purpose of the test. An ethical evaluation and justification of the intended and probable use of the test will make clear how much care language testers need to take with reliability and how certain they need to be of the results. Only the most elaborate test batteries, with multiple administrations of multiple methods of testing the multiple traits or abilities that make up language proficiency, are capable of producing rich and accurate enough profiles to be used for making critical or fateful decisions about individuals. Normally, testers use much simpler measures, which find their justification only in their accuracy for the group. Too often tests are used to play Russian roulette with the test takers. If the aim is to help a learner (a pedagogical diagnostic test) or if concerns are with group norms and not individuals (surveys or evaluations), using a single measure is justified, provided it is interpreted carefully. But if it is to make some serious decision affecting the future of the person being tested, language testers must accept full responsibility for the inevitable uncertainty of a powerful but flawed technology, and make sure not just of reliability but also of focused and relevant validity, and intelligent and sceptical interpretation of the multiple methods of measurement and assessment used. Like medicines, language tests need clear labels giving details of measurement error and validation, which should appear on the face of score reports rather than in manuals read only by experts.

It is, then, a fitting celebration of the centenary of Professor Edgeworth's papers analysing the difficulties and hazards of measuring human abilities, and of the Jubilee of the efforts of the Modern Language Study to assess control of a second language, that the two major industrialized language testing agencies, ETS in Princeton and UCLES, should recently have undertaken such radical reforms of their tests in English as a foreign language. Scepticism, as a book by Ellen Spolsky (forthcoming) will argue, need not be tragic.

Notes

1 I am indebted to conversations with Robert Gerwin, MD, for my introduction to this area.
2 I am grateful to Ellen Spolsky for drawing my attention to this work.
3 Growing up among those who were rebelling against Lado, it took me many years to appreciate the significance of *his* rebellion. Impressed by the psychometric sophistication of English language testers, I did not (until I was revising this book) appreciate how much we lost by the professional split from foreign language testers.

Bibliography

Adams-Fallon, M. and C.W. Stansfield. 1985. 'Report to the TOEFL Executive Committee'. Educational Testing Service Archives.

Agard, F.B. 1946. 'The University of Chicago language investigation tests'. *Hispania* 29/1: 31–7.

Agard, F.B., R.J. Clements, W.S. Hendrix, E. Hocking, S.L. Pitcher, A. van Ernden, and H.G. Doule. 1944. *A Survey of Language Classes in the Army Specialized Training Program.* New York: Commission on Trends in Education [of the Modern Language Association of America].

Agard, F.B. and H.B. Dunkel. 1948. *An Investigation of Second Language Teaching.* Boston, Mass.: Ginn.

Alatis, J.E. 1961. 'Testing the English language proficiency of foreign students' in Center for Applied Linguistics 1961c: 11–29.

Alatis, J.E. (ed.). 1990. *Georgetown University Round Table on Languages and Linguistics 1990.* Washington D.C.: Georgetown University Press.

Albert, M. 1978. 'Measuring second language speaking ability in New Brunswick's senior high schools' in J. L. D. Clark (ed.) 1978a.

Alderson, J.C. and C. Clapham. 1992. 'Applied Linguistics and language testing: a case study of the ELTS test'. *Applied Linguistics* 13/2: 149–67.

Alderson, J.C., and A. Hughes. (eds.). 1981. *Issues in Language Testing.* ELT Documents 111. London: The British Council.

Alderson, J.C. and B. North. (eds.). 1991. *Language Testing in the 1990s: The Communicative Legacy.* London: Modern English Publications and the British Council.

Alderson, J.C. and D. Wall. 1993. 'Does washback exist?'. *Applied Linguistics* 14/2: 115–29.

American Council on the Teaching of Foreign Languages. 1982. *ACTFL Provisional Proficiency Guidelines.* New York: American Council on the Teaching of Foreign Languages.

American Council on the Teaching of Foreign Languages. 1986. *ACTFL Proficiency Guidelines.* New York: American Council on the Teaching of Foreign Languages.

Anderson, C.C. 1960. 'The new STEP essay test as a measure of composition ability'. *Educational and Psychological Measurement* (Spring issue): 95–102.

Anderson, R.D. 1975. *Education in France, 1848–1870.* Oxford: Clarendon Press.

Andrade, M.J. 1922. 'Testing the Meras–Roth–Wood Scale'. *High Points* 4/10: 6–11.

Angelis, P.J. 1982. 'Academic needs and priorities for testing' in *American Language Journal* 1: 41–56.

Angiolillo, P.F. 1947. *Armed Forces' Foreign Language Teaching: Critical Evaluation and Implications.* New York: S.F. Vanni.

Bachman, L., F. Davidson, K. Ryan, and Inn-Chull Choi. 1989. *An Investigation into the Comparability of Two Tests of English as a Foreign Language: The Cambridge–TOEFL Comparability Study. Final Report.* Cambridge: University of Cambridge Local Examinations Syndicate. Also published in *Studies in Language Testing* 1: Bachman, Davidson, Ryan, and Choi. 1995. Cambridge: Cambridge University Press.

Bachman, L.F. 1990. *Fundamental Considerations in Language Testing.* Oxford: Oxford University Press.

Bair, R.L. 1965. 'The MLA Cooperative Foreign Language Tests in Russian'. *Slavic and East European Journal* 9: 308–14.

Baker, F. 1928. 'Test forms for classroom material'. *French Review*: 27–45.

Ballard, P.B. 1920. *Mental Tests*. London: Hodder and Stoughton.

Barber, E.G. 1972. Memo to Files. Ford Foundation Archives: PA66–60.

Barnwell, D. 1992. 'Foreign language teaching and testing during World War II'. *Dialog on Language Instruction* 8/1–2: 29–34.

Barzun, J. 1962. 'Foreword' in B. Hoffman, 1962: 7–11.

Bejar, I.I. 1985. *A Preliminary Study of Raters for the Test of Spoken English*. Research report. Princeton, N.J.: Educational Testing Service.

Benn, T.V. 1936. 'The reliability of French composition'. *Modern Languages* 18/1: 33–7.

Binet, A. and T. Simon. 1916. *The Development of Intelligence in Children*. Baltimore: Williams and Wilkins.

Block, N.J. and G. Dworkin. (eds.). 1976. *The IQ Controversy: Critical Readings*. New York: Pantheon Books.

Bloomfield, L. 1933. *Language*. New York: Holt, Rinehart, and Winston.

Boerner, A.V. 1962. Letter to Melvin Fox, 5 December. Ford Foundation Archives: PA63–213.

Booth, J. 1847. *Examination is the Province of the State; or an Outline of a Practical System for the Extension of National Education*. Cited in J. Roach, 1971.

Bottiglia, W.F. (ed.). 1957. *The Language Classroom: 1957 Northeast Conference on the Teaching of Foreign Languages*. Reports of the working committee. Cambridge, Mass.: MIT Press

Bottke, K.G. and E.E. Milligan. 1945. 'Test of aural and oral aptitude for foreign language study'. *Modern Language Journal* 29: 705–9.

Bovée, A.G. 1947. 'A study of the relationship between visual thought comprehension in English and in French'. *French Review* 21: 120–3.

Bovée, A.G. 1948. 'The relationship between audio and visual thought comprehension in French'. *French Review* 21: 300–5.

Boynton, D. 1962a. Letter to David Harris, 7 June.

Boynton, D. 1962b. Letter to David Harris, 27 July.

Boynton, D. 1962c. Letter to David Harris, 11 September.

Boynton, D. 1963a. Memorandum to members of Executive Committee, 5 June. College Board Archives.

Boynton, D. 1963b. Memorandum to members of the Executive Committee, undated. College Board Archives.

Boynton, D. 1963c. Memorandum to Members of the Executive Committee, 17 December. College Board Archives.

Bramson, L. (ed.). 1964. *Examining in Harvard College*. Cambridge, Mass.: Committee on Educational Policy, Harvard University.

Bree, G. (ed.). 1955. *Culture, Literature and Articulation: 1955 Northeast Conference on the Teaching of Foreign Languages*. Reports of the working committee. New York: New York University.

Breland, H. 1983. *The Direct Assessment of Writing Skill: A Measurement Review*. New York: College Entrance Examination Board.

Breland, H., R. Camp, R.J. Jones, M.M. Morris, and D.A. Rook. 1987. *Assessing Writing Skill*. New York: College Entrance Examination Board.

Brereton, J.L. 1944. *The Case for Examinations: An account of their place in education with some proposals for their reform*. Cambridge: Cambridge University Press.

Bretnall, W.B. 1961. Letter to Kay Salter, 9 February (with manuscript notes). College Board Archives.

Bretnall, W.B. 1965a. 'The TOEFL Program', 11 June. College Board Archives.

Bretnall, W.B. 1965b. Summary of CEEB–ETS Meeting on TOEFL, 1 July. Turnbull Papers, Educational Testing Service Archives.

Brière, E. 1969. 'Current trends in second language testing'. *TESOL Quarterly* 3/4: 333–40.

Brigham, C.C. 1923. *A Study of American Intelligence*. Princeton, N.J.: Princeton University Press.

Brigham, C.C. 1935 'Examining fellowship applicants: A report made to the Social Science Research Council on the method of selecting fellows for first year graduate study'. *Bulletin* 23. Princeton, N.J.: Princeton University Press.

Brinsmade, C. 1928. 'Concerning the College Board examinations in Modern Languages'. *Modern Language Journal* 8/2: 87–100; 8/3: 212–27.

British Council. 1961. *Anglo-American Conference on English Teaching Abroad, June 1961*. Jesus College Cambridge, British Council.

Brock, R.C. 1933. 'An experimental evaluation of various bases for prognosis in Spanish'. Unpublished MA thesis, University of Southern California.

Brooks, N. 1954. 'Report of the committee on tests' in H. E. Sollenberger (ed.) 1954: 49–56.

Brooks, N. 1955. 'Report of the committee on tests' in G. Bree (ed.) 1955: 64–8.

Brooks, N. 1959. 'Report of working committee IV: definition of language competences through testing' in F.D. Eddy (ed.) 1959: 49–56.

Brooks, N. and S. Sapon. 1957. 'Report of the committee on tests' in W.F. Bottiglia (ed.) 1957: 20–3.

Broom, M.E. 1927a. 'A silent reading test in Spanish'. *Journal of Educational Research* 16/5: 357–64.

Broom, M.E. 1927b. 'A silent reading test in French'. *Journal of Educational Research* 19/5: 385–6.

Broom, M.E., M.S. Contreras, and W.V. Kaulfers. 1927. 'A silent reading test in Spanish'. *Modern Languages Forum* 12/3: 7–11.

Brown, W. and G.H. Thomson. 1921. *The Essentials of Mental Measurement*. Cambridge: Cambridge University Press.

Bryan, M. 1966. 'The MLA Cooperative Foreign Language Tests: Tests with a new look and a new purpose'. *The DFL Bulletin* 6/2: 4–8.

Buck, P.H. 1964. 'Examinations: a retrospective view at Harvard' in L. Bramson (ed.) 1964: 4–37.

Buda, R. 1931. 'A French cultural test'. Unpublished MA thesis, College of the City of New York.

Buros, O.K. (ed.). 1938. *The Nineteen Thirty-Eight Mental Measurements Yearbook of the School of Education, Rutgers University*. New Brunswick, N.J.: Rutgers University Press.

Buros, O.K. (ed.). 1975. *Foreign Language Tests and Reviews*. Highland Park, N.J.: The Gryphon Press.

Burt, C.L. 1921. *Mental and Scholastic Tests*. London: London County Council.

Canale, M. and M. Swain. 1980. 'Theoretical bases of communicative approaches to second language teaching and testing'. *Applied Linguistics* 1: 1–47.

Canty, L.M. 1935. 'Twenty-five case studies of outstanding successes and failures in French classes'. Unpublished MA thesis, New Jersey State Teachers College, Montclair.

Carlson, S.B., B. Bridgeman, R. Camp, and J. Waanders. 1985. *Relations of Admission Test Scores to Writing Performance of Native and Non-native Speakers of English*. Research report. Princeton, N.J.: Educational Testing Service.

Carroll, B.J. 1980. *Testing Communicative Performance: An Interim Study*. Oxford: Pergamon.

Carroll, J.B. 1951. *Report and Recommendations of the Interdisciplinary Summer Seminar in Psychology and Linguistics: Cornell University, 18 June–10 August, 1951*. Ithaca, N.Y.: Cornell University.

Carroll, J.B. 1953. 'Some principles of language testing' in A.A. Hill (ed.) 1953.

Carroll, J.B. 1954. 'Notes on the measurement of achievement in foreign languages'. Unpublished mimeo.

Carroll, J.B. 1960. 'The prediction of success in intensive foreign language training (final revision)'. Laboratory for Research in Instruction, Graduate School of Education, Harvard University.

Carroll, J.B. 1961. 'Fundamental considerations in testing for English language proficiency of foreign students' in Center for Applied Linguistics 1961c: 30–40.

Carroll, J.B. 1962. 'The prediction of success in intensive foreign language training' in R. Glaser (ed.) 1962: 87–136.

Carroll, J.B. 1986. 'LT+25, and beyond'. *Language Testing* 3: 123–9.

Carroll, J.B. 1987a. 'Measurement and Educational Psychology: beginnings and repercussions' in J.A. Glover and R.R. Ronning (eds.) 1987: 89–106.

Carroll, J.B. 1989. Letter to Bernard Spolsky.

Carroll, J.B. 1993. *Human Cognitive Abilities: A Survey of Factor-analytic Studies.* Cambridge: Cambridge University Press.

Carroll, J.B., A.S. Carton, and **C.P. Wilds.** 1959. *An Investigation of 'Cloze' Items in the Measurement of Achievement in Foreign Languages.* Cambridge, Mass.: Laboratory for Research in Instruction, Graduate School of Education, Harvard University.

Cattell, J.M. 1890. 'Mental tests and measurements'. *Mind* 15: 373–81.

Cattell, J.M. 1905. 'Examinations, grades and credits. *Popular Science Monthly* 66: 367–78.

Cattell, J.M. 1973 (1947). *Man of Science.* New York: Arno Press.

Center for Applied Linguistics. 1959. *Proceedings of the Conference on Teaching English Abroad, May 1959.* Washington D.C.: Center for Applied Linguistics.

Center for Applied Linguistics. 1961a. Minutes of the Advisory Committee meeting, 18 March. Ford Foundation Archives, PA63–213.

Center for Applied Linguistics. 1961b. Testing conference: May 11th and May 12th. (agenda) Washington D.C. mimeo. Personal papers of Leslie Palmer.

Center for Applied Linguistics. 1961c. *Testing the English Proficiency of Foreign Students.* Report of a conference sponsored by the Center for Applied Linguistics in co-operation with the Institute of International Education and the National Association of Foreign Student Advisers. Washington D.C.: Center for Applied Linguistics.

Center for Applied Linguistics. 1966. 'TOEFL: Testing of English as a Foreign Language'. (Drafted by L[ois] M[cArdle].)

Chalmers, P.M. 1960a. Letter to Edward S. Noyes. 30 November. College Board Archives.

Chalmers, P.M. 1960b. Letter to Richard Pearson. 21 December. College Board Archives.

Cheydleur, F.D. 1928a. 'The construction and validation of a French grammar test of the multiple choice type'. *Journal of Educational Research* 18/3: 184–96.

Cheydleur, F.D. 1928b. 'Results and significance of the new type of modern language tests'. *Modern Language Journal* 12/7: 513–31.

Cheydleur, F.D. 1929. 'The relative reliability of the old and new type modern language examination'. *French Review* 2/6: 530–50.

Cheydleur, F.D. 1931. 'The use of placement tests in modern languages at the University of Wisconsin'. *Modern Language Journal* 15/4: 262–80.

Cheydleur, F.D. 1932. 'Mortality in modern languages students: its causes and prevention'. *Modern Language Journal* 17/2: 104–36.

Cheydleur, F.D. 1937. 'The case for more objective tests in higher education'. *Education* 17/7: 408–16.

Christie, T. and **G.M. Forrest.** 1981. *Defining Public Examination Standards.* Schools Council Research Studies. London: Macmillan.

Clark, J.L.D. 1965. 'MLA Cooperative foreign language tests'. *Journal of Educational Measurement* 2: 234–44.

Clark, J.L.D. 1977. *The Performance of Native Speakers of English on the Test of English as a Foreign Language*. Research report. Princeton, N.J.: Educational Testing Service.

Clark, J.L.D. (ed.). 1978a. *Direct Testing of Speaking Proficiency: Theory and Application*. Princeton, N.J.: Educational Testing Service.

Clark, J.L.D. 1978b. 'Interview testing research at Educational Testing Service' in J.L.D. Clark (ed.) 1978a: 211–28.

Clark, J.L.D. and S.S. Swinton. 1979. *An Exploration of Speaking Proficiency Measures in the TOEFL Context*. Research report. Princeton, N.J.: Educational Testing Service.

Clarke, F.M. 1931. 'Results of the Bryn Mawr test in French administered in New York city high schools'. *Bulletin of High Points* 13/2: 4–13.

Clarke, M.L. 1959. *Classical Education in Britain, 1500–1900*. Cambridge: Cambridge University Press.

Code, L. 1991. *What Can She Know? Feminist Theory and the Construction of Knowledge*. Ithaca, N.Y.: Cornell University Press.

Coffman, W.E. 1993. 'A king over Egypt, which knew not Joseph'. *Educational Measurement: Issues and Practice* 12/2: 5–8, 23.

Cole, R.D. and J.B. Tharp. 1937. *Modern Foreign Languages and Their Teaching*. New York: Appleton–Century–Crofts.

Coleman, A. 1929. *The Teaching of Modern Foreign Languages in the United States*. New York: Macmillan.

Coleman, A. 1932. *An Analytical Bibliography of Modern Language Teaching, 1927–1932*. Chicago, Ill.: University of Chicago Press.

Coleman, A. (ed.). 1934. *Experiments and Studies in Modern Language Teaching*. Chicago, Ill.: University of Chicago Press. 191–218.

Coleman, A. and C.B. King. (eds.). 1938. *An Analytical Bibliography of Modern Language Teaching, Vol. II, 1932–1937*. Chicago, Ill.: University of Chicago Press.

Coleman, A., C.B. King, C. Balluff, and R.H. Fife (eds.). 1949. *An Analytical Bibliography of Modern Language Teaching, Vol. III, 1937–1942*. Columbia University, New York: King's Crown Press.

College Entrance Examination Board. 1926. *The Work of the College Entrance Examination Board: 1901–1925*. Boston, Mass.: Ginn.

College Entrance Examination Board. 1929. *Twenty-ninth Annual Report of the Secretary*. New York: College Entrance Examination Board.

College Entrance Examination Board. 1930. *Thirtieth Annual Report of the Secretary*. New York: College Entrance Examination Board.

College Entrance Examination Board. 1931. *Thirty-first Annual Report of the Secretary*. New York: College Entrance Examination Board.

College Entrance Examination Board. 1932. *Thirty-second Annual Report of the Secretary*. New York: College Entrance Examination Board.

College Entrance Examination Board. 1933. *Thirty-third Annual Report of the Secretary*. New York: College Entrance Examination Board.

College Entrance Examination Board. 1934a. *Thirty-fourth Annual Report of the Secretary*. New York: College Entrance Examination Board.

College Entrance Examination Board. 1934b. *The Reading of the Comprehensive Examination in English: An Analysis of the Procedures Followed during the Five Reading Periods from 1929 through 1933*. New York: College Entrance Examination Board.

College Entrance Examination Board. 1935. *Thirty-fifth Annual Report of the Secretary*. New York: College Entrance Examination Board.

College Entrance Examination Board. 1936. *Thirty-sixth Annual Report of the Secretary*. New York: College Entrance Examination Board.

College Entrance Examination Board. 1937. *Thirty-seventh Annual Report of the Secretary*. New York: College Entrance Examination Board.

College Entrance Examination Board. 1939. *Thirty-ninth Annual Report of the Secretary*. New York: College Entrance Examination Board.
College Entrance Examination Board. 1940. *Fortieth Annual Report of the Secretary*. New York: College Entrance Examination Board.
College Entrance Examination Board. 1944. *Forty-fourth Annual Report of the Secretary*. New York: College Entrance Examination Board.
College Entrance Examination Board. 1945. *Forty-fifth Annual Report of the Secretary*. New York: College Entrance Examination Board.
College Entrance Examination Board. 1946. *Forty-sixth Annual Report of the Secretary*. New York: College Entrance Examination Board.
College Entrance Examination Board. 1948. *Forty-eighth Annual Report of the Secretary*. New York: College Entrance Examination Board.
College Entrance Examination Board. 1954. *Foreign Languages: A Description of the College Board Tests in French, German, Latin and Spanish*. New York: College Entrance Examination Board.
College Entrance Examination Board. 1961. 'Conversation between Richard Pearson and Kay Salter'. College Board Archives.
College Entrance Examination Board. 1963. Extract from minutes of Trustees. 'NCTEFL', 24 March. Ford Foundation Archives: PA63–213.
College Entrance Examination Board. 1966. Press release, 27 January. Ford Foundation Archives: PA66–60.
College Entrance Examination Board. 1967. 'Summary report: meeting of the National Advisory Council on TOEFL', 23 January. Private Papers of Leslie Palmer.
College Entrance Examination Board and Educational Testing Service. 1965. Agreement, 4 August. College Board Archives.
College Entrance Examination Board and Educational Testing Service. 1972. 'The Test of English as a Foreign Language (TOEFL): End of Grant Report', March.
Commission on Trends in Education of the Modern Language Association of America. 1944. 'Foreign languages and the army program'. *Hispania* 27: 382–3.
Committee on Resolutions and Investigations. 1917. 'Report of committee on resolutions and investigations appointed by the Association of Modern Language Teachers of the Middle States and Maryland'. *Modern Language Journal* 1: 250–61.
Commonwealth Education Liaison Committee. 1961. *Report of the Commonwealth Conference on the Teaching of English as a Second Language Held at Makerere College, Uganda*. Entebbe: Government Printer.
Conant, J.B. 1934. 'Notes and News: President Conant speaks again'. *Modern Language Journal* 19: 465–6.
Cooper, R.L. 1964. Memorandum reporting the results of the special comparison administration of TOEFL at Columbia University, Program in American Language Instruction.
Cooper, R.L. 1968. 'An elaborated language testing model'. *Language Learning* 7: 57–72 (special issue).
Cowan, J.M. and M. Graves. 1944. 'A statement on intensive language instruction'. *Hispania* 27: 65–66.
Coward, A.F. 1950. *The Method of Reading the Foreign Service Examination in English Composition*. Research report. Princeton, N.J.: Educational Testing Service.
Crawford, G.D., H.D. Argoff, and M.L. Adams. 1983. 'Oral language proficiency testing at the Foreign Service Institute'. Foreign Service Institute Archives.
Criper, C. and A. Davies. 1986. 'The ELTS validation study: report to the British Council and the University of Cambridge Local Examinations Syndicate'. Unpublished report.
Criper, C. and A. Davies. (eds.). 1988. *ELTS Validation Project Report*. ELTS Research Report Vol. I(i). Cambridge: University of Cambridge Local Examinations Syndicate.
Cuninggim, M. 1964. Letter to Dr Dangerfield, 27 October. College Board Archives.

Dandonoli, P. and G. Henning. 1990. 'An investigation of the construct validity of the ACTFL proficiency guidelines and oral proficiency interview'. *Foreign Language Annals* 23/1: 11–22.

Dangerfield, R. 1964. Letter to John W. Gardner, 18 August. Ford Foundation Archives: PA63–213.

Dangerfield, R. 1965. Letter to Charles Ferguson, 22 July. Personal papers of James E. Alatis.

Davidson, F.G. 1988. 'An explanatory modeling survey of the trait structures of some existing language test datasets'. Unpublished PhD dissertation, University of California, Los Angeles.

Davies, A. (ed.). 1968. *Language Testing Symposium: A Psycholinguistic Perspective*. Oxford: Oxford University Press.

Davies, A. 1990. *Principles of Language Testing*. Oxford: Basil Blackwell.

Davies, A. 1992. 'Is language proficiency always achievement?'. *Melbourne Papers in Language Testing* 1/1: 1–16.

Decker, W.C. 1925. 'Oral and aural tests as integral parts of Regents' examinations'. *Modern Language Journal* 9: 369–71.

deJong, J. and D.P. Stevenson. (eds.). 1990. *Individualizing the Assessment of Language Liabilities*. Clevedon, Avon: Multilingual Matters.

de la Salle, J.-B. 1838. *Conduite des ecoles chrétiennes*. Paris: J. Moronval.

de la Salle, J.-B. 1935. *The Conduct of the Schools*. New York: McGraw-Hill.

Department of State. 1967. *Foreign Affairs Manual, Uniform State/USIA Regulations, Revision*. Washington: Department of State.

Diederich, P.B. 1950. *The 1950 College Board English Validity Study*. Research report. Princeton, N.J.: Educational Testing Service.

Diederich, P.B., J.W. French, and S.T. Carlton. 1961. 'Factors in judgments of writing ability'. *Research Bulletin RB-50–58*. Princeton, N.J.: Educational Testing Service.

Dizney, H. 1965. 'Concurrent validity of the Test of English as a Foreign Language for a group of foreign students at an American university'. *Educational and Psychological Measurement* 25: 1129–31.

Dorcus, R.M., G.E. Mount, and M.H. Jones. 1953 (mistakenly dated 1952). *Construction and Validation of Foreign Language Aptitude Tests*. University of California, Los Angeles, for the Adjutant-General's Office.

Dunkel, H.B. 1948. *Second Language Learning*. Boston, Mass.: Ginn.

Dunkel, H.B. 1960. 'Review of the Modern Language Aptitude Test'. *French Review* 33: 634–5.

Duran, R.P., M. Canale, J. Penfield, C.W. Stansfield, and J. Liskin-Gasparro. 1985. *TOEFL from a Communicative Viewpoint on Language Proficiency: A Working Paper*. TOEFL Research Report No 17. Princeton, N.J.: Educational Testing Service.

Dyer, H. 1964. 'Proposed "merger" with TOEFL', 25 April. Turnbull Papers, Educational Testing Service Archives.

Dyer, H.S. 1954. 'Testing by ear'. *College Board Review*, 1–3 May.

Eddy, F.D. (ed.). 1959. *The Language Learner: 1959 Northeast Conference on the Teaching of Foreign Languages*. Reports of the working committee. Boulder: University of Colorado.

Edgeworth, F.Y. 1888. 'The statistics of examinations'. *Journal of the Royal Statistical Society* 51: 599–635.

Edgeworth, F.Y. 1890. 'The element of chance in competitive examinations'. *Journal of the Royal Statistical Society* 53: 644–63.

Educational Testing Service. 1961. Report of meeting, 4 May 1961. Educational Testing Service.

Educational Testing Service. 1965. *Annual Report, 1964–65: The Test of English as Foreign Language (TOEFL), Project 575*. Princeton, N.J.: Educational Testing Service.

Educational Testing Service. 1977. 'TOEFL Reserve Policy'. Princeton, N.J.: Educational Testing Service Archives.

Educational Testing Service. 1988. 'Welcome to TOEFL: Policy council and committee orientation'. Educational Testing Service Archives.

Educational Testing Service. 1989. *TOEFL 25: Celebrating 25 Years of Service.* Brochure. Princeton, N.J.: Educational Testing Service.

Educational Testing Service. 1991. *Understanding TOEFL.* Research report. Princeton, N.J.: Educational Testing Service.

Educational Testing Service and **Modern Language Association.** 1962. Letter of agreement, 1 July.

Eley, E.G. 1955. 'The test satisfies an educational need'. *College Board Review* 25: 9–13.

Eribon, D. 1991. *Michel Foucault.* Cambridge, Mass.: Harvard University Press.

Espinosa, A.M. and **T.L. Kelley.** 1927. *The Stanford Spanish Tests.* Palo Alto, CA.: Stanford University Press.

Evaluation and Advisory Service. 1961. Proposal to develop a test in English for Foreign Students. Turnbull Papers, Educational Testing Service.

Evans, M.K. 1937. 'The measurement of French pronunciation'. Unpublished MA thesis, Ohio State University.

Examiner. 1974. 'Eight taking a new lease on life' in *Examiner* 3 (20 June): 1/3.

Examiner. 1979. 'Good writing is more than just putting commas in the right place' in *Examiner* 8 (25 May): 3.

Farrand, W. 1926. 'A brief history of the College Entrance Examination Board' in College Entrance Examination Board 1926: 21–30.

Feder, D.D. and **G. Cochran.** 1936. 'Comprehension maturity tests: a new departure in measuring reading ability'. *Modern Language Journal* 20/4: 201–8.

Ferguson, C.A. 1966. Letter to George L. Anderson, 28 June. Ford Foundation Archives: PA63–213.

Ferguson, W.C. 1930. 'Aural and oral-oral tests in French'. *School* 18/8: 722–7.

Ficken, C.E. 1937. 'Intercorrelations of part scores in foreign language tests'. Unpublished PhD dissertation, University of Wisconsin.

Fife, R.H. 1937. 'Reading tests in French and German'. *Modern Language Journal* 22/1: 56–7.

Finch, H.F. and **O.R. Floyd.** 1935. 'The relation of chronological age to achievement in the study of French'. *Journal of Educational Psychology* 26/1: 52–8.

Finkelstein, I.E. 1913. The Marking System in Theory and Practice. Baltimore, Md.: Warwick and York.

Fisher, J.H. 1963. Letter to Damon Boynton, 23 October.

Fishman, J.A. (ed.). 1957. *Review of Research Activities of the College Entrance Examination Board 1952–1957.* New York: College Entrance Examination Board.

Fishman, J.A., A. Rubal-Lopez, and **A.W. Conrad.** (eds.). Forthcoming. *Post Imperial English: 1940–1990 Status Change.* Berlin: Mouton.

Ford Foundation. 1963a. Docket excerpt, Trustees meeting. Ford Foundation Archives: PA63–213.

Ford Foundation. 1963b. 'Grant to Modern Language Association', 8 April. Ford Foundation Archives: PA66–60.

Ford Foundation. 1965. 'Program action'. Ford Foundation Archives: PA66–60.

Ford Foundation. 1975. *Language and Development: A Retrospective Survey of Ford Foundation Language Projects, 1952–1974.* New York: Ford Foundation.

Ford, H.E. and **R.K. Hicks.** 1929. 'French tests in English, Canadian and American Schools'. *Modern Languages* 10/6: 181–5.

Foucault, M. 1975. *Surveiller et punir: naissance de la prison.* Paris: Gallimard.

Foucault, M. 1979. *Discipline and Punish: The Birth of the Prison.* New York: Vintage.

Fox, M.J. 1962a. Letter to David P. Harris, 17 October. Ford Foundation Archives: PA63–213.

Fox, M.J. 1962b. Letter to David P. Harris, 10 December. Ford Foundation Archives: PA63–213.

Fox, M.J. 1963a. Letter to David P. Harris, 21 January. Ford Foundation Archives: PA63–213.

Fox, M.J. 1963b. Letter to Malcolm D. Talbott, 14 February. Ford Foundation Archives: PA63–213.

Fox, M.J. 1963c. Letter to Edward S. Noyes, 21 February. Ford Foundation Archives: PA63–213.

Fox, M.J. 1963d. Letter to David P. Harris, 27 March. Ford Foundation Archives: PA63–213.

Fox, M.J. 1965a. Letter to Royden Dangerfield, 24 March. Ford Foundation Archives: PA63–213.

Fox, M.J. 1965b. Memo to Clarence H. Faust, 6 May. Ford Foundation Archives: PA66–60.

Fox, M.J. 1972. Memo to Elinor Barber. Ford Foundation Archives: PA66–60.

Fox, M.J. and D. Harris. 1964. *English as a Second Language: Development and Testing*. New York: Ford Foundation.

Franke, W. 1960. *The Reform and Abolition of the Traditional Chinese Examination System*. Cambridge, Mass.: Harvard University Center for East Asian Studies.

Frantz, A.I. 1939. 'The reading knowledge test in the foreign languages: a survey'. *Modern Language Journal* 23/6: 440–6.

Fraser, M.M. and C.C. Crawford. 1931. 'A comparison of adults with junior high school students as to progress in learning Spanish'. *Modern Language Forum* 16/2: 40–2.

French, J.W. 1951. *The Description of Aptitude and Achievement Tests in Terms of Rotated Factors*. Chicago, Ill.: University of Chicago Press.

French, J.W. 1962. 'Schools of thought in judging excellence of English themes' in *1961 Proceedings of Invitational Conference on Testing Problems*. Princeton, N.J.: Educational Testing Service.

French, S., J.B. Slater, M. Vassiloglou, and A.S. Willmott. 1987. *Descriptive and Normative Techniques in Examination Assessment*. Oxford: University of Oxford Delegacy of Local Examinations.

Fries, C.C. 1945. *Teaching and Learning English as a Foreign Language*. Ann Arbor, Mich.: University of Michigan Press.

Frith, J.R. 1953. 'Selection for language training by a trial course' in A.A. Hill (ed.) 1953: 10–15.

Fuess, C.M. 1950. *The College Board: Its First Fifty Years*. New York: Columbia University Press.

Gabbert, T.A. 1941. 'Predicting success in an intermediate junior college reading course in Spanish'. *Modern Language Journal* 8: 637–41.

Galton, F. 1883. *Inquiries into Human Faculty and Development*. New York: Macmillan.

Gerber, F.J. 1940. 'An analysis of the examinations for approval of oral work in French given by the State Department of Education of New York'. Unpublished MA thesis, State College for Teachers, Albany.

Ghigo, F. 1944. 'Standardized tests in the ASTP at the University of North Carolina'. *French Review* 17/6: 358–60.

Gibbons, H. 1940. 'The ability of college freshmen to construct the meaning of a strange word from the context in which it appears'. *Journal of Experimental Education* 9: 29–33.

Gibson, A.M. 1934. 'School examinations surveyed'. *Journal of Education* (London) 66/777: 199–201.

Gibson, A.M. 1935. 'University scholarship examinations: scope and standards, modern languages'. *Journal of Education* (London) 67/788: 131–3.

Giduz, H. 1942. 'The 1941 French placement tests at the University of North Carolina'. *High School Journal* 25/1: 36–9.

Gifford, B.R. (ed.). 1989. *Testing Policy and the Politics of Opportunity Allocation: The Workplace and the Law.* Boston, Mass.: Kluwer-Nijhoff.

Ginsberg, R.B. 1992. *Language Gains during Study Abroad: An Analysis of the ACTR Data.* Washington D.C.: National Foreign Language Center.

Girard, D. and **J. Trim.** 1988. 'Project no. 12: Learning and teaching modern languages for communication'. Report, Council for Cultural Co-operation, Council of Europe.

Glaser, R. (ed.). 1962 *Training Research and Education.* Pittsburgh, Pa.: University of Pittsburgh Press.

Glover, J.A. and **R.R. Ronning.** (eds.). 1987. *Historical Foundations of Educational Pscyhology.* New York: Plenum.

Godshalk, F.I. 1961a. 'Conference in Testing the English Proficiency of Foreign Students', 22 May. Educational Testing Service Archives.

Godshalk, F.I. 1961b. Memo to William Turnbull, 14 September. Educational Testing Service Archives.

Godshalk, F.I. 1961c. Memorandum for Mr Chauncey, Mr Dyer, etc., 14 November. Educational Testing Service Archives.

Godshalk, F.I. 1962a. 'Report on the January 12–13 1962 meeting', 29 January. Educational Testing Service Archives.

Godshalk, F.I. 1962b. 'Decisions of the National Advisory Council for TOEFL (Testing of English as a Foreign Language)', 16 May. Turnbull Papers, Educational Testing Service Archives.

Godshalk, F.I. 1962c. Memo to William Turnbull, 21 September. Educational Testing Service Archives.

Godshalk, F.I. 1963a. Letter to Damon Boynton, 4 February. College Board Archives.

Godshalk, F.I. 1963b. Letter to Edward Noyes, 4 February. College Board Archives.

Godshalk, F.I. 1963c. Information for Mel Fox, 8 February. Ford Foundation Archives: PA23–213.

Godshalk, F.I. 1963d. Letter to Edward Noyes, 16 September. College Board Archives.

Godshalk, F.I. 1964. 'Proposed concurrent CEEB and TOEFL administrations, with GRE overtones', 1 April. College Board Archives.

Godshalk, F.I., F. Swineford, and **W.E. Coffin.** 1966. *The Measurement of Writing Ability.* New York: College Entrance Examination Board.

Gould, S.J. 1981. *The Mismeasure of Man.* New York: W.W. Norton.

Greenberg, J. 1938. 'The relation of mental ability to achievement in foreign languages in the junior high schools of New York City'. Unpublished PhD dissertation, New York University.

Grieve, D.W. 1964. *English Language Examining: Report of an Inquiry into the Examining of English Language at the Examinations for the School Certificate and the General Certificate of Education of the West African Examinations Council.* Lagos: African Universities Press for the West African Examinations Council.

Hades, E. and **J.M. Stalnaker.** 1934. 'A new type of comprehensive foreign language test'. *Modern Language Journal* 19/2: 81–92.

Hagboldt, P. 1933. 'Reading for comprehension'. *German Quarterly* 6/2: 68–76.

Hale, G.A. and **F. Hinofotis.** 1981. *New Directions in Language Testing.* Research report. Princeton, N.J.: Educational Testing Service.

Hall, E.J. 1936. 'Oral examinations in Spanish for undergraduates'. *Hispania* 19: 461–6.

Handschin, C.H. 1919. *Handschin Modern Language Tests, Test A.* Yonkers, N.Y.: World Book Company.

Hansard. 1833. *Hansard's Parliamentary Debates.* London: T.C. Hansard.

Hansard. 1853. *Hansard's Parliamentary Debates.* London: Cornelius Buck.

Harris, D.P. 1961a. 'The American University Language Center Testing Program' in Center for Applied Linguistics 1961c: 41–53.

Harris, D.P. 1961b. Letter to Edward Noyes, 20 November. College Board Archives.
Harris, D.P. 1962a. 'Report of the Interim Executive Committee', May. National Advisory Council.
Harris, D.P. 1962b. Letter to Melvin J. Fox, 5 October. Ford Foundation Archives: PA63–213.
Harris, D.P. 1962c. Letter to Melvin J. Fox, 10 October. Ford Foundation Archives: PA63–213.
Harris, D.P. 1962d. 'Summary of questionnaire–survey'. National Advisory Council.
Harris, D.P. 1962e. Memorandum to TOEFL executive committee members, 13 December. Personal papers of Leslie Palmer.
Harris, D.P. 1963a. Letter to Melvin J. Fox, 16 January. Ford Foundation Archives: PA63–213.
Harris, D.P. 1963b. Letter to Melvin J. Fox, 11 March. Ford Foundation Archives: PA63–213.
Harris, D.P. 1963c. Letter to Melvin J. Fox, 19 March. Ford Foundation Archives: PA63–213.
Harris, D.P. 1963d. Letter to Leslie Palmer and the National Council, 4 April. Personal papers of Leslie Palmer.
Harris, D.P. 1963e. Letter to Edward Noyes, April 15. College Board Archives.
Harris, D.P. 1963f. Letter and agendas for the meeting of the Testing Committees, 3 June. Personal papers of Leslie Palmer.
Harris, D.P. 1963g. Progress report, June 6. College Board Archives.
Harris, D.P. 1964. Letter to Charles Ferguson, 7 October. Personal papers of James E. Alatis.
Harris, D.P. 1973. 'The American Language Institute' in *The Lado Years 1960–73*. Washington D.C.: Georgetown University Press. 24–7.
Harris, D.P. 1989. Letter to Bernard Spolsky, 7 June 1989.
Hartog, P. and E.C. Rhodes. 1935. An Examination of Examinations, being a Summary of Investigations on Comparison of Marks Allotted to Examination Scripts by Independent Examiners and Boards of Examiners, together with a Section on Viva Voce Examinations. London: Macmillan.
Hartog, P., P.B. Ballard, P. Gurrey, H.R. Hamley, and C.E. Smith. 1941. *The Marking of English Essays*. London: Macmillan.
Hartog, P. and E.C. Rhodes. 1936. *The Marks of Examiners, Being a Comparison of Marks Allotted to Examination Scripts by Independent Examiners and Boards of Examiners, together with a Section on Viva Voce Examinations*. London: Macmillan.
Hedgcock, F.A. 1933a. 'French at the First Certificate Examination'. *Modern Languages* 15/2: 57–61.
Hedgcock, F.A. 1933b. 'French at the First School Certificate Examination'. *Modern Languages* 14/5: 135–40.
Hedgcock, F.A. 1934. 'M.L.A. Trial Examinations in French'. *Modern Languages* 15/3–4: 111–16.
Heim, C.F. 1933. 'Comparative study of the Modern Language scores made in the Carnegie examinations at Temple University in 1930'. Unpublished MA thesis. Temple University.
Henmon, V.A.C. 1921. *Henmon French Tests—Tests 1, 2, 3 and 4*. Yonkers, N.Y.: World Book Company.
Henmon, V.A.C. (ed.) 1929. *Achievement Tests in the Modern Foreign Languages, Prepared for the Modern Foreign Language Study and the Canadian Committee on Modern Languages*. New York: Macmillan.
Henmon, V.A.C. 1934a. 'Recent developments in the construction, evaluation, and use of tests in the modern foreign languages' in A. Coleman (ed.) 1934: 191–218.
Henmon, V.A.C. 1934b. 'Recent developments in the study of foreign language problems'. *Modern Language Journal* 19/4: 187–201.

Henmon, V.A.C., J.E. Bohan, C.C. Brigham, L.T. Hopkins, G.A. Rice, P.M. Symonds, J.W. Todd, and R.J. Van Tassel (eds.). 1929. *Prognosis Tests in the Modern Foreign Languages: Reports Prepared for the Modern Foreign Language Study and the Canadian Committee on Modern Languages*. Publications of the American and Canadian Committees on Modern Languages. New York: Macmillan.

Henning, G. 1992. 'Dimensionality and construct validity of language tests'. *Language Testing* 9/1: 1–11.

Hill, A.A. (ed.). 1953. *Report of the Fourth Annual Round Table Meeting on Languages and Linguistics*. Washington D.C.: Georgetown University Press.

Hoffman, B. 1962. *The Tyranny of Testing*. New York: Crowell-Collier.

Hopkins, L.T. 1921. *The Marking System of the College Entrance Examination Board*. Cambridge, Mass.: Graduate School of Education, Harvard University.

Howard, J.B. 1963. Memo to Henry T. Heald, 8 March. Ford Foundation Archives: PA63–213.

Howard, J.B. and M.J. Fox. 1963. Memo to Henry T. Heald, 8 March. Ford Foundation Archives: PA63–213.

Howell, J.J. 1964. *College Board Scores of Candidates of Non-English Background Tested at Foreign Centers*. College Entrance and Examination Board Research and Development Report. Princeton, N.J.: Educational Testing Service.

Hubbell, A.F. 1963. Letter to James M. Nicely, Treasurer of the Ford Foundation, 9 April. Ford Foundation Archives: P63–213.

Huddleston, E.M. 1954. 'Measurement of writing ability at the college-level: objective vs. subjective testing'. *Journal of Experimental Education* 22/3: 165–213.

Hughes, A. and D. Porter. (eds.) 1983. *Current Developments in Language Testing*. London: Academic Press.

Hughes, M.M. 1935. 'Rate of acquisition of an English vocabulary by Spanish-speaking children'. Unpublished MA thesis, University of Chicago.

Hunt, T., F.C. Wallace, S. Doran, K.C. Buynitzky, and R.E. Scharz. 1929. *Language Aptitude Test: George Washington University*. Washington D.C.: Center for Psychological Service, George Washington University.

Huskisson, E.C. 1983. 'Visual analogue scales' in R. Melzack (ed.) 1983a: 33–7.

Hymes, D. 1967. 'Models of the interaction of language and social setting'. *Journal of Social Issues* 23/2: 8–38.

Interim Committee. 1962a. 'Proposed budget for the testing of English as foreign language', May. NAC/TOEFL.

Interim Committee. 1962b. 'Responsibilities of project director and his professional associate', May. NAC/TOEFL.

Jackson, P.W. (ed.). 1992. *Handbook on Research on Curriculum*. New York: Macmillan.

Joint Committee on English Examinations. 1941–65. (Executive Committee, 1957–65) Minutes. Archives of the University of Cambridge Local Examinations Syndicate.

Joncich, G.M. 1968. *The Sane Positivist: A Biography of Edward L. Thorndike*. Middletown, Conn.: Wesleyan University Press.

Jones, E.S. 1933. *Comprehensive Examinations in American Colleges*. New York: Macmillan.

Jones, E.S. (ed.) 1934. *Studies in Articulation of High School and College*. Buffalo, N.Y.: University of Buffalo.

Jones, E.S. 1937. 'Comprehensive examinations in the Humanities'. *Bulletin of the Association of American Colleges* 23/2: 211–318.

Jones, R.L. 1975. 'Testing language proficiency in the United States Government' in R.L. Jones and B. Spolsky (eds.) 1975: 1–9.

Jones, R.L. 1979. 'The oral interview of the Foreign Service Institute' in B. Spolsky (ed.) 1979: 104–15.

Jones, R.L. and B. Spolsky. (eds.). 1975. *Testing Language Proficiency.* Arlington, Va.: Center for Applied Linguistics.

Jones, W.K. 1934. 'Objectives as a prognostic test'. *Hispania* 17/3: 285–9.

Kamman, J.F. 1953. 'A comparison of factor patterns in a native language and an auxiliary language'. Unpublished PhD dissertation, University of Illinois.

Kandel, I. 1936. *Examinations and their Substitutes in the United States.* New York: Carnegie Foundation.

Kane, H. 1983. *A Study of Practices and Needs Associated with Intensive English Programs: Report of Findings.* Research report. Princeton, N.J.: Educational Testing Service.

Kaulfers, W.V. 1931. 'Present state of prognosis in foreign languages'. *School and Society* 39/8: 585–96.

Kaulfers, W.V. 1933a. 'Forecasting efficiency of current bases for prognosis'. Unpublished PhD dissertation, Stanford University.

Kaulfers, W.V. 1933b. 'Practical techniques for testing comprehension in extensive reading'. *Modern Language Journal* 17/5: 321–7.

Kaulfers, W.V. 1937. 'Objective tests and exercises in French pronunciation'. *Modern Language Journal* 22/3: 186–8.

Kaulfers, W.V. 1938. 'Review article'. *Hispania* 21: 218.

Kaulfers, W.V. 1939. 'Prognosis and its alternatives in relation to the guidance of students'. *German Quarterly* 12/3: 81–4.

Kaulfers, W.V. 1942. *Modern Languages for Modern Schools.* New York: McGraw-Hill.

Kaulfers, W.V. 1944. 'Wartime development in modern-language achievement testing'. *Modern Language Journal* 28/2: 136–50.

Kellenberger, H. (ed.). 1954. *Committee Reports: 1954 Northeast Conference on the Teaching of Foreign Languages.* Providence, R.I.: Brown University, Division of Modern Languages.

Kittson, E.C. 1918. *Theory and Practice of Language Teaching.* Oxford: Oxford University Press.

Klein-Braley, C. and D. Stevenson. (eds.). 1981. *Practice and Problems in Language Testing.* Frankfurt-am-Main: Peter D. Lang.

Klemm, F.A. 1942. 'The placement examination in college German'. *German Quarterly* 1: 32–5.

Koischwitz, O. 1934. 'A new method of testing extensive reading in contemporary literature classes'. *German Quarterly* 7/1: 9–18.

Kurath, W. and J.M. Stalnaker. 1936. 'Two German vocabulary tests'. *Modern Language Journal* 21/2: 95–102.

Lado, R. 1946. *Test of Aural Comprehension in English.* Ann Arbor, Mich.: English Language Institute, University of Michigan.

Lado, R. 1949. 'Measurement in English as a foreign language'. Unpublished PhD dissertation, University of Michigan.

Lado, R. 1951a. *English Language Test for Foreign Students.* Ann Arbor, Mich.: George Wahr.

Lado, R. 1951b. 'Phonemics and pronunciation tests'. *Modern Language Journal* 35: 531–42.

Lado, R. 1953. 'Test the language' in A.A. Hill (ed.) 1953. 29–33.

Lado, R. 1957. *Linguistics across Cultures: Applied Linguistics for Language Teachers.* Ann Arbor, Mich.: University of Michigan Press.

Lado, R. 1961. *Language Testing: the Construction and Use of Foreign Language Tests: A Teacher's Book.* New York: McGraw-Hill.

Larsen, R.P., J.R. Wittenborn, and E.G. Giesecke. 1942. 'Factors contributing to achievement in the study of first semester college German'. *Journal of Experimental Education* 10/4: 265–71.

Latham, H. 1877. *On the Action of Examinations Considered as a Means of Selection*. Cambridge: Deighton, Bell.

Lau, L.M. 1933. 'The use of the Symonds' Foreign Language Tests in beginning French'. Unpublished MA thesis, University of Chicago.

Leahey, T.H. 1987. *A History of Psychology: Main Currents in Psychological Thought*. Englewood Cliffs, N.J.: Prentice-Hall.

Libbish, B., F.J. Warne, and G.W. Wagstaffe. 1935. 'Report on the First School Certificate Questionnaire'. *Modern Languages* 16/3–4: 124–35.

Lind, M. 1948. *Modern Language Learning: the Intensive Course as Sponsored by the United States Army, and Implications for the Undergraduate Course of Study*. Provincetown, Mass.: The Journal Press.

Lowe, P., Jr. 1988. 'The unassimilated history' in P. Lowe, Jr. and C.W. Stansfield (eds.) 1988.

Lowe, P., Jr. and C.W. Stansfield. (eds.). 1988. *Second Language Proficiency Assessment: Current Issues*. Englewood Cliffs, N.J.: Prentice-Hall Regents.

Lowell, A.L. 1926. 'The art of examination' in College Entrance Examination Board 1926: 31–43.

Lundeberg, O.K. 1929. 'Recent developments in audition-speech tests'. *Modern Language Journal* 144/3: 193–202.

Luria, M.A. and J.S. Orleans. 1928. *Luria–Orleans Modern Language Prognosis Test*. Yonkers, N.Y.: World Book Company.

Macaulay, T.B. 1853. *Speeches, Parliamentary and Miscellaneous*. London: Henry Vizetelly.

Macaulay, T.B., Baron. 1899. *The Works of Lord Macaulay*. Boston, Mass.: Houghton Mifflin.

MacKenzie, N. 1961. 'English proficiency testing in the British Commonwealth' in Center for Applied Linguistics 1961c. 54–72.

MacLeod, N.W. 1963. Letter to Allan F. Hubbell. Ford Foundation Archives: PA63–213.

Madaus, G.F. 1990. *Testing as a Social Technology*. The inaugural annual Boise lecture on education and public policy. Boston: Boston College.

Madaus, G.F. and T. Kellaghan. 1991. 'Student examination systems in the European community: lessons for the United States'. Contractor report submitted to the Office of Technology Assessment, United States Congress.

Madaus, G.F. and T. Kellaghan. 1992. 'Curriculum evaluation and assessment' in P.W. Jackson (ed.) 1992.

Maley, A. 1989. 'Comments on the Final Report' in *Cambridge–TOEFL Comparability Study: Responses to the Final Report*. Cambridge: University of Cambridge Local Examinations Syndicate.

Manuel, H.T. 1930. *The Education of Mexican and Spanish-speaking Children in Texas*. Austin, Tex.: Fund for Research in the Social Sciences, University of Texas.

Manuel, H.T. 1960. 'Review of Modern Language Aptitude Test'. *Personnel and Guidance Journal* 38: 582–4.

Manuel, H.T. 1965. *Spanish-speaking Children of the Southwest*. Austin, Tex.: University of Texas Press.

Maronpot, R.P. 1939. 'Discovering and salvaging modern language risks'. *Modern Language Journal* 23/8: 595–8.

Marquardt, W.F. 1961. 'Can foreign student selection be based on aptitude for learning English?'. *International Institute of Education News Bulletin*.

Matheus, J.F. 1937. 'Correlation between psychological test scores, language aptitude test scores, and semester grades'. *Modern Language Journal* 22/2: 104–6.

Mathews, J.C. 1985. *Examinations: A Commentary*. London: George Allen and Unwin.

McClelland, C. 1980. *State, Society and University in Germany, 1700–1914*. Cambridge: Cambridge University Press.

McDaniel, J.M., Jr. 1963. Letter to G.W. Stone, 8 April. Personal papers of James E. Alatis.

Melzack, R. (ed.). 1983a. *Pain Measurement and Assessment*. New York: Raven Press.

Melzack, R. 1983b. 'The McGill Pain Questionnaire' in R. Melzack (ed.) 1983a. 41–7.

Michel, Sister Virgil. 1934. 'Prognosis in the modern foreign languages'. Unpublished MA thesis, University of Minnesota.

Michel, Sister Virgil. 1936. 'Prognosis in German'. *Modern Language Journal* 20/5: 275–87.

Miner, G.B. 1931. 'The measurement of achievement in Spanish'. *Hispania* 14/6: 457–82.

Minton, H.L. 1987. 'Lewis M. Terman and mental testing: in search of the democratic ideal' in M.M. Sokal (ed.) 1987: 96–112.

Moller, A. 1981. 'A study in the validation of proficiency tests in English as foreign language'. Unpublished PhD dissertation, Edinburgh University.

Monroe, P. (ed.). 1931. *Conference on Examinations, Eastbourne, England, 1931*. New York City: Teachers College, Columbia University.

Monroe, P. (ed.) 1935. *Conference on Examinations, Folkestone, England, 1935*. New York City: Teachers College, Columbia University.

Monroe, P. (ed.) 1939. *Conference on Examinations, Dinard, France, 1938*. New York City: Teachers College, Columbia University.

Monroe, W.S. 1921. 'The Illinois Examination'. *University of Illinois Bulletin* 19: 70.

Moreno-Lacalle, J. 1922. 'Report of the Committee on Realia'. *Hispania* 5: 96.

Morgan, W.J. 1953. 'A clinical approach to foreign language achievement' in A.A. Hill (ed.) 1953: 15–21.

Mosher, F. 1964. Letter to Mr Dangerfield, 8 September. College Board Archives.

Müller, D.K. 1987. 'The process of systematisation: the case of German secondary education' in D. Müller, F. Ringer, and B. Simon (eds.) 1987. 15–52.

Müller, D.K., F. Ringer, and B. Simon. (eds.) 1987. *The Rise of the Modern Educational Systems: Structural Change and Social Reproduction, 1870–1920*. London: Cambridge University Press; Paris: Editions des Sciences de l'Homme.

Munby, J.L. 1978. *Communicative Syllabus Design*. Cambridge: Cambridge University Press.

Myron, H.B. 1944. 'Teaching French in the Army'. *French Review* 17/6: 345–52.

Nairn, A. 1980. *The Reign of ETS: The Corporation That Makes Up Minds*. The Ralph Nader Report on the Educational Testing Service.

Nargil, W.M. 1992. 'The origins of Educational Testing Service'. *ETS Developments*. Winter issue.

National Advisory Council. 1962a. 'Conference for organization of program for testing the English proficiency of foreign students'. National Advisory Council.

National Advisory Council. 1962b. 'Proposal: That a new and improved program for testing the English proficiency of foreign students overseas be developed under the direction of the National Council on the Testing of English as Foreign Language'. 3 August.

National Advisory Council. 1962c. 'Proposal: That a new and improved program for testing the English proficiency of foreign students overseas be developed under the direction of the National Council on the Testing of English as Foreign Language.'

National Advisory Council. 1962d. 'Report of the January Conference for the organization of a program for testing the English proficiency of foreign students'. National Advisory Council.

National Advisory Council. 1962e. 'Report of the May 1962 meeting of the National Council on the Testing of English as a Foreign Language'.

National Advisory Council. 1962f. 'Summary description of the program for evaluating the English proficiency of foreign students'.

National Council. 1962a. 'Report of the May 1962 meeting of the National Council on the Testing of English as a Foreign Language'.

National Council. 1962b. 'Constitution of the National Council on the Testing of English as a Foreign Language'.

National Council. 1962c. 'Proposal: That a new and improved program for testing the English proficiency of foreign students overseas be developed under the direction of the National Council on the Testing of English as Foreign Language'.

National Council on TOEFL. 1963a. 'Description of the National Council on the Testing of English as a Foreign Language'.

National Council on TOEFL. 1963b. 'Report of the May 1963 Meeting'. College Board Archives.

National Council on TOEFL. 1963c. 'Report of the meetings of the Test Planning and Test Writing committees of the National Council on the Testing of English as Foreign Language'.

National Council on TOEFL. 1963d. 'Minutes of the 25 October 1963, meeting of the executive committee of the National Council on the Testing of English as a Foreign Language'.

National Council on TOEFL. 1964a. 'Minutes of the 25 March 1964 meeting of the Executive Committee'. College Board Archives.

National Council on TOEFL. 1964b. 'Report of the 18 April 1964 meeting of the National Council on the Testing of English as a Foreign Language'.

National Council on TOEFL. 1964c. 'Memorandum transmitting scores on the Test of English as a Foreign Language'. College Board Archives.

National Council on TOEFL. 1965. 'Report of the 15 May 1965 meeting of the National Council on the Testing of English as a Foreign Language'.

Neal, J.W. 1984. 'Standardized testing and international student admissions: the case of TOEFL'. Address to the Texas Association of International Education Administrators, Fort Worth, Texas.

Nemzek, C.L. 1938. 'The value of the Bernreuter personality inventory for direct and differential prediction of academic success as measured by teachers' marks'. *Journal of Applied Psychology* 22/6: 576–86.

Nemzek, C.L. 1939. 'The value of certain factors for direct and differential prediction of academic success'. *Journal of Experimental Education* 7/3: 199–202.

Nevo, D. 1986. 'Comments on Stansfield: A history of the Test of Written English: the developmental year'. *Language Testing* 3/2: 235–6.

North, B. 1992. *Options for Scales of Proficiency for a European Language Framework.* Occasional paper. Washington D.C.: National Foreign Language Center.

Noyes, E.S. 1961a. Letter to Sirarpi Ohannessian, 24 February. College Board Archives.

Noyes, E.S. 1961b. Letter to David Harris, 4 December. College Board Archives.

Noyes, E.S. 1963a. 'Notes on conversation, 6 February 1963, with Melvin Fox of Ford and Fred Godshalk of ETS about the CEEB's Interest in the National Council on Teaching (sic) of English as a Foreign Language (NCTOEFL)'. College Board Archives.

Noyes, E.S. 1963b. Notes on NCTOEFL test, 6 February. College Board Archives.

Noyes, E.S. 1963c. Letter to Melvin Fox, 18 February. Ford Foundation Archives: PA63–213; College Board Archives.

Noyes, E.S. 1963d. 'The National Council on the Testing of English as a Foreign Language'. March. College Board Archives.

Noyes, E.S. 1963e. Letter to David P. Harris, 25 March. Ford Foundation Archives: PA63–213.

Noyes, E.S. 1963f. Letter to Damon Boynton, 20 June. College Board Archives.

Noyes, E.S. 1963g. 'Notes on meeting in Washington D.C. with National Council on the Testing English as a Foreign Language'. College Board Archives.

Noyes, E.S. 1964a. NCTOEFL meeting 18 April. College Board Archives.

Noyes, E.S. 1964b. Letter to Lois McArdle, 24 November. College Board Archives.

Noyes, E.S., W.M. Sale, and J.M. Stalnaker. 1945. *Report on the First Six Tests in English Composition.* New York: College Entrance Examinations Board.

Noyes, E.S. and J.M. Stalnaker. 1938. *Report on the English Examination of June 1937.* New York: College Entrance Examination Board.

Odell, C.W. 1929. 'Educational tests for use in the high schools'. *University of Illinois Bulletin* 27/3.

Ohannessian, S. 1961. Letter to Edward Noyes. College Board Archives.

Oller, J.W., Jr. 1979. *Language Tests at School: A Pragmatic Approach*. London: Longman.

Oller, J.W. 1991a. 'Foreign language testing, Part 1: Its breadth'. *ADFL Bulletin* 22/3: 33–8.

Oller, J.W. 1991b. 'Foreign language testing, Part 2: Its depth'. *ADFL Bulletin* 23/1: 5–13.

Osgood, C.E. (ed.) 1954. *Psycholinguistics: A Survey of Theory and Research Problems; Report of the 1953 Summer Seminar Sponsored by the Committee on Linguistics and Psychology of the Social Science Research Council*. Baltimore, Md.: Waverly Press.

Osterweis, M., A. Kleinman, and D. Mechanic. (eds.). 1987. *Pain and Disability: Clinical, Behavioral and Public Policy Perspectives*. Washington D.C.: National Academy Press.

Otis, A.S. 1918. 'An absolute point scale for the group measurement of intelligence'. *Journal of Educational Psychology* 9: 238–61, 333–48.

Palmer, A.S., P.J.M. Groot, and G.A. Trosper. (eds.). 1981. *The Construct Validation of Tests of Communicative Competence*. Washington D.C.: TESOL.

Palmer, L.A. 1961. 'The Michigan Overseas Testing Service' in Center for Applied Linguistics 1961c: 73–85.

Palmer, L.A. 1965a. 'Material for ETS Annual Report'. Educational Testing Service Archives.

Palmer, L.A. 1965b. *Annual report, 1964–65: The Test of English as Foreign Language (TOEFL), Project 575*. Princeton, N.J.: Educational Testing Service.

Palmer, L.A. 1965c. 'Memorandum for Ms Jane Wirsig'. Private Papers of Leslie Palmer.

Palmer, L.A. and B. Spolsky. (eds.). 1975. *Papers in Language Testing 1967–74*. Washington D.C.: TESOL.

Paquette, F.A. and S. Tollinger. 1968. *A Handbook on Foreign Language Classroom Testing: French, German, Italian, Russian, Spanish*. New York: Modern Language Association of America.

Parker, W.R. 1954. *The National Interest and Foreign Languages*. Washington D.C.: US Government Printing Office.

Parker, W.R. 1961. *The National Interest and Foreign Languages*. Washington D.C.: US Government Printing Office.

Pasanella, A.K. (ed.). 1961. *Review of College Board Research 1952–1960*. New York: College Entrance Examination Board.

Paterson, D.G. 1925. *Preparation and Use of New-type Examinations: A Manual for Teachers*. Yonkers, N.Y.: World Book Company.

Pearson, R. 1955. 'The test fails as an entrance examination'. *College Board Review* 25: 2–9.

Pearson, R. 1960. Letter to Paul M. Chalmers, 16 December. College Board Archives.

Pearson, R. 1961. Letter to Katherine Salter, 24 May. College Board Archives.

Pearson, R. 1962. Letter to John Morse, 29 May. College Board Archives.

Pearson, R. 1964. Memorandum for Mr. Noyes, 21 April. College Board Archives.

Pearson, R. 1965a. Memorandum for Mr. Sims, 9 March. College Board Archives.

Pearson, R. 1965b. Memorandum for Mr. Sims, 29 March. College Board Archives.

Pearson, R. 1965c. Letter to Melvin J. Fox, 15 September. Ford Foundation Archives: PA63–213.

Pennycook, A. 1989. 'The concept of method, interested knowledge, and the politics of language teaching'. *TESOL Quarterly* 23/4: 589–619.

Pennycook, A. 1990. 'Critical pedagogy and second language education'. *System* 18/3: 303–14.

Percival, T.S. 1950. 'Achievement tests in French grammar and vocabulary'. Unpublished MA thesis, University of Durham.

Peters, W.F. 1961. 'Report of TDY Trip to Washington D.C. USAF Lackland Air Force Base'. Personal papers of Sydney Sako.

Phillipson, R. 1992. *Linguistic Imperialism*. Oxford: Oxford University Press.

Pike, L.W. 1979. *An Evaluation of Alternative Item Formats for Testing English as a Foreign Language.* Research report. Princeton, N.J.: Educational Testing Service.

Pimsleur, P., R.P. Stockwell, and A.L. Comrey. 1962. 'Foreign language learning ability'. *Journal of Educational Psychology* 53/1: 15–26.

Pitcher, B. and J.B. Ra. 1967. *The Relations Between Scores on the Test of English as a Foreign Language and Ratings of Actual Theme Writing.* Research report. Princeton, N.J.: Educational Testing Service.

P.K. 1965. TOEFL. Memorandum to Albert Sims, 15 April. College Board Archives.

Pollitt, A. 1991. 'Giving students a sporting chance: assessment by counting and by judging' in J. Alderson and B. North (eds.) 1991: 46–59.

Porter, D., A. Hughes, and C. Weir. (eds.). 1988 *Proceedings of a Conference Held to Consider the ELTS Validation Study.* ELTS Research Report Vol. I(ii). Cambridge: University of Cambridge Local Examinations Syndicate.

Pottle, F.A., N.S. Buck, W.C. DeVane, and H.M. Hubbell. 1944. 'Yale University: report of the president's committee on the teaching of modern foreign languages'. *Hispania* 27: 386–93.

Pressey, S.L. and L.C. Pressey. 1922. *Introduction to the Use of Standard Tests: A Brief Manual in the Use of Tests Both of Ability and Achievement.* Yonkers, N.Y.: American Book Company.

Program for the Testing of English as a Foreign Language. 1964. Press release. April. College Board Archives.

Raatz, U. 1981. 'Are oral tests tests?' in C. Klein-Braley and D. Stevenson (eds.) 1981: 197–212.

Reed, J. 1987. 'Robert M. Yerkes and the mental testing movement' in M.M. Sokal (ed.) 1987. 75–95.

Ricci, M. 1942. *China in the Sixteenth Century: The Journals of Matthew Ricci, 1583–1610.* New York: Random House.

Rice, F. 1959. 'The Foreign Service Institute tests language proficiency'. *Linguistic Reporter* 1: 2,4.

Richards, J.C. 1984. 'The secret life of methods'. *TESOL Quarterly* 18/1: 7–23.

Richardson, H.D. 1933. 'Discovering aptitude for the foreign languages'. *Modern Language Journal* 18/3: 160–70.

Roach, J. 1971. *Public Examinations in England 1850–1900.* Cambridge: Cambridge University Press.

Roach, J.O. 1934. 'Certificates of Proficiency'. Personal papers of J.O. Roach.

Roach, J.O. 1935. 'Modern languages and international relations'. *Education* (26 July): 80–1.

Roach, J.O. 1936 'The reliability of school certificate results'. *Overseas Education: a Journal of Educational Experiment and Research in Tropical and Subtropical Areas* 7/3: 113–8.

Roach, J.O. 1945. *Some Problems of Oral Examinations in Modern Languages: An Experimental Approach Based on the Cambridge Examinations in English for Foreign Students, Being a Report Circulated to Oral Examiners and Local Examiners for Those Examinations.* Cambridge: University of Cambridge Local Examinations Syndicate.

Roach, J.O. 1956a. 'Examinations in English as a foreign language: possible future developments'. Personal papers of J.O. Roach.

Roach, J.O. 1956b. 'Examinations in English as foreign language: Memorandum no. 2'. Personal papers of J.O. Roach.

Roach, J.O. 1971. *A Policy for Cultural Relations.* Cambridge: Heffer.

Roach, J.O. 1977. 'National tests in foreign languages'. Personal papers of J.O. Roach.

Roach, J.O. 1983. ' "My work" with the Local Examinations Syndicate 1925–45'. Personal papers of J.O. Roach.

Roach, J.O. 1984. 'Leaving the service of the University of Cambridge, 1925–1945'. Personal papers of J.O. Roach.

Roach, J.O. 1985. 'Service with the Local Examinations Syndicate'. Personal papers of J.O. Roach.

Roach, J.O. 1986. 'On leaving the Syndicate, 1945'. Personal papers of J.O. Roach.

Roach, J.O. 1989. Letter to Bernard Spolsky.

Robert, O.T. 1927. 'En marge des examens d'entrée au collège'. *French Review* 1: 29–39.

Rogers, A.L. 1929. 'French aural comprehension test' in V.A.C. Henmon (ed.) 1929: 311–21.

Rogers, A.L. and F.M. Clarke. 1933. 'Report on the Bryn Mawr test of ability to understand spoken French'. *Modern Language Journal* 17/4: 241–8.

Ronning, R.R., J.A. Glover, J.C. Conoley, and J.C. Witt. (eds.). 1987. *The Influence of Cognitive Psychology on Testing*. Hillsdale, N.J.: Lawrence Erlbaum.

Ross, L.W. 1937. 'Pronunciation quiz for French'. *High School Journal* 20/3: 96–7.

Ruch, G.M. 1924. *The Improvement of the Written Examination*. Chicago, Ill.: Scott Foresman.

Ruch, G.M. and G.D. Stoddard. 1927. *Tests and Measurements in High School Instruction*. Yonkers, N.Y.: World Book Company.

Rulon, P.J. 1943. 'Report on contract test constructed for the ASTD, ASF Contract No W-19–073 AST(Sc-1)-26: Report on scales for measuring ability to speak German and Russian, Term 5'. Harvard University.

Rulon, P.J. 1944a. 'Report on contract test constructed for the ASTD, ASF Contract No W-19–073 AST(Sc-1)-26: comprehension of spoken German, Term 6'. Harvard University.

Rulon, P.J. 1944b. 'Report on contract test constructed for the ASTD, ASF Contract No W-19–073 AST(Sc-1)-26: comprehension of spoken Russian, items proposed for use in War Department tests'. Harvard University.

Rulon, P.J. 1944c. 'Report on contract test constructed for the ASTD, ASF Contract No W-19–073 AST(Sc-1)-26: comprehension of spoken Russian, Term 6'. Harvard University.

Ryberg, D.C. 1968. 'Review of Pimsleur Language Aptitude Battery'. *Journal of Counseling Psychology* 15: 299–300.

Ryden, E.R. 1947. 'Vocabulary as an index to learning in a second language'. Unpublished PhD dissertation, Northwestern University.

Sako, S. 1961a. 'Conference on testing the English proficiency of foreign students. USAF Lackland Air Force Base'. Personal papers of Sydney Sako.

Sako, S. 1961b. 'English proficiency testing program at the USAF Language School' in Center for Applied Linguistics 1961c: 86–97.

Sako, S. 1991. Letter to Bernard Spolsky.

Salter, K.A. 1961a. Memorandum to Mr Pearson, 19 May. College Board Archives.

Salter, K.A. 1961b. Letter to Richard Pearson, 19 May. College Board Archives.

Salter, K.A. 1962. Memorandum for Mr Pearson, 29 May. College Board Archives.

Sammartino, P. 1931. 'Improvement curves in the comprehension of printed French and in the acquisition of French vocabulary'. Unpublished PhD dissertation, New York University.

Sammartino, P. 1938. 'A language achievement scale'. *Modern Language Journal* 22/6: 429–32.

Sandiford, P. 1928. *Educational Psychology: An Objective Study*. London: Longman; New York: Green.

Sandri, L. and W.V. Kaulfers. 1945. 'An oral fluency rating scale in Italian'. *Italica* 22: 133–44.

Sandri, L. and W.V. Kaulfers. 1946. 'An aural comprehension scale in Italian'. *Italica* 23: 335–1.

Sapon, S.M. 1956. 'Report of the committee on tests' in *Foreign Language Tests and Techniques: 1956 Northeast Conference on the Teaching of Foreign Languages: Report of the Working Committee*. Bryn Mawr, Penn.: Bryn Mawr College: 33–8.

Saretsky, G.D. 1984. 'History of the EEFS'. Unpublished manuscript, EEFS Papers, Educational Testing Service Archives.

Schwartz, S.T. 1937. 'The prediction of success in beginning French on the basis of IQ and marks in school subjects'. Unpublished MA thesis, George Washington University.

Scottish Council for Research in Education Examination Inquiry. 1934. *The Prognostic Value of University Entrance Examinations in Scotland.* London: University of London Press.

Seagoe, M.V. 1938. 'Prediction of achievement in foreign languages'. *Journal of Applied Psychology* 22/6: 632–40.

Searle, J.R. 1969. *Speech Acts: An Essay in the Philosophy of Language.* Cambridge: Cambridge University Press.

Seaton, I. 1981. 'Background to the specifications for an English Language Testing Service and subsequent developments' in J.C. Alderson and A. Hughes (eds.) 1981: 121–2.

Seibert, L.C. and **E.R. Goddard.** 1935. 'A more objective method of scoring composition'. *Modern Language Journal* 20/3: 143–50.

Seibert, L.C. and **B.D. Wood.** 1930. *Columbia Research Bureau Aural French Test.* Yonkers, N.Y.: World Book Company.

Sepmeyer, I.H. 1961. Letter to Joel B. Slocum. Ford Foundation Archives: PA63–213.

Shephard, W. 1989. Conversation with Bernard Spolsky.

Shohamy, E. and **A.R. Walton.** (eds.). 1992. *Language Assessment for Feedback: Testing and Other Strategies.* Dubuque, Ia.: Kendall/Hunt Publishing; Washington D.C.: National Foreign Language Center.

Sims, A.G. 1962a. Letter to David Harris, August.

Sims, A.G. 1962b. Letter to David Harris, 10 September.

Sims, A.G. 1964a. Letter to Edward Noyes, 2 April. College Board Archives.

Sims, A.G. 1964b. Letter to Melvin J. Fox, 10 September. Ford Foundation Archives: PA63–213.

Sims, A.G. 1965a. TOEFL and its financing, 15 February. College Board Archives.

Sims, A.G. 1965b. Conversation with Melvin J. Fox and Robert Solomon, 17 February. College Board Archives.

Sims, A.G. 1965c. Memorandum to Pearson and Hanford, 25 February. College Board Archives.

Sims, A.G. 1965d 'TOEFL', 25 February. College Board Archives.

Sims, A.G. 1965e. Letter to William Turnbull, 22 March. College Board Archives.

Sims, A.G. 1965f. Meeting at ETS with Turnbull and Solomon on TOEFL, 22 March. College Board Archives.

Sims, A.G. 1965g. Conversation with Mel Fox of the Ford Foundation about TOEFL, 25 March. College Board Archives.

Sims, A.G. 1965h. Conversation with Leslie Palmer, 25 March/26 March. College Board Archives.

Sims, A.G. 1965i. Meeting with Leslie Palmer of TOEFL, 26 March. College Board Archives.

Sims, A.G. 1965j. Luncheon meeting with Melvin J. Fox at Ford Foundation re TOEFL, 8 April. College Board Archives.

Sims, A.G. 1965k. Telephone conversation with Malcolm Talbott, 12 April. College Board Archives.

Sims, A.G. 1965l. Letter to Melvin J. Fox, 26 April. Ford Foundation Archives: PA66–60.

Sims, A.G. 1965m. Conversation with Melvin J. Fox of the Ford Foundation, 11 May. College Board Archives.

Sims, A.G. 1965n. Conversation with Melvin J. Fox, 14 June/16 June. College Board Archives.

Sims, A.G. 1965o. Letter to William Bretnall, 6 August. College Board Archives.

Sims, A.G. 1965p. Letter to Melvin J. Fox, 12 November. Ford Foundation Archives: PA66–60.

Skehan, P. 1986. 'The role of foreign language aptitude in a model of school learning'. *Language Testing* 3: 188–221.

Skehan, P. 1989. *Individual Differences in Second-language Learning.* London: Edward Arnold.

Slocum, J.B. 1961. 'Assessing the English proficiency of foreign students: point of view of US universities' in Center for Applied Linguistics 1961c: 99–102.

Smith, F.P. and H. Campbell. 1942. 'Objective achievement testing in French recognition versus recall tests'. *Modern Language Journal* 26/3: 192–8.

Sokal, M.M. 1987. 'James McKeen Cattell and Mental Anthropometry: nineteenth century science and reform and origins of psychological testing' in M.M. Sokal (ed.) 1987. 21–45.

Sokal, M.M. (ed.). 1987. *Psychological Testing and American Society 1890–1930*. New Brunswick, N.J.: Rutgers University Press.

Sollenberger, H.E. (ed.). 1954. *Foreign Languages Teachers and Tests: 1954 Northeast Conference on the Teaching of Foreign Languages*. Reports of the working committees. Providence, R.I.: Brown University.

Sollenberger, H.E. 1978. 'Development and current use of the FSI Oral Interview Test' in J.L.D. Clark (ed.) 1978a. 3–12.

Solomon, R.J. 1962. 'Further work on English test for foreign students', 2 March. Turnbull Papers, Educational Testing Service Archives.

Solomon, R.J. 1964. 'Future of TOEFL', 21 April. Turnbull Papers, Educational Testing Service Archives.

Spaulding, S. 1951. 'Two formulas for estimating the reading difficulty of Spanish'. *Educational Research Bulletin* 30: 117–24.

Spearman, C. 1904a. 'The proof and measurement of association between two things'. *American Journal of Psychology* 15: 73–101.

Spearman, C. 1904b. ' "General intelligence": objectively determined and measured'. *American Journal of Psychology* 15: 202–92.

Spiers, A.G.H. 1927. 'A French language teacher's scale'. *French Review* 1: 13–28.

Spoerl, D.T. 1939. 'A study of some of the possible factors involved in foreign language learning'. *Modern Language Journal* 23: 428 31.

Spolsky, B. 1977. 'Language testing: art or science' in *Proceedings of the Fourth International Congress of Applied Linguistics*. Stuttgart: Hochschulverlag: 7–28.

Spolsky, B. 1979. *Some Major Tests*. Washington D.C.: Center for Applied Linguistics.

Spolsky, B. 1981a. 'Some ethical questions about language testing' in Klein-Braley and Stevenson.

Spolsky, B. 1981b. 'The gentle art of diagnostic testing.' Unpublished manuscript. Paper given at IUS Symposium.

Spolsky, B. 1983. 'Fourteen years on: later thoughts on overall language proficiency' in A. Hughes and D. Porter (eds.) 1983. 39–42.

Spolsky, B. 1985. 'The limits of authenticity in language testing'. *Language Testing* 2: 31–40.

Spolsky, B. 1989a. *Conditions for Second Language Learning*. Oxford: Oxford University Press.

Spolsky, B. 1989b. 'Communicative competence, language proficiency, and beyond'. *Applied Linguistics* 10/2: 138–56.

Spolsky, B. 1990. 'Oral examinations: an historical note'. *Language Testing* 7/2: 158–73.

Spolsky, B. 1992. 'The gentle art of diagnostic testing revisited' in E. Shohamy and A.R. Walton, (eds.) 1992. 29–41.

Spolsky, B. (forthcoming). 'English in Israel after Independence' in J.A. Fishman, A. Rubal-Lopez, and A.W. Conrad (eds.) (forthcoming).

Spolsky, E. (forthcoming). *Satisfaction: Skepticism in Renaissance Poetry and Painting*.

Stalnaker, J.M. and W.A. Kurath. 1935. 'A comparison of two types of foreign language vocabulary test'. *Journal of Educational Psychology* 26: 435–42.

Stansfield, C. 1984. 'Request for funding of the writing project. Proposal submitted to the TOEFL Policy Council'. Princeton, N.J.: Educational Testing Service.

Stansfield, C. 1986. 'A history of the Test of Written English: the developmental year'. *Language Testing* 3/2: 224–34.

Starch, D. 1913. 'Reliability and distribution of grades'. *Science* 38: 630 ff.

Starch, D. 1914. *The Measurement of Efficiency in Reading, Writing, Spelling and English.* Madison, Wis.: College Book Store.

Starch, D. 1916. *Educational Measurements.* New York: Macmillan.

Starch, D. and E.C. Elliott. 1912. 'Reliability of the grading of high school work in English'. *School Review* 20: 442ff.

Starch, D. and E.C. Elliott. 1913a. 'Reliability of grading work in mathematics'. *School Review* 21: 254 ff.

Starch, D. and E.C. Elliott. 1913b. 'Reliability of grading work in history'. *School Review* 21: 676 ff.

Starr, W.H 1962. 'MLA Foreign Language Proficiency tests for teachers and advanced students'. *PMLA* 77/4, part 2: 31–42.

Starr, W.H. 1992. Letter to Bernard Spolsky.

Sternbach, R. 1983. 'The tourniquet pain test' in R. Melzack (ed.) 1983a. 27–31.

Stevenson, D P. 1981. 'Beyond faith and face validity: the multitrait-multimethod matrix and the convergent and discriminant validity of oral proficiency tests' in A. Palmer, P. Groot, and G. Trosper (eds.) 1981. 37–61.

Stevenson, D.P. 1985. 'Authenticity, validity and a tea party'. *Language Testing* 2/1: 41–7.

Stoddard, G.D. and G.E. Vander Beke. 1925. *Iowa Placement Examinations: Foreign Language Aptitude.* Iowa City: State University of Iowa.

Stone, G.W. 1963. Letter to Dr. Henry Heald, 14 March. Ford Foundation Archives: PA63–213.

Strevens, P. 1989. 'Comments' in *Cambridge–TOEFL Comparability Study: Responses to the Final Report.* Cambridge: University of Cambridge Local Examinations Syndicate.

Stubbins, T.E. 1940. 'The prognostic values of the subjects of a secondary school entrance examination'. *British Journal of Educational Psychology* 10/1: 16–24.

Sutton, F.X. 1992. Letter to Bernard Spolsky.

Swain, M. 1990. 'Second language testing and second language acquisition: is there a conflict with traditional psychometrics?' in J. Alatis (ed.) 1990: 401–12.

Swineford, F. 1955. 'Reliability of an interlinear test of writing ability'. *School and Society* 81/2051: 25–7.

Swineford, F. and M. Olsen. 1953. *Reliability and Validity of an Interlinear Test of Writing Ability.* Research report. Princeton, N.J.: Educational Testing Service.

Symonds, P.M. 1930a. *Foreign Language Prognosis Test.* New York: Teachers College, Columbia University.

Symonds, P.M. 1930b. 'A foreign language prognosis test'. *Teachers College Record* 31: 540–6.

Talbott, M.D. 1963. Letter to Melvin J. Fox, 12 February. Ford Foundation Archives: PA63–213.

Tallent, E.R.E. 1937. 'An analysis of certain relationships between intelligence quotients, English placement test scores, and scholastic'. Unpublished MA thesis, University of Tennessee.

Tallent, E.R.E. 1938. 'Three coefficients of correlation that concern modern foreign languages'. *Modern Language Journal* 22/8: 591–4.

Taylor, C. 1993. 'TOEFL 2000 Background and Developments'. E-mail letter to Bernard Spolsky, (Message ID: <199312032234.AA23760@gateway.rosedale.org>).

Teague, O.D. 1931. 'Predictive significance of pre-college data with reference to college success'. Unpublished MA thesis, University of Tennessee.

Terman, L.M. 1916. *The Measurement of Intelligence: An Explanation of and Complete Guide for the Revision and Extension of the Binet–Simon Intelligence Scale.* Boston, Mass.: Houghton Mifflin.

Terman, L.M. 1925. *Genetic Studies of Genius.* Stanford, CA.: Stanford University Press.

Terman, L.M. and M.A. Merrill. 1937. *Measuring Intelligence: A Guide to the Administration of the New Revised Stanford–Binet Tests of Intelligence.* Boston, Mass.: Houghton Mifflin.

Tharp, J.B. 1927. 'The new examination versus the old'. *School and Society* 26/674: 691–4.
Tharp, J.B. 1929. 'Examining knowledge of foreign language grammar'. *French Review* 2/6: 486–99.
Tharp, J.B. 1930. 'Effect of oral–aural ability on scholastic ability'. *Modern Language Journal* 15/1: 10–26.
Tharp, J.B. 1932. 'Review of Report of the Commission appointed by the College Entrance Examination Board to revise the definition of the requirements in French, German, Italian, Spanish'. *Modern Language Journal* 16/4: 369–72.
Thibault, P. 1953. 'Implications of experience with College Board language tests' in A.A. Hill (ed.) 1953: 21–9.
Thomson, G.H. 1939. *The Factorial Analysis of Human Ability*. Boston, Mass.: Houghton Mifflin.
Thomson, G.H. 1954. *The Geometry of Mental Measurement*. London: University of London Press.
Thorndike, E.L. (ed.). 1903. *Heredity, Correlation and Sex Differences in School Ability*. New York: Columbia University.
Thorndike, E.L. 1904. *An Introduction to the Theory of Mental and Social Measurements*. New York: The Science Press.
Thorndike, E.L. 1910. 'Handwriting'. *Teachers College Record* 11/2.
Thorndike, E.L. 1912. *Education: A First Book*. New York: Macmillan.
Thorndike, E.L. 1941. 'Mental abilities'. *Proceedings of the American Philosophical Society* 84: 503–13.
Thorndike, E.L., E.O. Bregman, J.W. Tilton, and E.Woodyard. 1928. *Adult Learning*. New York: Macmillan.
Thorndike, E.L. and I. Lorge. 1944. *Teacher's Word Book of 30,000 Words*. New York: Bureau of Publications, Teacher's College, Columbia University.
Thurstone, L.L. 1935. *The Vectors of the Mind*. Chicago, Ill.: University of Chicago Press.
TOEFL Programs and Services. 1990. *TOEFL Test and Score Manual*. Princeton, N.J.: Educational Testing Service.
Tollinger, S. and F.A. Paquette. 1966. *The MLA Foreign Language Proficiency Tests for Teachers and Advanced Students*. New York: Modern Language Association of America.
Toulmin, S. 1990. *Cosmopolis: The Hidden Agenda of Modernity*. New York: Free Press.
Traxler, A.E. 1941. 'A study of the Junior Scholastic Aptitude Test'. *Journal of Educational Research* 35/1: 16–217.
Turnbull, W.W. 1961a. Memo to Fred I. Godshalk, 2 February. Turnbull Papers, Educational Testing Service Archives.
Turnbull, W.W. 1961b. 'English exams for foreign students', 21 February. Turnbull Papers, Educational Testing Service Archives.
Turnbull, W.W. 1961c. Notes, November. Turnbull Papers, Educational Testing Service Archives.
Turnbull, W.W. 1963. Letter to John Fisher and Damon Boynton, 6 December. Turnbull Papers, Educational Testing Service Archives.
Turnbull, W.W. 1965. TOEFL. Turnbull Papers, Educational Testing Service Archives.
Turnbull, W.W. 1966. Note to Mr Solomon, November. Turnbull Papers, Educational Testing Service Archives.

University of Cambridge Local Examinations Syndicate. 1987. *English as a Foreign Language: General Handbook*. Cambridge: University of Cambridge Local Examinations Syndicate.
Upshur, J.A. 1962. 'Language proficiency testing and the contrastive analysis dilemma'. *Language Learning* 12: 123–7.
Upshur, J.A. and J. Fata. (eds.). 1968. 'Problems in foreign language testing'. *Language Learning* (special issue).

Valentine, C.W. and **W.G. Emmett.** 1932. *The Reliability of Examinations: An Enquiry with Special Reference to Secondary Schools, the School Certificate Examination, and the Award of Scholarships at Universities.* London: University of London Press.

Vernon, P.E. (ed.). 1957. *Secondary School Selection.* London: Methuen.

Villaréal, J.J. 1947. 'A test of the aural comprehension of English for native speakers of Spanish'. Unpublished PhD dissertation, Northwestern University.

von Mayrhauser, R.T. 1987. 'The manager, the medic and the mediator: the clash of professional psychological styles and the wartime origins of group mental testing' in M.M. Sokal (ed.) 1987: 128–57.

Wagner, M.E. 1934. 'Prediction of college performance' in E. Jones (ed.) 1934: 123–210.

Wagner, M.E. and **E. Strabel.** 1935. 'Predicting success and failure in college ancient and modern foreign languages'. *Modern Language Journal* 19/4: 285–93.

Wantman, M. 1961a. Memo to William Turnbull, 17 March. Turnbull Papers, Educational Testing Service Archives.

Wantman, M.J. 1961b. 'Notes of meeting on May 4 on EEFFS'. Turnbull Papers, Educational Testing Service Archives.

Webber, C. 1989. 'The mandarin mentality: civil service and university admissions testing in Europe and Asia' in B.R. Gifford (ed.) 1989: 33–60.

Werner, H. and **E. Kaplan.** 1950. 'Development of word meaning through verbal context: an experimental study. *Journal of Psychology* 29: 251–7.

Westaway, G., J.C. Alderson, and **C.M. Clapham.** 1990. 'Directions in testing for specific purposes' in J. deJong and D. Stevenson (eds.) 1990: 239–57.

Whitla, D.K. 1964. 'Uses of the multiple choice test' in L. Bramson (ed.) 1964.

Wigglesworth, D.C. (ed.). 1967. *Selected Conference Papers of the Association of Teachers of English as a Second Language.* Washington D.C.: NAFSA.

Wilds, C.P. 1961a. 'Assignment of + ratings'. Foreign Service Institute Archives.

Wilds, C.P. 1961b. 'Proficiency ratings for native speakers'. Foreign Service Institute Archives.

Wilds, C.P. 1975. 'The oral interview test' in R.L. Jones and B. Spolsky (eds.) 1975: 29–37.

Wilkins, D.A. 1976. *Notional Syllabuses: A Taxonomy and its Relevance to Foreign Language Curriculum Development.* Oxford: Oxford University Press.

Williams, S.B. and **H.J. Leavitt.** 1947. 'Prediction of success in learning Japanese'. *Journal of Applied Psychology* 31: 164–8.

Winterbottom, J.A. 1962. 'National Advisory Council: English test for foreign students'. (Report of meeting.)

Wittenborn, J.R. and **R.P. Larsen.** 1944. 'A factorial study of achievement in college German'. *Journal of Educational Psychology* 35: 39–48.

Wood, B.D. 1928. *New York Experiments with New-type Modern Language Tests.* New York: Macmillan.

Woodford, P. 1990. Conversation with Bernard Spolsky.

Woodworth, R.S. 1918. *Dynamic Psychology.* New York: Columbia University Press.

Yerkes, R.M. 1911. *Introduction to Psychology.* New York: Henry Holt.

Yerkes, R.M. (ed.). 1921. *Psychological Examining in the United States Army.* Washington D.C.: Government Printing Office.

Yerkes, R.M., J.W. Bridges, and **R.S. Hardwick.** 1915. *A Point Scale for Measuring Mental Ability.* Baltimore, Md.: Warwick and York.

Young, J.A. 1933. 'Deriving practical instruments for predicting success in high school French'. Unpublished MA thesis, University of Pittsburgh.

Zenderland, L. 1987. 'The debate over diagnosis: Henry Herbert Godard and the medical acceptance of mental testing' in M.M. Sokal (ed.) 1987: 46–74.

Index of personal names

References to chapter notes are indicated by page and note number, e.g. 'Barzun, J. 49n1'.

Subject index

References to chapter notes are indicated by page and note number, e.g. 'lexicon 171n29'. Names of examinations and tests are in italic.

Hungarian language 127

idioms 127, 134n9, 199–200, 201
  see also under names of individual tests
IELTS (formerly ELTS) 1, 343–6, 346nn1, 9; 350
Illinois, University of 94, 134n9
immigrants to USA 55–8
Immigration Act 1924 (US) 55–6, 59
industrialized testing 84, 283, 333
Institute of International Education 217, 229, 246, 247n4, 266n10
Institute of Language and Linguistics (US) 161
institutional inertia 2, 95
institutionalization 95
Instituto Cervantes (Spain) 347n13
integrative testing 49, 79, 201, 225, 230, 241, 283, 341, 353
  see also Carroll, J.B. *in index of personal names*
intelligence (I.Q.) 27–30, 63, 69, 117, 119, 120, 121, 123, 128, 134–5nn9, 10; 161–2, 163
intensive foreign language training 128–30, 139–41
Inter-American Tests 153n26, 214n7
interlinear exercise 166–7
International Conferences on Examinations 66, 69
International Cooperation Agency 218
International English Language Testing Service *see* IELTS
International Institute, Columbia (US) 66
International Language Testing Association 152n24
International Programme of Australian Universities 344
intonation 183
Investigation of the Teaching of a Second Language 106, 163
Iowa Foreign Language Aptitude Test 121–2, 170n20
Iowa Placement Examination 120, 124
Israel Academic Committee for Research on Language Testing 219
Italian language 44, 64, 186, 190

Japanese language 127, 128, 139
Jesuits (Society of Jesus) 16
Johnson Foundation 293, 299, 306
Joint Committee on English Examinations 207
Junior Scholastic Aptitude Test (US) 125

Kellogg Foundation 293, 299
King–Campbell Test 202
knowledge 15, 84, 352, 358
Korean language 130, 139

laboratories, language 3
Laboratory for Research in Instruction (Harvard) 128
Lackland Air Force Base 201–3, 300
Language Achievement Scale (Columbia) 89
Language Aptitude Test 118
language learning ability 117, 125, 131
Language Teaching (Lado) 214n7, 235n9
Language Testing 234n4
Latin examinations 18, 54, 91
learning a foreign language, definition of 149
Leaving Certificate Examination (UK) 125
Leeds, University of 144
lexicon 165–6, 171n29
limen-referencing 340
linguistic theory 230
listening *see* aural
Listening Comprehension Test 201
Listening Test for Students of English as a Second Language 214n6
literature examination for foreign students 63, 64, 65, 88, 90, 205–6, 212
London County Council 30
Long Beach Junior College 88
Lower Certificate see Cambridge Lower Certificate
LT + 25 Symposium 219
Lundeberg–Tharp test 78, 79
  Audition Test in French 94, 181–2
Luria–Orleans Modern Language Prognosis Test 118, 123, 135n10

Mandarin Chinese 126, 127, 132, 160
manipulation of system 23
marking
  analytical vs. holistic 323, 325, 328
  Cambridge examinations 339–41
  Cambridge Lower Certificate grading 109–10
  difficulty in grading 27, 53
  Godshalk *et al.* 324–7
  major variations 39, 67, 111, 325
  scoring guide 329–30
  survey of exemption practices 85–7
  three levels of pass 64, 83, 102
  tighter control 83
  TOEFL scoring 331–2
  written work 59–63
Massachusetts high schools 122
measurement, development of 27–30, 33–5, 86, 331, 340
measurement of pain as analogy 350–2
measurement in psychology 26, 30
mechanized testing 84, 94, 217
meetings of testers 158–63, 169nn13, 14
meetings of TOEFL 241–7, 247–9, 257–9, 277–8, 281–2